ARCHAEOLOGY AS LONG-TERM HISTORY

ARCHAEOLOGY AS LONG-TERM HISTORY

EDITED BY IAN HODDER

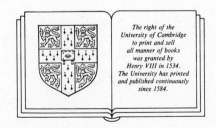

The right of the
University of Cambridge
to print and sell
all manner of books
was granted by
Henry VIII in 1534.
The University has printed
and published continuously
since 1584.

CAMBRIDGE UNIVERSITY PRESS
CAMBRIDGE
LONDON   NEW YORK   NEW ROCHELLE
MELBOURNE   SYDNEY

Published by the Press Syndicate of the University of Cambridge
The Pitt Building, Trumpington Street, Cambridge CB2 1RP
32 East 57th Street, New York, NY 10022, USA
10 Stamford Road, Oakleigh, Melbourne 3166, Australia

First published 1987

Printed in Great Britain at the University Press, Cambridge

British Library cataloguing in publication data

Archaeology as long-term history. –
(New directions in archaeology)
1. Archaeology and history
I. Hodder, Ian   II. Series
930.1   CC77.H5

Library of Congress cataloguing in publication data

Archaeology as long-term history.
(New directions in archaeology)
Bibliography.
Includes index.
1. Archaeology. 2. Man, Prehistoric.
I. Hodder, Ian. II. Series.
GN766.A66   1987   930.1   86-18848

ISBN 0 521 32923 X   *90-5660*

CE

CONTENTS

CONTRIBUTORS

David Collett, Department of Archaeology, University of Cambridge, U.K.

Kevin Greene, Department of Archaeology, University of Newcastle-upon-Tyne, U.K.

Knut Helskog, University Museum, Tromsø, Norway

Ian Hodder, Department of Archaeology, University of Cambridge, U.K.

Paul Lane, Department of Archaeology, University of Cambridge, U.K.

Henrietta Moore, Department of Anthropology, University of Kent, U.K.

Jacqueline Nowakowski, Boswednack Manor, Zennor, St Ives, Cornwall, U.K.

Ajay Pratap, Department of Archaeology, University of Cambridge, U.K.

Peter Timmins, Department of Anthropology, McGill University, Montreal, Canada

Alexander von Gernet, Department of Anthropology, McGill University, Montreal, Canada

Elisabeth Vestergaard, The Medieval Centre, Odense University, Denmark

James Whitley, Department of Archaeology, University of Cambridge, U.K.

PREFACE

Archaeology has, particularly over the past two decades, emphasised systemic interrelationships. Indeed systems theory is a primary concept within processual archaeology. More recently, the analysis of social and symbolic structures has become increasingly prominent in the discipline. Both systemic and structural analyses are concerned to place things in their contemporary setting – the aim is to explain an object or event as part of a synchronic whole.

Thus a dichotomy is set up between synchronic and diachronic, historical, analysis. The natural links between two disciplines specifically concerned with the past, history and archaeology, were explicitly decried by many anthropological archaeologists within the New Archaeology.

Yet, at about the same time, many social and cultural anthropologists were themselves embracing history. Turning to archaeology, anthropologists would often be surprised to find little interest in their historical questions. Archaeology had become to a great extent ahistorical.

More recently, however, within the post-processual phase in archaeology, the links to history are being resought, and it is within this renewed effort to capture the traditional links between archaeology and history that this volume seeks to play its part. The causes of this renewed archaeological interest in history may be varied. There is the awakened interest in history within anthropology itself. There is the emergence of a stronger and more theoretically vocal historical archaeology. There is, for example, the sustained denial by Bruce Trigger of the need for a split between history and archaeology. And there are the internal doubts within archaeology about the adequacies of the processual programme. Whether particular causes can be given or not, there is a recurring pattern, a stream of interest across a range of disciplines – an interest in, and a questioning of, history.

Archaeology can, in particular, offer its long time span to this debate. But, as this volume demonstrates, the incorporation of history involves more than recognising the long term. It also involves a wider discussion of historical method and the philosophy of history. The notion that archaeology provides additional data for the study of historical processes gives this book its title.

There is a close connection here between the discussion of history and the discussion of context provided in a companion volume (I. Hodder (ed.), *The Archaeology of Contextual Meanings*, Cambridge University Press). The historical context is one component in the overall context relevant to an understanding of any material culture product. The analysis of historical texts has much to contribute to the analysis of material culture 'texts'. In this volume, historical analysis is probed in relation to the wider concern with all forms of contextual interpretation.

The historical approach
in archaeology

Chapter 1

The contribution
of the long term

Ian Hodder

Most existing approaches in archaeology are able to explain neither the generation nor the specificity of cultural material. There is a need for an historical dimension to add to the processual and structural approaches. By 'history' is meant Collingwood's 'history from the inside'. Archaeology is particularly able to contribute to the history of the long term. For example, questions of the special character of European developments over the long term were asked by Weber. Although Weber's work has had little impact in archaeology, Childe asked similar questions and it is possible today to describe more fully the distinctive character of Europe in prehistory. Such information is directly relevant to recent anthropological and historical discussion. Long-term history raises problems about the relationship between the past and the present, but it opens up a fundamentally different perspective on issues such as the relationship between the material and the ideal; whether enduring structures are peripheral to, or at the core of, social systems; the relationship between structure, process and meaning content; and the historical role of material culture resulting from its durability. Processes such as diffusion, acculturation, and the production of skeuomorphs need to be reintroduced into archaeology as being explanatory and as playing an important role in any study of social change.

What is meant by an historical approach in archaeology? Responses to this question often refer to the notion that adequate explanation involves identifying the series of events that lead up to the event to be explained. This is certainly part of the definition of history used in this volume. Yet such a viewpoint is already widely found in archaeology. Within systems theory, the system at time n is affected by the system

state at time n−1. In Marxist approaches in archaeology, the new social system arises out of, and is already present within, the preexisting contradictions. In palaeoeconomic approaches the historical dimensions of Darwinian theory are often retained.

Nevertheless, it has been more common in archaeology to oppose historical and scientific, anthropological, explanations. Whereas the latter form of explanation often emphasises cross-cultural regularities, the former often seems to get involved in detailed descriptions of particular cases. I wish to argue that there are two interrelated debates which separate historical from non-historical accounts.

The first concerns the relationship between description and explanation. I have argued (Hodder 1986) that archaeological explanations can always be shown to be descriptions given in response to questions – questions such as 'why is this site near this stream?' or 'why was this site abandoned?' These descriptions can be either general (such as, 'people use nearby resources') or particular (such as, 'the river broke its banks and flooded the settlement'). Even the relevance of a particular answer to a particular question is based on general and/or particular descriptions. But when a particular description is used we can understand it, and its relevance, only in terms of some general principles. What historical explanation tries to do is limit the dependence on general statements, because it is believed that the relevance of a general statement to a particular statement has to be proven, not assumed.

Thus, in answering the question 'why did this event occur?', the archaeological historian – the archaeo-historian – initially answers as best s/he can by describing the sequence of preexisting events in great detail. In identifying the totality of relevant factors, "total history" (Braudel, 1973, p. 1238) is written. Often using an 'aquatic' metaphor, a 'stream' or 'flow' of events is produced, with no easily determinable beginning or end. It is rather like the problem of deciding when life begins – is the important point when the first breath is taken, is it at some stage in the development of the foetus, or immediately the egg is fertilised? But fertilisation depends on sperm, and hence one life depends on another in a continuous stream. Archaeologists often talk of the stream of continual variability and change as one artifact type is transformed into another, and Sayce (1933) has provided some elegant demonstrations of such continua.

With this viewpoint, it becomes difficult to talk of the cause of a life, or the cause of a type. The generalising procedure involves breaking up continua in order to make general statements about cause and effect. But in historical analysis, the attempt at total description (which is itself explanatory and often highly theoretical) leads to an emphasis on process rather than event. Unfortunately, in archaeology, the term 'processual' has come to be associated with an approach which is, in fact, fundamentally non-processual. Processual archaeology has been closely tied to systems theory, to causal functional explanation, and to a 'billiard ball' view of the past based on the interrelationships of events. In historical analysis, on the other hand, the billiard game is not an appropriate metaphor because the definition of the entities (the balls) will vary in different historical contexts, and because there is a fluid set of interrelationships between the balls such that the balls merge and become one. And this one ball has fuzzy edges, and it transforms itself, changes its appearance as it moves through time. A river, with changing banks, or perhaps the currents of wind, are better metaphors.

Historical explanation, then, involves an attempt at particular and total description, and it does not oppose such description to explanation and general theory. Rather, our generalising anthropological concerns can progress only through an adequate description, and hence understanding in our terms, of the particular. The relationship between the general and the particular, between 'our' context and 'their' context, is opened to doubt and scrutiny.

The second debate which distinguishes historical from non-historical accounts concerns the question of whether culture is reducible to things outside itself. The stance taken by non-historical approaches is clear. For example, in many types of structuralism the codes are reducible ultimately to the binary and other mechanisms of the human mind. In ecological and functionalist archaeology, culture is reducible to its effects on, for example, population survival. On the other hand, the historical approach as used in this volume argues that cultures

are produced as organised and organising schemes of action that are meaningful to the individuals involved. These schemes are organised because of the human need to categorise and arrange, in order to perceive and act upon the world. The organisational schemes are arbitrary in the sense that their forms and content are not determined by anything outside themselves. But they are not arbitrary in the sense that, once the continuous stream of human action begins, there are necessary historical links as one scheme is transformed into another. Culture is, then, not reducible. It just is.

The organisational schemes are universal in the sense that they may have more general beginnings, held in common with others, and in the sense that we can all come to an understanding of them. But they are also particular and unique, created out of circumstances by the human mind. The historical process, the continual stream of being, is directed. And here we see the distinction between action and event made by Collingwood (1946). Rather than looking at events from the outside, it is necessary to attempt an understanding of 'the insides of events', to grasp the intentions, values and organisational schemes within human action. There is certainly a semiotic orientation to this view (see for example Preziosi 1979) but linked to an emphasis on social practice.

An historical approach in archaeology thus involves contributing to anthropological discussion an understanding of the processes of social change by concentrating on the particular context and on meaningful action. Yet in understanding any event as a particular action, how do we define the relevant temporal context? Is what happened 1,000 years ago relevant, or only the last five minutes? And is the event to be understood in terms of what is in the individual actor's head or in terms of some collective assumptions? In so far as they can be distinguished, what is the relative importance of social, economic and ideational structures?

An important attempt at answering such questions in a way that is immediately relevant to archaeologists was made by Braudel (1958, 1973) and the Annales school in Paris. Braudel identified three scales in the historical process, although these were simply arbitrary divisions of a continuum. First, over the very long term, there are permanent, slow-moving, or recurrent features. Thus, in his great work on the Mediterranean (1973) he talks of the "constants" and of "the deep bone-structure of the Mediterranean" (*ibid.*, pp. 1239 and 1240). Second, there is structural or social history. This is a history of groups, collective destinies and general trends with still slow but perceptible rhythms. Finally, there is the individual and the event. This is the traditional history of individual men and women and of the ephemera of brief happenings. In what follows I intend to discuss Braudel's scheme and relate it to recent work in archaeology and to the papers in this volume.

Very long-term structures and contents

It is perhaps misleading that Braudel often refers to his first, long-term history as geographical. His concern is not simply to describe the physical environment and to argue that enduring Mediterranean values are a product of this environment. Rather, the physical, social and ideational are all inextricably linked. For example, instead of describing the mountains of the Mediterranean as those areas above a certain arbitrary altitude, he asks "what exactly is a mountain?" He discusses the distinctive character of Mediterranean mountains as opposed to ranges elsewhere in the world, and describes the Mediterranean mountains in terms of "the freedom of the hills" where people are difficult to conquer and control (*ibid.*, p. 41). He talks of the recurrent character of the Mediterranean mountains as empty or as refuges, with dispersed as opposed to village occupation and having "a separate religious geography" (*ibid.*, p. 35). The Mediterranean islands, on the other hand, led isolated, yet often vital, and precarious lives, as can be seen from the aggregate of events over long periods. Indeed 'island' becomes a concept, so that Braudel can talk (*ibid.*, p. 160) of "islands that the sea does not surround". In explaining why the Reformation never really took hold in the Mediterranean, he suggests (*ibid.*, p. 768) that, "possibly because of an ancient substratum of polytheism", Mediterranean Christendom remained attached to the cult of the saints and the Virgin Mary.

For Braudel, then, any particular event is part of, influenced by, very long-term continuities which are both the aggregate of previous events, and structures and beliefs which form those events. The physical geography of a region will play an important role here, as was emphasised in archaeology by C. Fox (1932). But also, human relationships and perceptions have enduring qualities, closely tied to the physical constraints and opportunities.

There is an increasing interest in such long-term processes in archaeology and anthropology. For example, Alain Testart (1982) has argued that the sexual division of labour in hunter-gatherer societies cannot be reduced to various 'external' functional needs. For example, the hypotheses that women cannot hunt because children make them less mobile, or that two types of knowledge (hunting and gathering) are most efficiently separated, or that men and women have different natural strengths and abilities which suit them to particular tasks, are not supported by the evidence collated by Testart. Instead, Testart identifies a symbolic problem to do with blood. Humans separate two different kinds of flowing blood – that from killing animals, and menstrual blood. Hence the sexual division of labour results from a symbolic concern. Testart supports his case by showing that the taboos of contemporary hunter-gatherers are concerned specifically with separating weapons from women.

Such a model has various expectations about changes through time and place. For example, as hunting increases at the expense of collecting, women are brought more into the animal economy, so that taboos, rituals of separation, domestic cultural elaboration to do with hunting, food preparation and eating increase. This hypothesis may help to explain variation in cultural elaboration in, for example, the European Upper Palaeolithic.

Haudricourt (1962, p. 40) suggests that a further problem develops when agriculture begins. Plants and animals are brought into the home, domesticated, made part of the interior world of human culture. But at some point there is harvest and slaughter. This involves killing 'one's own', and has to be surrounded in ceremonies and 'rites de passage'.

Braudel's concern, however, is with more concrete structures which have some historical specificity. It would be necessary carefully to examine the relevance of the models of Testart and Haudricourt before applying them to the ancient world. Such applications are often facilitated by noting long-term contrasts between regions.

For example, Haudricourt (1962, and see Demoule 1982) draws an analogy between western ideologies and western domestic species, and between eastern ideologies and eastern domesticates. Sheep need direct and immediate control. Without its shepherd the sheep is vulnerable and the image of the pastoral shepherd as leader is important in western religion and political philosophy. Wheat and barley are not fragile but they do receive rough treatment as they are sown, harvested and the grains are separated out with violent motions. The emphasis in the west is on control. In the east, rice involves careful preparation of the ground and the water buffalo remains independent. Philosophy and politics emphasise indirect and bureaucratic control.

To support these hypothetical links in evidence from west and east would be an enormous task, involving analyses of a wide range of materials. Prehistory too would have to play its role, supporting or refuting the validity of Haudricourt's hypothetical links by examining whether the two different 'styles' of life did emerge with domestication. Clearly such structures remain abstract, and it is only when linked with action and event in Braudel's third category of history that their force becomes apparent and they become archaeologically visible.

One area in which archaeology has already been involved in discussion of long-term structures is in the debate about the origin and nature of Indo-Europeans. It is not my concern here to summarise this large area of controversy and uncertainty. Unfortunately much of the archaeological involvement has been at the level of identifying Indo-European traits (such as pastoralism), which is always dangerous given the propensity of traits or groups of traits to change their meanings in different contexts. Perhaps more useful would be to identify the long-term underlying structure of Indo-European society. Such a structure has been identified by Dumézil (1977) and is discussed by, for example, Demoule (1980), Haudry (1981) and Benveniste (1969).

Dumézil identifies a 'trifunctional' structure. The first part is a magic-religious sovereignty, a judicial and religious authority. The second is the force of warriors, and the third is production and reproduction. This basic structure has different transformations in all the different Indo-European groups, and it occurs in different forms in all areas of culture – in thought, religion, institutions, in the concept of history, medical doctrine and even in colour symbolism. For Dumézil this is an historical structure since although other societies have similar divisions, only among the Indo-Europeans is the 'trifunctional' structure found in all aspects of life. He notes the difference with bipartite divisions in China and the unity of Jewish religion (Demoule 1980, p. 112). The structure as defined is unique and endures over long periods, despite regionalisation and wide separation of the varied Indo-European groups.

Archaeologists have long toyed with the idea of identifying some common cultural core from which the varied European societies developed. Hawkes (1954, pp. 167–8), for example, wanted to follow such a regional, historical approach in order gradually to peel off the later variety and get at the common core. But it was Childe who devoted much of his work to identifying the particular nature of European society (Trigger 1980).

Childe's first edition (1925) of *The Dawn of European Civilization* was intended to understand the particular nature of European culture and to identify a spirit of independence and inventiveness that led to the industrial revolution. He suggested that a distinctively European spirit, involving vitality, inventiveness, a lack of authoritarianism and autocratic power, and a modern naturalism, began in the Bronze Age. Even in the sixth edition of *The Dawn* he argued that "a distinctively European culture had dawned by our Bronze Age" (1957, p. 33).

Childe's descriptions of the fundamental differences between west and east differ somewhat from the account of Haudricourt (see above), perhaps underlining the difficulty of making interpretations at this level of generality. Nevertheless, it remains possible, as Braudel's own work suggests, to collect data to strengthen or weaken alternative hypotheses. Childe was particularly concerned with the greater local diversity in Europe, and the quicker change and progress, especially in the evolution of tools and weapons. He made his contrasts with the Near East, but the same conclusions are reached by Lechtmann (1984) in her comparison of the technological characters of New World and Old World metallurgy. The importance and elaboration of metals in Europe are linked to their wider use in warfare, transport and agriculture, whereas in the Andes, for example, metals had a more symbolic role in both secular and religious spheres of life.

There has been much other work on long-term continuities in the New World (e.g. Bricker 1981; Coe 1978; Vogt 1964, 1965; Flannery and Marcus 1983), but I wish to continue with the European scene in order to demonstrate how such archaeological work can contribute to debate within other disciplines. Weber's (1976) analysis of the relationship between the Protestant ethic and the spirit of capitalism is in answer to his question "why does capitalism emerge in western Europe and not in other parts of the world?" Similar questions seem to lie behind the work of Haudricourt and Childe. But Weber does not have the time perspective to identify the growth of the Puritan emphases on duty and continuous bodily or mental labour. Rather than seeing any one 'cause' of the Protestant ethic, Weber suggests that it 'unfurls' from Roman law, to the

western church, to Protestantism. Clearly Childe saw similar developments even farther back, in the European Bronze Age. These concerns with 'origins' *are* important. Without the longer perspective one might think that capitalism 'caused' Protestantism, or the other way round. In fact, however, the 'direction' towards Protestantism may have existed for longer periods, growing and changing, unfurling in different conditions, producing capitalism but also produced by it.

The European worlds described by Weber and Childe involve individualism, quick change and an economic and practical rationality. In a discussion of the origins of English individualism, Macfarlane (1978, p. 163) suggests the hypothesis "that the majority of ordinary people in England from at least the thirteenth century were rampant individualists, highly mobile both geographically and socially, economically 'rational', market-oriented and acquisitive, ego-centred in kinship and social life". However, although Macfarlane accepts that the same character might be identifiable in *The Germans* of Tacitus, he cannot identify the origins of this long-term style. "It will need other works before we can trace the elusive English back to their particular roots" (*ibid.*, p. 206). Although Macfarlane is here concerned with England rather than Europe, it is again apparent that adequate considerations of historical events and of the relative importance of the different factors involved in social change lead to a search for the long term. Prehistory can here contribute to history, and hence to anthropology.

There are, of course, many dangers here, and the methods of history and long-term history will be discussed below. One of the major difficulties has been outlined by Merriman (1987). It is certainly attractive today to imagine prehistoric Europe filled with individualistic, creative, free, rational entrepreneurs. Yet Merriman shows how our views of Europe north of the Alps are derived from Classical Mediterranean authors projecting their sense of 'barbarian' onto this other world. In the nineteenth century a Romantic interest in the Celts and their independent spirit revived. Yet through critical assessment of the historical origin of such ideas, coupled with detailed consideration of European prehistoric data, particularly when contrasted with those of other parts of the world, I would argue that scientific analysis of long-term continuities in social, economic and symbolic structures can be conducted.

All continuities exist through change since no two actions can ever be identical. What types of rhythm of change occur over the long term? Archaeologists have been little concerned with such questions. It would be interesting, for example, to compare the numerous cases in which periods have been divided up into Early, Middle and Late phases. Are there any common characteristics of, for example, Early phases? And what causes variation between them? And once a certain type of Middle phase has been reached, what sort of leeway exists for the Late phase? Answers to such questions would lead to an understanding of whether long-term rhythms do occur.

Few European prehistoric archaeologists would accept a

distinction between a 'hot' rhythm of fast change in societies which emphasise the continuous process of history and a 'cold' rhythm of slow change in societies which emphasise categorical distinctions (Lévi-Strauss 1962). Yet if continual change is everywhere to be found, how does it proceed? One view is that, once a new structure or scheme has been found, there is the possibility of endless permutation and expansion. Thus, "all classification proceeds by pairs of contrasts: classification only ceases when it is no longer possible to establish oppositions. Strictly speaking, therefore, the system knows no checks" (Lévi-Strauss 1962, p. 217). This practically unlimited capacity for extension can be seen in many archaeological sequences. Sayce (1933) noted that by the process of elaboration from a simple idea one could move from a grass stem, to a clarinet, to all wind instruments, to the church organ. He also suggested that the pace of elaboration increased through time, and he provided an explanation. The mind is always busy producing patterns, and innovation comes about from playing with what is already there. As what is already there increases so also the pace of innovation increases.

In Chapter 2, Whitley provides an example of such a process, although within the German idealist tradition it has a slightly different meaning. Here there is the notion of an underlying ideal which the producers of material culture are trying to attain. There is a gradual move towards the 'perfect' expression of some abstract quality.

Of course, the phenomenon of 'decline' or 'simplification' is also commonly met. It can be argued that oppositional structures do not lend themselves to endless elaboration. At some point the system gets 'stuck' or 'filled up' as everything is cross-referenced to everything else in a dense, complex network. A new structure is derived out of the old, and the cycle can start again.

Such discussion is premature until the relevant research has been carried out. And also it is abstract. Can one really talk of structures becoming more or less elaborate and complex as if they meant nothing and did nothing in the social realm? To a certain extent it can be argued that there may be constraints deriving from structures which are independent of other, shorter histories. Clearly, however, most structural variation and change are located within shorter-term strategies, to be considered below. It is the shorter-term changes which reproduce and create the longer term. It is important not to reify the long term. Yet, in so far as there is an interaction between the long and short terms, archaeologists, and particularly prehistorians, can play an indispensable role. That role will have to be argued by archaeologists in ways that have been largely ignored recently.

Social structures

If there is some degree of determinancy on human agency identifiable in long-term continuities, there may also be constraints provided by social structures. The individual event takes place within certain bounds set by the social conditions of existence, and it is the analysis of these constraints that Braudel

(1973) called social or structural history. In his work on the Mediterranean in the sixteenth century AD, Braudel gave many examples of this scale of historical analysis. Some of the social structures seem unchanging over the period considered. For example, a quadrilateral of cities (Genoa, Milan, Venice and Florence) formed the economic centre of the Mediterranean in the fifteenth and sixteenth centuries. Distance also remained a constant in this period (*ibid.*, p. 369). Average speeds for covering a set distance remained much the same before and after the sixteenth century so that administration, letters, orders and troop movements were all similarly affected. Any particular action occurring over space is influenced by constraints which take their form within a specific set of social, technological and ideational conditions.

Other social conditions which influence individual actions include temporal change. Braudel (*ibid.*) provided many examples of prices and wage curves for the sixteenth century, of demographic movements and the changing dimensions of states and empires. He also talked of sixteenth-century society tending to polarise through time into a rich nobility and a great and growing mass of the poor and disinherited (*ibid.*, p. 755).

Archaeologists have long been concerned to identify quantitative trends of similar types. Logistic and exponential growth curves for population increase, 'battle-ship' curves for the increase and decrease in the popularity of styles, the increasing separation of hierarchical levels in settlement pattern studies, the increasing dependence on certain resources, have all been charted by archaeologists, and the methods involved have become a regular part of the archaeological armoury.

Such analyses involve little more than the surface description of aggregates of events. It is difficult to argue that the events themselves are constrained by the quantitative trends which they produce. An alternative is to examine the relationship between structure and event which lies behind and produces the quantitative trends. Archaeological concepts of social structure have been greatly developed by Marxist critique and discussion (e.g. Spriggs 1984).

Incorporation of the notion of an underlying structure of social relations is seen in this volume in the work of, for example, Pratap (Chapter 8). Patterns of regional exploitation and domination in India have affected the subsistence strategies of individual groups and imply that generalisation or comparison with the subsistence economies of groups elsewhere may be difficult. Vestergaard (Chapter 7) discusses the way in which the different social structures of neighbouring groups may be linked to different ways in which material culture is given social meaning. Collett too (Chapter 10) shows that the ordering of the material world is dependent on a set of social meanings of some historical specificity.

However, as with longer-term structures, there is a danger that the social structure becomes reified such that the relationship between structure and action is obscured. Many Marxist studies of social structure have long been concerned to identify general evolutionary trends. More recently Parker Pearson (1984) and Bonte (1977) have been influenced by

Leach (1954) in their identification of cyclical social trends occurring within broad material constraints. Yet even within such studies of the rhythms of social-structural change, the individual often appears caught within trends beyond his or her comprehension.

While the importance of the social structure in delimiting human action can readily be admitted, and while the social structure as the unintended consequence of action can be accepted (Giddens 1979), what exactly is the relationship between structure and intentional action? What role can individual events play? What is the individual potsherd in the overall scheme of things? These questions will be considered further below, but first the individual event itself can be discussed as Braudel's third scale of historical analysis.

Individuals and events

For Braudel (1973, p. 901), every event, however brief, has some effect on larger-scale structures. But the writing of such history is more selective in that the historian has to pick out events that are considered 'important'. The definition of importance partly relates to the questions being asked. More specifically, Braudel (*ibid.*, p. 902) defines an important event as one that has consequences. He talks of chains of events, and picks out certain wars, the coming to power of particular kings and leaders, as significant in the phase by phase historical description.

Archaeologists dig up individual artifacts which are the results of individual events. They have to reconstruct the social structures, the groups, the societies, the regions, from the individual traces on potsherds, individual discard and constructional events. While considerable energy has recently been invested in the identification and explanation of archaeological variability, the relationship between variability and norm or structure has been largely ignored. The role of the individual has been denied, and archaeological variability has, wherever possible, been reduced to predictable, rule-governed behaviour.

Braudel remained unsure about the relationship between event and structure. His view that "the long run always wins in the end" (1973, p. 1244) has an internal logic, a tautologous character from which it is difficult to escape. Yet it does seem possible to argue that since societies are made up of individuals, and since individuals can form groups to further their ends, directed, intentional behaviour of individual actors or ideologies can lead to structural change. Indeed, societies might best be seen as non-static negotiations between a variety of changing and uncertain perspectives.

Nowakowski (Chapter 5), for example, shows the way in which different individuals and groups of individuals within 'one society' have different senses of 'place', and make different uses and interpretations of material culture items. A similar point has been made by Kent (1983) in relation to ethnographic and archaeological work. Nowakowski, Vestergaard (Chapter 7) and Helskog (Chapter 3), all demonstrate processes whereby individuals make different selections from within a cultural tradition, giving the same things different meanings and transforming them within new contexts.

It is not argued here that archaeologists should try to identify individual or named persons in the past. Rather the concern is to break down the notion that clear-cut aggregates and common structures exist within the entities that we construct as archaeologists. It is not enough simply to note variability and to explain it 'from the outside', by reference to general laws about social structures and behavioural trends. Each event can be seen, not as the passive by-product of 'the environment', but as an active force in changing that environment. Both the particularity and the meaning content of the actions need to be addressed if that force is to be reconstructed.

Of the myriad of individual events excavated by archaeologists, which are significant in shaping long-term and medium-term structures? The answer to such a question lies in our ability as archaeologists to recognise Braudel's chains of events. It is from analyses of such chains that archaeologists can begin to make contributions to understanding of the relationships between structure and event. Moore (Chapter 9) provides an example of a 'knock-on effect' which illustrates the need, even at this third scale of historical analysis, to consider the 'inside' of events.

She shows how an initial event – colonial pressure about hygiene in Kenyan Marakwet settlements – coupled with an indigenous desire to use the house for entertaining and display, had the consequence that males and females no longer had their own huts, but that kitchen and entertaining/living huts were separated. An indigenous, pre-existing principle connected burial places to houses. But, because of the reorganisation of hut use, men and women could no longer be buried separately in relation to houses. Another local principle linked the separation and discard of rubbish to burial. Now, no longer were different kinds of refuse kept distinct. The initial event has had a knock-on effect on settlement, burial and refuse disposal. But these systemic relationships make sense only in terms of the local principles of meaning and, as Moore shows, in terms of the directed strategies of individuals and sub-sections within society.

The replacement of stone axes by steel axes had many knock-on effects in Aborigine groups (e.g. Sharp 1952), the effects varying according to the social structures and systems of meaning within different groups (Melody Pope, pers. comm.). The ethnographer, like the historian or archaeologist, cannot be sure that a statistical correlation in time and place implies a relevant relationship. The notion that an event is relevant and important for another depends partly on inductive analyses of interrelationships, coincidences and differences, but also on the ability of the analyst to provide some theory to account for the interrelationships. We have seen that, to be plausible, the theory must include internal perceptions, motivations and cultural patterns.

Where do the individual events occur that ultimately lead

to major social and cultural change? Archaeologists have the ability to watch the way in which variability in one realm becomes adopted to take a dominant position. Do new social forms tend to have their origin in peripheral, subordinate areas of life or are they produced from within the centre? Does material culture behaviour in 'harmless' areas of activity provide an objectification of alternative models of society that ultimately challenge the dominant mode? In what ways can the event change the structure?

Continuity and change

In some ways Braudel's scheme as outlined above is best replaced by an examination of the relationships between structure (of various types and scales) and event (of various types and scales). This is a more flexible approach which directly faces the main problem raised by Braudel. To what extent do structures, aggregates and wholes have any real independent existence? Do objective historical processes exist independent of human agency?

It can be argued that ideational structures are the most lasting and determinant. The argument here might be that humans cannot live, eat or act without perception based on cultural-historical frameworks. In this case it is symbolic archaeology that will unearth the longest-term structures. Or else it can be argued that ideational structures endure only because they are peripheral and unimportant, the dominant structures being social and economic.

Throughout this volume, the view is taken that there is a two-way relationship between structure and action, and that this relationship is often more dialectic and antagonistic than smooth and systemic.

It is relevant here to consider the relationships between continuity and change and between tradition and novelty. A major contribution in this field was made by Redfield (1953, 1956). Moore (Chapter 9) follows Gluckman (1958) in making a distinction between continuity through change and change through continuity. In the first case practices persist in changing circumstances, and in the second case practices change in order to retain things as they are. These two strategies may be negotiated by different groups in relation to each other, and Moore provides some examples. Further illustration is provided by Vestergaard (Chapter 7).

Willis (1977) has shown the way in which strategies taken by individuals against the system in which they live may have the unintended consequence of maintaining the structure of that system. Lane (Chapter 6) also argues that the social structure as represented in settlement space is continually given new meaning, reordered but reestablished as individuals follow through their varying life strategies.

Material culture, especially in the form of buildings, as discussed by Lane, Nowakowski, Moore and Collett, has a particular importance in the relationship between change and continuity, event and structure. By their very durability (Donley 1982), material constructions provide a potential for the 'fixing' of dominant meanings, for making those meanings

seem lasting and unchanging. There is always the possibility for reinterpretation. Yet the material construction itself provides a limit to reevaluation. Or at least the construction provides a peg on which social strategies can be hung.

At the same time, notions such as 'continuity' and 'change' are very much matters of perception, involving the evaluation of similarity and difference. Temporal perspectives and structures are built in the present as much as they determine the present. It is necessary, then, to move from a consideration of space and distance as socially meaningful and historically particular, a realm already well covered in archaeology, to an equivalent consideration of time.

It can be argued that time has two natural characteristics. On the one hand it is continuous. In the chain of being life has no beginning and no end – there is only transformation and continuous change. On the other hand it has natural breaks – birth, death, day, night – a bird flies away, a rock falls. In the social and cultural realm it is the same. On the one hand history is a continual stream of becoming and doing. Yet this continuity can be broken, punctuated by changes that can be sensed.

In human society natural and cultural events are used to emphasise sameness, difference, becoming, death, and so on. Individuals may try to make two pots the same in order to build a continuity. Such strategies may have the effect of denying time, of timelessness. Hence ideologies involving naturalisation are invoked. The two pots can also be made substantially different, ushering in a new order, and an identification of past opposed to present. Nowakowski (Chapter 5) and Lane (Chapter 6) provide contrasting examples of how knocking down a house or wall, punctuating time, can have effects on the continuity of the social structure.

Diffusion and migration provide settings in which the often complex and subtle interrelationships between continuity and change can be played out. These processes are discussed in particular in the final section in this volume by Collett (Chapter 10) and Greene (Chapter 11), where the point is made that the impact of the new forms depends on their previous social meanings and on the new context in which they are placed. The identification of diffusion is itself explanatory in that it explains why a particular form is found in a particular area. But it can also be seen as a social and symbolic process requiring further historical probing.

Similarly, the term 'acculturation' often appears overly abstract and descriptive. As Moore (Chapter 9) argues, the word is often used in such a way as to imply culture contact between groups, emulation, borrowing and the possible absorption of one group by another. But the widespread use of such a term may hide important differences in the processes of social change in different historical circumstances. An alternative approach is to examine the forces of change and continuity as structural components of groups in contact with one another, and then to examine the event of that contact in relation to structure.

In the hands of traditional archaeologists the skeuomorph helps to explain the shape and decoration of artifacts. Thus,

Sayce (1933, p. 87) explained the decoration of a pottery vessel by saying that it derived from or copied a leather original. Von Gernet and Timmins (Chapter 4) define a skeuomorph as the reappearance of a shape or decoration that had previously occurred in a different medium or material. Such a process is again one in which continuity and change, structure and event, interplay. But the social effect of such ploys cannot be understood outside their particular historical contexts. Particular, 'inside' archaeo-history is required.

It might be suggested, then, that the old tired debates about whether cultural change is internal or external, autonomous or introduced (see Odner 1983b for a summary in relation to European prehistory), were necessarily of limited value since all change incorporates continuity and the archaeologist can emphasise one or the other at will. The problem here has been the failure to identify continuity and change as social-symbolic processes. They have been studied from the outside, as givens. An alternative approach is to examine the ways in which similarity and difference, continuity and change, are constructed through material culture, and to interpret the way in which these constructions play a role in the dialectical relationship between structure and event. Thus, each material act has the potential for reordering the past, for causing temporal breaks and for bringing about new perceptions of the past. How and whether it does so or not depend on the social-symbolic strategies of individuals and groups within particular historical contexts.

Methods and conclusions

The methods employed in all the applied examples in this volume suggest a certain coherence of approach. First, all the authors take Lane's (Chapter 6) point of view that we do not have to observe the act of novel writing to be able to understand a novel. Hypotheses about what was in the author's head may be part of that understanding, and an interview with the author might throw some further light. Yet all texts, written or material culture, have multiple meanings at different levels. The author's thoughts are part of the picture but they may be irrelevant to many types of enquiry about meaning and event. In this volume it is assumed that past words and cultural acts can be 'read' by placing them more fully into patterned, structured relationships – that is, within the wider 'text' of which they form a part. Such con-textual analysis is both particular and general, concrete and theoretical. Rather than translating the text into something other than itself, the aim is, as far as possible, to understand it in its own terms.

It is, then, incumbent on the archaeo-historian to demonstrate that arguments about long-term structures and about the significance of individual events do make coherent sense of the data as perceived. This is partly a pattern-playing, inductive exercise. The data are searched for recurring patterns of association and contrast, similarity and difference. Data may seem to be relevant to each other because of statistically significant patterning. But at the same time theory is imposed, both general and particular.

While the need to contribute to and use general theory is accepted within this volume, the authors remain wary of the uncritical application of general terms. This point is made specifically by Pratap (Chapter 8) in relation to 'shifting cultivation' and by Moore (Chapter 9) in relation to 'acculturation' and 'westernisation'. All such terms and general concepts have to be scrutinised in relation to the particular historical data being considered.

The transference of information from one society to another on the basis of some perceived likeness between them is often called indirect or cross-cultural analogy. Von Gernet and Timmins (Chapter 4) make the important point that many apparently indirect analogies may in fact be direct in the sense that the two societies being compared may have a common historical ancestry. Here again the need for archaeologists to examine the origin and divergence of long-term cultural traditions is apparent. Superficially two societies may appear very different. But at the structural level there may be similarities deriving from a common cultural core. This commonality is not only an essential part of any understanding of analogical comparison. It is also part of an understanding of the adaptive processes at work in the two societies.

Since historical method as described here is accommodative and, in an absolute sense, uncertain, and since the meanings of texts are seen as multiple and open-ended, the authority of the archaeological interpretation cannot reside solely in appeals to the data. It is equally important for archaeologists to be self-critical, not only in relation to the questions they ask of the data, but also in relation to answers given. This point is expressed by Pratap (Chapter 8) and is particularly important in relation to the search for long-term structures where the past and present are brought closer together. Where the past is in this way made relevant to the present it can all too easily become the mirror of the present. David Clarke's (1973) description of a new critical awareness, a loss of innocence in archaeology, in fact contributed to a continued blindness to the social construction of the archaeological past. It is only more recently that self-critical analysis has been encouraged in archaeology (e.g. Conkey and Spector 1984; Handsman 1980, 1983; Leone 1982). Such analysis of our own texts, our archaeological writings, is part of historical analysis and integrates the study of the present with that of the past. The idea and identification of long-term structures may derive from the present. But, equally, long-term structures, identifiable in the archaeological domain, may contribute to and form the present world and the archaeologist within it.

Chapter 2

Art history, archaeology and idealism: the German tradition

James Whitley

Some aspects of the German archaeological scene often appear to Anglo-American archaeologists as overly concerned with description rather than with scientific explanation. German archaeology is decried as old-fashioned, out-of-touch. Whitley demonstrates, however, that an idealist tradition in German archaeology and art history leads to a distinctive view of material objects and their interpretation which needs to be understood in its own terms. In examining nineteenth-century art history and some examples of German archaeological interpretation, Whitley demonstrates close links to Kant and Hegel and to a concern less with explanation of material culture by reference to function and context, and more with identifying abstract issues which formalise and contribute to the generation of art and material culture. Anglo-American archaeology would benefit from an incorporation of these more humane yet scientifically idealist aims and methods within a broader contextual approach.

To many British and American archaeologists, particularly to those influenced by the so-called 'new' archaeology of the past two decades, German archaeology often appears strange and unlovely. It seems narrow in its almost exclusive concentration upon artifacts and unnecessarily exhaustive in their description. It appears to lack the geographical, economic and anthropological dimensions of Anglo-American archaeology. But this judgement is superficial. German archaeology is a separate tradition, almost a separate discipline, whose concerns are often quite different from our own. This difference in part stems from a much closer relationship with art history, with aesthetics, and ultimately with philosophy; in particular with that philosophical perspective often referred to as 'idealism'. These are the relationships I wish to examine. I shall therefore be concerned with three related themes: the notion of 'Idealism' as a part of philosophical thought; its appropriation by German art historians and its application to the study of stylistic change; and the use of 'idealist' theories derived from art history in the study of prehistoric material.

In contrast to these overtly philosophical concerns, Anglo-American archaeologists have recently dealt with the phenomenon of 'style' in one of two ways: either they have approached material culture from a sociological standpoint (where cultural items become the currency for the endless renegotiation of power relations); or they have treated artifacts as the products of universal behavioural norms (where artifacts are judged by purely utilitarian standards). Aesthetics as such has not been regarded as a proper subject of archaeological interest. Yet at a time when there is a much greater theoretical interest in material culture among British and American archaeologists, the German tradition should not be ignored. It is in the hope that this perspective still has something to contribute, if only by way of balance, that this article is written.

The word 'idealism' can have many meanings, but the attempt to bring them all into play simultaneously can result only in confusion. The political and moral connotations of the word should first be dispensed with. Equally there have been many definitions of the term recently adopted which are, to say the least, inappropriate. Idealism did not originally mean the possession of ideas by the writer or author. Similarly the use of the term 'idealism' to denote the attempt by some historians to attribute ideas to people in the past (ideas conceived of as thoughts or concepts) and then to seek an explanation of historical change in terms of those ideas is of recent coinage. In the twentieth century it is true that some German art historians have seen works of art as the physical manifestation, the embodiment as it were, of ideas and/or ideals held by the artists themselves, and sometimes these art historians have been called 'idealist'. There is thus in many ways a similarity between the German art historian Panofsky and the English historian Collingwood. Just as Panofsky (1957) thought it necessary to reconstruct the ideas of the Abbé Suger before one could begin to understand the abbey church of St Denis, so Collingwood (1946, p. 199), quoting Croce, felt that, in order to write the history of a Neolithic Ligurian one had to reenact in one's own mind the thoughts and feelings which led a Neolithic Ligurian to act in the way that he did. But, Panofsky's idealism is not Kant's, and to use the term 'idealism' in this way is to mistake its original meaning. With respect to nineteenth-century art history the term has a more restricted, a more precise, sense, one that bears a closer relationship to its usage in western philosophy. To understand this sense we have to return to one of the originators of the western philosophical tradition, Plato.[1]

Plato did not have a notion of idealism, but he did have a theory of ideas or forms. Briefly stated, he noticed that while individual horses, humans, tables and the like have a transient material existence, the forms of humans, horses, etc. not only reappear but persist apparently eternally. What makes humans human and horses horses therefore cannot be the material from which they are composed, but an eternal essence in which they partake, Humanity or Horseness. (Sometimes he expressed this relationship differently: particular horses were imitations of the eternal form, Horseness.) These essences must be eternal otherwise the examples of such forms could not repeat themselves with such fidelity to type. The Forms were therefore, in a sense, more real, and certainly to be more highly regarded than any individual man or horse, and the notion that it is an abstract principle which animates the phenomenal world is a thread which links many features of western, particularly German, thought. Strangely, if logically, this led Plato to devalue art. Art is an imitation of the phenomenal world which in turn is an imitation of the world of Forms or Ideas. Art is therefore the least real of all things, and of least value. Yet western thought has frequently used Platonic metaphysics and Platonic arguments to turn Plato's own evaluation of art on its head. Later Christian writers, particularly those Byzantine theologians who stood opposed to the image-breaking Iconoclasts, wished to show that the religious art of their own age was of real spiritual value, indeed that it served a spiritual purpose. They therefore argued that images, icons, were a medium through which the divine spirit could enter the phenomenal world to be apprehended by human eyes. For

them art played a transcendental role in human experience (see Runciman 1975, pp. 81–9; Ware 1964, pp. 38–42). In a similar vein, Panofsky has traced the influence of the neo-platonic notion of Idea, as providing both an ideological justification for the making of works of art and an intellectual tool for understanding its purpose, in western Europe from Antiquity through the medieval period to the seventeenth century (Panofsky 1968). German art historians, standing at the end of this tradition, admiring art as much as they admired Plato, seemed to have thought along lines not dissimilar from earlier Christian apologists. Even E. H. Gombrich, the least mystical of German art historians and the one most influenced by British empirical modes of thought, could say (1979, p. 84): "I would still defend the position that Mozart has found means of giving real pleasure to human beings which are as objectively suited to this purpose as are aeroplanes to flying, that Fra Angelico has discovered ways of expressing devotion or Rembrandt of hinting at mysteries anybody can learn to see because they are 'there'."

It is important to note that Gombrich is not simply claiming that Fra Angelico had an 'ideal' of devotion or Rembrandt of mystery that they wished to express. He is also saying that, in a timeless sense, Rembrandt's paintings are about mystery and Fra Angelico's about devotion. It is possible for someone from an age or culture quite different from that of either painter to come to an understanding of these works, to an appreciation of their timeless qualities. This attitude has affected most German art historians, though it is a notion which we, in our relativist age, encouraged to believe that whatever claims to be art is art, find difficult to credit. The critical art historians, however, sought to justify the timeless claims of art, and moreover sought to understand how it is that something in a Platonic sense, transient and material, can possess 'timeless' qualities. How did this come about?

Art history began as a discipline separate from the related enquiries of aesthetics and archaeology in the early nineteenth century. With aesthetics it continues to share a philosophical interest in the questions of perception, judgement and knowledge. With archaeology it shares a concern with the material and cultural forms of the world and with historical change. The word archaeology in art historical parlance has however now come to mean a restricted interest in the particular historical conditions surrounding a work or style; in detailed problems of technique and craftsmanship; and in patronage and explicit intention. It is not that the idealist or critical school of art historians disdains to consider such questions. They are considered important, but secondary, and as regards stylistic change there has been very much a tendency to seek non-functional explanations. I will try to trace some of the reasons for this below.

What must also be remembered about the early art historians, apart from the fact that their education was strongly absorbed by philosophical issues, is their knowledge of and affinity to the art of the antique world. Throughout the nineteenth century the art of the Greeks was thought to be exemplary, and it was in relation to this art that most judgements were made. At the same time their knowledge of the ancient world led them sometimes into the consideration of older civilisations, particularly the Egyptian, and their acquaintance with archaeology enabled them to expropriate the art of many cultures into their enquiry. Their ideas thus had, in the nineteenth century, an effect upon archaeological thinking, particularly in Classical Archaeology. In the twentieth century, art history tended to restrict its interest to the specifically western and post-Roman traditions of oil painting and architecture, and this earlier breadth of concern was dissipated, though never lost. For this reason I shall be concentrating upon nineteenth-century art historians and their effect upon archaeology.

There were perhaps three men who initiated the project of German art history: Winckelmann, Kant and Hegel. Winckelmann was the first to try to write a history of antique art as opposed simply to treating the Classical world as a repository of Great Works. Kant is important not primarily because of his few remarks on art nor for his idea that 'freedom' is to be found in the contemplation of works of art, but for his philosophy. Kant offered a critique of the empiricist concept of knowledge. He argued that the mind is not a tabula rasa upon which the order of the world impresses itself, but that we can make sense of the world only through our reasoning faculty, which exists prior to any experience. Our knowledge and judgement of the world are thus products of our reasoned engagement with it. Kant and many other German thinkers placed an especial value on art as opposed to other material things as an object for the mind's engagement and sought to understand what was distinctive in this form of experience. This was one of the reasons why functional explanations were thought to be dissatisfactory to many German thinkers. For the contemplation and retrieval of the past had to possess a moral dimension. To reconstruct the intentions and purposes which an object was meant to serve, or to uncover the details of its manufacture or to discern its relationship with contemporary antecedent or precedent works was not thought to be an exercise capable of a morally as well as an intellectually reasoned engagement. Thus though explanations of, for instance, the details of the form of certain Egyptian statuary in terms of the funerary rituals and commemorative functions they were meant to serve were quite common at the beginning of the nineteenth century, such explanations never found favour with the major critical art historians, who felt they should be doing something more. Their conception of the retrieval of the past necessarily involved an aesthetic evaluation. An account of the circumstances surrounding any work of art, of its cultural context, or even of the artist's stated intentions and ideals, was for them a purely descriptive exercise.

To turn to Hegel, he was not the first to write about art in a manner that was both historical and aesthetic but he was the first to relate artistic development to an aesthetic and philosophical system. There is a vulgarised belief that Hegel was responsible for that form of explanation which attributes all cultural forms to 'the spirit of the age'. Hegel's notion of Idea and Spirit are in fact quite different. Hegel saw historical progress teleologically as the gradual realisation of Spirit. Human achievement lies in the ever more subtle articulation of Spirit in all cultural forms, from philosophy to art. Thus though the pyramids may be a great and noble achievement for their age, as a refined expression of Spirit they were not to be compared with a Gothic cathedral, whose form was not simply massive but was subtle and aesthetically refined in its construction.

It would be an exaggeration to say that Hegel's thought cast a shadow over nineteenth-century art history. But the tendency to combine an historical account of change, particularly in architecture and sculpture, with a lack of attention to the purposes which that art was meant to serve is a persistent feature of art history in this period. This tendency is most evident in Hegel's immediate successor, Schnaase. Schnaase's main field of interest was medieval, particularly Gothic, architecture, and he payed special attention to the problem of how such an architecture could have developed from antique forms. A key phase in this development was the transformation of the Roman basilica into the Christian church. Schnaase did not see this change as the natural response to ideological (particularly liturgical) needs nor as the expression of the new Christian spirit. He saw it primarily as a logical development, the logic being a movement from an emphasis on a building's exterior (the most obvious examples of this type being Greek temples, which were architecturally impressive only from the outside) to the interior (examples being the fifth- and sixth-century churches in Ravenna and Istanbul), to the extent that the shape of the interior began to determine the form of the exterior. To give the flavour of this type of account, Schnaase himself is worth quoting. On ancient architecture he has this to say (quoted in Podro 1982, p. 34): "Ancient architecture was less capable of creating a beautiful interior because it placed greatest importance on the self-contained, firm forms, defined by circles and straight lines. It was not only the religious and domestic morals of the ancient world which made the interiors of their buildings unimportant, but also its formal sense."

This formal sense cannot be equated with any beliefs the people of that age might have held, but with an Idea which can be seen only retrospectively. Michael Podro has this to say on Schnaase (Podro 1982, p. 40): "Schnaase's explicit prising free of the work of art from its functional and symbolic purpose can be seen to enforce a strong reading of his transformation thesis; the strong reading of the thesis is that we understand a work as modifying its antecedents and as carrying intimations of its successors. This way of interpreting works becomes more plausible once their visual form is released from contextual functions and contingent meanings. For then the works can be seen exclusively in the context of each other, and so as progressive modifications of each other: the rationale of each can be identified with its role in the developmental sequence."

What must be underlined in Schnaase's approach is his

Fig. 2.1 Continuity in the
decoration of capitals
(examples taken from
Riegl 1923)

complete separation of works of art from the culture that
produced them. In seeing the transformation as a sequence of
forms governed by an internal logic, and in disregarding context
and function, Schnaase treats artistic development as
autonomous. As Podro points out (1982, p. 41), "to be
autonomous is to have a separate history". The idea that
artistic development was autonomous was strongly to affect
later accounts, in particular that of Schnaase's successor, Alois
Riegl.

Before dealing with Riegl, a brief word is required on
another form of explanation current in nineteenth-century
German art historical thought. This focussed upon craft
traditions and sought to explain them in one of two ways.
Either changes in form were seen as the outcome of the
interpenetration of motifs and techniques from one craft
tradition to another, or the craft tradition as a whole was
viewed as the progressive realisations of potentialities inherent
in the medium. Thus the history of pottery can be seen as the
unfolding of the possibility of plasticity, the history of sculpture
that of stone. Riegl reacted strongly against this type of
explanation. In his earlier work (Riegl 1893, p. 192) his
Stilfragen (on which I would like to concentrate because it
ranges over examples which are as much archaeological as they
are artistic), he developed a different theory of overall stylistic
change. The theme of this work is the development of the
acanthus and palmette motif from ancient Egypt onwards. In
common with much German thought he saw the transformation
of the lotus to the palmette not as a motif whose change was
due to the differing imitation of natural forms, but as possessing
an internal dynamic. To quote Podro again, he saw in its
development "the urgencies of design" (1982, p. 71) and a
striving towards "richer and more integrated form" (*ibid.*,
p. xxv). A key feature of his thesis is that antecedent artistic
forms have the greatest effect on subsequent development, and
not natural forms which can be observed in the present. This
led him to stress the continuity in the decoration of capitals
(though this continuity was interrupted when at one stage the
decorative motif linking the Egyptian with the Greek, the
palmette, was for a brief period to be found only on the surface
of pots) from the Egyptian through the Greeks and Romans to
the Romanesque and beyond (see fig. 2.1). For him the forms
of art resembled the forms of the natural world not because the
former were imitations of the latter but because they shared the
same evolutionary urge. In the organic as in the cultural world
variety not only is the result of a development from antecedent
forms but also exhibits a natural tendency towards exuberance.
The sequence of change from lotus through palmette to
acanthus and later capitals may stand as the paradigm for such
development.

The central dilemma of the idealist tradition came to a
head in the personality of Heinrich Wolfflin. The questions
which most preoccupied Wolfflin concerned how we come to
understand the expressive character of art, and in particular the
expressive character of periods and styles. In this sense he was
concerned with stylistic change, and how we can understand not

only the process but the logic of such change. In the late nineteenth century this general question had occupied the minds of many thinkers. Do we see the expressive character of art as immanent in the works themselves, as individual manifestations of some indefinable Zeitgeist, as many followers of Hegel would have done? Or, more concretely, do we see art as the outcome of a particular social context, the complex interplay of ideology, social relations, patronage and the artist's skill, reading, as it were, out of a work of art those concrete cultural forces which originally went into it? Wolfflin found such forms of explanation unsatisfactory, and sought, by contrast, to understand the nature of a work or style in terms of formal principles. Wolfflin had a particular affection for the art of the Renaissance and Baroque and he devised a set of formal categories not simply to describe, but to analyse the art of these two periods. Whereas the art of the High Renaissance is characterised by linear (draughtsmanly) definition, is 'planimetric' in its suggestion of space, uses 'closed' forms, and achieves its unity by a harmony of parts, Baroque art is characterised by a 'painterly' definition of line, aims primarily, in its use of recession, to emphasise depth, employs 'open' forms and achieves its unity by concentration on a single theme. In his most important work, *The Principles of Art History* (Wolfflin 1950), he comes close to identifying these formal properties with the expressive characters of Renaissance and Baroque art respectively. That is to say these formal attributes are not merely ways of describing the difference between Renaissance and Baroque styles in a typological sense, nor are they the means whereby an effect is achieved, an effect whose character is ultimately determined by ideological requirements,

but are, in themselves, constitutive of the nature of the art of these two periods. Wolfflin's approach has been widely criticised (see Gombrich 1966; Podro 1982, pp. 98–151), and Wolfflin himself was well aware of the inadequacies of his formal analysis. But no art historian would deny that his approach and his categories have added immensely to our understanding of the nature of both Renaissance and Baroque art. In particular his refinement of the technique of formal comparison, where verbal arguments are constructed through a series of contrasting images, has had enormous influence. This has extended beyond the realm of art history proper and has become an integral part of much German archaeological argument.

It is perhaps time to provide an archaeological example. This comes from the prehistoric Aegean, where archaeologists of many nationalities work and where the Germans in particular have long been strongly represented. In the Aegean one of the most puzzling and longstanding problems is the radical discontinuity, in almost every feature of life from house forms, burial customs and metal-working to canonical vase shapes, between the Late Bronze Age (Mycenaean) and the period of the introduction of iron-working (Protogeometric and Early Geometric). The example is taken from the work of the German archaeologist Bernhard Schweitzer, and deals with the form of explanation he adopts for the change from Late

Fig. 2.2 Mycenaean piriform jar (from Schweitzer 1971)

Fig. 2.3 Protogeometric neck-handled amphora (from Schweitzer 1971)

Mycenaean to Protogeometric. This example, I believe, exemplifies the influence which this tradition has had upon archaeology. He contrasts a Late Mycenaean (LHIIIB) three-handled piriform jar with its Protogeometic successor (figs. 2.2 and 2.3). He regards them as functional equivalents, and any change in shape or decoration cannot therefore be due simply to functional criteria. His remarks deserve extensive quotation. On the earlier LHIIIB piriform jar he has this to say (1971, p. 24): "Three shoulder handles emphasize the many-sidedness, the spatiality, and the circular dynamic of the volume of the vase. The foot and the neck at the extremities of the vertical axis accentuate the effect of volume, giving it firmness and stability within the concrete exterior space, while forming as far as possible an integral part of the total system of expression." On the other hand, he has this to say of its Protogeometric and Geometric successor, the neck-handled amphora (*ibid.*): "These handles were called 'ears' in Greek, expressing the newly developed double bilaterality of form: the separation of front and back and the affinity of the vessel with the human body, with its pairs of limbs and visible organs around a symmetrical axis. The sense of verticality increases in Ripe and Late Geometric. The vertical axis begins gradually to predominate over the dimensions of volume and depth. The whole vessel is constructed around the vertical." He becomes almost lyrical in his account of the implications of the new form (*ibid.*): ". . . here it becomes the opposite of the Mycenaean principle of voluminosity, and produces a preponderance of physical, sculptural anthropoid structure over the expression of volume." And he goes on to say (*ibid.*): "Here we see that prevalence of the sculptural form over the feeling for space and painting which characterizes the entire art of historical Greece."

To me these passages resound with the voices of German art history and their philosophical precursors. In his use of the technique of formal comparison, in his analysis of the formal principles which characterise two different epochs, he remains indebted to Wolfflin. In his emphasis upon the abstract, ordering principles of Geometric art, in what he makes of the contrast between Mycenaean voluminosity and Geometric verticality, he echoes not only the type of account favoured by Schnaase but also the major presuppositions of Platonic metaphysics. In his sense of anticipation of what Geometric art will lead to, he echoes Hegel. In his strong feeling for the dynamics of form, in his notion that, once the canons of Geometric art are established, progress along these lines, in the direction of a more expressive articulation of form is as inevitable as it is desirable, he follows Riegl. This is not to say that he belongs to any one school, or that his debt to any one person is very great, but that he employs a form of explanation which, I believe, could have been arrived at only by someone whose patterns of thought had been deeply influenced by German art history. It is a form of explanation to be found in the works of many English-speaking archaeologists, especially those working in Classical periods.

Yet to uncover the historical influences upon Schweitzer's choice of words is not to understand what is of value in his account. For his words are not chosen simply to display his appreciation nor to convey, impressionistically, his aesthetic response to the two objects which he compares. On the contrary, his language is precise. But again this precision of vocabulary and syntax is not governed primarily by typological requirements. He is not concerned with an account of the shape of the objects that aims simply to be clear and unambiguous, that aims to be, in short, purely descriptive, but with an analysis of form. He contrasts two objects and in so doing he contrasts the abstract principles which they embody. In this way he is attempting to pinpoint the difference in the formal sense (to use Schnaase's term) of two different epochs. Thus his purpose is historical. But in being historical he clearly feels no need to relate the form and decoration of the vases to the economy and society of either the Mycenaean or the Early Iron Age worlds. It is enough to realise that these objects were part of the lives of the people in their respective periods, and that to understand their formal sense is a step in the direction of understanding the epoch from which they came. It is in this manner that he is seeking to make the objects of the past intelligible to the present and to do so more directly than if it was demanded that objects continually be mediated by some all-encompassing social or economic theory. The two vases exemplify the contrast between two different periods or cultures. That, for Schweitzer, is enough.

One other possible area of confusion must also be cleared up. Schweitzer is not attributing to the potters and painters of the Mycenaean and Protogeometric periods certain ideals. He is not saying that Mycenaean potters had a notion of voluminosity, nor that those of the Protogeometric possessed an idea of verticality. Nor is Schweitzer a structuralist. He is not claiming that the polarities of verticality and voluminosity somehow govern all cultural forms and originate, ultimately, from the ordering principles of the human brain. The formal sense he analyses has nothing to do with words or with universal psychological propensities. His own words are used to underline an argument which is primarily visual. The terms 'verticality' and 'voluminosity' are labels attached to an understanding of form arrived at first by a sensuous response to the objects illustrated, a response which is only then given a rational reconstruction. The appropriateness of the terms can be gauged only when we, following his argument, have looked at the objects and compared them.

It may be objected that, in taking my examples from historical periods or from those periods in prehistory which immediately precede what to us is 'Classical', I have not dealt properly with the problems of prehistoric art. For it is psychologically easier to make aesthetic sense of what we consider to be ancestral to ourselves. But the rapacity of American museums in acquiring art from all periods and cultures should remind us that, in the modern age, what we regard as our own aesthetic tradition is highly malleable. Similarly it has been put to me that the Mediterranean is much richer than northern Europe in 'fine' artifacts and that therefore this tradition is most appropriate where it is presently most used. This is to ignore the cultural richess of much of central and northern Europe in prehistoric times, particularly in metalwork. The tradition is as relevant here as it is in the Mediterranean (Sandars 1968). Forms of art historical analysis continue fruitfully to be applied to prehistoric works of art. Taylor (1987) has shown the potential of iconographic and iconological approaches towards our understanding of 'Thraco-Getic' art. If there is a fault, it does not lie in the material.

To sum up, the value of encountering this tradition lies in the recognition that art history has faced, and continues to face, a dilemma (one that it shares with archaeology) from its very inception as a discipline. Both archaeology and art history share the task of dealing with the material remains of the past and of translating those objects into the present. At a very early stage in its development, art history became dissatisfied with the two most obvious paths towards this translation, these two being the task of exact and painstaking reconstruction of the functions and purposes of art within a particular cultural context, and an interest in the past that was purely a reflection of contemporary concerns. The former was thought to be a 'scientific', descriptive exercise, devoid of any higher value or purpose, the latter as self-evidently meretricious. What German art historians have been seeking (not, it must be said, with any measurable success) is what Panofsky has termed an 'Archimedean' view on past art. By this he does not mean scientific objectivity, for that would be value-free and therefore value-less. Rather he means a perspective on the art of the past that would be as true for a nineteenth-century observer as it would be for one from the twentieth; as valuable for a Nigerian as it would be for an Englishman or a German. That is to say, German art history aimed to discover a standpoint from which to give a rational account of the intrinsic aesthetic properties of

a work or style, one of universal validity. Though this is not a question which has much exercised Anglo-American archaeologists, it remains central to any general enquiry into the past, and should not be dismissed. The importance of the German tradition to contemporary archaeological discursive practice should, I believe, be as a corrective. For there is in Britain and America today a tendency for archaeology to become no more than a second-class sociology of the past. Archaeology is subordinated to history and history to sociology in the pursuit of a final, abstract truth. We have for a long time been travelling down the second of those paths, the dangers of which were noted long ago by the Germans. Thus we have long accustomed ourselves to see artifacts simply as outcomes, as products, valuable only in the information they convey, not in themselves. Whether the perspective be economic and technological (objects as tools) or social (objects as counters in some endless social game) the effect is much the same. German art history on the other hand, in relating objects to abstract concerns, does not thereby devalue them. In this respect at least, in treating its raw material as more than props to its arguments, German art history has remained closer to the old-fashioned ideal of a humane discipline.[2]

Notes

1. I have omitted references to Plato, as there are too many editions of his work for particular references to be of much value. The arguments for the Theory of Forms are to be found chiefly in two dialogues, the *Phaedo* and the *Republic*. His views on the illusory and transient nature of art are to be found in Book X of the *Republic*.

2. I would like to thank Ian Hodder for encouraging me to revise what was originally a seminar paper for publication. I am also most grateful to Tim Taylor, Chris Chippindale, Colin Renfrew and Anthony Snodgrass, and most especially Paul Binski of Caius College, Cambridge, for reading and commenting on earlier drafts of this paper. Any faults are of course my own.

**Continuity and change:
the very long term**

Chapter 3

**Selective depictions.
A study of 3,500 years
of rock carvings from
Arctic Norway and their
relationship to the Sami drums**

Knut Helskog

Throughout Scandinavia, prehistoric rock art depictions are characterised by the absence of domestic scenes – huts, hut interiors, food preparation and consumption in the home. The 'inside', possibly largely female roles, are 'denied' in the art. Rather it is 'outside' activities such as hunting, fishing, boats and rituals which are accorded importance. And, of course, the art itself occurs outside settlements and domestic pottery, and the domestic sphere in general, are often not the focus of decoration and symbolic elaboration. Spatially, the 'outside' realm is often associated with death (burial) and rituals (such as ritual hoardings). In the Neolithic in southern Scandinavia, it is the 'outside' world which is particularly associated with symbolic elaboration and decoration. Through time, the boundary between inside and outside, domestic and wild, receives different emphases in changing social contexts. In this chapter Helskog examines one aspect of this structure, the rock art of northern Norway in the Neolithic and Bronze Age. Despite alterations through time, continuities can be discerned with depictions on the Sami drums used by shamans in medieval Norway. Such long-term continuities in the nature and locus of ritual and art have major potential implications for our understanding of the formation of contemporary European society.

Introduction

Like the previous chapter, this chapter considers the processes of cultural selection. In this case the concern is with the selection of figures carved into rock surfaces, and those painted on the membranes of the drums of the Sami.[1] The changes and the continuities of the selection will also be compared to the general prehistoric cultural sequence to illustrate some of the relationships to other spheres of culture.

Work on the rock carvings in Alta in the province of Finnmark, Arctic Norway (fig. 3.1) led to the conclusion that there was an unusually solid basis for reconstructing the chronology of these carvings (fig. 3.2). The chronology, based on multivariate analysis of morphologically classified carvings, the relationship of groups of carvings to the Holocene shore displacement (fig. 3.3), and field observations, consists of four or five diachronic phases between 4200 and 500 calendric years BC (K. Helskog 1983, 1984a, n.d.a). Furthermore, it became apparent that the phases were synchronous with other changes in the general archaeological record (fig. 3.4) (K. Helskog n.d.b).

The beginning of each phase in the general archaeological record is characterised by changes in material culture, and there are indications in some phases of population increase as well as changes in house and household size and organisation (fig. 3.4). It is this general chronology which provides the cultural framework to which the carvings can be meaningfully related. Yet it must be emphasised that the framework is general and based mainly on evidence from outside the Alta Fjord (E. Helskog 1983; Engelstad 1985; K. Helskog 1974, 1980, 1984b; Simonsen 1961, 1979, pp. 363–496). The collection and preliminary analysis of the fjordal material indicate that the same general development also took place in Alta. On this basis it has been possible to start a discussion of the relationship between changes and continuities in the figures and other cultural data (K. Helskog 1984a, n.d.a, n.d.b). This paper is a continuation of this discussion with an emphasis on the selectivity of the depictions. Selectivity will be discussed at the phase level, and in relation to cultural and natural phenomena. By cultural phenomenon is meant any human or human-type activity, object or structure. By natural phenomena are meant animals, plants or geographical/topographical features. It is quite obvious that these two definitions do include phenomena which fall into both categories such as the scenes in the carvings which include both people and animals.

The second part of the paper concerns the relationship between the selectivity of the carvings and the selectivity of the figures on the drums of the Sami (figs. 3.6, 3.15). Authors such as Manker (1938, pp. 224–5; 1971) and Simonsen (1979, pp. 479–82) have observed that there are pictorial similarities between the depictions on the rock surfaces and on the drums, yet there exist no analyses of possible relationships. The use of the drums is also associated with shamanism, an interpretation which is also often associated with the rock art of northern

Eurasia and Siberia (Gjessing 1945, pp. 312–16; Ravdonikas 1936; Hagen 1976, pp. 152–4; Gurina 1980, pp. 21–4; Siikala 1984). It is quite unlikely that shamanism as reported among the Sami is a recent arrival from Norse and Christian religion. Rather, Sami shamanism seems to be part of a cultural tradition among northern Eurasian hunters and fishers (Hultkrantz 1978a, b), and should be explored within that framework. Therefore, and due to the possibility of shamanistic representations on the carvings, the figures on the drums might represent a continuation of some of the principles and meanings of the figures depicted on the rock surfaces in Alta as well as at other places in northern Scandinavia. It has been suggested (K. Helskog 1984a, pp. 25–7) that there is some continuity in beliefs and rituals from those expressed in the carvings to those which existed among the Sami from the twelfth to the nineteenth centuries AD. This pertains for example to the beliefs and rituals associated with the cult of the bear. Thus I have found it logical to turn to these drums as a part of the analysis of the carvings. The second part of this paper, then, is an examination of the selection of the figures on the Sami drums for principles and meaning which might aid in interpreting their historic relationship to the rock carvings and the meaning of the carvings themselves.

The archaeological sample and the analysis of the carvings

The carvings were discovered during systematic field research in three areas: Hjemmeluft, Bossekop and Amtmannsnes (fig. 3.1). There is one more large area with carvings, and two small areas with paintings (Simonsen 1979, pp. 454–7). These are not included in this analysis because the data are not yet systematised. Additional fieldwork is also needed. The sample under consideration includes an estimated 50% of the carvings in the three mentioned areas. Of a sample of 1,252 carvings, approximately 52% belong to phase 1, 25% to phase 2, 15% to phase 3 and 8% to phase 4. The analysis is based on relative numbers because the exact number of carvings which belong to the different phases is not known, and secondly, because of the unequal representation of the phases (Helskog n.d.b). The material under analysis is considered to be representative for the carvings in Alta, as are the main trends which are revealed by the analysis. Phase 4 is significantly less represented than the other phases. Since the time span of phase 4 is longer than that of any of the other phases there seems to be a distinct reduction in the number of figures made.

Adjacent to the carvings there are approximately 36,000 m^2 of occupation sites in which flakes and a few tools have been found by extensive test pitting and excavations. Traces of only two houses which could indicate some degree of permanency were found. Most of the traces of such houses are found at other places around the fjord, in the bottom as well as along the sides and on the outside islands.

In what follows, each of the phases will be discussed in relation to the archaeological evidence from Alta and the rest of the archaeological record from Arctic Norway.

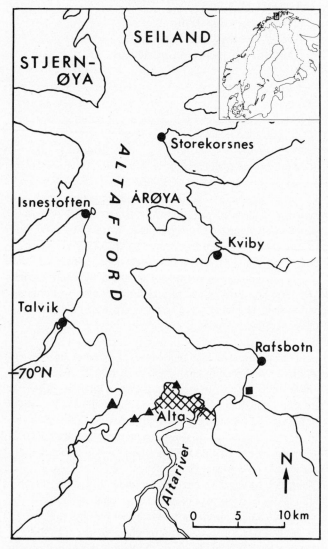

Fig. 3.1 Locational map. ▲ = rock carving sites, ■ = rock painting site, ● = main population centres

Phase 1 (4200–3600 BC)

A classification of the human figures into active figures (those who seem to be doing something) versus passive figures (those who seem to be doing nothing) (K. Helskog 1984a) showed that the active dominated over the passive (fig. 3.7). The active figures are mainly hunting or participating in a dance/procession, carrying some tool/item/weapon, or they are in a boat. Household or indoor domestic activities have not been found. The emphasis is on activities which take place outdoors and on a land surface. Furthermore, the meaning of these scenes seems to be associated with the activities rather than with only the humans themselves.

It is sometimes possible to distinguish between men and women on the basis of depicted genitalia and breasts, assuming a fair degree of naturalism (fig. 3.8). (It has recently been suggested to me that the straight line interpreted as a downhanging penis is in reality an overdimensioned clitoris or a symbolic vagina. Perception clearly plays a role here and this is a problem which will be dealt with in another analysis.) Sometimes sex can be inferred by association between human figures. For example, when two figures are depicted side by side and one has an erect penis (the male) and the other a big stomach, wide hips, or even no distinguishing features (the female) (fig. 3.9). This leads to only a slight increase in the number of females. In essence, sometimes it was important to depict genitals or breasts to distinguish between males or females, in order to communicate the meaning of the figures.

But in the majority of cases, the communication of the meaning is also associated with other features, such as the moose-headed poles or the boats (fig. 3.10). If sexuality was important then it was probably connoted by associations between human figures and material culture objects.

Among the land mammals, reindeer and moose are clearly dominant. The other mammals are considerably less common (0.05%). Similarly, the few birds and fish and sea mammals depicted (3%) are all species which would be caught for their food value. With the exception of some of the fish, the hides of these animals were also used for clothing, containers, rope, etc. In essence, the selection of the terrestrial animals and the birds depicted could be connected with their value as a food and raw material source, a possibility which comes as no surprise, and which has been noted in other areas with rock carvings. Fish and sea mammals, on the other hand, are hardly depicted (Table 3.1), a phenomenon which is also common elsewhere among the carvings of northern Scandinavia (Hallström 1960, pp. 326–8; Gjessing 1932; Simonsen 1958). This is somewhat surprising since fish and, to some extent, sea mammals must have been the mainstay of the diet. In the White Sea area the carvings of, for example, fish are equally rare although sea mammals are quite common (Savvateyev 1970; Bakka 1975, pp. 108–10).

Seen in relation to the cultural and natural environment in general there is a large variety of phenomena not depicted (or not recognised by me). Activities and items associated with

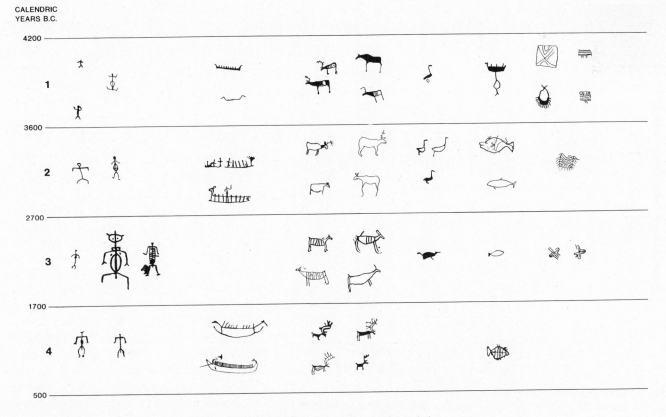

Fig. 3.2 Chronological chart of the main classes and types of figures according to phases 1–4

preparing food, making clothes or other domestic chores are lacking as well as depictions of plants and insects. As such, the carvings clearly depict a special selection of phenomena.

From the rest of the archaeological record it is known that the people of northern Troms and of Finnmark were hunters and fishers who lived in small coastal/fjordal settlements (fig. 3.4) (Simonsen 1965, 1979, p. 367; Renouf 1981; E. Helskog 1983, p. 150; K. Helskog 1984b; Engelstad 1985). They lived in small band societies whose subsistence economy was based on the seasonal exploitation of resources. The settlement pattern did include some seasonal transhumance (Simonsen 1965, 1979, pp. 397–405; H. Olsen 1967). There are reasons to suggest that there were different choices of residential stability due to a high degree of adaptability and flexibility in relation to fluctuations and variations in the seasonal resources (Engelstad 1984). The direct evidence for settlements in the Alta fjord itself is sparse since most of the sites have not yet been properly dated. However, the excavations at a site in 1925 (Nummedal 1929, pp. 29–35) and in 1979–80 have given a typological date of a similar age to the

adjacent rock carving in Hjemmeluft. The site which covers an area of 4000 m^2 has no visible house remains. The excavation, of approximately 55 m^2, revealed only an assortment of lithic tools and flakes.

Phase 2 (3600–2700 BC)

Approximately 3600 BC there were distinct changes in the form of all the main types of depictions with the exception of the stick figures. The selection of cultural versus natural figures is as in the previous phase (table 3.1). There is a slight change in emphasis among those figures which are depicted. First of all, birds are more commonly depicted than in the first phase (0.3% to 5.0%). The emphasis is on the larger land animals, while the marine fauna are still selected out. Second, boats are more frequent (K. Helskog 1984a, n.d.a) and the activities in which human figures are engaged are to a larger extent associated with boats and water than in phase 1 (fig. 3.11). As in phase 1, the meaning of most of the human figures seems to be given by the activity in which they are engaged, rather than by the individual figure itself (K. Helskog

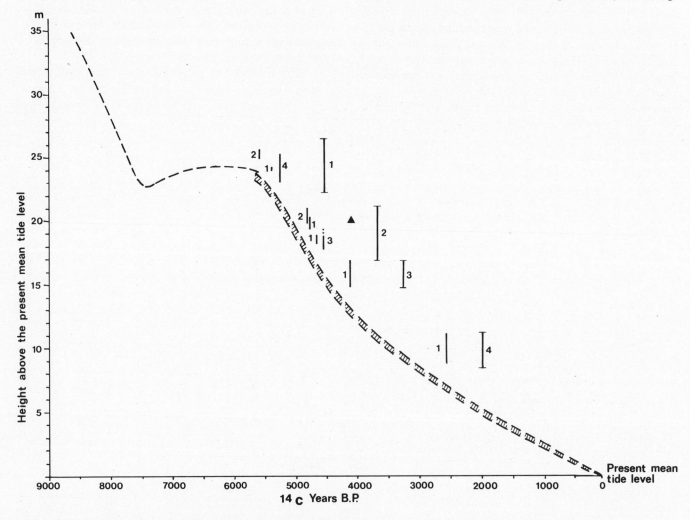

Fig. 3.3 Shore displacement chart with the altitudinal location of the phases. Numbers equal the number of sites (|) at the same altitude, and indicate the altitude of the majority of the depictions from the four phases (I)
▲ = the site Storsteinen

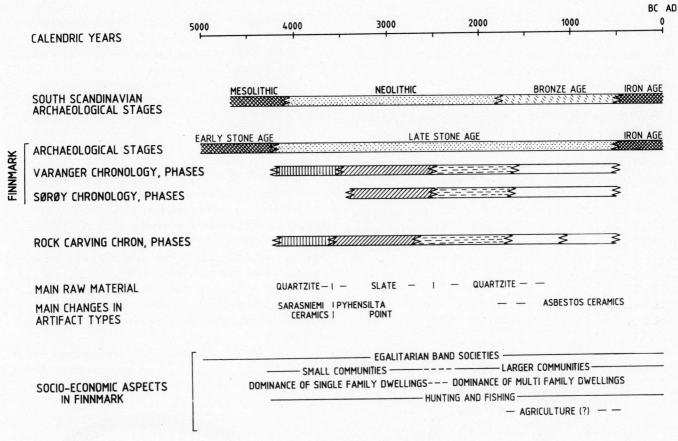

Fig. 3.4 Chronological chart of the rock carvings and the general archaeological development

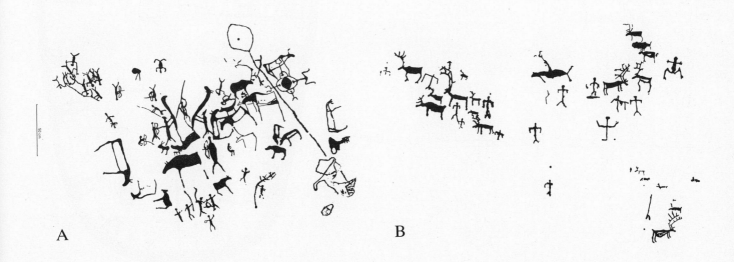

Fig. 3.5 Examples of rock carvings sites. A = Ole Pedersen IX, phase 1 (4200–3600 BC); B = Apana Gård I, phase 4 (1700–500 BC)

Table 3.1. *The relative distribution of the main classes of figures in phases 1–4.*

The percentages are based on 1,252 classified figures. The total number of figures is between 2,500 and 3,000. An inclusion of all the depictions will increase the percentages of reindeer/moose in phases 1–3, and reduce the percentages of the other classes. Phase 4 will remain fairly unchanged because the total number of figures is only slightly greater than that recorded to date.

Classes	Phases			
	1	2	3	4
Human figures	31.5	13.0	45.3	23.4
Reindeer/moose	60.0	63.0	45.3	51.1
Bear	2.6	2.0	1.0	—
Other terrestrial animals	0.6	—	—	—
Marine animals	1.5	0.6	1.6	3.3
Birds	0.3	5.0	0.5	—
Designs	1.8	0.6	6.3	—
Boats	1.7	15.8	—	22.2
No. of figures	653	317	192	90

1984a). The frequency of men versus women is also similar to that in phase 1.

The rest of the archaeological record indicates that there are general changes in material culture at the beginning of the phase. However, the socio-economic organisation and the subsistence settlement pattern seem to be a continuation from phase 1.

Phase 3 (2700–1700 BC)

As in the previous phases there were distinct changes in the form of the figures, with the exception of the stick figures. In phase 3 these are mainly depictions of humans. The selectivity of cultural and natural phenomena is as in the two previous phases (table 3.1). Among the animals the emphasis is on the larger land mammals. There are no birds, and among the marine life the halibut is represented by three and the salmon by one depiction. With the main exception of form (see below) there is overall continuity in selectivity from phase 2. The main selective changes are to be found in the lack of boats and associated activities.

Among the human depictions there appears a new type of figure (fig. 3.2), two to ten times larger and more elaborate than those in the two previous phases. Some of these figures

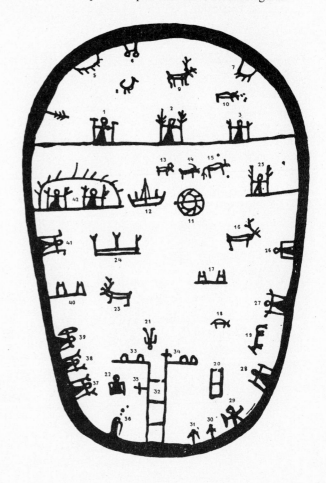

Fig. 3.6 Examples of northern type drums (Manker 1950, drums 44 and 64)

have facial features and/or hair, and there appear to be both men and women. Adding to the facts that 80% of the figures are passive in contrast to the dominance of active humans in phases 1 and 2 (fig. 3.7), and that there are few scenes, the change might be one of meaning and principle aside from form (K. Helskog 1984a). Such a change is also indicated by the general layout of the carvings. In contrast to phases 1 and 2 the depictions are now frequently overlapping and sometimes impossible to separate and distinguish. Since there is no shortage of rock surfaces in Alta, the overlapping is more a difference in choice than a consequence of the presence or absence of suitable rock surfaces.

Approximately contemporary with the beginning of phase 3 there is, as with the beginning of the other phases, general evidence of changes in material culture as well as changes in social organisation (Simonsen 1975, pp. 242–74; 1979, pp. 371–9; E. Helskog 1983, pp. 49–77; K. Helskog 1980) and a population increase (K. Helskog 1984b). The evidence from the Alta fjord is only tentative so far, but seems to correspond to the pattern from Sørøy and Varanger (Simonsen 1979, pp. 371–9). The subsistence settlement patterns are believed to have been as flexible as in the two previous phases. The social change is connected with the change from a dominance of one-room sod houses with an average floor space of 11–12 m² to sod houses with an average floor area of 25 m². This is interpreted as a change from nuclear to extended or multi-family households (Simonsen 1979, p. 371) or as an organisational change rather than a change in family structure (K. Helskog 1984b).

Phase 4 (1700–500 BC)

The changes, in form and partly in content, of the figures are as distinct between phases 3 and 4 as between any of the other phases. The numbers of carvings, however, are considerably less, and it has been suggested that there was a real reduction in the use of depictions on rock surfaces as

carriers of meaning. The selection between natural and cultural phenomena is similar to the previous phases. Reindeer are the only animal depicted aside from one moose. Boats are again represented and they are now of a clear south Scandinavian type. The humans are depicted only as stick figures. Among the human figures in the boats there are a few which seem to be engaged in activities other than simple transportation. As an example can be mentioned one boat with 12 persons dancing, of whom two seem to be holding a drum (fig. 3.12). Among the active people on a land surface there are only two scenes, one with three swordsmen and one with a hunter and a moose. Only men can be singled out by genitalia and by the assumption that swordfighting is an activity of men. Seen as a whole, the active humans (including crew members) are again more frequent that those that are passive.

As in the earlier phases marine life is selected out. Only three halibut have been depicted. Halibut are the only marine fauna which are repeatedly depicted throughout the approximate 3,700 years during which the carvings in Alta were made.

The rest of the archaeological record indicates that other types of changes occurred at the beginning of phase 4. Pollen evidence indicating the possible cultivation of barley (*Hordeum*) has been discovered on Isnestoften at the west side of the Alta fjord, dated to 3420 ± 100 BP (Vorren 1983, pp. 19–23). This is the first evidence of a possible change in the subsistence economy among the population this far north-east in Arctic Norway. It is comparable with the evidence from the southern part of this Arctic coast (Vorren 1979; Vorren and Nilssen 1982; Johansen 1979, 1982; Hultgreen 1983). The boats in the carvings are also of a type traditionally associated with agricultural societies further south in Scandinavia (Larsen 1972; Marstrander 1963, 1970; Burenhult 1980; Malmer 1981; Rygh 1908). It should be noted that agriculture, if it was practised in Alta, due to environmental and climatic constraints, would have been only a small and probably insignificant part of the subsistence economy. The population would, of necessity, have relied mainly on hunting and fishing. In general, there is also some tentative evidence of changes in material culture (Johansen 1979; Simonsen 1975, pp. 254–80; K. Helskog 1980).

The youngest carvings correspond approximately to the

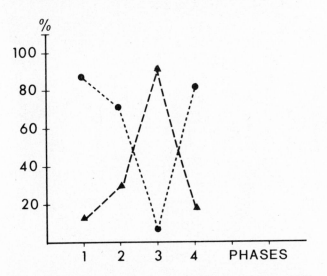

Fig. 3.7 The relative frequency of active (●) versus passive (▲) human figures

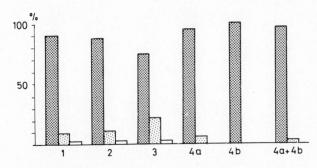

Fig. 3.8 The relative frequency of males and females
= males and females   = males
= females

transition between the Late Bronze Age and the Early Iron Age further south in Scandinavia, or between the Late Stone Age and the Early Iron Age in the arctic.

Phase 4 has been divided into two diachronic phases (4a and 4b) on the basis of two distinct types of boat (K. Helskog n.d.a). These boats are located at different altitudes above the sea level. It has not yet been possible to include other types of figures into phase 4b with perhaps the exception of the immediately adjacent moose hunting scene and a pair of foot soles and a whale (?). It is evident that in Alta, as among the carvings of the Late Bronze Age in southern Scandinavia, boats are the most common type of figure.

Summary and discussion

The rock surfaces possibly represent only one of several types of surface which were used for making depictions. It is reasonable to believe that clothes, tools, weapons and structures were ornamented, as is known among recent hunters and fishers in the circumpolar area. Good and well documented examples are the Inuit of the Bering Sea area (Fitzhugh and Kaplan 1982), the ornaments on the dress of the shaman of the Samoyeds (Graceva 1982, pp. 315–23), or the drums of the Sami (Manker 1950). The preservation of organic material from the Late Stone Age populations is fairly good for certain sites in northernmost Norway, and a few ornamented artifacts have also been found. This is the case especially at sites in eastern Finnmark (Simonsen 1961, 1975). As such, the rock carvings (or petroglyphs) are a part of a whole spectrum of depictions and could perhaps best be understood within that whole. To date, however, there are not sufficient archaeological data to follow this line of enquiry.

Overall, there are at least four abrupt changes in the form (or style) of the figures (fig. 3.2). In addition comes the appearance and the disappearance of the carvings. Each of these changes corresponds roughly to some changes in the rest of the archaeological record. Similarly, there are changes in the content as well as in the frequency of the boats, of active versus passive figures, of men versus women, and in the depiction of

certain types of animals. Birds are absent in phases 3 and 4 while only moose and reindeer are depicted in phase 4. Furthermore, there is the change from very little overlapping of figures to a high degree of overlapping in phase 3 and back to very little overlapping in phase 4. There are the large and elaborate depictions of humans found in phase 3 and the lack of geometric patterns in phase 4.

On the other side there are the continuities. First of all, there are no recognisable natural phenomena except for the animals. These animals, although their internal frequency varies between the phases, are mainly the largest land animals such as reindeer and moose, although there are also some depictions of bears, foxes/dogs/wolves, beaver and large aquatic birds. In essence, the selection has been for animals which were important both in the subsistence economy and perhaps also in ritual. There is also continuity in the discrimination against marine fauna, despite the fact that the marine fauna must have provided the mainstay of the diet. (Note that the coastal and fjordal waters of Arctic Norway do not freeze during the winter and that fish, seals and whales are available.) Hunting and fishing were the main subsistence pursuits throughout the whole of the period in which the carvings were made – a fact which is only partly illustrated in the fauna depicted in them. Therefore, the selection of the fauna which are depicted might be associated with other, including mythological aspects.

Seen as a whole, the continuities and discontinuities in the carvings and in the rest of the archaeological record do present a complex picture of the relationships between

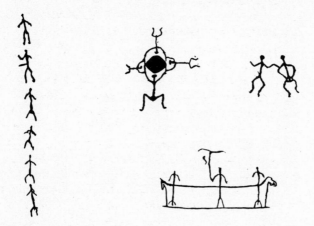

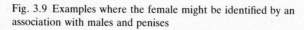

Fig. 3.9 Examples where the female might be identified by an association with males and penises

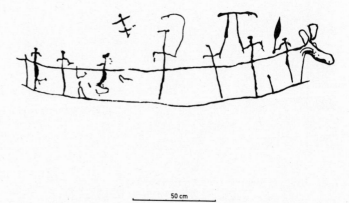

Fig. 3.10 Human figures with moose-headed poles and boat with a moose head adorning the bow. Phase 1 (4200–3600 BC)

depictions and other spheres of culture. Despite very clear changes in form (style), and at times in content, which correspond roughly with general changes in material culture, there are also equally clear continuities in the classes of figures which are depicted. Seen in relation to the sphere of cultural activities, there is a clear selection for activities associated with animals, people and boats. The activities depicted seem to be conducted outdoors and to be connected with subsistence, travel or religion (ritual). Indoor domestic or household activities are never depicted (or recognised by me). This is a feature which Alta has in common with all other rock carvings in Scandinavia. In essence, the main principles behind the selection of the classes of figures to be depicted show little change during 3,700 years.

The carvings are also seasonal in the sense that they were probably made sometime during spring to autumn when the rock surfaces were free from layers of snow. This seasonality is also reflected in most of the fauna which are depicted, and some of the carvings might have a meaning which only can be understood in a seasonal context. For example, the reindeer fence depicted at Bergbukten I (fig. 3.14) does have a meaning in connection with reindeer drives within the time span from spring to autumn. Ethnographically, the reindeer migration back to the winter pastures in the interior was probably the time of the most important hunt. Furthermore, a fence would have been effective only during the snow-free months of the year. So, in this case both the making and the meaning are likely to have had some connection with seasonal subsistence activities. Similarly, the fishing of salmon and halibut is seasonal as is the hunting and presence of migratory birds like swans, geese and ducks. Overall, there is a 99% selection in all the phases for fauna which is seasonal (spring–autumn) in this Arctic fjordal area. There are, however, also depicted activities such as a single person or groups of persons dancing or in boats, activities which are not necessarily seasonal.

There are some indications of a spatial arrangement in the sense that figures are grouped on the rock surfaces. For example, there are areas which are dominated by certain types of figures, such as the boats (K. Helskog n.d.a). This is the case both for sites taken as a whole and for areas within a site in all the phases. This statement is based on field observations and visual inspection of the site maps.

The correspondence of the chronology of the carvings to the rest of the archaeological record, and the typological similarity of the carvings in Alta to carvings in the White Sea and the Lake Onega area, to central north Sweden and the Norwegian west coast, suggest that the transformations were not altogether a local phenomenon. They were also part of a common sphere of form, selectivity and change over a large geographical area. This indicates that there was some form of unity in communication/beliefs/ideology over large areas, and that the causes of change could be somewhat similar in different areas.

The rock carvings seem to disappear all over Scandinavia

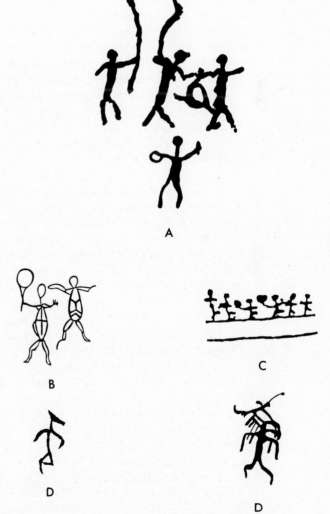

Fig. 3.12 Example of human figures holding possible drums, and possible shamans. From: (A) Phase 1, Alta; (B) Skavberget, Troms (Simonsen 1956); (C) Phase 4, Alta; (D) phase 3, Alta

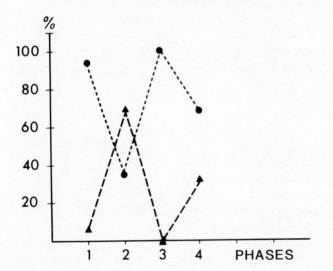

Fig. 3.11 The relative frequency of activities on land (●) versus on water (▲)

at the end of the Bronze Age or during the first part of the Iron Age. The distances within Scandinavia are considerable, up to 3,000 km, and there must have been strong and viable impulses which caused such a change. There are three exceptions to this. In eastern Finnmark there is found a rock surface with a few carvings (a Sami attacking a wolf, and two reindeer) which are dated to the medieval period or later (Simonsen 1979, pp. 479–82). In Lyngen in Troms are found a carving of a boat with sail and a bow with a dragon (?) head, and a reindeer of possibly recent date. In interior north Sweden, in a medieval Sami camp in the upper Lule river area, there is found a carving on a stone, possibly of a person aiming a bow and arrow (Mulk, 1985). The data are still inadequate to show whether those instances represent a continuation of the tradition of making carvings or separate occurrences.

From the end of the Late Stone Age there was continuity in band societies whose subsistence was based on hunting and fishing, in addition to the maintenance of decoy reindeer and draught animals and small (e.g. 10–15 animals) herds of reindeer. This tradition continued up to the sixteenth and seventeenth centuries AD in northern Scandinavia. The maintenance of small herds might be of historic origin although it has been suggested that such maintenance could also have existed back in the Late Stone Age (K. Helskog 1983) or the early Iron Age (Simonsen 1982, pp. 563–4). Historically, members of these societies used depictions of animals, humans,

objects, items, structures or other cultural or natural phenomena in connection with their communication with the spirit world, in healing and in magic. In particular the depictions on the drums of the Sami are the closest we can come to a regional and early historic pictoral resemblance to the rock carvings. In the following pages I will briefly discuss these depictions to examine any continuity or discontinuity from the selectivity and the principles seen in the rock carvings.

The Sami drums
Their use, age and affiliation

The time span between the population at the end of the Late Stone Age and the early Sami population might be relatively short. Views vary, based on historic and archaeological evidence, from direct continuity to a gap of a thousand years. It is therefore possible that the historic Sami culture can contain elements which are a product of or a continuation of prehistoric cultural tradition. These are elements such as the depictions on the drums of the Sami (figs 3.6, 3.15).

The drums consist of hide stretched over an oval frame or bowl of wood. They are between 30–40 cm long. Both the drum membranes and the frames are decorated. The decorations on the membranes are painted while those on the frame are normally carved. Different types of pendants can also be attached to the frame. The figures are painted with red colour extracted from the bark of the alder. They are mainly outline drawings. In some cases the figures have interior patterns or body fill (Manker 1938, 1950). In essence, the variation in the form of the figures is similar to that of the rock carvings, and Zachrisson (1983, p. 86) also asserts that in the ornaments of the frames of the drums is found a continuation of the geometric style found at the site of Kjelmøy in Varanger. This

Fig. 3.13 The bear hunt scenes at (A) Bergbukten I (Phase 1), and (B) Ole Pedersen I (Phase 1)

Fig. 3.14 The reindeer corral at Bergbukten I (Phase 1)

site, which is dated to around the time of Christ, is ascribed a Sami ethnic identity (Simonsen 1967; Kleppe 1977; B. Olsen 1984). When used, the drums were held in one hand and beaten with a T-shaped object held in the other hand.

The drums were used to establish contact between man and the supernatural powers, to secure a good outcome in any type of undertaking. The depictions played a part in aspects such as curing, hiring spirits, ecstatic divination and drum divination, in sacrifice service and in magic (Hultkrantz 1978a, pp. 40–58). Drums were used and owned both by the male head of a family and by the shaman. As such, any male could probably own a drum and foresee the future through divination without being considered a shaman (Bäckman 1978, p. 86). The shamans, who performed within small communities and on the family level, were mostly men who could resort to trance whenever spirits had to be called upon in connection with, for example, curing the sick, divination and hiring the dead (Hultkrantz 1978b, pp. 105–6). It is also probable that the shaman could and did use his powers to his own personal benefit. The drum and the associated cultural practices are believed to be old and genuine aspects of Sami culture. From

this point of view it is of some interest to know the age which has been attached to the Sami.

The Sami as an ethnic group were described in the late ninth century AD, probably in the seventh century, and probably in the first century AD by Tacitus in the *Germania* (Hætta 1980b; Withaker 1978, 1983). In northern Troms and Finnmark they were described as the only existing population in the late ninth century AD by the tradesman Ottar in a narration to King Alfred of England. Archaeologists such as Kleppe (1974, 1977) and Simonsen (1982, p. 549) suggest that the Sami as an ethnic group in Arctic Scandinavia can be traced back in time to the era around the birth of Christ, or to the early part of the first millennium BC (B. Olsen 1984, p. 216). Others, such as Baudou (1978a, 1978b), suggest that the Sami arrived in the early second millennium BC. Odner (1983a, pp. 101–10), on the other hand, suggests that the Sami were recognised and recognised themselves as an ethnic group in the middle of the first millennium AD. From the burial customs, the northern part of Troms and Finnmark seem to have been areas settled mainly or solely by Sami as late as the ninth century AD (Reymert 1980). Many Sami have claimed that

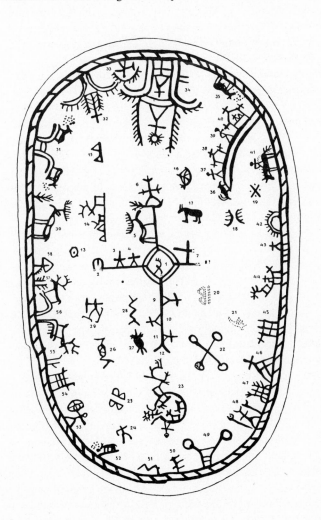
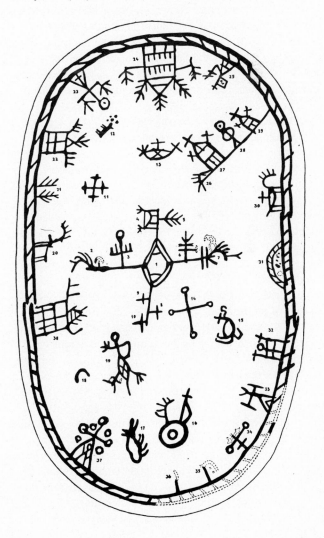

Fig. 3.15 Drums of the southern type (Manker 1950, drums 14 and 31)

they have roots extending back into the hunting–fishing population of Fenno-Scandia (Hætta 1979, 1980a). There is, in other words, some dispute concerning when the population was recognised as one ethnic group. But, whenever this ascription occurred it is safe to assume that elements from the prehistoric or preceding cultures continued, as for example the cult of the bear (Zachrisson and Iregren 1974; K. Helskog 1984a). The specific activities in fig. 3.13 certainly had a long continuity. There is no reason, either archaeologically or historically, to assume that there was a total cultural change.

The earliest indications of the use of drums stem from the rock carvings in Alta (fig. 3.12). First there is the figure of a person beating a possible drum while walking behind a group of hunters, dated to between 4200 and 3600 BC. Then there are two persons holding a circular object which may be a drum, among the 12 dancers on a boat dated to approximately 500 BC. Lastly, there are those figures in all the phases which can be interpreted as shamans, such as the dancing figure in one of the bear hunt scenes in phase 1 and the masked and dressed figures in phase 3 (fig. 3.2): drums are traditionally associated with shamanism in Eurasia. Outside Finnmark there is a human figure from Skavberget in Troms (Simonsen 1955, 1958) holding a circular object while in movement together with another person (fig. 3.12). The circular object can be interpreted as a drum. Then there are the depictions in both Eurasian rock carvings and rock paintings which have been interpreted as shamans (Gurina 1980, pp. 21–4; Ravdonikas 1936; Hagen 1976, pp. 152–4; Gjessing 1945, pp. 312–16; Siikala 1984). Although the evidence is circumstantial, both rock carvings and rock paintings seem to point towards a long tradition in the use of drums, and shamanism.

The Sami drum was first described in *Chronicae Norwegicae* from the late twelfth century, in a narrative from a coastal Sami community in Finnmark. This drum was ornamented with figures of a whale, reindeer and sledge and a boat with oars. The next descriptions of a drum are from Olaus Magnus in 1555 and from Peucerus in 1560. There are also numerous descriptions from the seventeenth to nineteenth centuries (Manker 1938, 1950).

There seems to be general agreement that the ancient religion of the Sami and Sami shamanism were connected with the Arctic Eurasian and Siberian hunting and fishing cultures and that the influences from Norse and Christian religion are of a more recent date (Bäckman 1978, p. 67). Indeed, there is much about the drums the origin of which cannot be explained by Christian and Norse influences. The most obvious examples are the depictions of the animals, Sami gods and spirits, and the use of the drums. There are, however, also figures which quite clearly have a meaning influenced by or associated with Christianity (such as the depictions of saints and churches), or associated with Norse mythology (such as the depictions of Thor (Tiermes, Horagalles), the god of thunder (Karsten 1955)).

The figures on the drum might also reflect seasonal and geographical as well as functional and cultural contexts. First of all there are differences between the drums in different regions,

such as northern and southern Fenno-Scandia. Manker (1938, 1950) suggests that there was also a difference between the drums of the coastal and the inland population in the sense that more marine life should be expected to have been depicted on the drums of the coast than in the interior. Unfortunately, the sole surviving drum from the coastal area of Finnmark does not give any support to Manker's suggestion. There might also have been drums used in different functional contexts (Bäckman 1978, pp. 73–4). In 1642, for example, a Sami described a drum as only a half drum which was used for 'luck in hunting and fishing' (Manker 1950: 143–4). The Sami, from Semijaure in northern Sweden, then drew a 'real' drum.

The analysis

The analysis of the figures on the drum membranes is divided into two steps. The first step includes only the drums which are from the northernmost regions of Scandinavia. These are the 15 drums of the Lule, Torne-Kemi, and Finnmark types (Manker 1938, 1950). If there is any historical continuity in the carvings in Alta it is among these drums that it should be expected. Only one drum is from Finnmark although it is evident that drums did exist here as among the Sami in any other region of Scandinavia. They were destroyed during the change to Christianity during the eighteenth to nineteenth centuries. The second step includes both the northern and the southern drums, to try to gain an increased understanding of the principles by which phenomena are depicted. In both steps of this analysis the drums will be seen in relation to the rock carvings.

There are a few hundred years between the drums, but they are in this analysis regarded as belonging to a single phase, similar to the rock carving phases. The figures on the drums are classified into main classes using the same principles as for the rock carvings. In addition, the interpretation of the figures by Manker and others (Manker 1950) is drawn upon in a discussion of the principles by which the figures are identified, as an aid for interpreting the carvings.

The 409 figures on the 15 northern drums were classified into four main categories. The relative frequencies of these are illustrated in table 3.2. Only 75% of the depictions could be classified in this way. Manker (1950), on the other hand, has identified approximately 99% of the figures. The main difference with the former classification is found in the larger percentage of identified human figures.

Compared with the rock carvings the closest similarity in frequencies is found with phases 1 and 2, and not with phase 4, as should be expected from the argument of historic continuity. There is also a greater variety of classes and types of figures on the drums than on the carvings of phase 4. Yet in relation to the trend of what is or is not depicted through the 3,700 years of carvings, there is some similarity. The emphasis is on people and animals, items and patterns, and similar cultural and natural phenomena are omitted both on the drums and on the carvings. Among the animals the emphasis is on the reindeer, while birds, fish and sea mammals are hardly depicted at all. In

Table 3.2. *The relative frequency of types of figures on the northern and the southern drums, including all northern drums (n=15) and a sample (n=15) of the southern drums*

A=northern drums according to my classification. B=northern and C=southern drums according to Manker's (1950) classification. B and C are divided into two columns where the left-hand column illustrates the frequencies of the types within the main classes of people and animals while the right-hand column illustrates the frequencies of the total number of figures.

	A	B		C	
Human figures	34.3	47.0		39.3	
Gods, spirits		75.0	35.2	70.0	27.9
Shamans		3.0	1.4	3.7	1.4
People		22.0	10.4	26.3	10.4
Animals	22.0	18.4		25.5	
Reindeer	7.4	28.3	5.2	61.2	15.0
Moose		—	—	3.4	1.0
Bear		7.6	1.4	10.2	2.3
Birds	1.5	10.9	2.0	2.5	.7
Fish	1.5	9.8	1.8	—	—
Other	9.4	43.4	8.4	22.7	6.5
Natural phenomenon		15.0			7.8
Cultural phenomenon	2.2	8.2			23.6
Boats	1.5	1.6			2.6
Concepts		2.8			1.8
Miscellaneous	42.4	8.8			2.0

this there is a similar emphasis. Furthermore, there are no insects and no plants, with the exception of a few trees. In essence, the only continuity which can be observed is on a general level, a level which might be common for all Arctic hunters and fishers. It is of some interest that fish and birds are hardly represented on the drums, as in the carvings.

The second step is to analyse the depictions on both the northern (n=15) and the southern (n=56) drums. As on the northern drums, the human figures on the southern drums vary from naturalistic to schematic and abstract in form (Manker 1950, pp. 15–19). Most of these figures are standing and seen from the front. Some are larger than others, a few have body patterns and genitals, while some bodies are depicted as a single straight line. The depictions are mainly gods, spirits, or saints, but there are also hunters, farmers, Sami, magicians and ghosts. Only rarely is sex identified by genitals or breasts. A figure can be identified by an object or by its position on the drum. As an example can be mentioned Juksakka, the goddess of male children who is identified by a bow; and the god of hunting, Væraldenolmai, who is identified as standing beside a tree (alder). These two figures might easily have been interpreted otherwise if they had been among the rock carvings.

The principle of identifying figures by specific objects or design is found among the carvings of all the three first phases. The figures with the moose-headed poles of phase 1, with T- and C-shaped poles of phase 2 and with horizontal body patterns of phase 3 might all be examples of this (fig. 3.16). Otherwise, the identification is given by the maker and the user of the drum. It has not been possible to identify figures by their position on the rock surfaces as within the confined and closely structured environment of the drum.

As on the carvings, activities connected with households or domestic activities are not depicted. The activities which are repeatedly depicted are people in fishing boats and in sacrificial boats, and persons holding some sort of tool/implement or a bow. There are only two or three scenes, aside from those associated with boats, where more than one person is present. One of these scenes shows the three goddesses Juksakka (the bow woman), Uksakka and Sarakka standing at the bottom of a drum. Others include a few cases where people are aiming a bow at some animals (reindeer) or birds. Otherwise, there are a few depictions of people in a sledge pulled by reindeer, or people going to church.

Among the animals on the drums the emphasis is on reindeer, then bear and then moose, while on the carvings the emphasis is on the reindeer, then moose and then bear. As a whole the selection towards the animals and birds which are important food or raw material sources is a shared trait on the drums and the carvings. Marine fauna are, as on the carvings, depicted significantly less than mammals and birds. Figures of fish are rare. There is one exception, namely Manker's drum 63 (Manker 1950, p. 409) where fish and aquatic birds comprise 32%. This might be an example of the more specialised drums which were mentioned earlier. Even though there are a few fish on the inland drums, fishing is represented in other ways,

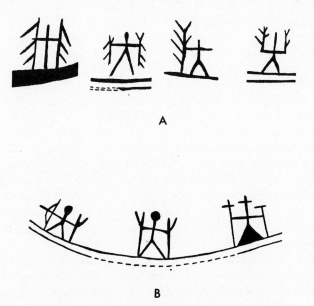

A

B

Fig. 3.16 Human figures identified by an object depicted on the drums. (A) The god of hunting (Væraldenolmai) and (B) the three goddesses Juksakka, Uksakka and Sarakka

namely by depicting fishing boats, lakes with boats, and lakes. The importance of fish seems to be represented by the means by which they are caught or the activity which resulted in their being caught rather than by the fish themselves. In the same way fishing might also be represented in the carvings. In addition to the animals and people, natural objects such as holy stones, mountains, earth, water, sun, rain and thunder are frequently depicted on the southern drums. It is also of interest to note that dual concepts like justice and injustice, good luck and bad luck, war and peace are also depicted. However, these concepts are known only because of the early historic descriptions of the drums and have not been recognised in the carvings. Seen in relation to natural and cultural phenomena, the depictions on the drums are more varied than those on the carvings.

Summary and discussion

The northern and the southern drums have different and specific internal organisation of figures. This organisation is different in principle, yet most of the figures are somewhat similar in form and seem to have had a similar meaning to those who used the drums. The repetition of specific depictions and their internal organisation point towards the repeated formalised use of the drums, formalised in ritual and meaning, as well as towards the common ideological background shared by those who practised and believed in the drums. Likewise, it is possible that the repetition of figures and scenes within and between the phases of the carvings do refer to formalised and repetitive behaviour which in some form at a later date is continued in the drums. In the carvings, the exact repetition of *specific* scenes is rare, though there is repetition in the selection of figures depicted. There are also some indications of spatial arrangements between carvings. On the drums the regularity of the spatial arrangement of the figures is much greater than on the carvings, a phenomenon which may partly be due to the confined surfaces of the drums. The rock surfaces provide no such strict confinement but allow for a more or less continuous expansion, as long as there are suitable surfaces. However, if desired, such regularity could certainly have been emphasised.

Comparison with the figures on the drums suggests that the active humans on the rock carvings identified by means of the objects they hold could be various gods or spirits identified by that object rather than people actively engaged in some type of mundane undertaking. Furthermore, the majority of the human figures on the carvings might be gods/spirits rather than mortal humans. The animals depicted on the drums are mainly (95%) regarded as spirit animals associated with shamans or animals to be sacrificed rather than game to be hunted. This might also have been the case on the carvings.
A main difference between the carvings and the drums is seen in the different emphases on animal, especially reindeer, and human figures. The reindeer is the most frequently depicted class of figures on the carvings while human figures

(gods and spirits) are emphasised on the drum membranes.

One explanation for this different emphasis might be that reindeer among the historic Sami were a domestic/semi-domestic animal and, as such, more easily accessible as a food and raw material resource and as a sacrifice to the gods than among societies where reindeer mainly, or perhaps only, were acquired by hunting. Therefore, there could have been more of an emphasis on the acquisition of the reindeer as a food resource in the religion of hunting–fishing societies than in societies where reindeer were tended and associated with private ownership. Here the emphasis was mostly on the reindeer as a spirit helper or spirit animal and as a sacrifice. This explanation contradicts somewhat an earlier hypothesis (K. Helskog 1983) that there could have been some form of domesticated reindeer in the Early Late Stone Age. Alternatively, the hunting/trapping of reindeer may have remained a prime concern during the Late Stone Age despite possible domestication of decoy animals and animals for transportation. In any case, the reindeer, and any other animal, might always have served as a shamanic spirit animal.

The lack of depictions and the selectivity is also a misrepresentation of life. The domestic world (perhaps perceived as female-based) of child care, the home, domestic craft and production is not shown, while the outside world (perhaps male-based) of trade, ritual, hunting, shipping etc. is shown. This gives power to ritual (the outside world etc.) and whoever is associated most clearly with it, and denies the importance of whoever is associated most clearly with the domestic world. As such, the depictions on the rock surfaces and on the drums emphasise the importance of the ritualistic and shamanistic world at the expense of the mundane domestic world, so that power could have been gained through the control of meaning in ritual.

The data on the more recent carvings are inadequate to show whether they represent part of a systematic trend. The depictions on the drums, on the other hand, are part of a systematic pattern which has some similarities to the rock carvings despite influences from Norse and Christian religion. The possibility that drums and shamans existed in prehistory, and the knowledge that drums were a commonly used instrument among the Sami in early pre-Christian history, indicates that the use of depictions in connection with rituals might have a long tradition in northern Scandinavia. This tradition existed 6,000 years ago, and is probably represented in its last stage by the drums and their associated rituals.[2]

Notes

1. The Sami are the indigenous population of northern Scandinavia also known as the Lapps.
2. I am grateful to Ian Hodder for the discussions we had in Cambridge in the early summer of 1984 when the idea for this paper was conceived, and for his later comments. I am equally grateful for the critical comments which I received from Ericka Engelstad, Alf Isak Keskitalo and Per Mathiesen.

Chapter 4

Pipes and parakeets: constructing meaning in an Early Iroquoian context

Alexander von Gernet and Peter Timmins

How can meaning be given to a unique pit, containing an assortment of artifacts (parakeet bones, pipe, slate tool and antler object) excavated on an early Iroquoian site in Ontario, dated to the early second millennium AD? Cultural continuity with historically attested groups allows the controlled use of analogy in order to assess the significance of the pit's contents. The bird–pipe association can be shown to be produced as the result of pipe-smoking ceremonies, the use of hallucinogenic plant substances and shamanistic practices. The analogy is supported by the quality and quantity of similarities with the archaeological pit, but also by a consideration of the possibility of a long-term historical context – a basic substratum or commonality of ideas which makes the varied comparative contexts used relevant to the particular case being examined. The ancient substratum of beliefs resurfaces in different forms at different times, without necessarily involving contact between the occurrences.

Introduction

Although archaeologists have always been interested in the symbolic dimension of culture, their frequent preoccupation with functions and activities has kept many from exploring structure and content within their own logic and coherence (Hodder 1982c, p. 4). Recent arguments for a symbolic or structural archaeology (which should not be confused with the analyses often associated with French structuralism) have found fault with a number of traditional approaches:

In processual analyses of symbol systems, the artefact itself is rarely given much importance. An object may be described as symbolising status, male or female, or social solidarity, but the use of the particular artefact class, and the choice of the symbol itself, are not adequately discussed. Similarly, traditional archaeologists use types as indicators of contact, cultural affiliation and diffusion, but the question of which type is used for which purpose is not pursued. The symbol is seen as being arbitrary.

(Hodder 1982c, p. 9)

In developing an alternative approach to the study of symbol systems archaeologists have been challenged to explore the manner in which items of material culture achieve meaning within their cultural contexts (*ibid.*, p. 9; Wylie 1982, p. 40). It is argued that the material record must be understood in terms of its interactive role in the socio-cultural world, a constitutive process that instils meaning in material objects. Moreover, it is suggested that the resultant symbolisation of material culture may serve a mediating or legitimating role in ideology or social relations (Hodder 1982c, pp. 9–10).

Although both Hodder (1982b) and Wylie (1982) have outlined the importance of analogical reasoning in the archaeological study of symbolisation processes, few studies have employed arguments from analogy to elucidate the crucial link between structural constraints and the generation of symbols in prehistoric contexts. In this study several associated artifacts are scrutinised in the light of structures and conditions independent of the observable data. Information concerning the formal and contextual data of the artifacts is combined with a substantial body of arguments from analogy in an attempt to demonstrate the manner in which material objects may achieve symbolic meaning under specific cultural conditions. This latter evidence is derived from a large data bank of books and articles relating to native pipe smoking and tobacco use, which von Gernet has compiled and indexed for a separate project.

The problem

During a recent analysis of faunal material from the Calvert site, an Early Iroquoian village in south-western Ontario, the bones of a Carolina parakeet were identified (Prevec 1984). The Carolina parakeet has been extinct since the 1930s and had never been found north of the Great Lakes prior to this discovery in an archaeological context. Of considerable interest is the fact that the bones were found in direct association with three relatively unusual artifacts: a stone pipe bowl, a slate tool and an antler artifact. The artifacts and the bones occurred together within a small pit, virtually devoid of other occupational debris, and appeared to have been purposefully buried rather than discarded as refuse.

Given the unique contextual association of these artifacts in the present, we feel there is reason to believe they were similarly associated in the systemic context of the past. If this association was entirely idiosyncratic our ability to provide a culturally meaningful interpretation is severely hampered. On the other hand, a recognition of the degree to which the association occurs in a larger spatial and temporal framework may help to illuminate the processes by which such associations are generated in the first place. If, indeed, similar associations are found in other contexts, it becomes necessary to assess the relevance of these if they are to serve as informative analogical arguments. The original problem thus becomes one of understanding why such correlations occur elsewhere. The premise involved here is that human symbolisation processes are sufficiently patterned to allow analogies to shed light on specific archaeological problems.

Before proceeding to these interpretive considerations, however, it is necessary to describe the archaeological context of the finds and the formal characteristics of the artifacts themselves.

The archaeological context

The Early Iroquoians

As an *in situ* development in north-eastern North America, Iroquoian prehistory can be traced at least as far back as Middle Woodland times (c. AD 700), and probably much further. Most Iroquoianists today recognise a transitional early Late Woodland culture known as Princess Point in southern Ontario, characterised by incipient corn agriculture as an addition to what was still essentially a hunting and gathering economy. Princess Point settlement patterns involve riverine (usually flood plain) summer village locations and winter dispersal to smaller inland camps (Stothers 1977).

By AD 900–1000 a well developed Iroquoian culture

pattern had emerged, as manifested in the Early Iroquoian Glen Meyer and Pickering cultures in south-western and south-central Ontario and the largely contemporaneous Owasco culture in New York State. Settlements shifted from river valleys to higher inland locations, usually on sandy soils. Although corn figured more prominently in the diet, hunting remained an important economic activity. Most Iroquoian villages of this period are small communities of 100–500 people living as extended families in a cluster of bark-covered longhouses, usually encircled by a fence or palisade. Such villages are often surrounded by numerous special purpose sites used for hunting, fishing, and collecting of a variety of resources.

Fortunately, the basic Iroquoian culture pattern continues (with only minor modifications) well into the period of European contact, at which time excellent ethnohistorical records fill in much that is archaeologically irrecoverable.

Just as elements of a hunting and gathering economy persisted throughout Early Iroquoian times, aspects of an ancient shamanic ideology also continued to be expressed among the Iroquoians well into the historic period (e.g., Whitthoft 1949, p. 84; Chafe 1964; Tooker 1970, p. 83). As Hultkrantz has pointed out, the tendency of farming cultures to superimpose religious beliefs on the ideology of previous hunting cultures is widespread in the New World (1979, pp. 144–5; see also Furst 1973–4, p. 35).

The Calvert site

Archaeological evidence for the survival of shamanic traits into the Iroquoian period has been found at the Calvert site, a 0.3 ha Early Iroquoian settlement near London, Ontario, excavated by the Ontario Ministry of Citizenship and Culture (Fox 1982). In opening approximately 80% of the site to view these excavations revealed a complex series of overlapping structures and features indicative of at least three separate and sequential episodes of rebuilding. This intra-village settlement pattern data indicates a degree of rebuilding and structure maintenance involving a relatively long period of site occupation. The five radiocarbon dates from the site suggest extended use sometime between c. AD 1100 and c. AD 1200 (Timmins 1984).

Archaeological features at Calvert range from large, complex stratified refuse pits rich in archaeological remains, to small, shallow depressions almost devoid of cultural material. The analysis of these features is currently being formalised in an attempt to document their variability, and to determine their function, the process involved in their formation, and the significance of their spatial distributions. For the purposes of the present paper, however, only one of these features needs to be described in detail.

A small, relatively unimpressive pit was located in the centre of a dense concentration of features on the western half of the site. At least two structures overlap in this area: thus it is not possible, at present, to assign the feature to any one house or phase of occupation.

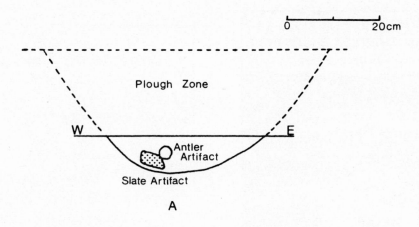

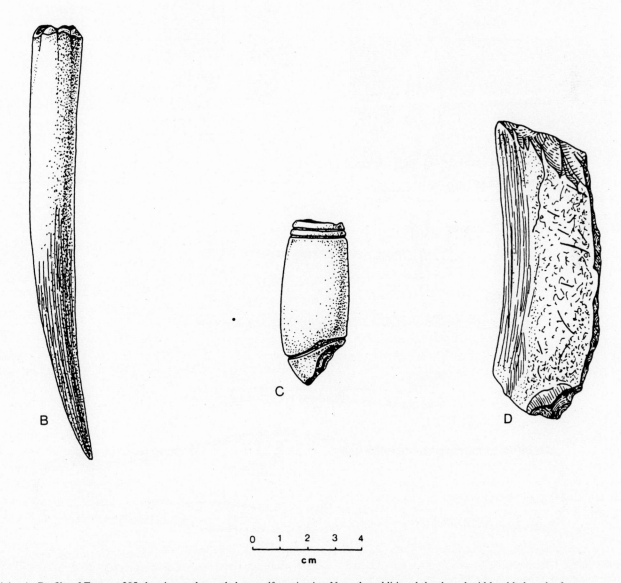

Fig. 4.1   A. Profile of Feature 285 showing antler and slate artifacts *in situ*. Note the additional depth and width added to the feature dimensions in consideration of plough zone material removed prior to excavation   B. Antler artifact   C. Limestone pipe bowl. Note encircling groove at base of bowl that may have been used for the attachment of a safety string   D. Slate tool

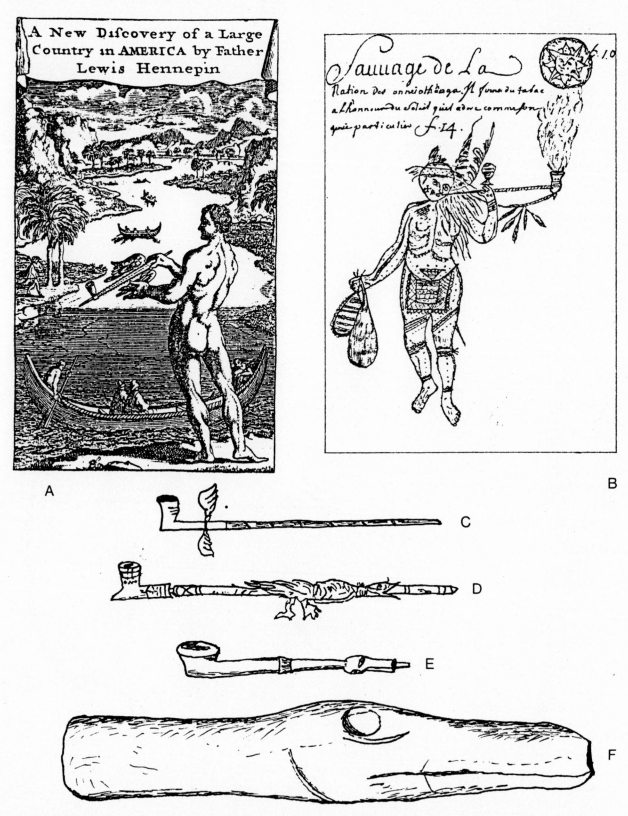

Fig. 4.2   A. One of the earliest depictions of a feathered pipe stem. Frontispiece to Lewis Hennepin's *A New Discovery of a Large Country in America* (1698). Courtesy McGill University Rare Book Libraries   B. Early illustration of an Oneida smoking his pipe. Note the typical Iroquoian vasiform pipe bowl and the feathers attached to a 'safety string'. From the *Codex Canadensis* (c. 1700). Artist unknown
C. Stone pipe bowl with long reed or wooden stem. From Robert Beverley's *History and Present State of Virginia* (1705, p. 227). Beverley claims to have seen this pipe himself and contrasts it with the prowed calumets described by explorers returning from the Mississippi area. Adapted from the original edition. Courtesy McGill University Rare Book Libraries   D. Early nineteenth-century calumet-like smoking device with bird skin impaled on stem. Based on Catlin 1841: 1, Plate 98   E. Twentieth-century wooden pipe of the Gros Ventres showing bird effigy near mouthpiece. Based on Clare 1955, p. 58   F. Side view of Adena stone tubular pipe in shape of Shoveler Duck. The bill serves as the mouthpiece. Maximum length is 14.5 cm. Based on Baby 1969, p. 17
Note: Specimens are shown at a variety of scales

Feature 285 was roughly circular in plan view, measured 24.5 cm in diameter, and was only 8 cm deep (from the plough-zone–subsoil interface). It would have originally been somewhat deeper since the actual occupation floor was above subsoil, within the plough-zone material that was removed prior to excavation. Figure 4.1A provides a reconstruction of the probable dimensions of the feature prior to plough disturbance, illustrating that the excavated portion of the pit represents only the basal level. In terms of form it is not unlike many other small features found at Calvert, yet the contents of Feature 285 established it as a highly unusual find.

Aside from the bird bones, the feature yielded a stone pipe bowl, an antler artifact and a slate tool (see fig. 4.1B–D). Although the latter two artifacts are important and have been discussed elsewhere (von Gernet and Timmins 1985), for the present discussion the bird bones and the stone pipe bowl are of central concern. With the exception of 0.2 gm of carbonised wood, the bones and the three artifacts, the feature contained no other occupational debris.

Through comparison with reference skeletons at the Smithsonian Institution in Washington, DC, Prevec (1984) positively identified the avian material from the feature as the remains of a Carolina parakeet (*Conuropis carolinensis*). Despite its having been relatively common in the south-eastern United States, the discovery of this extinct species on an archaeological site was of considerable ornithological interest as only sixteen skeletons of this bird are known in the world (Hahn 1963). Of the three bones discovered in the Calvert feature, one came from the head (a premaxilla), another from the wing (the proximal half of the left carpometacarpus) and the third came from the tail (a pygostyle).

Although the stone pipe bowl from Feature 285 is a rather plain specimen (fig. 4.1C), it nonetheless exhibits fine workmanship and represents something of an anomaly in an Iroquoian collection of this period. Stone pipes of any description are extremely rare finds on early Iroquoian sites (e.g. Noble 1975, pp. 23, 75). The elongated ovate bowl of the Calvert specimen is made of a soft grey limestone and has been drilled to form the bowl cavity. The only decoration consists of two horizontal lines encircling the bowl just below the lip. A deep groove encircles the base of the bowl near the elbow junction. It appears to be heavily worn and may have been functional rather than decorative.

The pipe is broken at the elbow and consequently lacks a stem. The question of whether this pipe had a non-detachable stone pipe stem or a detachable stem of wood or reed may have interesting implications in the light of non-archaeological data presented later in this paper. There is evidence to suggest that the Calvert pipe may have been equipped with a detachable wooden pipe stem (von Gernet and Timmins 1985). The average stem hole width of Early Iroquoian pipes with non-detachable stems is between 3.0 and 3.5 mm (Noble 1975, p. 24; Reid 1975, p. 23). The Calvert specimen displays a stem hole width of 5.7 mm which is larger than would be expected for a pipe with a non-detachable stem.

Another common feature of pipes with detachable stems is the presence of modifications on the bowl for the attachment of a 'safety string' or 'fob' running from the bowl to the stem (see fig. 4.2B; also Wright 1972, p. 81, Plate 21C; Rutsch 1973, p. 103; von Gernet 1985c, Plates 4b, 15f-g). With reference to the stone pipe bowl from Calvert, it is possible that the encircling groove at the base of the bowl was used for the attachment of such a string. This interpretation accounts for the evidence of wear within the groove and is consistent with the suggestion that the groove was non-decorative in nature. There is thus some formal evidence to suggest that the stone pipe bowl from Feature 285 at Calvert was fitted with a wooden pipe stem.

The search for meaning

The relationship between the objects found in the Calvert site feature would, at first glance, appear to have little significance, and the pit contents might be dismissed as a fortuitously associated set of artifacts. While analysing the parakeet bones, Prevec observed, however, that they came from the extremity areas of the head, wing, and tail, and concluded that "since these bones are left in a skin if it is to resemble the living creature, it is probable that the identified bones formed part of a skin that had ritualistic use" (1984, p. 7). This finding has important implications since we are no longer dealing with three disarticulated bones which were haphazardly thrown into the pit, but rather, with a *complete skin* of an unusual bird. We believe there is a considerable amount of evidence to suggest that the presence of an unusual bird skin in close proximity to a stone pipe bowl is not accidental and represents a well documented association recurring in a diversity of cultural contexts.

Bird skins and pipes

The most obvious bird/pipe association is the frequently discussed *calumet* – a class of ritual smoking devices, accounts of which span three centuries of ethnohistorical and ethnographic literature. Seventeenth-century European observers such as Marquette and the author of the De Gannes Memoir describe Illinois pipe stems as being ornamented not only with brilliant plumage but also with bird skins (Thwaites 1896–1901, Volume 59, p. 131; Pease and Werner 1934, p. 391). One of the more interesting accounts from this period is found in the work of Father Louis Hennepin:

> the *quill*, which is commonly two foot and a half long; is made of a pretty strong reed or cane, adorn'd with feathers of all colours, interlac'd with locks of womens hair. They tie to it two wings of the most curious birds they find, which makes their *Calumet* not much unlike *Mercury's* wand, or that staff ambassadors did formerly carry when they went to treat of peace. They sheath that reed into the neck of birds they call *Huars*, which are as big as our geese, and spotted with black and white; or else of a sort of ducks who make their nests upon trees, though water be their ordinary element, and whose

feathers are of many different colours. However, every nation adorns the *Calumet* as they think fit according to their own genius and the birds they have in their country.

(Hennepin 1698, p. 74)

Hennepin's description is supplemented by one of the earliest known illustrations of such a pipe (see fig. 4.2A) which served as the frontispiece to his *A New Discovery of a Large Country in America* (1698). Throughout the eighteenth century, accounts of calumet pipe stems consistently refer to attractive bird feathers and skins, often specifying that the head, neck, wings and tail were included (Beverley 1705; Lafitau 1724; Le Page du Pratz 1758; Charlevoix 1761; Rogers 1765).

More recent ethnographic reports parallel these early accounts in almost every detail. An emphasis on bird feathers or skins, especially those of eagles, woodpeckers, owls and ducks, characterises descriptions of pipe stems that were employed in a number of cultural and ceremonial settings (e.g. LaFlesche 1884, p. 614; Wissler 1912, pp. 159–61; Thomas 1941, p. 606; McClintock 1948, pp. 8–9; Wildschut 1960, p. 121; Murray 1962, p. 17; Bowers 1965, p. 48; Springer 1981, pp. 220, 222). During his extensive travels among North American natives in the 1830s, George Catlin often noted pipe stems ornamented with the skins, beaks and tufts of woodpeckers' heads (1841, Volume 1, pp. 147, 235). One of his many famous illustrations depicts a pipe stem with an unidentified bird skin literally impaled upon it, such that the mouthpiece protrudes from the bird's beak (Catlin 1841, Volume 1, Plate 98 (reproduced in fig. 4.2D); see also Ewers 1979, p. 13).

The practice of impaling bird skins on stems was relatively widespread. Among the Pawnee of the Central Plains a stem used in the *Hako* ceremony not only had tails, wings or heads of eagles, owls and woodpeckers attached to it, but was also thrust through the dried skin of a duck's neck and breast (Fletcher 1904, pp. 20–1, 40; cf. 1884, p. 309). In this case the stem was observed to protrude "a little through the bill of the duck, so that the bowl of a pipe could be fitted to it" (Fletcher 1904, p. 40; see also Hall 1977, p. 514). Dorsey describes a similar pipe stem among the neighbouring Omaha and notes that the lower mandible of the duck was sometimes removed (1884, p. 277).

Of considerable relevance to our present discussion of the Calvert find are two pipes secured for the Public Museum of Milwaukee by Alanson Skinner in 1923. The first specimen belonged to the Wolf gens of the Iowa, and on its highly ornamented stem "is impaled *the skin of a Carolina Paroquet*, the head of which is missing but had been pointed toward the bowl" (Skinner 1926, p. 229, Plate 32, Figure 2, emphasis added; see also West 1934, p. 273, Plate 185, Figure 2). A second example, from the Thunder gens (Iowa), also has bound to the stem "a well preserved skin of the rare Carolina Paroquet, with the head towards the bowl and the bill bent back" (Skinner 1926, p. 233, Plate 32, Figure 4; see also West 1934, p. 274, Plate 185, Figure 5). Skinner recognised the unusual and interesting nature of his museum purchases, especially since contemporary ornithologists maintained that

the bird had reached extinction fifteen years earlier (Skinner 1926, p. 229).

This rather brief sketch of ethnohistoric and ethnographic literature reveals a well documented association between pipes and bird skins, and even includes references to precisely the same rare species of parakeet found in the prehistoric feature we are attempting to illuminate. It will be noted, however, that these descriptions of smoking devices (which serve as potential sources of our analogies) are not derived from the same geographical or 'cultural' area as the archaeological context under scrutiny. It thus becomes necessary to establish what (if any) relationships exist between these non-Iroquoian accounts originating primarily in central North America, and an early or proto-Iroquoian manifestation in south-western Ontario.

Calumets

It has been observed that the feathered stem was prominent in a diversity of Amerindian groups (Fletcher 1904, p. 279) and a number of studies have attempted to examine its geographical distribution within an historical framework. Fenton argued that the spread of the calumet ritual from the western Great Lakes into the Iroquois area was primarily facilitated by the French who ostensibly adapted it for commerce and exploration (1953, pp. 156, 164–5).

In recent articles Turnbaugh accepts Fenton's claim that the calumet ceremony spread to most areas in relatively recent times and argues that with the increase in cultural disruption caused by European influence, the pipe, stem and associated rituals underwent a florescence representing a nativistic response or revitalisation movement (Turnbaugh 1979, 1984, pp. 61–2). Springer has, however, correctly observed that many descriptions of the Calumet Dance (in a variety of cultural contexts) were written by authors who were among the first Europeans to visit the tribes, suggesting that diffusion had occurred earlier and without help from the French (1981, pp. 225–6). Blakeslee agrees that the calumet was present in the area of the western Great Lakes and Mississippi River Valley before the arrival of French explorers (1981, p. 760). He also provides evidence (*ibid.*) from the records of the Spanish Inquisition that the calumet ceremony was already celebrated in 1634 by the Plains Apache (who probably received it from earlier Caddoan-speaking tribes) and attempts to trace the calumet pipe to at least 710 BP. Although Blakeslee's analysis goes far to demonstrate a definite prehistoric origin for this type of smoking implement, we are still left with Fenton's convincing evidence that calumet ceremonialism spread into the Eastern Woodlands and hence to the area of the Calvert site only during the historic period (circa 1680–1750 among the Five Nations Iroquois), a diffusion that postdates our archaeological feature by a full six centuries.

It would appear from our discussion thus far that the pipe/parakeet association present in the early Iroquoian context has no historical relationship with similar associations found in the paraphernalia of calumet ceremonialism. We believe, however, that the two examples are connected in a relationship of a different sort. A fuller understanding of this connection requires a broader appreciation of native pipe smoking that extends well beyond the stereotypic image of the 'peace pipe' wielding Indian, so popular in general public consciousness. As Wissler noted earlier this century, "most certainly every pipe was not a calumet and every smoking ceremony not a calumet ceremony" (1912, p. 168). There are indications that the intertribal diplomacy and attendant ritualism associated with the calumet made use of smoking implements that were symbolically charged with a much more fundamental and ancient belief system common to many Amerind societies. We have provided ethnohistorical and archaeological evidence elsewhere (von Gernet and Timmins 1985) suggesting the existence, among Iroquoians, of calumet-like smoking devices long before the historic diffusion of similar implements into the Eastern Woodlands. These earlier long-stemmed pipes (resembling the one shown in fig. 4.2B) presumably were not calumets in the traditional sense, in the same way that the feathered pipes found in Plains Indian medicine bundles were not employed in intertribal peace treaties such as those often found in the Mississippi Valley (see Wissler 1912, p. 168; Springer 1981, pp. 229–30). In other words, the association of smoking and birds forms part of an underlying substratum common to a variety of pipe complexes and not specifically linked to the famous calumet ceremonialism.

Effigy pipes and skeuomorphs

Besides the calumet, the most familiar bird/pipe associations, known to many North American archaeologists, are found among the Adena/Hopewell (c. 500 BC–AD 500) pipes of the Ohio–Mississippi drainage. Instead of (or perhaps in addition to?) the use of actual dead birds for decoration, these smoking implements often have stone bowls consisting of elaborately carved bird effigies (e.g. West 1934, pp. 604–15; Crouch 1965, pp. 8, 13, 34–54). At least two of these have been identified as 'paraquets' (West 1934, p. 613, Figure 2; Crouch 1965, pp. 13, 35, Plate 7).

Fenton was among the first to recognise the conceptual similarity between the ethnographically documented feathered stems of the Pawnee *Hako* and the much older Hopewell duck effigy pipes (1953, p. 205). More recently Hall has suggested an even greater similarity between the flat-stem gens pipes of the Iowa (such as those having Carolina parakeets impaled on their stems) and the platform pipes of 1,200 to 2,100 years ago (1977, p. 504; 1984, p. 2). This conclusion is based partly on his belief that some of the Hopewell forms originally had long, flat stems much like the ethnographic examples (Hall 1977, p. 504; 1984, p. 17; cf. Crouch 1965, p. 5).

Some researchers have alluded to an historical link between Hopewell smoking and the calumet ritual (Whitthoft *et al.* 1953, p. 90). Turnbaugh believes "it may yet be possible to follow the significance of Hopewell bird effigy pipes down through the subsequent use of eagle, owl, duck, and woodpecker feathers and parts on the Hako-type calumet" (1979, p. 686). Others have postulated Hopewellian influence

for the effigy pipes of the Iroquoian-speaking tribes around the eastern Great Lakes (Brasser 1980, p. 96). These latter ceramic or stone effigy pipes become increasingly common in Iroquoian archaeological sites after the fifteenth century and over half of the faunal representations are birds (Noble 1979, pp. 70–1; Mathews 1980, p. 297; 1981a, p. 33). Owls, woodpeckers, eagles and ducks are frequently reported in Ontario samples (Noble 1979, pp. 70–1;· Mathews 1981a, p. 34; Kenyon 1982, pp. 119, 121, Figure 78) and recall similar species found on the skinned and feathered stems mentioned earlier. Extinct or otherwise unusual birds such as great auks, razor-billed auks, flamingoes, parrots and parakeets have also been reported (e.g. Hart 1978, p. 223; Mathews 1981a, p. 34; Kenyon 1982, pp. 99–101, 197, 212, Plates 93, 189).

Of major importance in any attempts to demonstrate (or even suggest) an historical relationship between stone platform pipes, feathered stems, or ceramic effigy pipes is the concept of *skeuomorphs*. This refers to the reappearance of a shape or decoration that had previously occurred in a different medium or material (see Turnbaugh 1984, p. 61). One of the most striking examples of a skeuomorph is the aforementioned impaled bird motif which has the stem of a pipe thrust through the body of a duck or other bird, so that the mouthpiece protrudes from the bill. Precisely the same idea is replicated in a Gros Ventres (Montana) sacred pipe, in which a wooden carving in the shape of a duck's head replaces an actual bird skin in exactly the same location, and with the stem protruding from the bill (Clare 1955, pp. 55–6, 58; reproduced in fig. 4.2E). Wooden pipes with carvings of birds' heads are also occasionally reported in the ethnographic literature on the Plains Hidatsa (Bowers 1965, pp. 345–6).

We believe this concept is of considerable antiquity in North America and that recognition of its historical continuity may be masked by its oscillation between perishable and non-perishable materials. The most easily discernible manifestations of this motif in the archaeological record are stone bird effigies having a long tube drilled through the length of their bodies. These straight-tubular effigy pipes are usually associated with the Adena culture of the Northeast and have been found at Welcome Mound, dated 350 BC ± 200 years (Ritchie 1980, p. 205). The pipes are often carved to represent the neck, head and bill of shoveller ducks (*Spatula clypeata*) with the bill serving as the mouthpiece (Setzler 1960, pp. 455–6, Plates 2, 4; Ritchie and Dragoo 1960, pp. 15–16; see fig. 4.2F). The recovery of a number of identical examples from various sites prompted Baby (1969, pp. 16–17) to add the motif to a list of diagnostic Adena traits.

Is it too farfetched to surmise that these representations are part of the same ancient substratum of beliefs that resurfaces as perishable or near-perishable skeuomorphs throughout eastern and central North America? The possibility that Adena/Hopewell symbolic concepts had ample opportunity to influence early Iroquoian skeuomorphs has been raised (von Gernet and Timmins 1985), although a direct historical continuity may never be demonstrated.

Similar problems of cultural continuity are found in discussing relationships between Hopewell pipes and historic calumets. Although Blakeslee has provided evidence that the calumet pipe may be as much as five centuries older than previously realised (Blakeslee 1981, p. 763; Hall 1984, p. 4) he has found no direct continuity between it and Hopewellian forms (Blakeslee 1981, p. 764). Hall is convinced, however, that the evolution of the calumet pipe replicated the evolution of Hopewellian platform pipes, by which he is "not suggesting direct continuity of particular cultural forms as much as the persistence of culturally transmitted beliefs and understandings which manifest themselves in many different but recognizably related ways" (Hall 1977, pp. 504–5; 1984, p. 2; cf. Blakeslee 1981, p. 764). There is no reason to deny a concurrent process linking Adena/Hopewell symbolic subsystems with antecedent skeuomorphs in twelfth-century south-western Ontario. Our archaeological example from Ontario and the historic feathered calumets further west may well have had a common ancestry; yet, as will presently be suggested, uninterrupted lines of design persistence need not be documented for analogues to be heuristically useful in illuminating prehistoric symbolic meaning.

The presence of the bird motif on smoking pipes or other tobacco-related objects has an enormous distribution in the New World. It may even be found among the relatively rare incised effigy pipes of prehistoric south-western North America (Simmons 1968, pp. 15, 143–4). Alden Mason mentions a number of prehistoric Mexican examples with conventionalised representations of ducks and other birds, in which the head forms the bowl and the beak faces the smoker as part of the stem (1924, pp. 9, 37, Plates 1, 2). Ornithomorphic pipes, which Stahl considered 'precolumbian' (1926, p. 114, Plate 18), have been recovered in Bolivia. Among the Guaporé tribes of South America tobacco snuffing tubes are often made to resemble birds and are reminiscent of archaeological bird-shaped pottery snuffers from Costa Rica (Wassén 1965, pp. 25–6, Figure 2, 3; 1967, pp. 243, 285, Figures 4, 34; Furst 1974, pp. 10–11). Although some components of tobacco ritualism may have diffused throughout the Americas over a period of thousands of years (e.g. Hall 1984, pp. 6, 11–12, 24), there is evidence that bird/pipe associations are at a level of universality beyond particular cultural peculiarities, and diffusionist explanations may be rendered unnecessary to some degree. It becomes of crucial importance to explore, in well documented ethnographic contexts, patterns in the conditions or mechanisms that generate such symbolic associations and give them meaning.

Bird symbolism and altered states of consciousness

Ethnographic accounts of feathered pipe stem ritualism often contain interpretations or explanations of bird symbolism. Eagles are said to be associated with day, owls with night, woodpeckers with trees and ducks with water (Fletcher 1904, p. 40; Gilmore 1933, p. 18; McClintock 1948, p. 3). These and other birds are also associated with an impressive inventory of

more specific attributes (Fletcher 1904, pp. 20–1; Linton 1923, pp. 2, 6; Gilmore 1933, p. 18; Fenton 1953, pp. 167, 195, 205; Wildschut 1960, p. 115; Bowers 1965, pp. 345–6; Ubelaker and Wedel 1975, p. 448), and it becomes apparent that natives selected a number of birds precisely because of their unusual capabilities or habits. There is a considerable amount of evidence to suggest that Amerindians valued species with particularly colourful plumage. Among the Huichol of Mexico, for example, the brilliantly coloured macao plumes are associated with "the flames of the greatest shaman of all, Grandfather Fire" (La Barre 1975, pp. 32, 71). The most extraordinary native preoccupation with coloured bird feathers is the South American practice of employing frog or toad poisons to alter artificially the natural plumage of live parrots. This involved application of the potent substances to the bird skin with the intention of gradually changing, for example, green feathers to yellow and red (Furst 1976, p. 163). A similar preference for specific colours may have led an individual in prehistoric south-western Ontario to seek out (either through trade or in the immediate environment) a Carolina Parakeet, which was known for its striking green, red, and yellow plumage (Prevec 1984, p. 4; Kennedy 1984, pp. 56, 57–8). Such perceived outstanding qualities, however, fail to relate birds and smoking devices in a meaningful fashion, and we thus reverse the association and ask what it is about smoking that leads to ornithological symbolism.

In a recent study, von Gernet (1985a) has established that Amerindians of the Northeast smoked a variety of entheogens (mind-altering plant substances) presumably to produce altered states of consciousness and enhance visionary experiences. Using evidence from botany, psychopharmacology, ethnohistory, and ethnographic descriptions from a variety of cultural contexts, he has shown that *Nicotiana rustica* (the potent native tobacco employed in most of eastern North America) and a number of other species were capable of producing major dissociational states and were consumed in quantities sufficient to reach the pharmacological threshold at which most humans experience the sensation of flight or other out-of-body phenomena. This confirms earlier suspicions that native tobacco species might legitimately be added to the long list of 'hallucinogens' used by New World peoples (Janiger and Dobkin de Rios 1976).

When the physiological effects of tobacco consumption and fasting are combined with cultural suggestion, trance states and concomitant visual imagery frequently occur. Ornithological symbolism is not uncommon in a variety of such 'visions' or 'dreams' (e.g. Lowie 1919, p. 181; cf. La Barre 1975, p. 71). After consuming tobacco or other entheogens the Jibaro of eastern Ecuador and Peru "see tucans, wild turkeys, parrots, and other magical birds" (Karsten 1935, pp. 446–7). That these pseudoperceptions may have led to the transformation of birds into pipes (or vice versa) is dramatically illustrated by the account of a twentieth-century Plains Sioux vision quester:

The heat, the steam, the tobacco had made me giddy and

light-headed. It had emptied my mind so that the spirits could enter it. I felt weak, but I also felt power streaming through my veins, a new, strange power. As I stared into the glowing stones, I thought I saw a small bird in them. I recognized it as an eagle. I had hardly done so when it turned into a pipe. It all happened in a flash, in a twinkling of an eye, but it was very real to me.

(quoted in Halifax 1979, pp. 81–2)

It is equally conceivable that in the past such experiences can be related to the practice of impaling bird skins on smoking devices and to the production of ornithomorphic pipes. During an altered state of consciousness these birds (occurring, as they do, within 5 to 60 cm of the smoker's visual field) may, in turn, have been regarded as live creatures. Throughout North America feathers are often endowed with life in themselves and stuffed bird skins are said to come alive during ceremonies (e.g. Johnson 1967, Volume 1, p. 177; Skinner 1920, p. 297). During a vision Black Elk (an Oglala Sioux) observed a pipe which had a spotted eagle outstretched upon the stem and noted that it "seemed alive, for it was poised there, fluttering, and its eyes were looking at me" (Neihardt 1972, p. 23). Iroquoian mythology also contains references to 'pigeons' who, while perched on pipe stems, rustled their wings and cooed happily whenever the pipe was smoked (Hewitt 1918, p. 140; Curtin 1923, p. 383). This is reminiscent of many smoking devices, particularly the stone pipes having elaborately carved bird effigies sitting or perched on them (e.g. Thruston 1890, pp. 194–5, Figures 92, 93).

Bird effigies perched, mounted, or impaled on sticks of all kinds frequently symbolise the soul journey of the shaman (Kirchner 1952, pp. 256–7; Eliade 1964, p. 481; Furst 1976, p. 155). Indeed, birds have a ubiquitous role in shamanism, and feathers are often mentioned in descriptions of healing wands, staffs, and shamanic costumes (Kirchner 1952, pp. 255–9; Eliade 1964, p. 156; Halifax 1979, p. 16). One explanation for this occurrence is that many birds, such as owls, eagles and vultures, possess very keen eyesight, and ornithological paraphernalia allow shamans to "see better into the world of spirits" (Wassén 1965, p. 28; 1967, p. 283; Wilbert 1975, p. 451). In South America, their intimate connection with the visionary realm of hallucinogens has prompted some researchers to consider birds as 'patrons for ecstatic intoxication' (Wassén 1967, p. 283). This may also explain their prominence in the symbolism of peyotism (La Barre 1975, pp. 39, 56, 69–72).

A second explanation for bird/tobacco/shamanism associations involves the concept of flight. Crow warriors of the Western Plains tied eagle heads and feathers to their bodies to "absorb the power of flight" (Wildschut 1926, pp. 287–8), while Siberian Tungus shamans claim that ornithomorphic accoutrements are indispensable for the flight to other worlds and say "it is easier to go, when the costume is light" (Eliade 1964, p. 157). The Warao of South America keep their body 'light' by smoking tobacco and eating very little (Wilbert 1972, pp. 68–9). This may have been the intention of

seventeenth-century Iroquoian individuals who are reported to have fasted as much as eighteen days without consuming anything but tobacco (Thwaites 1896–1901, Volume 10, p. 203; see also Sagard [1632] 1939, p. 112). The importance of tobacco in the aerial symbolism of the Akawaio (a South American group) is shown by Audrey Butt, who notes that the tobacco spirit and bird spirit helpers combine to get the shaman airborne (Butt 1966, pp. 56–8; see also Wilbert 1975, p. 448). For many natives of Guiana bird spirits *are* tobacco spirits and the use of tobacco accompanies every act of the medicine man (Wassén 1965, p. 25).

Tobacco and the guardian soul

Man/animal metamorphoses, and indeed transformation rather than creation, is a central shamanistic concept (Furst 1976, p. 6) which has been identified as a pervasive theme in Iroquoian ideology (Parker 1924, pp. 49, 59). A common ability of shamans in various parts of the world is the transformation of their souls into birds during the out-of-body experiences of trance (Zerries 1962, p. 906; Eliade 1964, pp. 157, 403, 481; Schultes and Hoffmann 1979, p. 122), and in the Americas such metamorphoses are frequently associated with the ingestion of psychoactive plants (Dobkin de Rios 1976, p. 61; Schultes 1972, p. 21). Among natives of El Gran Chaco 'bird-shaped human souls' are created through the dissociational states induced by hallucinogenic snuff (Wassén 1965, p. 29). Seventeenth-century Iroquoians reported that what is known as the 'dream' or 'free' soul routinely flew away during visionary experiences and became associated with spirits in the shape of owls, eagles, ravens, and a host of other creatures (Thwaites 1896–1901, Volume 17, p. 153; Volume 26, p. 267; Volume 33, p. 191; Volume 39, p. 19; Hewitt 1895, p. 110). Von Gernet has argued elsewhere (1985b) that a better understanding of protohistoric Iroquoian visionary experience requires the notion of a fusion between dream-soul and guardian spirit, resulting in an entity known as the 'guardian soul' (see Hultkrantz 1953, pp. 375–6).

Eliade suggests that in many instances tutelary animals can be regarded as one of the shaman's 'souls', or the 'soul in animal form' (1964, p. 94). The most extreme manifestation of this process is nagualism, which involves such an intense identification of an individual with his guardian spirit that it is sometimes called the 'alter ego concept' (Hultkrantz 1979, p. 71). Although commonly an attribute of the religions of aboriginal Mexico and Guatemala, nagualistic-type theories have been identified among the Penobscot of the Northeast, where shamans are said to have been able to change into their guardian spirits (Hultkrantz 1979, pp. 72–3).

Much has been written on the conception of the alter ego and its relation to birds (e.g. Zerries 1962, passim). Furst has interpreted the famous 'Eagle Dancer' design on a Spiro Mound conch shell as a classic illustration of the shaman's ecstatic ascent "as he and eagle, his tutelary spirit, merge into one" (1965, p. 58). Ojibwa vision questers frequently transformed themselves into their ornithomorphic tutelaries

(Hallowell 1966, p. 284), and Halifax also speaks of the dissolution of any distinction between the shaman and his bird-shaped 'ally' (1979, p. 16).

Several archaeological artifacts, such as a snuffer from Monte Alban, Oaxaca (c. 300–100 BC), possess both human and animal effigies, suggesting a metamorphosis (Furst 1974, pp. 18–19). Among the Mohawk Iroquois personal tutelaries could reside in objects such as pipes (Carse 1949, pp. 37–8) and a number of researchers have interpreted the effigies found on Iroquoian smoking implements as guardian spirits (Mathews 1976, p. 27; 1978, pp. 164, 180; 1980, p. 303; 1981b, p. 161; Latta 1976, pp. 263–5; Kenyon 1982, p. 99). Marlene Dobkin de Rios believes the Adena/Hopewell effigies might also correspond to shamanistic animal familiars available to manipulation by tobacco-using natives (1977, p. 242). Birds might be envisioned as particularly powerful tutelaries since many successfully mediate between air, land, and water (see Fletcher 1904, p. 21; Gilmore 1933, p. 18). Furst observes:

> it is axiomatic of shamanic symbology that it selects precisely those animals that can shift between different environments or that by virtue of unusual life histories or habits are perceived as mediators between disparate states. Where the bird motif is unspecific, it seems to stand for the power of flight that is the shaman's special gift and that is activated by the hallucinogen. It should be noted that birds are often regarded as guardian spirits or even manifestations of specific psychoactive plants, especially tobacco; this observation provides one clue for the meaning of bird-shaped tobacco pipes in North American Indian art.
>
> (Furst 1976, p. 154)

An explanation that postulates a conceptual fusion between 'guardian spirit' and 'soul', however, gives the interpretation of ornithomorphic smoking devices a slightly different dimension. If the bird on the pipe bowl or stem represents a guardian soul, then it is symbolically the smoker himself, or at least the aspect of the self that is externalised during the out-of-body experience of a dissociational state. Ethnopharmacologists interested in the cultural use of hallucinogens have often noted that spirits and deities are said to be 'addicted' to tobacco to the same degree as their human counterparts (Furst 1976, p. 24). Thus, Iroquoians offered the plant to birds (Carse 1949, p. 36), a sacrifice which the Winnebago of the western Great Lakes called "filling the spirits' pipe" (McKern 1928, p. 149). The neighbouring Menomini sometimes held their pipes by the bowl, twirling the stem about "so that all the gods may partake" (Skinner 1913, p. 96). As Speck notes, the sub-Arctic Naskapi hunter "proceeds toward further communion with his own soul-spirit by smoking tobacco in his stone pipe", his intention being "to feed the soul" and thus encourage continued assistance from external potencies (in Hultkrantz 1953, p. 384). We believe that this may partially explain why many ornithomorphic smoking implements are represented so that smoke actually issues from the beak or through the body of the creature. By smoking a pipe (i.e. blowing and sucking 'power') an individual may therefore simultaneously 'feed' his body and his guardian soul.

Bundles

Although we have provided a considerable amount of evidence suggesting that, during its use-life, the parakeet skin found in our archaeological context may actually have been impaled or otherwise mounted on the pipe stem, there is a possibility that the two objects were physically separate (albeit symbolically connected) components of a buried ritual bundle. If this interpretation is accepted there is, of course, little relevance to a demonstration of the presence or absence of long detachable pipe stems in early Iroquoian contexts. In this case, despite being physically (and perhaps conceptually) separate objects, it is clear that the pipe and the bird may still be inextricably associated.

Bird skins and pipes are, in fact, commonly found in sacred bundles of the historic Hidatsa (Bowers 1965, pp. 345, 346, 364), Blackfoot (Wissler 1912, pp. 137, 160–2, 169–71; McClintock 1948, p. 6; Clare 1955, p. 8), Teton Dakota (Smith 1967, p. 26), Gros Ventres (Clare 1955, pp. 57–9) and Winnebago (McKern 1928, pp. 149–50), as well as other tribes. Hanson's survey of medicine bundles among 17 Plains Indian tribes revealed that 65 per cent contained *both* pipes and birds (J. R. Hanson 1980, Table 1; see also Ubelaker and Wedel 1975, p. 446; Sidoff 1977, p. 177). Of particular interest is a Plains Arikara bundle which contained, among other birds, the skin of a Carolina parakeet (Ubelaker and Wedel 1975, p. 447).

The presence of an analogous collection of ritual paraphernalia in early Iroquoian contexts is not totally unexpected since 'medicine bundles' occur in later times (e.g. Whitthoft and Hadlock 1946, p. 420). Seventeenth-century missionaries among the Huron also described tobacco pouches which contained "charms" and "other little necessities" (Thwaites 1896–1901, Volume 10, p. 209; Volume 17, p. 209; Volume 44, p. 295). The "charms" were frequently birds or bird parts (Thwaites 1896–1901, Volume 10, p. 209; Volume 26, p. 267; Volume 33, pp. 211–13) and there is more recent evidence that some were 'fed', wrapped in ancient rags, and buried (Shimony 1970, pp. 250–1). Parts of birds are occasionally found in Iroquoian burials (Mathews 1978, p. 186) and it is unfortunate that their contextual significance is rarely explored in any detail. In the light of our present discussion, for example, can it be entirely chance that in an excavation of an historic Iroquoian (Neutral) cemetery the wing bones of a trumpeter swan were found within 15 cm of a ceramic bird effigy pipe (Kenyon 1982, pp. 197, 204)?

An interpretation that envisions the parakeet skin at Calvert as a 'charm' originally buried with other objects in a bundle is entirely in harmony with our previous guardian-soul model. Iroquoian 'charms' were frequently recognised in everyday life as some form of familiar spirits (Thwaites 1896–1901, Volume 17, pp. 159, 207, 211) and are thus analogous to the talismans of the northern Plains which were identified with, or supplied by, tutelaries (Hultkrantz 1979,

p. 76). In fact, components of Crow medicine bags and Hidatsa personal bundles were symbolic representations of guardian spirits seen during visions, while in other instances the whole bundles were identical with such spirits (Bowers 1965, p. 246; Sidoff 1977, p. 194; Hultkrantz 1953, p. 347). The frequent emphasis on smoking and visionary experiences during ritual procedures connected with the bundle-complex suggests a conceptual similarity with the ancient symbolic subsystem of shamanism that linked pipes with birds through visions of guardian souls.

Conclusions

The present exercise has been a search for meaning in the archaeological record that ventures well beyond the archaeologically observable. Two artifacts, a stone pipe bowl and the remains of a bird skin, were discovered within centimetres of one another on a twelfth-century Iroquoian site in south-western Ontario. Traditionally, such a combination of objects might receive little further attention, beyond a rather vague conjecture that the pit (or even the house) in which they were contained had some 'ceremonial' or 'ritual' function, and a claim that additional interpretations are mere guesswork. Following Wylie (1982, p. 42) we argue that often, in cases of symbolic or structural interpretations, a scepticism about the possibility of any reliable, empirically grounded knowledge of the cultural past is unfounded.

Of crucial importance here is a recognition that some symbolic associations crosscut archaeologically delimited 'cultural' boundaries and may reach levels of generality beyond specific spatio-temporal contexts. It was demonstrated that historically and ethnographically documented associations between smoking devices and bird skins are widespread and in some instances even include the same rare species of parakeet found at the Calvert site. It remained to show in what manner a postulated analogical relationship between ethnographic source and the archaeological subject has relevance (see Salmon 1982, p. 63).

The homology between the source and subject of specific analogical arguments has frequently been scrutinised by archaeologists (e.g. Ascher 1961; Chang 1967; Binford 1967; Tringham 1978; Gould 1978; Charlton 1981). Although most researchers agree that the source is somewhat removed from the initial raw data or archaeological subject, there is generally little consensus on the degree of externality allowable in any given inferential argument. Childe felt that an analogue "drawn from the same region or ecological province is likely to give the most reliable hints" (1956, p. 51), while Schiffer decries such limitations as "spurious methodological advice" (1978, p. 233). Restricting the use of analogies only to those data that appear to have immediate relevance or applicability (Binford 1967; cf. Tringham 1978, p. 187) is to deny the possibility that the boundary conditions for any given inference or generalisation might be broader than was originally conceived. Thus, Steward's (1942) *direct historical approach* or Gould's (1974, pp. 37–40) *continuous* models are not always demonstrably

superior to or more useful than *discontinuous* models in which the sources of analogies are historically unrelated to the archaeological subjects under consideration. It seems clear that not all inferential arguments need to be solidly entrenched in some substantive historical connections linking the two sides of an analogy.

The principal sources of our analogy (i.e. smoking devices with well documented bird associations) are historically unrelated to our archaeological sample only in the sense that most do not originate in specifically Iroquoian contexts. The possibility that we may be dealing with an ancient shamanic tradition underlying much of New World culture illustrates the fuzziness that characterises the interface between *continuous* and *discontinuous* models. At one level, symbolic meanings in our archaeological feature presumably are linked to the ecstatic shamanic experience which Eliade has designated as "a primary phenomenon" known to the "whole of archaic humanity" (1964, p. 504). With a few exceptions, American Indians were in ethos still hunters, and the extraordinary persistence of shaministic traits in the New World has led La Barre to recognise many aspects of native religion as "a kind of mesolithic fossil" (1970, p. 79; 1972, pp. 270, 272, 278; see also Furst 1973–4). Various authors have postulated (and provided convincing evidence for) an Asiatic origin for the shamanistic substratum underlying most Amerindian cultures (La Barre 1970; Wilbert 1972, p. 83; Furst 1976, pp. 5–6). Furst provides a long list of core elements common to the New World and Asia and argues that "there are demonstrably so many fundamental similarities between the core elements of the religions of the aboriginal New World and those of Asia that almost certainly at least in their basic foundations the symbolic systems of American Indians must have been present already in the ideational world of the original immigrants from northeastern Asia" (1976, pp. 5–6). An Asiatic origin for some of the circumpolar shamanistic practices found in the Iroquoian area at the time of European contact has been acknowledged as a definitive possibility (Trigger 1978, p. 799).

The ritual use of tobacco and its association with birds is extremely widespread in eastern North America (Springer 1981, p. 229) and we have provided evidence that cultural continuity in specific design motifs and attendent symbolic associations may be interrupted in the archaeological record through the oscillation of perishable and non-perishable skeuomorphs. More importantly, the evidence offered in this study indicates that a particular motif or symbol need not even be transmitted from generation to generation, but rather may be replicated independently, given the existence of certain cultural preconditions. We have identified possible causal mechanisms which define the conditions under which the symbolic associations might be expected, and have suggested that these are linked to the altered states of consciousness so typical of shamanism.

Tobacco use (although certainly not as old as shamanism, soul-flight, and bird symbolism) is in itself a logical extension of a now widely recognised ancient New World cultural predisposition for the use of psychoactive plants (La Barre 1970; Furst 1972, p. ix; 1976, pp. 2–3). Although the postulated causal mechanism used to explain bird/pipe associations has an element of biological reductionism (i.e. the link between a symbol and the physiological effects of consuming an entheogen), this should not be considered universally applicable, and it must be remembered that cultural determinants help to organise hallucinatory experience (Wallace 1959; Furst 1972, pp. xiv–xv; Dobkin de Rios 1972, p. 148). Thus, while certain alkaloids set the stage for similar symbolic representations by giving the taker the kinesthetic sensation of being weightless (Wassén 1965, p. 29; Dobkin de Rios 1973, p. 1222; 1975, p. 407), images of parrots, macaws, and other magical birds are culturally patterned and expected during the soul journeys of visionary experiences (Langdon 1979).

It is unlikely that we will ever know the precise reason why an early Iroquoian individual carefully buried a pipe and a parakeet skin in a particular pit at a particular time, and what meaning he assigned to this association. As Hodder has suggested, however, the problem of unique context is not as difficult to overcome once we begin to understand the link between general principles of meaning and symbolism and specific cultural arrangements (1982b, pp. 24–6). Since the Calvert site feature was not only produced within a uniquely 'Iroquoian' ideological framework, but may also be given meaning within the much broader context of Amerindian ecstatic religion, analogical inferences involving similar cultural conditions have relevance, even when originating in entirely different ethnographic regions of the New World. The general methodological principle involved in such an archaeology is simply that

> known contexts may be expected to provide guidelines for the reconstruction of mechanisms or conditions that would have been capable of producing a given body of data. It is at least more plausible to expect that something

like known mechanisms, or mechanisms governed by the same parameters as known mechanisms, operated in the past than to postulate such total discontinuity that the past is considered completely unreconstructable from its material record and knowledge of contemporary cultural phenomena.

> (Wylie 1982, p. 43)

We have undoubtedly failed to exhaust the full range of interpretations bearing upon the Calvert site feature; yet there appear to be compelling reasons for accepting the model offered, and until a superior explanatory strategy is put forward, these empirically grounded observations seem better than arbitrary speculation.[2]

Note

1. Many of the ideas developed in this paper were formulated during a graduate seminar entitled 'Analogy and the Interpretation of Archaeological Data', given by Professor Bruce Trigger at McGill University during the fall and winter of 1984–5. Professor Mike Bisson, Rosemary Bernard, David Denton, Bruce Jamieson, Mary Ann Levine, Moira McCaffrey and Gary Warrick participated in this seminar and provided valuable insights into many of the issues discussed here.

An earlier version of this paper was presented at the first McGill–Université de Montréal Joint Archaeology Seminar, held in February 1985.

The global survey of aboriginal pipe and tobacco use from which material for this paper was derived was prepared while von Gernet was a recipient of a Social Sciences and Humanities Research Council of Canada Doctoral Fellowship. Timmins' analysis of the Calvert site material has been assisted by members of the Ontario Archaeological Society and supported by the Ontario Heritage Foundation, the Max Bell Foundation and McGill University. He would also like to thank William Fox, Regional Archaeologist, Ontario Ministry of Citizenship and Culture, for his advice on the Calvert investigations, Rosemary Prevec for her exacting faunal analysis, and Janie Fox for her fine artifact drawings.

Both authors acknowledge the assistance of Bruce Trigger and Ian Hodder who read and commented upon earlier versions of this paper.

Chapter 5

**Staddle-stones
and silage-pits:
successional use in an
agricultural community**

Jacqueline Nowakowski

**Continuity and change:
the past active in
the present**

*Nowakowski looks at a contemporary example of how meanings
associated with surviving material culture objects from the past are
transformed and distorted as they move into new contexts, but
nevertheless the objects themselves and their meanings influence the
new situation as part of an active social process. She looks at the
successional re-use of traditional farm buildings on Bodmin Moor,
Cornwall, England. The meanings which are associated with past
buildings depend on one's social position and perspective.
Nowakowski isolates five sections of contemporary society on the
Moor and shows how their attitudes to the re-use of older buildings
vary – some integrate the older buildings if they can be given a
practical use, while for others it is the symbolic connotations which are
important.*

Introduction

Historical knowledge is that special case of memory where the
object of present thought is past thought, the gap between
present and past being bridged not only by the power of the
present thought to think of the past, but also by the power of the
past thought to reawaken itself in the present.

(Collingwood 1946, p. 294)

This paper is not an attempt to explain the nature of
historical knowledge, but is an attempt to explore some of the
avenues along which a rural community travels in acquiring and
experiencing a sense of that knowledge. It also tries to assess
how important such knowledge is in influencing present
behaviour.

It has been well documented elsewhere that material
culture can provide many valuable insights into the behaviours
of human societies (e.g. Deetz 1977; Gould and Schiffer 1981;
Hodder 1982a, 1982b). I will describe and analyse here an
exercise that was developed to explore the way material culture
that is particular to a local community articulates and sustains
an important link and dialogue between that community's
present local life and its known or perceived past. This is
largely a phenomenological exercise in so far as I shall
concentrate on the analysis of a particular behavioural
phenomenon that affects material culture, rather than on an
analysis of the material culture itself. My approach has been
influenced by Billinge's observation that "facts and objects
cannot exist independently of man's consciousness", and the
importance of his remark that, "it is what phenomena *mean*
that defines their reality, not what they are" (Billinge 1977,
p. 57). I hope to demonstrate in this paper that by examining
individual strategies and behaviours towards a particular
inherited material environment, we increase our understanding
of the wealth of meanings we are prepared to allow materials to
contain. This affects the richness of our reconstructions of the
behaviour of individuals and societies, past and present, and
the usefulness of our explanation of this behaviour.

In order to achieve the above aims, I will explore just one
aspect of behaviour towards inherited material culture: the
process of recycling and maintaining historical material objects
in successive cultural contexts. I hope to show that this process,
'successional use', is important and fundamental to all

developed societies that have a sense of historical awareness and an understanding of change. I would like to show that this topic is of particular importance in the analysis of cultural change and, as such, demands serious consideration by archaeologists and historians alike.

Schiffer's book, *Behavioural Archaeology* (1976), fired an interest in the many cultural, and non-cultural, processes that affected behaviour towards, and use of, cultural objects. This paper looks in detail at one of the cultural processes, or 'C-transforms', that Schiffer identified, and hopes to demonstrate that a close study of this particular behavioural phenomenon is valuable in its ability to reveal a wealth of information about the ways in which societies deal with and may, in the past, have dealt with the problems of abandonment and the disposal of outmoded cultural material.

'Successional use' is a cultural behavioural process (Schiffer 1977, pp. 39–40) in which a particular cultural object undergoes a change in function (though not necessarily a change in physical form), through a process of successional use. An extension of use-life and a change in the function of an object bring into question the initial value attached to the object and thus may well suggest a change in its 'meaning'. Questions about values which are intrinsic to material objects and which transcend their outwardly functional attributes and thus affect the use-life of an object are raised. Investigating motives behind 'successional use' may reveal how material culture is used in the process of cultural change. To explore the reasons behind this phenomenological behaviour, the activity itself has to be isolated and seen in action in a context which itself is undergoing change.

As little work on this issue has been undertaken by archaeologists there are few models to draw upon and few hypotheses to work with. However, in a short paper, Nicolaisen (1979, pp. 223–35) attempts to unravel the fundamental reasons why societies, both past and present, within our western culture, actively recycle selected, redundant cultural 'debris'. Nicolaisen closely analyses the behavioural phenomenon of the transference of 'rural-type' objects, (i.e. objects whose function and meaning are particular to, and derived from, their 'natural' rural contexts), to public display in suburban and urban situations. His conclusions add to the mundane explanations derived solely from the functional interpretation of an object. He argues that the object in question, be it a milk churn or cart-wheel, is given a value or meaning, when it is reused, which transcends any derived from its original functional role. The secondary use of an object may "distort" (*ibid.*, p. 224) its initial meaning, but at the same time elevates and stresses its symbolic value. A purely practical explanation of successional use can indeed satisfy one level of understanding, but if we ignore the often deliberate and symbolic act which has taken place with such behaviour, then we may gloss over more important and significant motives that reveal deeper social and psychological concerns to preserve and maintain what is important in reminding society both of its material past and the values that pertain to that past, as well as

revealing experiences of cultural change. Nicolaisen's findings highlight important behavioural processes that are all too often by-passed and explained by that "age-old campaign of thriftiness imposed by circumstances as well as by outlook" (*ibid.*, p. 224). They show more importantly that the deliberate re-use of material objects may serve a fundamental purpose in linking present behaviour to that of the past; to show that history does not play a passive role but affects present behaviour, and that what actually takes places through successional use is not a nostalgic and random process of the "accidental preservation of the outdated" but a "deliberate infusion of the anachronistic into the contemporary modern context" (*ibid.*, p. 230).

During the course of a study of the spatial organisation of abandoned farmsteads on Bodmin Moor in east Cornwall, England, it became clear that the process of site abandonment was apparent and not real (Nowakowski 1982). Many of the seemingly derelict farmsteads in an abandoned sample were not completely abandoned insofar as many of them fulfilled secondary uses within the working landscape. It was clear that certain cultural agencies were preventing 'uninhabited' farmsteads from becoming complete ruins. The same phenomenon appeared also on working farms; farmers were re-using and often deliberately maintaining older buildings which were, within modern mechanised farming systems, obsolete. Although the physical forms of many of these older buildings had not changed, their original functions had; an intentional re-use of outmoded material culture was thus seen to be taking place. There were numerous instances of, for example, old cowsheds and shippons being used as generator houses or storage places or even housing modern farm animals (Nowakowski 1982, p. 29). These buildings (stationary cultural objects), erected in former times to serve now obsolete farming regimes, were, through the practice of successional use, being maintained within a new agricultural, economic and social context. The very existence of this practice appeared to betray certain attitudes and reactions to social and cultural changes that were taking place within the local moorland community.

By focusing only on the primary use of a material object, be it a structure or an artifact, we restrict our understanding of the various roles that material culture may perform within societies both past and present, and we may deny ourselves the opportunity to confront the importance of values that are attached to objects within particular societies. The fact that an object is re-used may be noted, but why a particular object has been selected for re-use and what its secondary use actually implies, are questions that are often left unexplained and unexplored. In doing this many assumptions about societies are made which can only satisfy the functionalist's adaptive and integrative views of culture. As Broner has pointed out, many functionalist thinkers maintain that "continuance of tradition does not occur in a haphazard manner based on a superorganic effect of culture, but rather on practical considerations of participants in a culture" (1979, p. 147). A clear criticism of such material functionalism is that function and utility only reveal, "dubious surface explanation" (*ibid.*, p. 148). Deeper meanings that may exist are rarely sought or even acknowledged. Broner continues, "folk act not only out of practical motivations . . . but also from philosophical considerations that affect perception" (*ibid.*, p. 148). Both past and present societies may be seen to be selective in their preservation and conservation of outmoded material culture, which inevitably results in the clear imbalance of cultural relics which survive. I would like to show that this process of selection is not accidental but subconsciously motivated, and can reveal much about the psychological experiences felt within local rural communities as they undergo social and economic changes.

I returned to Bodmin Moor in the spring of 1984 to observe and record in more detail the conditions of, and individual strategies involved in, the 'successional use' of outmoded and traditional farm buildings. Before I describe and outline the results of my investigation, I would like at first briefly to describe my methodological approach.

Methodology

I have always found that farmers in the west country and the northern counties are more interested in the history of their farmsteads and farms, partly because these have not changed their old identity so much as the large-scale arable farms of the eastern side of Britain.

(Hoskins 1970, p. 11)

If Hoskins' observation (above) is accepted, the importance of local history and tradition for the behaviour of certain rural communities has also to be accepted.

In order to investigate the perceived 'historical awareness' within the Bodmin Moor community I had, at first, to develop a programme of fieldwork that would allow attitudes and interests to be voiced through various members of the community itself. An ethnoarchaeological approach was considered the most appropriate since it would provide a corpus of first-hand experience and attitudes to life on the moor. Here I played not only the role of archaeologist, but also those of rural sociologist, historian and ethnographer. After familiarising myself with the general history of agriculture and settlement of the moor I set out to record life on the moor as revealed through both behaviour and attitudes (obtained via oral testimony).

I interviewed a cross-section of the present population of Bodmin Moor, expecting the older people, who have spent their whole lives on the moor, to have a stronger regard for the past than the younger settlers who have come from elsewhere.

In devising the interview technique, which became the major tool in this study, I was conscious of the danger of so influencing conversations that only answers that would favour my thesis would be elicited. To overcome this problem a basic set of questions was posed to all interviewees so that I could place each individual within a controlled context. This also facilitated an easier classification of behavioural strategies that is fully described below. Once such information was collected the interview became less rigid and individuals were encouraged to speak for themselves and reveal, through conversation, their attitudes towards their local environment.

I have decided to present and analyse my results within a framework made up of the five main groups of modern inhabitants of the moor. I would like to stress that these groups do interact with each other and are not as isolated from, or as antagonistic towards, each other as my presentation may make them appear. The grouping is arbitrary and was undertaken solely to give greater clarity to the following sections.

Bodmin Moor

Bodmin Moor is an upland granite moorland in eastern Cornwall. Modern settlement is dispersed; isolated farmsteads typically exist on sites which can be traced, through documentation and archaeological fieldwork, back to the medieval period at least (Herring forthcoming).

Settlement and agricultural history – the past 100 years

Up until three or four decades ago, agricultural activity on the moor was characterised by small, inter-related family farms (Pounds 1945, p. 310). Family farming was typical of Cornwall as a whole throughout the post-medieval and early modern periods (*Penny Magazine* 1836, p. 196; Pounds 1945, pp. 61 and 310; Fussell 1958–9, p. 344). This tradition, it can be argued, retarded the taking-up of many of the technological innovations made in agriculture in the eighteenth and nineteenth centuries. Cornwall, therefore, did not experience to such an extent as counties further east the 'High Agriculture' of the 1860s (Harvey 1970). New machinery was adopted only gradually and farming practices changed slowly. These general conditions sustained an inward-looking aspect to farming, maintaining it as 'a way of life' which worked on a relatively low commercial level and thus contrasted strongly with the larger farming estates in other parts of the country (Williams 1963, p. 75).

During the post-medieval period most agricultural land in Cornwall was held by tenants holding 'three lives' leases (Hamilton-Jenkin 1945, pp. 320–22). Such leases were granted to three named people and were held until all the 'lives' had expired, when the land returned to the landowner (Worgan 1811, pp. 19–21). During the nineteenth century on Bodmin Moor many landowners had their estates improved as farmsteads were built by 'three-lives tenants' in areas that were newly taken in; the tenants benefited from relatively low rents and the perceived security of possibly renewing their leases if they wanted to. This system became illegal early in this century and was replaced by leases on numbers of years. In the pre-war years many farmers on the moor were tenant farmers: however, since the Second World War access to landownership has become easier with the fragmentation of the larger farming estates (see for example Latham 1971, p. 13).

Throughout the post-medieval and early modern periods up to the 1940s, the moor supported a tight-knit community of a few tenant farming families. (The local graveyard at Bolventor is, for example, dominated by a few surnames only).

Since the war, many of these farming families have dispersed or disappeared and an increasing number of 'outsiders' have moved onto the moor. The nature of the moorland community today is less closely interrelated, and is more disparate and individual, resulting in the loss of a cohesive communal identity.

Agriculture on Bodmin Moor has always been essentially pastoral, with crops grown mainly for fodder. It still is today, although emphasis changes from stock to dairying according to the demands of the market. Around the turn of this century, for example, dairying became rather more important (Rowe 1959, p. 148) and that agricultural regime continued until after the Second World War, when the trend turned towards stock farming in response to national subsidy policies (Brewster 1975, p. 242).

The smaller farms of Victorian and earlier periods had been able to support the economy of family farming, though often tenants' incomes were augmented by wages from outside part-time labour in the local china clay quarries and tin mines. Today these farms are too small to support extensive modern farming programmes. The business-like nature of the modern farming world and the new age of consumerism mean that these traditionally small family farms are unable to compete on an equal basis with larger concerns, and have either been amalgamated or absorbed by the latter (Hine 1972, p. 58). The resulting increase in the area farmed by any one farmer has led to the abandonment of many homesteads which today stand empty or in partial ruin. Walls of the smaller enclosures around such sites are often destroyed to create larger fields.

These economic changes go hand in hand with social changes, both of which need to be outlined and understood since they provide a contextual background to the different behavioural strategies seen on the moor today. Fewer 'local' people live on the moor – a number of 'non-local' people have moved into farmsteads no longer inhabited by working farmers, and other such farmsteads now stand abandoned and uninhabited. The far-reaching social changes have ensured the breakdown and fragmentation of a tight-knit community centred traditionally around family farming. Community identity has changed with the arrival of 'outsiders' or people 'not of the moor' to the moorland scene, and the present population of moorland farmers are largely unrelated.

We can today identify five distinctive types of occupant living on the moorland farms of Bodmin Moor. Each will invariably have differing attitudes towards the farms that they inhabit, as well as having different constraints on their farming behaviours and strategies. They can be identified within the following groups:

 i Farmers with familial links to the moorland's traditional economic and social lifestyles – the older generation.
 ii Farmers with familial links to the moorland through their respective families – the younger generation.
 iii Farmers with no familial links to the moorland – newcomers to the moor; the young (or old) 'outsider'.
 iv Non-farming residents with familial links with the indigenous community, usually elderly.
 v Non-farming residents who have come to live on the moor from the 'outside'.

It is important, at first, to outline the needs and constraints of modern farming on Bodmin Moor so that an understanding of the meaning of change and its implications for each of these groups may be emphasised.

As was mentioned above, Bodmin Moor is now farmed more extensively. Efficiency, economy of labour and space, and practical convenience are high priorities of any modern farmer. To many farmers these needs are paramount to the smooth running of a successful farming business. Extensive moorland farming involves larger stocking numbers and thus larger acreages. All modern farming relies heavily on mechanisation to reduce time and labour expenditure.

Modern farming takes place on the sites of older farms on the moor. These sites were once adequately equipped to support subsistence farming but in terms of modern farming they are obsolete. The farm buildings existing are often too small and too specialist. They are often grouped together and cramped in small yards, and their surrounding fields are too small for modern machinery to manoeuvre easily. Farmers working these sites today are therefore confronted with decisions about how best to integrate modern farming into old sites.

The following sections will deal with the five types of occupants listed above. They will outline the general conditions and constraints within which each group on the moor works and will describe their general attitudes towards farming (and living) on the moor as revealed through interviews. These attitudes will subsequently be compared with their strategies vis-à-vis inherited material culture. An attempt then will be made to understand how each group perceives and experiences change, and how their attitudes towards change are reflected in their use of inherited material culture – in this case the older farm buildings.

i. Farmers with familial links to the moorland's traditional economic and social lifestyles – the older generation

Very few farmers farm in a traditional way on Bodmin Moor today. The older generation of farmers form a discrete social group known as 'old timers'. For many the moor has always been their place of work and home, and their ties to the land are therefore emotionally deep-rooted. Many 'old timers' were born in the late nineteenth and early twentieth centuries when the moorland community was still characterised by a tight local population of family tenant farmers. Today some of these people continue to farm, but the majority are slowly 'running down' their farms as they approach retirement.

Many among this group started their working lives as farm labourers, only later becoming tenant farmers in their own right. Today many of them are still tenant farmers who have never actually owned the farms they work. There are advantages in being a tenant farmer. Capital outlay is obviously limited and failure is therefore less financially damaging to the farmer. Greater mobility is also permitted to tenant farmers – they are more able to move to more attractive property, when it becomes available, than an owner-occupier who has stronger ties, through investment, with a particular farm. In the Bolventor area, for example, individual tenant farmers have occupied, in their working lives, as many as five separate tenements.

These older tenant farmers often tend to see their present roles within the moorland community as guardians of certain values which they feel are intrinsic to a tradition of moorland farming. A middle-aged tenant farmer at Dozmary Hill Farm is proud to carry on his family tradition of tenant farming. His father and grandfather were both tenants of the large Trebartha estate, his son is presently a Duchy tenant on the southern edge of the moor, and he himself has been a tenant on at least three different farms: Harrowbridge, Pinnockshill, and today at Dozmary Hill. For him, moorland farming is and has always been a family tenancy affair. Another middle-aged farmer at nearby Trezibbet philosophied that as farmers lived and farmed for a small fraction of time on the moor, the social and economic changes that faced them were minimal in relation to the passing of time itself. "The land remains", he said, "and farmers are guardians of the land only for short episodes." Both farmers felt themselves to be custodians of economic attitudes and social traditions local to the moor; they identified with, and indeed practised, the traditional system of tenant farming and the ethics of that tradition. Both showed their respect for the historical tradition of land and buildings by practically re-using the traditional material fabric which they had inherited. They both felt also that the appearance of technological and social change within the local landscape resulted in a loss of 'real values'. They coped with the physical and psychological changes by asserting the older values through re-using and preserving older buildings and by adopting overtly conservationalist stances. The farmer at Dozmary Hill, for example, mocked the all-too-easy life of the newer farmer by remarking that mechanised 'modern' farming dehumanised the struggle and challenge to farm in an area such as Bodmin Moor. Although he admitted that the moor needed to be farmed economically, he also felt that it was an individual farmer's duty to farm carefully and with discrimination; to have respect for the struggles that had taken place in the past which had "made today possible". He felt that it was important to preserve practically the traces of past human endeavour and hardship so that they could remain as relics of a past whose values were now slipping away; values which, he considered, through personal links, were 'real', compared to those of today. Through such attitudes and through the practical re-use of older buildings, these two farmers were not necessarily asserting that past traditions were the best, but were suggesting that the new ways of doing things and therefore the ethics of that new regime, were also not necessarily the best.

I also met a couple of 'old timers' who, after lifetimes of working as farm labourers, had acquired enough capital to buy their own farms, which they work today. One, near Bolventor, bought his relatively small farm thirty years ago and has worked and maintained it now as he did when he became its owner. He has not increased the farm's acreage and has contentedly carried out a practical strategy of re-using all the traditional buildings on the farm. His behaviour may be explained as an indirect reaction to the changes that he has lived through and witnessed over the seventy years that he has lived on the moor. He feels that the new breed of moorland farmer has a rather cavalier attitude to the place, and that often the newer farmers exploit the moor purely for economic gain, rather than respecting it as a place in which to live and work as part of a living community. Some of the homesteads he has known since childhood today stand derelict and in partial ruin, including the one on which he grew up, which is now on land owned by one of the newer landowners. He ostensibly regrets this state of affairs, stating that these new farmers "ranch the moor", rather than farm it in "the proper way". He openly dissociates himself from this type of behaviour and attitude through the upkeep of the traditional fabric of his farm – its older buildings. He re-uses, for instance, an old shippon on his farm which, although it is too small for today's cattle, has been adapted for use as calves' housing.

Another elderly farmer at Carkeet in the Fowey valley shares these attitudes. Carkeet itself is a splendid old farm built in the 1840s. The wealth and energy invested in the farm buildings by the original owners are impressive, and successive farming occupants on the farm have clearly deliberately maintained the buildings in their original state over the past 140 years. The present occupier has re-used all the buildings and carefully maintained its traditional feel; carrying out only piecemeal repair work when necessary. His behaviour towards the site speaks of the respect that he has for the original energy manifested in the buildings and is typical of his overall farming outlook. Through fifty years careful farming at Carkeet, he has managed to make all the buildings work for him; they appear to have exerted little or no restraint on his farming strategies since he is now one of the most successful stock farmers on the moor. He has a reputation in the neighbourhood of being a farmer who does things 'in the old way' and is sometimes regarded as extreme and perhaps stubborn. He, together with a few other older farmers on the moor, has continued, for example, to cut peat for domestic fuel, thus carrying on a moorland tradition and drawing attention to the 'old way'. It appears that he too is subconsciously asserting his position as a true 'moorlander' by adhering to the older values of hard work which make up, in his view, the true morality of a moorland way of life; a morality which may become threatened with eradication as farming becomes less labour-intensive through modern farming technology.

The few examples presented above have described individual attitudes to local change and strategies employed in support of those attitudes. Changes that have completely altered the social and economic orders of the moorland community over the past forty years are most keenly experienced within this group. Reactions to the changes are broadly similar in this group insofar as the few remaining local moorlanders with personal contact with the local history have tried to maintain some of the perceived and felt 'substance' (and subsequently 'identity') of a known moorland existence, through the upkeep and preservation of the older buildings on their farms in the process of 'successional use'.

ii Farmers with familial links to the moorland through their respective families – the younger generation

There is also, farming on Bodmin Moor today, a small group of younger farmers who form the latest working generation of traditional moorland families. For those within this group, their relatively new positions as responsible farmers offer opportunities to demonstrate individual abilities at carrying on with the family's traditional occupation of farming. Most of them are farming farms which had previously been in their families' possession or occupation, and so they are to some extent constrained in the way that they might work a site by the knowledge that they are continuing to farm on sites that have deeply felt familial connections.

One young farmer, for example, recently took over the tenancy of St Luke's Farm in Bolventor from his father, who had been its tenant for over forty years. The new farmer is therefore carrying on a tradition of farming on a site that has been farmed by successive generations of his family. He grew up on the farm and learnt to farm from his father. In the years since he took over, he has made very few alterations to the physical character of the place and he has re-used all the old standing buildings on the site, despite stocking slightly larger numbers of animals and experimenting with farming methods different from those of his father. The farmstead is about 130 years old. The buildings therefore date mainly from the mid-nineteenth century and although not especially grand, they are solidly moorland: traditional in physical form and design.

This particular farmer has a sensitive and careful approach to farming; he takes good care of his animals and is concerned to keep up a generally neat appearance on the farm. He reuses all the older buildings on the farm, maintaining that they "have life in them yet", and so he consciously integrates them into the general running of his modern farm. Since he outwinters his stock, the animals are rarely brought into the farmyard at the same time, so the buildings in the yard are mostly used for storage purposes or to house newly born and pregnant animals. He sees himself as a conservation-conscious farmer; an attitude that he has nurtured and inherited from his father, and one that he instinctively regards as 'appropriate' and in keeping with the family tradition. Although he has adapted the farm to suit his own way of farming he has made a deliberate effort to retain as much as possible the familiar traditional character of the place. His attitudes and behaviour imply a gentle respect for the traditional lifestyle of the farm which has a personal link and meaning for him through his own family.

Personal histories and familial associations with particular farmsteads need not always be good; when they are not,

destructive and less positive attitudes towards the upkeep of an old site may occur. In general, it is fairly uncommon to witness the complete demolition of a whole farm on Bodmin Moor. Usually empty sites are allowed to fall to ruin or are reused in some way (see below). However, the recent demolition of Carneglos farm in the Fowey valley has caused some local disquiet. Carneglos was one of the earliest farms in the central part of the moor and stood in an area which is known to be archaeologically rich in extensive prehistoric and medieval settlement remains. It was recently pulled down by its owner, who lives nearby in a modern bungalow. In recent years the farm was lived in by non-farming tenants. On their departure the owner, a middle-aged moorlander, destroyed the site. When asked why he had carried out such a drastic move, the owner quietly indicated that he wanted to eradicate the site since it held bad memories for him. His brother had hanged himself there some years before and since that time "bad things" had occurred at the farm. His own family had farmed at Carneglos all their working lives and his familial associations were clearly strong. Rather than allowing the bad memories to continue to exist for him through successional use of the site, he decided to demolish the whole farm and to reuse the building material to repair walls and hedges. His somewhat extreme behaviour has already entered the local mythology, as his action clearly transgressed unspoken rules of accepted conduct amongst the true locals. However his action does indicate that psychological motives play an important part in behaviour towards inherited material culture.

Psychological motives of a different nature underlie the behaviour of another young farmer and landowner who has recently moved into Fernacre, a farmstead high up on the desolate north-west part of the moor and a portion of his father's large moorland estate. This young farmer shares with the St Luke's farmer (above) a concern for practical conservation, though his background and actual relationship to the farm are somewhat different. He farms part of his father's land, and he is perhaps more emotionally independent of the place since the farm has never actually been lived in by his family, and so there is less chance of his behaviour breaching or offending an established code of familial conduct. Fernacre has a long occupational history going back to the fourteenth century at least (Herring, forthcoming), although the present buildings on the site are mostly nineteenth-century in date and, in architecture, are very formal. The dwelling house itself is one of the moor's larger houses, built by a professional architect for a well-to-do family in the late nineteenth century. Alongside this stand the ruins of an earlier farmstead which are probably seventeenth- to early eighteenth-century in date. The new farmer has carried out a deliberate programme of renovation on the site, carefully repairing the older buildings so that they can be used for his own farming purposes. Original architectural features such as the mullioned windows in the stable have been left *in situ*, and walls have been repointed. He is also in the process of erecting a large covered yard in the farmyard which he intends to use for all his major farming operations. Rather than erect a 'modern' prefabricated structure, he has deliberately chosen to put up one whose walls are built entirely of granite and which will eventually be slate roofed. Although it is relatively expensive to erect a building such as this today, it is part of his deliberate policy to maintain the traditional feel and character of the place by erecting a building 'of the moor'. (Granite and slate are the moorland's traditional building materials.) The other older buildings at Fernacre are to be reroofed so that the use-lives of these structures can be extended for purposes of storage. Fernacre is now the only inhabited farm in this isolated part of the moor, although previous to this young farmer's occupancy it had been empty for years. The farmer intends to restore it to its former working condition and views his reoccupation of the farm as a new stage in its history, "bringing life back to the old place". By re-using the older buildings he is consciously blending the old with the new, integrating both the new and old orders and making them work together.

In the cases described above, I have tried to show policies that aim at practical preservation and respect for traditional farming regimes by re-using older buildings, while at the same time satisfying modern farming needs and goals. These policies have come from people who have more than just an economic interest in the moor. They also have a social interest in the place and are conscious of its changing physical character and its past physical identity, and are thus concerned to perpetuate the links with its material past through the upkeep of material elements pertaining to that past. I have also presented one case where psychological needs have overriden practical adaptation and economic rationality, and this particular example, which resulted in offensive destructive behaviour, demonstrates that practical concerns may not necessarily take precedence over emotional ones.

I would now like to examine the behaviour of people who have recently moved onto the moor. As will be shown, this type of occupant may be motivated by a different set of needs, which may often entail fairly extensive alterations to the landscape which they farm.

iii Farmers with no familial links to the moorland – newcomers to the moor; the young or old 'outsider'

The arrival of newcomers to the moor, which largely began as a result of post-war sales when the larger estates were broken up and sold off, has not only completely altered the moorland's traditional social character, but has also precipitated the demise of its traditional economic way of life. The extensive nature of farming today inevitably results in individual farms being areally larger than before and this, in turn, has led to a large number of farmsteads being redundant. The land belonging to any one particular farm is often scattered and dispersed, as purchased farms are not always contiguous. Empty redundant farmsteads on some of these dispersed parcels of land may be reused within modern farming programmes for storage and shelter, but some are left to

dereliction. The new farmer may not even live on the moor and so may essentially be an absentee landowner and farmer.

While some farmers may try to integrate obsolete buildings within their farming operations and may make just piecemeal alterations to these buildings to allow for greater efficiency, others may not. The attainment of efficiency can be destructive in its effect on the traditional character of these sites. A middle-aged farmer who has moved to the Bolventor area has completely altered the physical character of his home farm. He has demolished all the older granite buildings in the farmyard and replaced them with new standardised corrugated iron and breeze-block farm buildings. He has also completely remodelled the farmhouse, thus transforming the whole character of the site. He has embarked too on a scheme of amalgamating the smaller nineteenth-century fields around the site through wall removal. Stone from these walls is sold to construction firms. Another 'outsider' has completely altered the traditional character of his farm near Warleggan, by erecting in place of the older farm, a 'hacienda-type' collection of buildings, which look very incongruous in a bleak moorland landscape. A similar physical reorganisation of the landscape recently took place on Twelve Men's Moor in North Hill. Here an extensive area of enclosed moorland was reclaimed by a small syndicate of farmers. They saw fit to record their work by inscribing onto the faces of some of the larger cleared boulders their names, the date and the total cost of the operation. While the behaviour outlined above is not yet common on the moor, the cash incentives recently offered to upland farmers by the EEC to improve marginal agricultural areas and intensify their exploitation will no doubt result in more widespread physical alteration of the inherited material landscape.

Destructive behaviour such as that described above is mostly manifested by farmers new to the moor who have no direct familial links with the area's past. They are relatively alienated from the landscape into which they have moved and have fewer cultural constraints on their behaviour. Such emotional alienation clearly makes it easier for them to alter elements within the landscape in order to suit their own needs. Redundant material culture inherited from the past may be seen as impeding economic farming and thus may be removed. Older buildings that are not destroyed or left to fall into ruin by these 'outsiders' are retained and 'successively used' only for purely practical purposes. For example, any buildings that stand in exposed areas on the edge of the open moorland may incidentally be re-used for animal shelter or fodder storage by the absentee farmer, though their sporadic use often means that they are not deliberately maintained (Nowakowski 1982, p. 29).

The 'outsiders' apparently come to farm on the moor for purely economic reasons, and may not therefore be fully accepted by the remaining indigenous farmers, who often regard these newer farmers as being ambitious only to exploit the moor for as much financial gain as possible, and not interested in contributing to community life. They are often seen as having implanted onto the moor a totally new regime with its inflexible economic ethics which show little respect towards the past lifestyle of the moor. Although the relationship between these two groups is not overtly antagonistic, a mutual suspicion is revealed in different behaviour. Many of the indigenous farmers, for example, quietly argue that the 'outsiders' (for among this group that is how they are truly perceived) have brought a competitive spirit to farming on the moor, as one individual tries to outclass the other; while many of the 'outsiders' feel that the way they farm is more realistic and is part of the ethos of the modern industry. The older folk are stubbornly introspective as a matter of pride.

iv. Non-farming residents with familial links with the indigenous community; usually elderly

Normally a retiring Bodmin Moor farmer either goes to live with his farming children on the moor, or moves out to live in one of the small villages dotted around the moor. Some however remain on the moor, despite the fact that they ceased to farm, in order to resist being uprooted from a place in which they have lived in and known all their lives. I spoke to a couple of elderly women who had once been involved in farming and who had remained, in retirement, in the areas where they had spent their working lives. They now live in Bolventor, a small settlement high upon the central part of the moor which has no facilities. Most of the other people living in Bolventor work in towns off the moor, but the settlement was once occupied by farm labourers who worked on the Trebartha Estate and in the local tin and china clay works (Axford 1975, pp. 144–5). One of the women has lived in this part of the moor all her life; she was born at Codda Farm and farmed with her husband for over forty years in a neighbouring farm. She has never left the moor and has not moved more than a mile from the place where she was born. She has a wealth of local knowledge and can remember vividly the days when the area was populated by several close-knit interrelated farming families who were associated with particular farmsteads. For survivors of truly 'local' communities such as she is, individual farmsteads are important emotional markers. The older people on the moor possess a mental template of the community of which they were once part and which for them now no longer exists. The social changes that have taken place over the last forty years on the moor distort that template, as familiar farms and landmarks get taken up by 'outsiders' and the community becomes more disparate in its social make-up. The loss of 'place' is most deeply felt. As regards material culture, regret is expressed about the many farmsteads which are now left to fall down and "go back to the granite". Quiet bitterness is expressed about those who seemingly take the moor for granted and thus fail to either acknowledge the uniqueness of sites or the traditional values (based on hard manual labour) that made up the moorland community. Impotence is felt, in old age, to effect any change or to express, other than through the odd grumble, the way they feel about local change. While many of these elderly observers reluctantly admit that 'progressive attitudes' will ultimately prevail, they applaud those older folk who still live in the isolated farmsteads and maintain them through

successional use. It is as if only through such behaviour can they maintain a link with their own individual pasts and histories; and through such behaviour as successional use of their material culture they can feel that their identities as the original 'true moorland folk' are being respected.

v. Non-farming residents who have come to live on the moor from the 'outside'

This final descriptive section will look at the behaviour of people who have come to live on the moor but do not farm it.

Many within this group are true 'outsiders' in the sense that they have come to live in a rural environment but do not participate in its agricultural way of life. They can be characterised as refugees from the hectic materialistic environs of city life. Their appearance on the moor marks another change in the moorland's social and economic structure. They buy old, sometimes partially ruined 'pretty' farmsteads (often outbidding local offers), and then renovate them. They often bring with them certain idealised expectations of the place which seem to be reactions to urban life. Rural life is seen as wholesome and simple, more agreeably paced and soothing, unpretentious and traditional. These images become encoded in their renovations of older farm buildings as the traditional becomes romanticised and subsumed by preconceptions of what the vernacular should be like.

Many of these people whom I interviewed were particularly interested in the individual histories of the places which they had bought. Discoveries of past material cultural objects such as old pieces of farming equipment, discarded by previous occupants, are often made during renovations. Rather than being thrown away, these objects may be put on prominent display around the farms; they might, for instance, adorn front lawns and gardens. Old staddle stones and granite troughs often become garden furnishings. The functional use-lives of such objects are now obsolete, and any successive use made of them is symbolic. The deliberate retention of past material objects associated with the former life of a place are indicative of a respect for that particular place's history. The public display of such objects reinforces the new occupant's idealised interpretation of the place, and acknowledges the changes that are taking place within the local landscape by hinting at the lost life-style associated with that place. Such behaviour may indicate a wish within this group to communicate this knowledge to the rest of the community.

Discussion

In the sections above, I have attempted, through the presentation of a range of individual viewpoints and behaviour, to outline various reactions to cultural change in a local rural community. While the phenomenon of 'successional use' of past material culture may be common to each of the groups discussed, the underlying motives for the appearance of such a phenomenon vary according to different social, economic and psychological needs. The interview technique has allowed individual needs to be heard. What becomes apparent is that in a local environment, certain material objects appear to have specific meanings and values. In response to different needs, these meanings elicit differing behavioural responses. For some members of the local community, outmoded material culture is integrated within present working strategies only if it can be seen to be useful and practical, while for others, the symbolic value of the outmoded material culture ensures its survival, overriding any utilitarian or functional demands. The dual role that material culture plays is highlighted when the context in which it is found is undergoing fundamental changes. As a local community becomes less cohesive in its social make-up, the behaviour of its individual members will vary according to any set of meanings and values that each individual attaches to the inherited material environment. These various responses can be used to analyse attitudes, both functional and emotional. Material culture therefore can be used to assess a community's personality.

For many of the 'old timers' the older farmsteads are poignant emotional landmarks in their own personal histories and remind them of a former social order in the community. For many in this group, a sense of stability and continuity is assured through the maintenance of sites that have strong familial associations. These farms gave the moorland a secure identity which was once fixed in time and space. Embedded within these older farmsteads are a whole set of values and aspirations that were once common to a particular economic and social order and world view. The social order was once, for example, comprised of interrelated family units centred around domestic production on the family farm. The economic and social outlook was highly ordered in terms of hierarchy, familial pride, priorities and structured work roles. Such orders had been maintained through the inheritance practices that assured the regular transference of familial resources from one generation to the next. Economic changes since the war, which have ensured a fragmentation and breakdown of those formerly secure social and economic orders and the demise of the family farm, have, for many of the older folk, resulted in a sense of 'placelessness' (Seamon 1979, p. 64). No longer are land and farm so religiously defined by familial units. No longer do the older generation know their place in the local landscape; the former community identity has lost its distinctive and familiar place. By attempting to preserve and maintain any older material elements within the local landscape, the older folk are subconsciously reacting to the new order by reverting to symbols of the old and familiar. For as Berger has pointed out, the 'true' local "cannot contemplate the disappearance of what gives meaning to everything he knows" (1979, p. 9).

The younger farmers on the moor, both those with familial ties to the land and the newcomers ('the outsiders'), represent the moor's new order. Being the farming and working groups on the moor today, they are effectively the active agents of change, and potentially have considerable influence in effecting change in the indigenous material culture. For both groups, their needs are not only psychological (i.e. establishing themselves as heirs apparent of the new social order), but also pressingly economic too, since they have to find ways to maintain viable farming businesses within a traditionally fashioned material environment. For those who have strong family links to their farms, their behaviour may to a large degree be conditioned and constrained by traditional ideologies. For such individuals, as with the 'old timers', family and farm identity may be inextricably tied to each other and permanently fixed in space. Family identity, through tradition, may be closely intertwined with family owned/associated land so that ties are deep-rooted, and almost sacred. These ties will have bearing on behaviour on the farms, and any violation of the traditional family domain may be domestically perceived as breaches of loyalty against the family's traditional morality. It becomes especially important for this group to behave in the appropriate manner since they are possibly the last generations of the moorland's traditional economic unit: the family farm. The case of the young farmer at St Luke's in Bolventor is an example of this, showing that long familial connections with a particular farm influenced this young farmer's perception of the place, and thus affected his behaviour on the site. Clearly psychological needs do greatly influence in such cases individual behaviour and attitudes. The local indignation and uneasiness felt within the neighbourhood when Carneglos Farm was demolished was indeed very eloquent of traditional morality within the local community; the local farmer had so clearly transgressed unspoken rules of conduct by his action.

Many of the newer farmers on the moor, the 'outsiders', are faced with a different dilemma. They are alienated in emotional terms from the material environment which they farm and therefore cannot be expected to experience any sense of disorientation or 'loss of place' that may be felt by the true locals. Their subsequent behaviour and attitudes may be viewed as insensitive and ruthless by others as they physically reorder their farms. Their casual neglect, and sometimes eradication, of distinctive places in the making of a more efficient and standardised landscape may arise out of an insensitivity to the uniqueness of a place. For some, the older farm buildings are stubborn relics which may stand as obstacles to expansive farming programmes. These buildings, regarded often as non-viable in modern economic terms, may even be subconsciously perceived as symbols of a past that has fortunately been left behind. Modern farming is businesslike, and it is an industry which is regarded as successful when progressive in its outlook. When these farmers reorganise the physical material environment, it is, in their view, for the better; to farm the moor more efficiently, more economically. As the new economic and social order the members of this group are now claiming the moor. The case of the Bolventor farmer cited above is perhaps an extreme example of the attitude of a newcomer to the moor, who by his behaviour in remodelling his whole farm is validating his claim as a new landowner, and heralding the superiority of the new ethos over the old.

The arrival and presence of this type of farmer on the moor could spell dramatic physical changes within the landscape, as newer symbols of the industrialised face of farming readily begin to appear; the survival and maintenance of older farm buildings is often merely incidental, serving strictly utilitarian needs.

The attitudes expressed by the fourth group (the older non-farming generation) interviewed in this study are important in helping us achieve a closer understanding of the emotive values that a particular material base may sustain within the 'local' human landscape. They help us to perceive clearly the various conflicting ideals, and the inter-group antagonism that is often seen to occur between different generations of working farmers. The feelings voiced by this group provide a valuable insight into the interactive nature of a material environment and its living and working community. For those in this group, who were once farming but are now observers within the local community, the casual and careless neglect of buildings and farmsteads by up and coming farmers may be seen as a stubborn inability to acknowledge the importance of 'place', and part of a failure to understand that the notion of 'place' is grounded as much in the community's history as it is in the physical fabric of its immediate environment. Such attitudes manifested in destructive behaviour towards the inherited material environment result in an emotional denial and estrangement from the community's physical past. This inevitably leads to a scenario in which younger members farming on the moor react in an extreme manner to the traditional conservatism sustained by the older members of the farming community, who may hopelessly strive to uphold an outlook on work and the community which the modern age has more or less banished. Yet the motives and ideals underlying the older farmers' behaviours become subconsciously strengthened by a need to sustain and satisfy for themselves a physical link between their home and work environments and their deep-rooted perceptions of 'place' within the local landscape. The material culture may provide that link in helping to uphold a mental template of the community of which they feel a part, despite the sweeping changes that have come about through shifts in the technological and economic spheres. The older farm buildings are part of the local community's personality: its history and its emotional fabric and hence older values and roles become even more strengthened when the human landscape is itself undergoing wider contextual changes.

The non-farming moorlanders are relatively new to the moorland scene. Often within this group certain attitudes and expectations about the rural landscape are held which in many ways cloud their perceptions of the real changes in the human landscape. A sense of 'place' is often essential to the way in which they see and regard the rural landscape. Yet this sense is not one which they have a familial claim to, but one which they seek and may construct. Many non-farming moorlanders may escape to the moor rather than arrive on it; and by this I mean that they seek to live in a place that may fulfil aspirations that an urban environment fails to satisfy. This is reflected in the desire to reoccupy a place "with a sense of history", a place that is rooted in its natural environment and one which has

links with traditions. A lack of emotional understanding of the traditional does, however, often result in the misinterpretation and sentimental romanticising of the vernacular in the renovation of old farm buildings. The symbolic nature of the traditional is stressed and emphasised through 'successional use' of old buildings and the deliberate public display of traditional objects. This group, too, is in the process of establishing its 'place' in the local moorland scene, and the individuals involved use their perceptions of the past in an attempt to define their place in the rural community.

In all the cases that I have summarised there is one unifying theme that brings together the various behavioural responses to change in the local community. The different strategies all reveal a concern to establish a sense of 'place' in an arena of change (cf. Relph's 1978 definition of 'place'). This may be achieved by recalling the past in resisting the forces of wider cultural change, or by referring to the past in acknowledging the inevitable consequence of change, or by embracing inevitable change by rejecting the past and all traces of that past. All these reactions are concerned to establish the notion of 'place', be it a familiar one or an entirely new one. For as has been shown, the notion of 'place' will vary for different group members, according to how they relate to their local surroundings and the meanings that they attach to their inherited material environment.

Conclusion

In this paper I have tried to demonstrate that by close analysis of the behaviour of individuals within a community towards their 'historical' material base, we may have at our disposal an invaluable pool of information that reveals undercurrents of various reactions to community change. The internal stresses and conflicts experienced as a traditional community moves forward to a more modern age can be monitored by examining specific forms of cultural behaviour. In my study I have shown that one behavioural activity, 'successional use', can reveal much about the experience of change on an individual and local level. The reuse of outmoded cultural objects within the community under study has fulfilled various needs, but the fact that this activity does occur is significant in reminding us of the communicative nature of local material culture. It is a medium through which a community may define itself, both to its participating members and to the outside world. Traditional artifacts and elements within a particular human landscape can both generate a sense of continuity to its older members by reinforcing a collective awareness of 'rootedness', and realise the notion of 'place' and the significance and importance of 'locality' for a local community.

In the introduction to this paper I quoted from Collingwood's discourse on the nature of historical knowledge. It is "the power of the past to reawaken itself in the present" that constitutes an experience of historical knowledge. I have tried to show that such power, as evoked by the survival of local material objects specific to a past age, may have an important and significant effect on the behaviour of later successive cultural systems. The material objects and buildings which become symbols measuring the progress and development from that past to the present survive solely on their ability to satisfy various needs in a new cultural regime. Within the local community on Bodmin Moor, these needs range from practical ones to those of a psychological nature. The study of behaviour towards inherited material objects reveals a wealth of information about the psychological state of the cultural system in which such behaviour occurs. A community undergoing internal change recalls the past in its evaluation of the new.

My study has been a phenomenological one in order to demonstrate that cultural behaviour is historically linked and that action does not exist without reference to what has occurred before in a particular setting. Cultural change is a complex issue, and if it is outlined and described in general terms, this may result in an unbalanced and partial reconstruction of events. Mead once wrote that "change must be examined from the point of view of the individuals who are exposed to change . . . the individual person (in their attitude and behaviour) is both the recipient and the mediator or agent of change" (1955, p. 15). Successional use forces us to consider the nature of cultural change and to examine the individual experience of change. It has also highlighted the important role that material culture may perform in providing various links between changes, and augments both a perceptual and an emotional experience of local historical awareness.[1]

Note

1. This work could not have been carried out without the patience and understanding of many people. I would like to thank all those on Bodmin Moor who gave me their time and trust and who made the fieldwork most enjoyable. I would also like to thank Ian Hodder for his patience, encouragement and interest and for inviting me to write the paper. My particular thanks go to Pete Herring for sparing time to critically edit the paper. I would also like to thank Helen McIlroy for additional editing. Finally I would like to dedicate the paper to my mother who died whilst I was writing; she has been and always will be my inspiration.

Chapter 6

Reordering residues of the past

Paul Lane

Lane discusses Collingwood's view that it is the thoughts which lie behind sequences of events which are the stuff of historical explanation. But this did not, for Collingwood, imply transcendentalism. Rather than entering into the mind of the historical agent, the aim is to recognise and interpret the value-laden nature of material events. Thus it is the meanings of space as much as its physical configuration that have an impact on the use of space by people. Yet the traces of events (the inherited material environment) have a recursive relationship with the narrative of those events, and this is demonstrated in a study of the Dogon in West Africa. In the Dogon village studied, physical settlement space is reclassified as individuals move through their lives, even though the settlement remains largely the same. The emphasis on continuity is made in a number of different ways. The organisation of space and the placing of pots within houses are linked through a set of beliefs to societal stability and to lineage dependence on the reproductive fertility of women. Yet this set of attitudes has internal contradictions leading to change and variation from the supposed traditional ideal.

An action leaves a 'trace', it makes its 'mark' when it contributes to the emergence of such patterns which become the *documents* of human action.

(Ricoeur 1981, p. 206, emphasis in the original)

Introduction

In this chapter I present some results of an investigation of contemporary village life amongst the Dogon of Mali, West Africa. My intention in so doing is to examine the manner in which the dominant representation of the past moulds settlement growth. In other words, I aim to demonstrate how narrated 'history' is actively used within contemporary Dogon society in such a way as to affect the actual history of settlement.

In the previous sentence both of the conventional meanings implied by the term 'history' have been employed. On the one hand I have used the term to signify 'narratives' in the broad sense of that word. Alternatively, the term can refer to 'events', the effects of which become the object of historical study. It is the latter which is implied where I use the phrase 'the history of settlement'. Within the discipline of archaeology we conventionally employ the traces or effects of events that took place in the past to construct historical narratives, explanations of those events. Our temporal position in relation to those events is such that we cannot directly observe them and thereby ascertain what caused these things to occur. Instead we must get by with making causal inferences from the traces of past events.

Accepting that these traces can be manifested in a variety of different ways, from written documents and census figures to artifacts and environmental impact, which often require different analytical and interpretative techniques, all have one thing in common – they were generated by human agency. Yet most efforts to explain changes in the pattern and morphology of settlement regularly make use of models which consider only human action *en masse* to be purposeful, and that of the individual as random and unpredictable, although intrinsically rational. Whereas we might be able to model human behaviour via the application of general laws – that is, define a set of conditions under which a rational agent is expected to act in a predictable manner – we can never reach an explanation of that action via a general law except in a tautologous manner. Leaving aside the problem of cultural relativity, which argues that rational behaviour is culturally specific, and can anyway be accommodated by hypothetico-deductivism (see Hanson 1975, pp. 85–96 for a discussion) a circularity in argument remains. In such models individuals are bearers of states rather than intentions, and their behaviour is viewed as governed by external forces, such as adaptation or the principle of least effort, rather than being intersubjectively motivated. One consequence of the application of this kind of model is that rational actions come to be explained by rationality alone. Our explanations should aim instead to reach an understanding of the construction of a particular rationality. Since systems of rationality are constructed by means of symbolic structures, the focus of inquiry into the nature of a particular configuration of events must be, at least to start with, the context of values, beliefs and meanings within which these events took place. Since individual events in the main are rational acts, their effects stand as expressions of that rationality, or, to use the term employed by Ricoeur, 'documents of human action', and by extension are made accessible to others by their expression.

I see this position as being closely similar to that favoured by Collingwood in his philosophical treatise *The Idea of History* (1946). The problem that Collingwood attempted to resolve was 'how is historical understanding possible?'. His argument was that the events that are of interest to the historian are the products of human thought, and the aims of history are to understand that thought, since to do so would also be to understand the events of history. This was not to be achieved by recourse to general laws, rather by "the re-enactment of past thought in the historian's own mind" (1946, p. 214). Because Collingwood does not provide in *The Idea of History* any methodological demonstration of how this re-enactment is to be achieved, his thesis has been poorly received within both history and archaeology. Recent efforts to reinstate Collingwood as a philosopher (e.g. Dray 1980, pp. 9–26) have largely gone unnoticed within archaeology, and the most commonly held view is that he favoured a highly speculative history or even transcendentalism. Renfrew, for example, has linked Collingwood's approach, by a deft sleight of the pen, with the writing of fiction. Thus, of Collingwood's thesis he claims "for the prehistorian and archaeologist such an approach is ... altogether inappropriate, and to follow it implies embarking on the sort of 'imaginative recreation' which leads on to the historical novel" (1979b, p. 4). This opinion is largely unfounded, and I want briefly to argue the case for the reinstatement of Collingwood's ideals.

In his rejection of the use of general laws in historical explanation, Collingwood identified a crucial difference between the processes of nature and those of human history. It was argued that the former can be "properly described as sequences of mere events" (1946, p. 215), and as such are phenomena presented for observation. Natural scientists are not concerned to discern the thought behind these phenomena. The events of history, however, "are never mere phenomena, never mere spectacles for contemplation, but things which the historian looks, not at, but through, so as to discern the thought within them" (*ibid.*, p. 214). In stating this Collingwood was arguing that human actions are normatively informed, and this is clearly the sense implied when he uses the term 'enacted'. Thus, these acts, and these alone, form the subject-matter of history, for it is the thought behind the action which historians ultimately want to discover.

Whereas one might concur in general with this view, it can seem to be more problematic to achieve in the absence of any kind of written documentation. The apparent lack of an exegesis on society by members of that society has been used as a damning criticism of Collingwood's thesis. The argument runs, how can we rethink past thoughts where no record of those thoughts exist? Hence it is suggested that whereas Collingwood's thesis might be feasible for the historian whose sources are written ones, it is entirely inappropriate where the bulk of the data is material culture. This was the stance taken by Lowther, who argued that it is harder for the prehistorian, unlike the Romanist, to rethink past thoughts, when "only a devolved expression of that thought is available for study" (1961, p. 175). Lowther is at fault however in thinking that of itself, material culture "can give little indication of the abstract ideas of the people by whom it was made" (1961, p. 174). Collingwood clearly did not hold such views, and was quite adamant that 'history' is not restricted to the time period following the invention of writing. I think the crux of the matter lies in how 'events' and 'thoughts' are conceptualised. As we have seen, Collingwood felt that events were the product of thoughts, an aspect which he characterised as the 'inside of the event'. His use of a quasi-spatial metaphor was unfortunate, since it can imply the need to enter into the mind of the historical agent. It is clear from his text, however, that the "fact that thought has an *inward* expression as well as outward ones does not give the former any privileged status as 'the thought'" (Dray 1958, p 203). By extension this also entails that these outward expressions, whether behavioural or material, should not be seen as 'thought-free' but as 'value-loaded'. Such a reading of Collingwood implies that, far from favouring a kind of transcendentalism, he appreciated that artifacts are not merely the residues of events, but are also representations of those events. This, I believe, liberates us from the anxieties and narrow strictures that Lowther wished to impose.

The efforts in recent years of researchers to elucidate a theory of material culture bear this opinion out. I therefore chose to consider, along with other contributors to this volume, that the material world, and its spatial arrangement, stands in a recursive relationship with the social world. Since my argument concerns the organisation and use of space I shall elaborate on a few points which have a direct bearing on the matter in hand.

In the first place it must be emphasised that space itself has no meaning, because it is a socially constructed phenomenon. This is a view forcefully reiterated by the urban geographer Manuel Castellis, who has written extensively on the historical relationships between space and society. He writes,

> space is not, contrary to what others may say, a reflection of society but one of society's fundamental material dimensions and to consider it independently from social relationships, even with the intention of studying their interaction, is to separate nature from culture, and thus to destroy the first principle of any social science: that matter and consciousness are interrelated and that this fusion is the essence of history and science.
>
> (1983, p. 311)

The importance of this statement is to stress that it is the meanings of space as much as its physical configuration that have an impact on the way people use, manipulate and interact within it.

Having said that, the physical arrangements should not be overlooked. The pre-existing configuration of buildings and spaces between strictures is not merely the environment of daily activities, it is also constituted by those activities. For instance, amongst the Dogon the processing of different crops takes place in certain restricted localities. Typically, these activities are performed outside the limit of inhabited village space. Generally, the reasons given for the localisation of this class of tasks concern attitudes to hygiene: for instance, millet chaff is said to cause severe skin irritations. However, Dogon medical knowledge is intricately linked to spiritual knowledge, and so one is told that a malevolent spirit is the root cause of an affliction of this kind. The regular use of this particular space creates thick deposits of millet chaff on which women work daily, and remain untroubled by it. Their physical actions not only generate chaff deposits but, through their actual performance, help to transform that space into a named place on everybody's mental map of the village. To perform these tasks elsewhere, such as within the bounds of the residential area of the village, would be to bring the malevolent spirits closer into the village.

Alternatively, acts of social classification of space will also serve to reinforce the boundaries that are imposed by those categories. For example, by redefining a house as 'a widow's room', as opposed to 'family house', a need for widows to have their own space is realised. On the bereavement of a husband a Dogon woman enters a new stage in her life, with different obligations and expectations than those which she held as a married woman. Hence the act of moving from one social category to another can have the effect of transforming one kind of space into another, without any physical alteration to the space itself.

It is conventional in archaeology, and in social science in general, to view space and time as mere environments of action. However, as I have suggested, human agents are not simply presented with a set of conditions with which to construct endlessly possible configurations. Because the spatial ordering of the everyday world is imbued with meaning which defines and excludes certain social categories, the options are never limitless. The constraints of ascribed roles and what is considered to be acceptable behaviour, defined by what has gone before, serve to circumscribe actions, making them in a sense predictable. Knowing that a particular arrangement is conventional, normal even, lets an individual know how s/he should arrange space. However, it must be clearly stated that social action is not characterised by rule following, but by negotiation. The possibility for breaking, bending or restricting a rule always remains, precisely because most kinds of social action involve the agent in an articulation with other people. It is this process of negotiation which gives social forms their dynamism and social action its potency.

The Dogon

In the second part of this paper I present some results of an ethnographic study of representations of the past and their bearing on the organisation and use of settlement space. My intention here is to demonstrate that what is represented as 'tradition' and constitutes that dominant image of the past is in part constructed from and sustained by a particular configuration of buildings, spaces, and material culture that constitutes, for the Dogon, the humanly constructed world. The argument has two themes, the representations of 'the past', in verbal and material forms, and the importance attributed to 'the past' in Dogon society. These two aspects, the traces of events and a narrative of those events, act in a recursive fashion upon each other, both in turn reconstructing and transforming the history of the settlement.

The Dogon are sedentary agriculturalists who live in an area to the south of the Niger Bend in Mali, West Africa. They are divided into four tribal groups by a process of lineage segmentation. Marriage is polygynous and virilocal, and descent is traced agnatically. Settlement is in the form of nucleated villages comprising the compounds of numerous nuclear families linked together by lineage ties. The extended family forms the basic unit of production, consumption and reproduction. The next largest social unit is the minimal lineage group, several of whom occupy space in the same village ward, and all of whom are descended from the same founding ancestor. The minimal lineage group like the extended family is an exogamous unit and so is linked by marriage to other patrilineages. Consequently villages can be composed of several village wards, and are related, though at a greater remove, to members of the same tribal group occupying other villages. I shall be restricting my remarks to the extended family, minimal lineage and village, although the general conclusions to be drawn are of equal relevance to the inter-village and tribal levels of social organisation.

In common with many other ethnic groups in the region, the Dogon trace their origins back to the kingdom of Mande, from whence they migrated in the fifteenth century AD. Led by the descendants of the founding ancestors of the four tribes, the early migrants established settlements in the area, at first in the west and later spreading east and north. The sequence of foundation is important, and the kinship links which were established then are maintained to this day, often over considerable distances. Although this era of migration, and of contact with the original inhabitants of the region, lies on the edge of 'mythological' time, the foundation of the first villages marks the start of a different kind of 'past'. In the sense that the events which subsequently took place were no longer those of a spiritual and mythical world, but were human, these foundations mark the beginnings of 'history'. For the most part, settlement history is recorded in the form of genealogies. However, notable and extraneous events, such as famines, inter-tribal wars, severe epidemics, the coming of Europeans and the like, are also recorded in oral tradition. Closely linked with genealogical knowledge is an awareness of the changes in the physical fabric of the settlement. For instance, most family heads could tell me the names of the individuals who had built the houses which belonged to their lineage, even those which remain merely as eroded traces of former houses. However, rather than simply being the tangible evidence of an ancestor, the house sites mark the stage of growth or decline the lineage had reached at a particular point in time, and its relationships with the other lineages of the village. It is to the contemporary manifestation of this process of 'settlement' that I now turn.

The particular study village[1] lies on the talus scree slopes of the Bandiagara escarpment. The latter is a vertical cliff face, reaching in places 200 metres in height, which marks the scarp slope of a sandstone plateau. The cliff line runs along a south-west–north-east axis for approximately 250 km. To the east lies a vast expanse of sand, known as the Plain of Gondo, and to the west the dip slope of the plateau. Village fields are located among the scree and at its base, in the piedmont valley. The latter, about five kilometres wide, is defined on its eastern edge by high sand dunes. The staple crop is millet and for the most part lineage-based production is self-sustaining.

Authority over both the extended family and the village is in the hands of the male elders. The head of each extended family, known as the 'ginu bana', is the eldest living male of that group, which is called the 'ginna'. He is responsible for both the daily and seasonal organisation of production, and controls the product of the collective labour of the extended family. He is also responsible for ensuring the distribution of this product, since he controls, through usufruct rights, access to the lands of the extended family, which includes compounds, houses and fields. The 'ginu bana' resides in a compound known as the 'ginu na' (great house), or more colloquially, the 'ginna'. Other members of the extended family occupy other compounds and houses in the village ward to which they belong.

The categorisation of residential space

Given that people live in, and arrange according to their desires, physical space, it is to be expected that there will be an isomorphic relationship between people and space. It would be mistaken, however, to expect this correlation to be always

based on strictly utilitarian or formal grounds. In fact the conceptual separation of form and function from the symbolic and historical dimension is likely to obfuscate rather than clarify. In what follows I shall discuss how a sense of belonging, of historical situation, is maintained in relation to the categorisation and organisation of dwelling space.

Physically a compound means a house or collection of up to three houses, enclosed by a dry-stone wall with one or sometimes more entrance ways. Also contained within the bounds of this space are granaries, used variously to store food staples, secondary crops and personal possessions. The open area that is enclosed by the compound walls can contain other facilities, such as animal byres, hen coops and weaving looms. The remaining space is used for a variety of tasks including craft production, food preparation, cooking, eating and socialising. Adults and children make use of the facilities and spaces within compounds to a greater or lesser degree according to their gender and age. Despite a certain uniformity in outward appearance, compounds, or strictly speaking the houses they contain, are divided into several categories.

This categorisation is made according to the social rank of the occupant(s) of the dwelling. Thus, houses occupied by groups of young males are called 'sagata:rau dunoy' (young men's room), those by widows 'ya:na peyne dunoy' (widow's room). Those used by elementary families are termed 'ginu sala' (ordinary house) and the residence of the 'ginu bana', the head of an extended family, is known as the 'ginu na' (great house).

Changing residential locations are a feature of the developmental cycle of the domestic group, and an individual will occupy several houses during his or her lifespan. Although the same logic applies to both men and women – that is, one based on the precautions taken against incest and prohibited sex – members of different sexes follow different spatio-temporal trajectories (Lane, in press). More importantly, because of this continually shifting pattern of residence, structures and compounds belonging to the 'ginna' (descent group) also come to be reclassified. For example, a house occupied by a widow ('ya:na peyne dunoy') might on her death be refurbished to house young males ('sagata:rau dunoy') or a young married couple (ginu sala). Of all the house categories only one, the 'ginna', is never reclassified, and each successive 'ginu bana' moves from his previous residence, with his wives, into the 'ginna'. If we consider the rules of residence in more detail, we see that they establish an isomorphic relationship between the place of residence of the eldest male of the minimal lineage and the eldest residential structure belonging to this group. However, this pattern is not necessarily adhered to by other lineage members. The next eldest male could easily live in a newly constructed house, whereas a junior member might live in one of the older buildings. This implies that, unlike other residential buildings, the notion of the 'ginna' as a structure is as important as the idea of the agnatic descent group.

The 'ginna' houses are regarded as at least very ancient if

not the oldest buildings in the village. Only particular shrines and certain abandoned houses are considered to predate the 'ginna' houses. Significantly, the latter are said to be the residences of the founder of the village, his sons and grandsons, the founders of all the existing minor lineages. The terminological equivalence of the words for the residence of the 'ginu bana' and the collective group he heads stresses the importance of the links between kin and place of residence. These compounds stand as durable evidence of the continuity through time of the patrilineage. A 'ginu bana' without a 'ginna' is unimagineable. Considered in conjunction with genealogies, these spaces define an individual's relations with other members of the village and also with the outside world. It is these relationships which provide the individual with an awareness of his or her identity and place in the social world. One feature of the life cycle is that the relationships which pertain between individuals change as people mature, get married, have children, grow old and die. As I have described above, this change in status is frequently marked by a change in residence. However, it is important to bear in mind that although the social fabric is reordered, and physical space is reclassified, the form of the settlement remains largely the same. The reasons for this are not strictly to do with meeting utilitarian demands or the limitations of a particular architectural style. Rather they have to do with the constraints that are placed on the expansion of the settlement via the ideological control over the relations of production and reproduction. The gist of the remaining part of my argument will demonstrate how this is achieved.

Symbolic power

As I have argued, an aspect of the village dynamic is a continuous changing pattern of residential location. Along with the process of ageing, two causal factors in this dynamic are the rule of post-marital virilocal residence for women and an idealised stricture on patrilocal residence for men. One of the practical necessities of the first rule is the provision of dwelling space. Since each wife occupies her own house within the confines of her husband's compound, a man is obliged to provide a house for each of his wives. This can be achieved by either constructing a new one, or by repairing and/or appropriating older structures belonging to his lineage. Hence, there is often a 'spatial consequence' to a marriage over and above the simple addition of an individual to the village. Since access to building land is controlled by the lineage head, residential space becomes a scarce resource for all junior members of the lineage. In the normal course of affairs, housing space is allocated to meet the needs of the younger males, allowing them to follow the ideal biography of a male, getting married, fathering children and later becoming an elder, and perhaps a lineage head. However, a situation of competition, and consequently tension between agnates, can also arise, which is in direct contradiction to the lineage-based ideology of cooperation. In extreme cases this can lead to lineage fission. Where this occurs the more junior member will

establish his own residence, which will eventually be categorised as a 'ginna', although maintaining ritual links with the senior segment. In such an eventuality the newer of the two 'ginna' would post-date many of the 'ginu sala' in the village. It is therefore necessary to emphasise that a 'ginna' need not be one of the earliest structures in the whole village (although many are), but simply the oldest belonging to a particular lineage segment. Because segments maintain links, principally for ritual purposes, the 'ginna' of the more senior segment is structurally superior to that of the junior.[2]

It is worth noting here that a concern expressed in both ritual orations and by the village elders in conversation was that members (male) of the 'ginna' and village were dispersed throughout geographical space (in Abidjan, Bamako, Mopti and the plains). The point of these comments was that this prolonged separation required powerful assistance and interference on the part of the ancestors if the traditions of the Dogon and the identity of the 'ginna' were to survive. However, the reasons for this spatial distribution have arisen largely because of the constraints placed on, in particular, young men by the ideology of the lineage. The system of land tenure, for example, by which usufruct rights in agricultural land are controlled by the 'ginna' head, ties other men to this collective and their natal village. These men, and this can include brothers of the 'ginu bana' as well as those of the younger generation, can establish a certain degree of independence by out-migration and settling in the less densely populated Plain of Gondo.

The opportunities for wage labour outside the region can offer an alternative way out. This alternative, however, has given rise to some unanticipated consequences, affecting marriage transactions. The traditional pattern of bridewealth is still largely maintained, and, unlike the case in many other patrilineal societies, does not present too great a burden on young men. However, the expectation of brides have changed. Several young women expressed the view that they preferred to marry men who had plenty of clothes and 'western' possessions, such as a bicycle or a cassette-radio. This level of expectation acts as a powerful incentive for men to go in search of wage labour. The opportunities for this lie only outside the region. This option is, as has been noted, in conflict with the desires of the lineage elders.

Paradoxically, this kind of outmigration is not a new phenomenon. Lifszyc and Paulme (1936), for instance, describe the status acquired by individuals who could dress up in 'exotic' clothes at the annual sowing festival ('bulu'), and record that these youths at that time went by the name of "Les Goldcoasts". Most of the elder men in the study village had indeed been absent from the region for a period of years and some were even conscripts in the colonial army and had been taken to France and North Africa. In other words, the elder males are choosing to emphasise an idealised pattern of residence (remaining in the village) which they did not adhere to themselves.

Such a concern to ensure the survival of the lineage via

the maintenance of traditions is a key element of Dogon society. It would be inappropriate, however, to characterise the society as conservative and unchanging. The past is used here as a strategy for coping with the present. This is seen more clearly in statements about the social order. For example, a regular feature during ritual ceremonies is the use of the phrase, 'It is a tradition of the past', following an allusion to some kind of event or action, and indicates the importance attached to contextualising certain practices. To cite only one case, during a sacrifice concerned with the propitiation of the female ancestors of the lineage ('ya:yinu'), the principal officiant, the lineage head, referred to the role of women in beer production and cooking in the following manner:

> With women it is a custom,
> That the hearth should have three stones.
> We depend on God for our customs.
> We hope that God does not abandon us,
> If we err, may God put that to one side.
> Thank you, thank you, thank you.
> Tomorrow we [the lineage] depend again on you [the women].
> The white calabash has done its work,
> The calabash which is held has drunk,
> The women, they have done their work,
> Their duty to give [beer and food] to be eaten, [is]
> A tradition of the Dogon.
> Do not think of it as a sufferance,
> It has been this way since there were women,
> We thank you for the respect [that you have shown],
> We depend on you.[3]

The metaphors used in this text require some explanation. The hearth is a potent symbol of the family for the Dogon. The sense implied by the phrase "a hearth should have three stones" is one of cooperation between the sexes. Its interpretation requires a certain familiarity with the features of Dogon cooking hearths. It is normal practice to use three large stones, arranged, in plan, in the form of a triangle, so as to support the cooking vessel over the flames. Similarly the phrases "the white calabash has done its work" and "the calabash which is held has drunk" stand as metaphors for the female tasks of food and beer production respectively. These two metaphors are more simply interpreted. 'White calabash', 'koro pilu', is the name given to all calabashes used during the food preparation process, and the name derives from the fact that those used for the winnowing of millet turn white from the millet flour and chaff. These calabashes are contrasted with the calabashes 'which are held', 'koro si', which are kept clean and are used as drinking vessels for beer, gruel and water. In this instance it is the sexual division of labour, and the products of female labour that are being represented metaphorically. The use of these particular symbols is entirely appropriate in this context since women had prepared the beer and food which were redistributed among agnatic and affinal kin.

The purpose of this kind of statement is twofold; on the one hand, the definitions of the social world which are represented are those most consistent with the interests of the dominant group – that is, male elders. In this case, the phrases naturalise and legitimate a sexual division of labour, by emphasising the 'traditional' nature of this division, and the mutual benefits which arise from it. What becomes obscured is the actual appropriation of part of the surplus product of the collective labour of the lineage for ritual and political purposes. On the other hand, it must be recognised that these statements are also *specifications* of the social relations which have to be reproduced in order that social reproduction as a whole is achieved. The subsistence needs of the lineage group are fulfilled by the collective labour of its active members. Once these demands have been met women and men have considerable autonomy over the disposal of their labour and products of that labour. In the absence of any selective appropriation of female labour within lineage production, the structures which need to be reproduced are, in effect, the social relations which permit control over the *reproductive capacity* of women. In patrilineal and gynaecomobile societies such as the Dogon these are essentially the relations between affinal males. It is toward the maintenance of these inter-lineage links that the exchange of bridewealth and the prestations of beer and food in certain ritual contexts are directed. Furthermore, this is most probably the social purpose of certain building and marriage rites which employ important material symbols of women and the patrilineage.

For instance, it is interesting to note that in the past, part of the foundation rites entailed the deposition of a calabash and the symbolic marking of the hearth in the outlines of the house sketched out prior to the start of building. Later, following the construction of the roof, a task performed communally by men from the village, women married to the male agnates and affines of the 'builder' prepared a celebratory meal. In contrast to normal practice, the men provided the culinary equipment and the women the 'food', which was in fact sand (Calame-Griaule 1955). As with the sacrifice referred to above, these prestations are distributed amongst affines and also agnates, with whom men have entered into some kind of obligation. The young man who constructs a new house needs the support of his agnatic and affinal kin to help with the building. In return his helpers receive beer and meals of rice with meat. The relationships which ensure the presence of affines at a funeral or a sacrifice, as was the case at the 'ya:yinu' sacrifice, may be more complex, but are based on the same principles of obligation and due. Of all affinal relationships the most prominent is that of the mother's brother : sister's son, 'niñu : sa i'. The two maintain throughout their lives a joking relationship, and the eldest of a man's sons often spends his childhood in his mother's natal village, living with and working for his maternal uncle. As a young adult, after his return to his natal lineage, he can be recalled to help on days of sacrifices, funerals and other ceremonies to distribute the beer that is provided on these occasions. In return, the 'sa i' can during these visits, and usually do, steal chickens from compounds, and act in a lawless fashion whilst in their uncle's village with impunity (Griaule 1954). More practical benefits are provided by a 'niñu' when a young man is trying to accumulate bridewealth.

Returning to the issues of residential space, when a young wife finally leaves her natal ward for that of her husband, in the case of a first wife usually after the birth of the couple's third child, she brings with her several personal possessions. However, she must also bring with her a waterpot, 'loy', which is to be used by her husband. Moreover, her first task as a new member of her husband's lineage is to fetch water for the 'loy' in his 'ginu na' and then for her husband. The next job to be performed in the 'ginu na' is to prepare and cook a meal for the members of the 'ginna'. Both of these acts require that pots are placed in their appropriate places, in the central room and on the hearth respectively. This gesture is known as 'ginna loy di kobu dana', or 'the fetching and placing of water for the pots of the "ginna"'. Through its performance "la nouvelle venue apporte, à son tour, dans la maison de famille, les âmes des enfants à naître qui siègent, avec le Nommo, dans la mare" (Dieterlen 1956, p. 141).[4] Dieterlen also records that where a woman is still contemplating whether to stay with her husband or not, she asks another member of the family to place the cooking pot on the hearth for her (1956, p. 141, note 6). These minor rites also mark, in a material sense, the transition of a wife from her natal 'ginna', and the space that occupies, to that of her husband. The significance of the hearth, cooking pot and water pot in these contexts is not simply derived from their practical associations with women. Admittedly the sexual division of labour ensures that women perform the tasks of cooking and fetching water. However, although these are in a certain sense wifely duties, they are also performed by other women of the 'ginna'. All the womenfolk of the 'ginna', above the age of ten or eleven, daily help to fetch water from the well, in the morning and evening. The 'loy' of the 'ginna' are filled first, then each wife will fetch water for those pots in her own house; unmarried girls help the widows with whom they lodge and also fill the waterpots of their unmarried brothers. The lineage group normally eats as a group at the 'ginna'; however, preparation of meals is carried out on a rota system, each married woman cooking the two daily meals in turn. Hence, it cannot really be argued that it is for her labour that a wife is valued. Instead, as suggested above, the real reason for a woman to cross the boundaries of a lineage group is to ensure its biological reproduction. One finds that the reason cited most often by men as to why it should be necessary for a woman to have given birth at least once before she takes up residence with her husband is 'so that her husband and his family knows

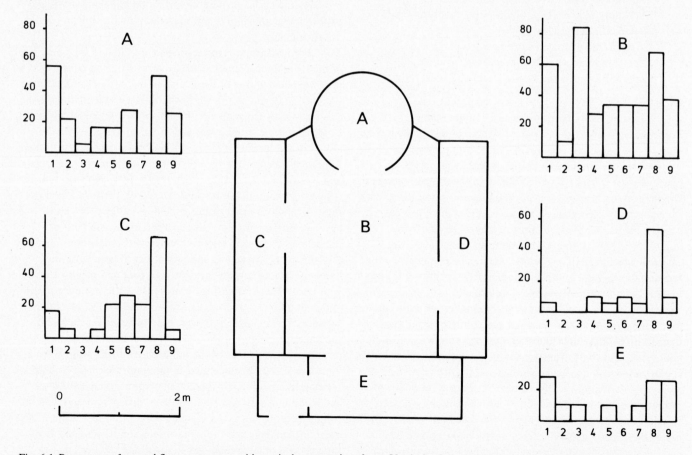

Fig. 6.1 Percentage of ground-floor room types with particular categories of pot. Vertical axis = percentage of rooms with pot type. Horizontal axis = type of pot: 1–2 cooking; 3 'loy' (waterpot); 4–6 beer brewing; 7 beer storage; 8–9 other (mainly storage). Rooms: A = kitchen; B = bedroom; C and D = stores; E = hall

that she is not infertile'. So in marking her entry into a new physical and social domain, the incoming wife can be said to be marking the arrival of her fertility, and so redefining in both social and material terms the space of the 'ginna'. Her arrival, in a sense, validates the attention, in the form of prestations, devoted to affinal links.

This suggests that the importance of the artifacts used in the rites described above is to do with fertility and reproduction, a fact substantiated by their symbolic meanings. The waterpot, as we have seen, is closely related to female fertility. This association derives from Dogon ideas about procreation and conception. In essence, the model holds that the foetus is formed in its mother's breast from a mix of seminal fluid and menstrual blood. During pregnancy the foetus is likened to a fish, swimming in the amniotic fluid; apart from meaning 'waterpot' the word 'loy' can be used to describe 'the amniotic sac' (Calame-Griaule 1968, p. 186). The hearth, among other things, symbolises for the Dogon, the prosperity of the lineage. Hence the aphorism, 'Where there are many hearths firewood is quickly finished', emphasises the benefits of cooperation, a point I shall return to below.

Some of these significances are retained in the use and organisation of domestic space. An analysis of the spatial distribution of objects within houses indicates that amongst the different types of pot used by the Dogon, only waterpots and those placed in first-floor shrines (stores) are consistently found in the same category of room (fig. 6.1). The other pots, such as cooking pots and those used for the storage and brewing of beer, are found more evenly distributed throughout the various rooms of a house. Moreover, despite considerable daily and monthly variations in artifact distributions within a house, waterpots, although regularly moved when used to fetch water, are always returned to the same room from which they were taken (see table 6.1). While there are several pragmatic reasons for this state of affairs, such as accessibility and a desire to keep the water cool, the close association of the central room of a house with the human torso in the recorded symbolism of the house (Calame-Griaule 1955) and the symbolism of the waterpot cannot be overlooked.

We have then a model of the domestic cycle, which despite constant changes, such as the recategorisation of residential space, the influx of new members into the kin group, and the process of biological ageing, still succeeds in replicating the pre-existing relations of production and reproduction. The changing pattern of relationships and interactions is geared so as to ensure the reproduction of the 'ginna'. Due to the rule of exogamy, their women are destined not to reproduce for the group and must be brought in from outside. To ensure this, relations must be sustained between lineages, as evidenced by the importance attached to honouring affinal relations. This desire for lineage reproduction is reinforced by a symbol system which emphasises female fertility via an association with moisture. This in turn is transposed back onto residential space in a variety of ways, such as on the arrival of a new wife, in the daily rearrangement of space and, in the past, during

foundation rites. Each re-emphasises at the level of practice a dependence on women in order to sustain the continuity of the lineage.

Yet, despite this emphasis on stability, the Dogon world has been in the past, and is in the present, undergoing change. The evidence is sparse, but it is clear that in some cases, and for a variety of reasons, pre-existing lineages no longer maintain a human presence in the village. Traces of their compounds remain, at first as locked houses with upstanding walls that later collapse into ruined footings. A strict rule limits access to and use of these spaces to lineage members only. Although they are a convenient source of raw materials for house building, no member of another lineage would presume to take stones or wood from these abandoned sites. The usual reason elicited for this is that the owners might at some future date wish to reoccupy the compounds. However, almost as an aside, a remark would be made about the failure in filial duties that led to the collapse of a 'ginna'. It is generally held that when a man chooses not to occupy his 'ginna' when he has the right, it is still his duty to maintain it. Where this does not occur, and the house falls into disrepair, disrespect of one's father and lineage is implied. Strictly speaking the fortunes of a lineage are its own affair, and other villagers must maintain a distance, careful not to pillage the 'history' of other lineages, as manifested in their residential structures. But, just as the wealth and riches of a family, though carefully hidden in granaries and trunks, are made visible by these same facilities, and more overtly at ceremonial occasions, so the 'misfortunes' of a lineage are there for all to see, for those who know how to read the signs. The locked houses of the contemporary scene tell a similar story. Young men have parted for the towns in search of work, or with their wives and children have cleared their own fields and built new compounds out in the plains.

Conclusion

I began this chapter with a discussion of Collingwood's exposition on the nature of historical understanding, a work generally overlooked in contemporary archaeology. The intervening section on Dogon ethnography detailed a study of their approaches to 'the past'. The reader by now may be pondering as to the relevance of these details to archaeology. Indeed, a common response to ethnoarchaeological studies that deal with belief systems but do not fall under the heading of 'cautionary tale', is to group them into a 'so what?' category. The following remarks are made in an attempt to rectify this view.

As Collingwood argued, in order to reach an historical understanding worthy of that name, it is our notions about the nature of events which require revision. It is inappropriate to see events entirely in terms of effects, the working out of a particular law or principle of human behaviour, precisely because actions in the real world are never so clear-cut, so dogmatic or so law-abiding. It is *because* individual actions appear to the passive observer as random that 'models of predictability' are oversimplifications of the aggregates of like

Table 6.1. *Absolute distribution of different functional categories of pot, by room, on different visits to a house (Room letters correspond to those in fig. 6.1)*

Pot function	Cooking					Water storage					Brewing					Beer storage					Other				
Room:	A	B	C	D	E	A	B	C	D	E	A	B	C	D	E	A	B	C	D	E	A	B	C	D	E
Month																									
Oct 1982	3	6	0	0	3	0	4	0	0	0	2	2	3	0	0	0	0	1	2	0	0	4	4	5	0
Nov	2	3	1	1	1	0	5	0	0	0	4	1	5	0	0	0	2	0	1	0	0	4	5	2	0
Feb 1983	1	2	0	0	6	0	3	0	0	0	1	2	2	1	1	0	1	2	0	0	0	1	4	4	0
Mar	0	1	0	0	3	0	5	0	0	0	5	0	4	0	0	0	2	0	0	1	0	4	3	3	0
Apr	2	2	0	2	7	0	6	0	0	0	4	0	3	2	0	0	1	1	4	0	1	4	2	4	1

events. Yet the same individual acts are understandable to those involved in them. It is this intersubjectivity, which we all experience and understand as social agents in our own societies, that permits a reading and interpretation of events. In short, an event *is* an exegesis. Admittedly it may not be immediately comprehensible, and is often open to misinterpretation, but these are problems of interactions in general, and are not just specific to the social sciences.

Where the archaeologist and historian are disadvantaged is that they are not in a position to observe the actions under study. However, and this I believe was the purpose of Collingwood's analogy with detective work (1946, pp. 266–78), this problem is not unique to the historical disciplines, but a feature of human knowledge in general. It suggests that the act of observation is not necessarily an essential part of understanding. To make use of a literary analogy, I think it would be accepted that we do not have to observe the act of novel writing on the part of an author to be able to understand a novel. If, as I have suggested, an event is an exegesis, then the traces of that event must be, at least in part, exegetical.

Hence a recut ditch, an abandoned structure, a resharpened stone axe are not merely the effects of utilitarian desires. As visible statements of a particular rationale they encompass and go beyond these strategies. The realisation of utilitarian ends is not achieved in a cultural vacuum. Although those ends have already been culturally defined and the limits of acceptable means for achieving them set by precedent, risks can be taken to go beyond these boundaries and establish new definitions. Younger Dogon men and women are seeking these modifications, so as to gain a perceived freedom from the autonomy of the family patriarch. Dogon elders, by invoking the past, are trying to contain the actions, on the part of the younger generations, which threaten their position of authority. By stressing lineage solidarity in verbal forms, which, like the metaphors of the hearth, emphasise the material evidence of the success of a particular order, the elders attempt to legitimate and naturalise that order. The sedimentation of meanings in objects which this encourages allows for historical understanding to take a specific form. Thus the past is

presented as a period of adherence to tradition, and despite traces of the ravages of famine, disease and war over the centuries on the population, of survival. But, as evidenced by the contemporary pattern of out-migration, this ideology sets up its own internal contradictions which cannot simply be reduced to population pressure, changing patterns of resource exploitations or the emergence of agricultural specialisation, although all of these phenomena have made their appearance in recent years. In the same vein, the ordering of domestic space meets pragmatic concerns which are at the same time symbolically loaded actions, helping to reproduce structures of authority and power. As a particular combination of events, the domestic tasks of food preparations, cooking, fetching water and brewing beer leave material traces which become 'the *documents* of human action'.[5]

Notes
1. Fieldwork was carried out between May and November 1981, and October and May 1982/3.
2. *Stricto sensu*, the term 'ginna' should refer only to the house of the senior members of the maximal lineage, and smaller social units, e.g. minor and minimal lineages, be called 'tire togu'. In practice, the latter maintain an economic independence and make use of the term 'ginna' to describe their members and the residence of the individual who heads that group.
3. 1982/3 Fieldnotes, Text 5. The word 'we' should be understood as referring to the collective whole rather than a section of the community.
4. In the past lineages collected their water from lineage 'lakes', or large ponds. Today, wells and a system of dams provide a more reliable water supply for the whole community.
5. Fieldwork was carried out with the permission of the Office of the Directeur Général des Enseignements Supérieurs et de la Recherche Scientifique, permit nos. 0626/DNERS & 1596/DNERS. I would like to thank Dr Kléna Sanogo, Director L'Institut des Sciences Humaines, Bamako, for his assistance and Michel Raimbault for his support and hospitality. My research assistants Ana Dolo and Missidou Dolo helped ease my introduction to Dogon life and kindly suffered my foolishness. I am grateful to Henrietta Moore, Elisabeth Vestergaard and Ian Hodder, who read and commented on earlier versions of this chapter.

Chapter 7

The perpetual reconstruction of the past

Elisabeth Vestergaard

Vestergaard compares two medieval transformation of an epic tradition, particularly in relation to descriptions of material culture. In the Scandinavian Vǫlsunga cycle a non-feudal society is described in which the patrilineal kin group is primary. There are relatively few descriptions of material objects in the texts but feasting, gift giving and the movement of artifacts are sources of prestige and power. Material culture often has an active social force. In the Nibelungenlied, on the other hand, a feudal society is depicted in which political and contractual links (vassal–lord, husband–wife) are primary. There is frequent mention of large amounts of clothing and material goods, although often described in aggregate, abstract terms. Power is not gained through specific artifacts, but material wealth in general expresses power obtained through one's position in society. This paper argues that we cannot assume that all artifacts are socially active to an equivalent degree in different social and cultural contexts. Vestergaard also demonstrates the way in which a long tradition of material culture use (such as hoarding) and of epic accounts can be transformed so that the same or similar things have new meanings in new contexts. Ultimately it will be possible to investigate Vestergaard's reconstructions by archaeological study in the areas of the two epic traditions. For the present, this paper discusses historical accounts of material culture usage.

The past is constantly reconstructed to produce meaning for a changing present. The history of archaeological research shows this clearly. The rendering and interpretation of history by historians also demonstrates how different epochs derive different meanings from the same material. Classical dramas are transformed during the centuries, either rewritten by other poets or performed and interpreted in new ways.

This perpetual reconstruction of the past is closely connected with social change. In this paper, one of the basic theses is that a structural congruity between the literary work and the social contexts is an important condition for the popularity of the literary work. This is especially so when the texts deal with problems which are essential to the social organisation. In what follows I will demonstrate how an epic tradition is transformed in relation to the social context.

Literary texts differ from other historical sources, such as law texts, because they do not contain any exact historical evidence about the societies concerned, and they are not just mechanical reflections of society. The literary representation of human relations allows us to get fuller insight into norms, into values, into how actions and personal relations ought or ought not to be – in short, insight into the world of ideas more difficult to catch through the traditional historical sources.

The literary sources
The literary material is the Scandinavian Vǫlsunga cycle and the German Nibelungenlied. They have a common origin partly in historical events from the age of the great migration in central Europe and partly in mythological and legendary material. The texts have developed rather independently up to

the oldest MSS, though the same persons and principal events are found in both cycles.

The oldest Scandinavian Eddic lays concerning this tradition are assumed to date from the beginning of the Viking Age. But they were not taken down in writing until the first half of the thirteenth century.[1] The oldest preserved MS *Codex Regius* is from around 1270, and is a copy of a MS that is now lost.

The German Nibelungenlied is assumed to have found its known form just before AD 1200, and the oldest MSS are slightly younger. None of them, however, is the original.[2]

Summary of the Vǫlsunga cycle

Sigurd, the young hero of royal and divine descent, revenges the murder of his father. He fights a huge dragon Fafnir and wins a hoard. He is the greatest hero the world ever saw. He awakens the valkyrie Brynhild and they promise each other eternal love. Later he arrives at Gjuke's hall. Gjuke's wife Grimhild wants to affiliate Sigurd to the Gjukungs and pours him a drink that makes him forget Brynhild. Sigurd then becomes the sworn brother of Gunnar and Hogni, the two oldest sons of Grimhild, and he marries their sister Gudrun. By means of sorcery he helps Gunnar to woo Brynhild as he assumes the appearance of Gunnar. Years later Brynhild and Gudrun start a quarrel over whose husband is the more glorious. Gudrun shows Brynhild the very ring and belt which Sigurd got from Brynhild when he wooed her and slept in her bed in the shape of Gunnar. Brynhild now wants Sigurd dead and Gunnar proposes to Hogni that they kill him. First Hogni refuses because Sigurd is their sworn brother. Then they agree to have their youngest brother Guttorm do it. He was too young to take part when the oldest brothers swore brotherhood with Sigurd. Sigurd is killed and Gudrun is inconsolable. But Hogni remarks that she would have been even more broken-hearted had her brother been killed instead of her husband. Gudrun takes no revenge.

Later on King Atle of Huneland woos Gudrun. Atle is the brother of Brynhild, hence Gunnar's brother-in-law. Not until her mother has poured her a drink of oblivion is Gudrun persuaded into this marriage. They get two sons together. After several years of marriage Atle wants the hoard which Sigurd once won. The hoard is now in the charge of Gudrun's brothers, and they have hidden in at the bottom of the river Rhine. Atle invites his brothers-in-law to a feast. In order to warn her brothers of the treachery behind the invitation Gudrun sends them a golden arm ring to which wolf's hair is attached. Nevertheless the brothers leave for Huneland. On their arrival they are fought by Atle and his men. The only survivors of the Gjukungs and their men are Gunnar and Hogni. In order to make Gunnar reveal where the hoard is hidden, the heart is cut out of Hogni while he is still alive. As Gunnar then proclaims that he is now the only one who knows about the hoard, he is thrown into a snake pit where he dies. Gudrun serves Atle a delicious meal. Then she tells him that it was the hearts of his own sons which he devoured and shared

out to his men. Atle becomes dead drunk during the night and Gudrun kills him with a sword, sets the house on fire and burns his men to death. Only Gudrun survives.

Summary of the Nibelungenlied

Like Sigurd in the Volsunga cycle Siegfried too is the greatest hero ever, and he has also won a hoard and fought a dragon. He lives at his parents' court, but when he sees a painting of the princess Kriemhild – the equivalent of the Norse Gudrun – he wants to woo her, and leaves for Worms on the river Rhine where she lives with her brothers, her mother and her uncle. They are all eager to win the famous Siegfried as an ally, so therefore Kriemhild's brother Gunther promises Siegfried Kriemhild if Siegfried helps Gunther to win Brünhild as a wife. Brünhild only wants to marry the world's greatest hero, and that is Siegfried. So in order to deceive Brünhild he has to play the vassal of Gunther. By means of his powers and magic tools Siegfried helps Gunther to win the trial of strength with Brünhild. The two couples are married the same day. When Gunther tries to make love to Brünhild on the wedding night, she beats him and hangs him against the wall, so he asks Siegfried to assist secretly the following night. He manages to beat Brünhild. Before leaving her Siegfried takes her belt and one of her finger rings. Siegfried and Kriemhild settle at his parents' court. Several years later they are invited to Gunther's court. During the tournaments the two women start a quarrel about which of them has precedence over the other according to the rank of their husbands. Kriemhild says that Siegfried is not a vassal as Brünhild thought, but the mightiest king, and she ends by showing Brünhild the very ring and belt which Siegfried took from Brünhild secretly, and in public she calls Brünhild a whore. King Gunther is persuaded by his uncle and supreme vassal Hagen that Siegfried must be killed, and so he is.

Siegfried's hoard is brought to Worms, but as Hagen fears that Kriemhild will buy allies in order to revenge the homicide of Siegfried, he seizes the hoard and lowers it into the Rhine. Kriemhild then marries King Etzel of Huneland and later her brothers and uncle are invited to a feast. In spite of bad omens they leave for Huneland. Kriemhild has won Etzel's brother Blödel as an ally. Etzel knows nothing about the conspiracy. The banquet ends in a huge slaughter and Kriemhild tries to burn her brothers to death. Ten thousand men are killed; only Gunther and Hagen survive of the Nibelungs.[3] Hagen refuses to tell Kriemhild where the hoard is hidden as long as his lord Gunther is alive. In order to make Hagen reveal this, Kriemhild has Gunther beheaded and as Hagen still refuses she beheads him herself. Then she is beheaded by Hildebrand, the vassal of an independent king, and the epic ends.

These summaries of the two versions of the very same tradition demonstrate at an empirical level how a literary tradition is reconstructed and transformed from one social setting to the other. The social relations of importance here are the ones associated with solidarity.[4]

In the Vǫlsunga cycle the most binding obligations of solidarity are to be found inside the patrilineal kin group. Sigurd revenges the murder of his father.[5] Brothers unite in conspiracy[6] and in fighting against a brother-in-law.[7] Love between spouses is secondary to patrilineal intra-group solidarity.[8] Even after Sigurd's death Gudrun is the ally of her brothers. The fictitious kinship relation of blood brotherhood contains binding obligations similar to the ones between brothers.

The Scandinavian societies were not feudal. The power base of kings and chieftains was income from their own property – ðal land – from trade and from plunder. The family provided the most important internal resources. Upon this basis the kings and chieftains built up relations of alliance to others and formed the 'hird' (retinue) around them. In the case of the king, the 'hird' had a character of bodyguard and private army. Also, hirdmen were able to get their income from their own family land. They voluntarily became the men of the king because they strove for honour, royal gifts and booty.

In the Nibelungenlied, kinship is not without importance either, but in situations of conflicting obligations the basis of solidarity turns out to be political and other contractual relations. Though Hagen is the consanguineal uncle of King Gunther, Hagen does not derive his power and influence from being a close relative of the king, but from the fact that he is the supreme vassal of Gunther. When Siegfried is killed, Kriemhild becomes the enemy of her brothers.[9] The relationships of vassal–lord, and of husband–wife are the major binding obligations in social and political life according to the universe of the Nibelungenlied.[10]

The Nibelungenlied takes place in a feudal system. Income follows from position in society. The vertical structure forms the backbone of state and society. Free men had no part in political power as free men, but through social relations which connected them with the source of power: vassalage. The form of social relation which the 'hird' represents in the Norse societies – the relation of personal associations with superiors – is in feudal society no longer a private and voluntary matter, but has become the public basis of the social and political system which no one can escape. Thus the relations of solidarity in the epics are transformed systematically, and are in accordance with the socio-political organisation of Norse and feudal European societies.

Material culture

If we look at the Vǫlsunga cycle and the Nibelungenlied in relation to material culture there are striking differences.

There are few descriptions of dress in the Vǫlsunga cycle. Gold rings and weapons are the items most frequently referred to. Red coats or red shirts are mentioned a couple of times, but not described. The splendour of the few banquets mentioned is implied by the brief references to mead, red wine and drinking horns. If, in the Vǫlsunga cycle all references to material culture were left out (dress, food, weapons, gold etc.), the total length of the cycle would hardly be reduced by more than a page or two. If the same was done to the Nibelungenlied, we would get a really abridged version.

Clothing is a matter of utmost importance in the Nibelungenlied. Before Gunther starts the voyage to Brünhild, he wants to know how to dress appropriately at her court.[11] Approximately 20 stanzas are then devoted to descriptions of the material used for preparing their dress: silk from Arabia, Morocco and Libya, foreign furs, Indian jewels, Arabian gold; and in their boat they have the most precious food and wine. The descriptions of the clothes are not only overwhelming throughout the epic, but the number of people dressed in beautiful clothes is also excessive. When Siegfried as a young man was knighted, 400 pages at the court were knighted too, and they were all given dresses for that day by Siegfried's parents: on garments of golden brocade gem was placed next to gem.[12]

The hoard Sigurd the Vǫlsung won was of such a size that up to the measure it could fill an otter skin.[13] It consisted of gold, golden rings, beautiful weapons and a golden coat of mail.[14] Riding his horse Sigurd carried away the hoard in two chests. The German hoard was of such a size that it could fill 144 huge wagons and its value would not diminish even though all human beings were given something from it.[15] It consisted of gold and gems.

In the Vǫlsunga cycle, the king's lavishness is implicit in the terms used. The number of men surrounding the kings or chieftains is very low when compared to the Nibelungenlied. Gunnar and Hogni leave for Huneland with a few men,[16] whereas Gunther and Hagen bring ten thousand men along. Neither the dresses nor the armour of Gunnar's and Hogni's men are described. They join their kings on the journey to Huneland, fight bravely and are killed – that is the information we get from the Eddic poems.

In the universe of the Nibelungenlied, kings are also obliged to be lavish with gifts. Land, clothing, weapons and gold are the gifts frequently mentioned. Though the items themselves are not that different from those given away by Scandinavian kings and chieftains, there are, however, important differences. The Nibelungenlied emphasises the external descriptions: costly attire and metals. Boundless riches consist of gold and gems, not specified items. In spite of the 'materiality' of gold and gems, they appear in this context to be expressions of abstract and overwhelming riches. Riches are for display. Royal and noble persons demonstrate their wealth by having huge trains of attendants, all lavishly dressed up. Every time royal persons meet there is a display of wealth. This has the function of symbolising the relative position of the principal characters, whether they are of equal rank[17] or have a relation of superiority/inferiority.[18]

The question is then: why are the descriptions of riches, dress and food so different in the two text corpuses? Explanations such as greater wealth in southern Germany than in Scandinavia, are not sufficient answers, as there is no immediate relationship between a certain amount of riches in a historical society and the epic descriptions of it. Besides, international trade was of importance to the people of the Scandinavian Viking Age, and we have plenty of archaeological evidence which proves that the previous foreign items found in the world of the Nibelungenlied had also reached the Scandinavian sphere. The explanation has to be sought for at the level of the basic structural transformations of the society and epic.

The descriptions of material culture are different and so are both the social and symbolic significances of riches. The hoard appears to have lost its function in the Nibelungenlied. Before I elaborate on these points a short discussion of two papers by the Russian historian Aron Gurevich (1968, 1974) will be of use.[19]

Aron Gurevich: Discussion

Gurevich tries to construct what might be labelled psychological social history of medieval societies (1968, pp. 126–7). For this purpose he utilises law texts, mythology, sagas, courtly poetry etc., and analyses the importance and function of wealth and gift-giving.

In Scandinavia, gift-giving had a magico-religious dimension added to the social links it established. Objects – whether land or movables – carried certain of their owner's qualities, from which the receiver would benefit. The expression RIKR MAÐR (rich man) covered the fact of being wealthy and powerful, but the 'rikr maðr' was also a darling of fate. Therefore, other men were eager to receive presents from him in order that his presents should bestow luck upon them too. They strove to share his luck. If gifts were not exchanged, but only received, the receiver was thereby accepting a social status inferior to that of the giver. The receiver became the man of the giver.

> A leader could not demonstrate his wealth without distributing it; he bestowed 'the shadow of his name' on the recipients of his gifts, thereby extending the scope of his own power. (1968, p. 129)

The generosity of the chief was the basis of all his relationships with his entourage. A chief who was stingy with feasts and presents could not count on the support and fidelity of his companions. By distributing swords, rings and other booty to them, the chief built up his power and confirmed his social prestige (1974, p. 15).

As in Scandinavia, "wealth, for a feudal lord, was not an end in itself nor a means of developing or bettering his economic state" (1974, p. 16). Wealth was distributed in public.

> All these ruinous acts were carried out in public in front of other lords and vassals who were to be subjugated. Without this aim such extravagance would have had no meaning at all. (*ibid.*)

Gurevich's statement on this topic also explains the emphasis on outward descriptions in the Nibelungenlied. Gurevich labels the generosity of the feudal lords 'an aggressive generosity'. The idea was to crush the guests under it, and to

carry off the victory in this original social 'game' where the prize was prestige (1974, p. 17).

The careful combination of proper historical research with literary evidence from the periods under study and with anthropological theory makes Gurevich a most inspiring medievalist. A consequence of the position that 'no social, political or economic institution, including wealth, can be adequately understood outside the systems of values current in society, or rather, outside a wide cultural context' (1974, p. 22) is that the incredible scale of splendour and gift bestowal in medieval society no longer appears to be irrational, but is shown to have a logic of its own.

There is a lack, however, in Gurevich's studies. He does not point out the essential differences between the two social systems under study. Neither does he include any discussion of the systematic transformation of the main concepts. Wealth and superiority/inferiority are some of the basic concepts in both social systems. But they are part of different systems. With the Vǫlsunga–Nibelungen tradition as an empirical base I shall discuss these questions.

Conclusion

The transformations which the epic tradition and the social contexts undergo, imply that wealth has several functions in the totality. In Scandinavian societies the family and the 'oðal' were the most important assets in the striving for political position. Family and 'oðal' may be regarded as the internal resources, allies as the external resources. Income was based on one's own farms, trade and plunder, and was the pre-condition for position and power in political society.

In a feudal system the most important asset was the relation to others in positions of power. The political ties had gained importance over the social ties. A position in the political hierarchy was a guarantee of income – taxes received from vassals and commoners.

In the Vǫlsunga cycle wealth is described as concrete objects of kinds usable in social exchange between allies to be or between chiefs and followers. In 'Atlaquiða' King Atle invites Gunnar and Hogni for a feast. His messenger offers gifts to Gunnar and Hogni from Atle if they would come: shields, beautiful weapons, golden helmets, red shirts, horses, several Huns, gold, land, etc.[20] These gifts are refused by Gunnar who says that he does not think that Atle has as much riches as they themselves have. They have seven rooms full of swords with gold hilts and other valuables too.[21] The gifts are refused by references to the possessions of the family. Atle's offer of gifts might be interpreted as part of a social exchange, where he tries to establish ties of alliance to his brothers-in-law. To me, it seems more likely that Atle attempted to make Gunnar and Hogni accept a status of being inferior to himself by offering these valuable gifts. It also must be taken for granted that Atle knew that they would reject this insulting implication that they were less rich and hence less powerful than he.

This passage is important as it demonstrates that power is derived from possession of wealth, and it illustrates which items were used for social exchange and the implications which follow from accepting gifts. Gunnar's reference to his seven rooms with swords and the like also contrasts with the way in which riches are described in the Nibelungenlied.

In the Nibelungenlied, wealth is described as immense masses of riches. Riches are here conceived abstractly as gold and gems in general. The riches are not the means by which one gains political power: they are a basis of prestige and they are mainly used for display. This display and squandering of wealth are expressions of the position one has and not the means by which one gets this position.

In the Vǫlsunga cycle and in Scandinavian society, particular kinds of wealth like rings and weapons were used as means to gain followers, allies and thus political power. Wealth used in this way had an active function, having a part in the formation and maintenance of social relations. Opposed to this are passive riches which are not redistributed or exchanged, and hence do not contribute to the formation of social relations – like the hoard in the Vǫlsunga cycle. When the hoard lost its social significance, even its guard Fafnir lost his existence as a social being, as he, guarding the hoard with no intention of using it socially, turned into a monster.

The contradiction between active and passive riches is functional in the Scandinavian societies. Possession of riches in general is of no use, though it shows that the rich man is a darling of fate. Riches are a precondition for establishing social links outside the family group in the competition for power. Passive riches do not furnish a man with allies; he will be excluded from gaining or keeping a power position. The social use of wealth is to exchange it, otherwise inter-group social relations would wither away.

The relation between what may be labelled active and passive riches is different in the Nibelungenlied and in feudal Europe where it is blurred. In one respect it is possible to claim that a distinction can be made in so far as Gurevich points out (1974, pp. 21–2) that noblemen looked down upon merchants accumulating wealth instead of displaying it. Relative political power is not created by wealth, as the wealth which matters is derived from the political position in society, and not from what one has earned by one's own work. This is the difference between the rich merchant and the nobleman. It is not exchange that creates society. Society organises transfers of goods along specified channels between specific categories of people. Beyond these transfers, the question of active or passive uses of wealth is not of any basic importance.

The Nibelungen hoard as such is wealth in excess. It is a symbol of high position and has no other functions whether hidden, displayed or spent. The hoard need not consist of specific kinds of items, but merely of wealth. It no longer has any function, but may be regarded as a picturesque but stunted relic of the tradition which had had its day by the time of the Nibelungenlied. Fafnir as hoard-guard is not found in the Nibelungenlied. He would have had no function because the opposition between active and passive riches is not important to the feudal system.

Through centuries and under changed social systems the transmission of an epic tradition is on the one hand faithful to the tradition. On the other hand, it keeps its viability as it is perpetually reconstructed to produce meaning for a changing present. It is elements and events which are preserved. But the preservation has not been determined by fidelity to the text, but by the changing relations which ascribe significance to some events and elements, and not to others.

Notes

1. Holtsmark (1970) pp. 224–31, and Dronke (1969) pp. vii, 42–5. The following summary of the Vǫlsunga cycle is compiled from the Eddic lays and the Vǫlsunga Saga.
2. Brackert (1970) I, pp. 265–6, 286–9, and de Boor (1972) pp. v–vi, xlvi-lii.
3. After having left for Huneland, Kriemhild's brothers and their men are called Nibelungs.
4. For a detailed discussion of transformation of social relations and of the concept of transformation, see Vestergaard (1985).
5. 'Reginsmál', prose text and stanza 26.
6. Brót from 'Sigurðarqviða', stanzas 1–4, 'Sigurðarqviða' in scamma. stanza 25.
7. 'Atlaqviða' and 'Atlamál'.
8. 'Guðrúnarzviða' (Qnnor), stanza 10 – Gudrun would have been more miserable had her brothers been killed instead of her husband Sigurd.
9. Nibelungenlied, stanza 1904.
10. The conflicting relationship: sister or wife, is demonstrated in Vestergaard (1984).
11. Nibelungenlied, stanza 343ff.
12. Nibelungenlied, stanza 30.
13. 'Reginsmál', stanza 5 and prose text.
14. 'Fafnismál', prose text following stanza 44.
15. Nibelungenlied, stanzas 1122–5.
16. 'Atlamál', stanzas 30.
17. Brünhild's arrival to Worms, stanzas 560, 568ff, 587–92.
18. Nibelungenlied, stanzas 249–55.
19. 'Atlaqviða', stanzas 4–5.
20. 'Atlaqviða', stanza 6–7.

Chapter 8

The Savariya Paharia: shifting cultivators of the Rajmahal Hills

Ajay Pratap

Preceding chapters have concerned the relationships between history and symbolic meanings. Equally, however, economic systems are forged within and create particular histories, as is demonstrated by Pratap in this chapter. Like Moore (Chapter 9) Pratap points out the inadequacy of general categories. The term 'shifting cultivation' has been widely employed for prehistoric economies. But to what extent are its structure and archaeological indicators widely comparable? The Savariya society in India today has been used as a model for Neolithic 'shifting cultivation'. However, it can be shown that the nature of the Savariya economy is linked into other economic and social systems involving domination and interference from the outside. There is little that is 'pristine' in their economic strategy. When set into its context of present-day and historical processes and into the context of the particular expectations of anthropologists, this example of shifting cultivation can be seen to be a particular historical product. Colonial influences and the activities of money-lenders have produced a set of circumstances within which shifting cultivation is carried out. Similar criticisms can be made of other societies which have been taken as examples of general economic categories, such as hunter-gatherer. Like the Savariya, these have been shown to be very 'modern' in nature, affected by a long history of external intervention.

A long time ago during the *Ingreji Raj* [The British Empire], one day the sahib (District official) summoned us to discuss our problems. So we went to see him. We talked about various things, then finally we came to the subject of *khallu* (shifting cultivation). He said to us, "Why do you people keep moving here and there and cutting new forests. Why don't you, like the Hindus, stay in one place and cultivate the land?" One of us replied, "Sahib, while doing *likha parhi* [revenue book-keeping]

why do you keep taking fresh sheets of paper? Why don't you keep writing on the same piece of paper again, and again and again?" We were soon told to return to the hills.

  (Chongdo Paharia's oral testimony, collected in 1984)

Introduction

Models for early agriculture, from Asia to Europe, have a noticeable tendency to gravitate towards shifting cultivation as a likely model for Neolithic revolution food producing strategies. That this cultivation itself remains poorly understood is the initial emphasis of this essay. Characteristically, the archaeologist trying to use shifting cultivation to generate a model for pre-settled agriculture follows a three stage programme:

1. In order to understand the mechanics of shifting cultivation, s/he distils a model from a mass of reports and monographs. However, this agriculture, wherever it is available for study today, presents a very complex structure, not easily amenable to functional definitions.

2. From these readings s/he tries to operationalise or to find a suitable set of indicators (such as decline in species of trees, burnt patches of land, and so on) which may be recognisable in archaeological deposits.

3. Then, finally, comes the act of survey and excavation. From one simplification to another, practically nothing

remains in the archaeological model which has much resemblance to the historically derived complexity of ethnographic instances of shifting cultivation. In this series of problems this essay sets itself the limited task of examining the first: how is the archaeologist better to understand shifting cultivation?

Central to the appeal that shifting cultivation has as the predecessor of early settled agriculture (as in Northern Europe) is its predicated archaic form – both its 'anti-surplus' (Sahlins 1972) mode of production, and the consequent absence of 'state' in its historically recorded development. Thus, although examples occur (see Bronson 1978) where it is associated with considerable societal complexity – Tikal (Maya), Angkor (Khmer), Prambanan (Javanese), and Anuradhapura (Sinhalese) – its 'stone age' affiliations have provided prime time characterisations (e.g. Sahlins 1972). In the evolutionary sequence of economic complexity, shifting cultivation systems seem to appear and exist only so long as they are required to convert primal forests to mixed secondary forests. Thereafter, having created the possibility of plough agriculture, and destroying in the process the ecological bases of their viability, they decline and disappear silently like the woolly mammoths, to the nether world of sediments and pollen charts. Rowley-Conwy's criticisms (1981) of slash and burn hypothesis (Iversen 1941; Clark 1952; Iversen 1973; Steensberg 1980) for the origins of agriculture in Neolithic temperate Europe are of immediate relevance here. He argues, convincingly, that shifting cultivation in Neolithic temperate Europe was unlikely. More significantly, he also argues that a reiteration of the slash and burn model is based largely on the archaeologist's primary quest for finding a 'Primitive and Archaic' economic practice to place at the 'head of the sequence' that culminates in settled agriculture. One may well ask how the archaeologist, without primary ethnographic experience, not only accepts but abets the idea that contemporary shifting cultivation, on which archaeological models are inevitably based, is a primitive and archaic practice? It is, therefore, important to comprehend the methodological nexus that seeks and creates the primitive and archaic, where the "primitive totality which formed social anthropology's traditional object – the tribal microcosm – is rapidly disappearing and will, within a few decades, entirely cease to exist" (Banaji 1970, p. 85).

Ethnoarchaeological studies of the economics of shifting cultivation have not yet got off the ground. Hence, biases inherent in the intuitive translation of contemporary shifting cultivation systems into archaeological models have escaped criticism. Unlike hunter-gatherer ethnoarchaeology, which is both profuse and, of late, sensitive to 'historical' checks and balances (Schrire, 1980), an historically aware ethnoarchaeology of shifting cultivation is yet to come into its own. Scarcity of fieldwork has denied the archaeologist the knowledge of the modern transformed basis of this economy, and the potential significance of this to the archaeological understanding of the dynamics of this agriculture. This transformation has, in most cases, come about through the economic contact of shifting cultivators with either feudalism and/or colonialism.

Explanatory generalisation about shifting cultivators in anthropology (Conklin 1957; Freeman 1955; Leach 1954; Vidyarthi 1963) have been based on perceptual approaches that disregard the recent history of the studied group. We encounter, repeatedly, cultivators who exist, seemingly, in splendid isolation. Others have found substance worth analysing only among those cultivators who are, it is implied, still in their pristine state, having stayed outside 'native-reserves' (Sahlins 1972, p. 42). Contrarily, the argument has to be made that a reserve-like situation, of externally imposed economic and social relations on essentially autonomous economic systems, has come about historically, even in non-colonised nations. In Thailand, which was never colonised in the same way as India, the 354,387 shifting cultivators (FAO/UNFPA Thailand 1980) have, today, to contend with state policy no less restrictive than in colonial and post-colonial India (for a historical analysis of pre- and post-British forestry in India, see Guha 1983). The possibility of pre-colonial structure of shifting cultivation being any more pristine must await historical research. Meanwhile it is important to underline the fallacy of intuitive and *a priori* extraction of the 'Neolithic' from current systems of shifting cultivation.

This essay, arising from research which is still in progress, is a discussion on the Savariya, a 'Scheduled Tribe', who live in the Rajmahal Hills of the Santal Parganas district in the State

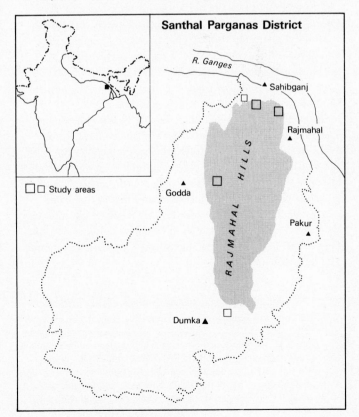

Fig. 8.1 The Santhal Parganas district

of Bihar (see fig. 8.1). By outlining the reconstruction of their history in the past two hundred years, the aim here is to address the *preconditions* of making direct historical analogies, rather than to demonstrate a test for locating shifting cultivation in the archaeological record. In this respect the general argument of the essay is that both shifting cultivation itself, and the evolutionist views governing its archaeological application, when contrasted with the course of historical developments within this economy, need to be thoroughly reconsidered.

The Savariya, although classified as a Scheduled Tribe, and for census enumerations considered a distinct ethnic group, appear not to have as distinct an 'identity' as it has been traditionally assumed (see Pratap 1987). The questions being raised in this essay form only part of the research on the archaeological sites which came up in the course of my site survey. The survey itself was carried out in what forms substantially the Savariya territory on the hills. This essay, then, outlines the results of an ethnohistoric investigation into the Savariya past, which was undertaken as a preliminary step towards formulating a working model for the Rajmahal Neolithic. The primary area of study is located in northern section of the hills (fig. 8.1), in the vicinity of villages: Baragutibera, Jhokmari, Demba, Hathidari, Marikuti and Pachrukhi. Visits were also made to the north-eastern (Targacchi) and southern (Sundarpahari, Gando) parts of the hills to gain a wider appreciation of the regional context.

The Savariya dialect, Malto, has been considered by Grierson (1927) to be the northernmost occurrence of the Intermediate Dravidian. It is by linguistic means, as also the fact that they are the only shifting cultivators existing, since antiquity, in the middle Gangetic region, that Savariya have been historically 'visible' since the mid-eighteenth century. The larger identity, 'Paharia' (meaning 'the people of the hills'), subsumes two other sub-identities – the Mal Paharia (39,950 individuals) and the Kumarbhag Paharia (7,568 individuals). The Savariya, numbering around 53,576 individuals (census 1981), are the largest of the sub-groups. On the question of the sub-identities, Sarkar (1933) has raised the possibility of the dispersal of the original Paharia in the north, on account of the military oppression which ensued when the hills first came under colonial jurisdiction in c. 1771. It is suggested, although on weak evidence, that they have inhabited the hills since the time of the Greek traveller Megasthenes' visit to the imperial Mauryan court in 302 BC.

Colonial and post-colonial projections of the 'primitive'

The hill man is much shorter than the Santhal, of a much lighter make, is beardless or nearly so, is not of a cheerful disposition, nor is he so industrious; his great delight appears to be attending the neighbouring markets where decked out with beads and chains, his hair fastidiously combed, oiled and ornamented, he will in company with his friends both male and female, while away the greater part of the day. Labour is the hillman's abhorrence but necessity compels him to cultivate a small portion of his land for his actual existence; beyond this trifling labour he never exerts himself. He will nevertheless fish or hunt or roam over miles . . . but to have to clear away the forest for his crop he considers a great hardship.

(Sherwill 1851, p. 555)

The candour with which Colonel Sherwill set about this description is perhaps the most recurrent and revealing element of the colonial prose on the Savariya. The colonial impressions, survey records, sketches, essays, notes and even an ethnographic novel used here cover the period c. 1770–1910. Viewed in relation to one another, even though the personality of each author provides interesting diversions, there is a perceivable stratigraphy of the successive refinement of the discourse on the 'primitive'. About the 1780s, the understanding of Savariya ethics and ritual is couched in metaphors which, to say the least, are a mixture of the Bible and the Bacchanal. Hodges, an itinerant English artist visiting the hills in the company of Augustus Cleveland, the colonial official credited with the first 'pacification' of the 'hill-men', was so moved by the spectacle of their annual buffalo-sacrifice, which he calls the "rites of Bacchus", that he "could have wished, for the honour of the fair sex, that these latter excesses had been restricted to the men" (Hodges 1793, p. 92). In contrast, Lieutenant Shaw, in a rare exposition of Paharia morality, brings to life their gods in first person: ". . . God answers, 'I saw that you behaved well, and kept my commandments; I will exalt you; in the meantime remain with me'" (Shaw 1807, p. 35). Even in the 1820s when the so far amorphous 'mountaineers' or 'hill-men' had been 'civilised' through the efforts of Cleveland, we find Colonel Francklin invoking the "inhabitants of the boundless wastes of Tartary" and the "Scythians" (1821, p. 8) as contrasts to the Savariya, for the benefit of the intrepid readers of the Calcutta Annual Register.

The growth of a more exhaustive study of the 'tribe' in India begins from the mid-nineteenth century, by which time the so-called tribal areas had, in political terms, simmered down from large-scale movements to 'insurgence'. In Santal Parganas district, which was itself born from the 'Jungleterry districts' after the great Santal 'Hul' of 1856–7, the settling down of colonial prose and imagery comes after this upheaval. The idyll of a devastated land provided, nevertheless, a fertile setting for the creation of ethnic stereotypes. With the growth of the tea gardens of Darjeeling, Duars and Assam, the Savariya and Santhal were transported, among many others, as plantation labourers. In the wake of the plantations, there now grew a pragmatic prose that marks the differences between the early cloyingly romantic one and one which is closer to the beginning of the twentieth century. Now we find Risley preparing exhaustive typologies of the 'People of India' (1908), while the Chairman of the Tea Districts Association exhorts newly recruited plantation managers with his bootleg version of Frazerian anthropology. In the *Hand-Book of Castes and Tribes of India* (Crawford, 1928), which was intended to improve the control of the managers over tribal plantation labour, the golden rule outlined is that it is only by grasping their 'culture' that the labourers can be managed better. "In dealing with the labouring classes of India", it explains, "we are dealing with the 'child-races' of mankind; their mental outlook is limited, their religions crude . . ." (*ibid.*, p. 16).

The first most striking tendency of this genre is the preparation of charters of 'Native Institutions' such as local versions of kinship, marriage, religion, totem and taboo, folk lore, customs surrounding birth and pregnancy, ethics and morals (e.g. Shaw 1807). The method used for this was to move directly into recordings of the so-called institutional arrangements, the idea being that the sum total of these specific practices was typical of their 'culture', the structure of which did not constitute a problem. This method of disinterested classificatory research can be explained by the purpose for which these studies were carried out. They were primarily intended to be encyclopaedic accounts for the consumption of administrators, to acquaint them with the people they were governing. The armed suppression of the Savariya 'insurgence' in the Santhal Parganas from 1765 to 1780, the Kol uprising in 1831 in Singhbhum and the 1855 Santhali rebellion had highlighted the need for such information as a means of better control. A second reason for such a method, and the discourse from which it was ultimately derived, is to be found in the immense social popularity of the Victorian naturalist tradition. Organisations such as the Asiatic Society of Bengal reflected this discourse in the prolific publications of the numerous 'observations' made by "naturalists, chemists, antiquaries, philosophers, and men of science in different part of Asia . . ." (Jones 1852, p. 1). Within this 'paradigm', which to Said (1978, p. 6) is "a system of knowledge, an accepted grid for filtering through the Orient into the Western consciousness . . .", lies the critical locus from which the bulk of Paharia documents can be understood, their value as historical documents also being contingent on this.

The now accepted stereotypes of Savariya 'isolation' found classic exposition in Bradley-Birt's 'Story of an Indian Upland' (1905). Forestry and land legislation, preceding and continuing at the time of his travels, were irreversibly 'opening' the non-existent 'isolation' of the Savariya. Despite the benefit of this ongoing spectacle, which is also eloquently embellished, he nevertheless depicts them as: "The most uncivilised of all the aboriginal tribes, [who] looked down from their rocky barrier on the chief highway of civilisation in Northern India" (*ibid.*, p. 3). Also, not unexpectedly, for the benefit of Street's (1975, p. 4) "claustrophobic Victorian drawing room" audience, Bradley-Birt juxtaposes the Savariya with the stereotypic colonial officer, who is, in contrast, "strong, quick to grapple with unforeseen events, fair, impartial . . . responding ably to the call to evolve order out of chaos and to inspire a people who had hitherto known no restraint save their own crude tribal customs and primitive institutions". Naturally, then, they are men "of whom the Empire may well be proud" (*ibid.*, p. 15).

This examination is necessary in so far as we consider it basic to the processes by which shifting cultivation developed into an object of study. To begin with, as far as shifting cultivators marry, produce, and worship, elaborations on them do not differ from similar elaborations of other people who are hunters, fishermen or use the plough. The unifying theme is the idea that all were primitive. Dalton's (1872) *Descriptive Ethnology of Bengal* and Risley's *Ethnographic Glossary* are critical landmarks in the effort of Orientalism to provide a 'fit' between the colonial stereotypes of ethnicity (caste and tribes) and the real cultural and economic variability which to this day confounds simple definitions. "Within this totalisation of colonial anthropology", as Goddard (1979, p. 64) argues, "there is nothing more than the idea of an aggregate of social relations (the social structure), maintained in being by the ongoing 'process of social life'. The primitive totality is merely an empirical whole which has a certain manifest pattern or arrangement, institutional or normative in character."

Post-colonial anthropologists writing on the Savariya have used the previous colonial accounts uncritically, in most cases as an easily accessible 'source'. Hence, the colonial terms of discourse on social structure have had a predetermining impact on them, and shifting cultivation along with its artificially appended social structure has been accepted as an object of study unquestioningly. This simplistic recording of phenomena to some extent survives intact in the post-colonial anthropological studies carried out through fieldwork among the Savariya. It must be emphasised that this inheritance consists not merely of a single 'method', but of a whole language of perception and research. This makes the projections of shifting cultivation of the Savariya mere instances of the larger legacy of the 'colonial encounter' (see Asad 1973). If anthropological 'information' is a product of the contact between the researcher (where the contrast between the colonial officer and the post-colonial anthropologist seems obvious) and the studied group, then a transformation in language should have occurred logically. Pathy *et al.* (1976) in their appraisal of tribal studies in India, have shown cogently the historical persistence of colonial approaches to studying the 'tribe'.

Intuitive functionalism is the main theoretical approach of Mohan (1959) and Verma (1959) who have essentially replicated a gazetteer brand of ethnography. Bainbridge's (1911) essay on Paharia religion becomes, for Verma and Mohan, the vital means of cross-checking their observations even though their own work comes half a century after that of Bainbridge. Their observations also employ the same analytical categories which have been in use since Risley (1892). 'Social organisation' is left to be deduced from a specific treatment of its constituents: marriage customs, puberty rites and so on. 'Economic analysis' is construed as merely elaborating on the various activities in the process of subsistence, such as shifting or plough cultivation, collection of forest product, or fishing. It is completely divorced from any institutional or historical aspects of wider consideration.

What these recent approaches amount to is a 'popular' view of the Savariya reality. As presented in the only monograph on the Savariya (Vidyarthi 1963), this view has some fundamental biases and theoretical limitations. Firstly, in keeping with colonial projections, Vidyarthi dwells on their 'excessive primitiveness', a statement that is more a pejorative assertion than a plausible working concept corresponding to reality. This is justified by the employment of earlier colonial theses of 'geographical and cultural isolation' and by liberally asserting that shifting cultivation as it exists today represents Neolithic behaviour in its modern guise. He says:

> Khallu (shifting cultivation), as is evident from prehistoric as well as ethnographic studies, resembles the primitive method of cultivation and takes us back to the Lower Neolithic (?) period ... it reminds us of the prehistoric transformation from hunting economy to the full fledged agricultural economy ... In the state of Bihar, the remnant of this primitive cultivation is found, on a large scale, among this Maler Paharai.
>
> (*ibid.*, p. 32)

He invokes Childe's (1951) concept of the Neolithic revolution, but his belief that such was the course of events in the history of the Savariya remains to be supported by any actual archaeological evidence, and he obviously does not regard this as necessary. It is amply clear that his 'discovery' of the remnants of a fossil of the Neolithic fulfils a romantic desire to see the past as in some mysterious manner in the present. Excavations have yet to reveal evidence for prehistoric shifting cultivation. A Neolithic dimension, at best, can only be introduced at the level of a hypothesis to be tested, but for Vidyarthi it has a strong rhetorical value, and what starts as a speculative analogy for him becomes real. Inevitably, actual historical evidence points in a different direction.

The problem, for the greater part of my fieldwork, has been to develop sufficient theoretical and empirical bases from which to comprehend the socioeconomic structure of Savariya society. Focussing on the more striking 'shifting cultivation' offsets the importance of the other activities which figure together in their process of production. Savariya hunting, which from Sherwill's sketches (1851) seems to have been a major economic activity, has with the striking decline of the Rajmahal ecology been reduced to mere entertainment for adolescents. In comparison, gathering of forest produce for subsistence and for sale in the neighbouring market has emerged as the fundamental strategy for survival. In fact, gathering and processing of forest goods constitute a strategy that can be considered separately from, but interdependent with, the more noticeable shifting cultivation. In 1810, in the course of his journey through the Jungleterry, Buchanan observed that the Paharia sold to the plains merchants "... firewood, posts, ploughs, mortars, planks, Junera [millet], Makayi [maize], cotton, Bora [beans], orohor [lentils], charcoal, and sabe [*sabai* grass]". In the place of which they bought "... rice, cloth, tobacco, salt, beads, brass ornaments, cattle, milk ghi [clarified butter], oil, fish, dry and fresh, pepper and other seasoning and iron implements" (Oldham 1930, p. 104). The implications of this trade relation, the significance of which seems highlighted by the fact that shifting cultivators were making and selling *ploughs* to the plainsmen, cannot be fully discussed here. But there is today a decline and change within this trade, giving gathering and internal product manufacture the misleading appearance of being a mere supportive strategy. It is, in fact, still the primary means of subsistence for a number of the Savariya. Besides, even for those who depend on cultivation as their primary means of survival, gathering is a year-round, essential activity. This is related to the fact that shifting cultivation in the Rajmahal Hills has not 'shifted' since the first decades of this century. It is now a process that is neither 'primitive' nor 'self-sufficient'. The contradictions that have grown within the Savariya economy, and the evident breakdown of shifting cultivation as traditionally understood, can more appropriately be seen as a consequence of Savariya existence within the larger sociopolitical context, in a historical framework.

Situating the Savariya Paharia

The people of these mountains, and all the hilly country between this place and Burdwan are a race distinct from those of the plain in features, language, civilisation, and religion. They have no castes, care nothing for the Hindoo deities, and are even said to have no idols. They are still more naked than the Hindoo peasants, and live chiefly by the chace [sic], for which they are provided with bows and arrows, few of them having fire-arms. Their villages are very small and wretched, but they pay no taxes, and live under their own chiefs under British protection. A deadly feud existed, within the last 40 years, between them and the cultivators of the neighbouring lowlands, they being untamed thieves and murderers, continually making forays and the Mohommedan Zemindars killing them like mad dogs or tygers, whenever they got them within gunshot.

(Bishop Heber 1828, pp. 195–6)

It is important to mention at this point that the villages of our study were not isolated from other peoples. Though there are considerable distances between their settlements, there are at least two other ethnic groups whose ongoing impact on, and interaction with, the Savariya it is necessary to emphasise. The Savariya villages are located on the plateaus and ridges of the hills and they practise thereon shifting cultivation, gathering and hunting as well as, minimally but crucially, plough agriculture. All shifting cultivation in the hills belongs exclusively to the Savariya. Where there is extensive plough agriculture, mainly on the foothills, but sometimes also on the high plateaus, this indicates the presence of the Santhals, who are mainly wet-rice cultivators. The Santhals, who migrated to this district in the early nineteenth century from Chotanagpur district lying to the south of Santhal Parganas, now live in the valleys and foothills of the range. However, the exact nature of their inter-territorial relationship is, at the moment, not clear. There appear to be no strict restrictions over the Santhals' movements, and even hunting, within the Savariya territory, though this activity frequently results in tensions.

The Savariya have also had a long political and economic contact with the Hindu and Muslim populations of the plains. Of particular relevance here are the lowland money-lenders generically called Mahajans. The money-lenders are cultivators living in the alluvial strip that exists between the northern face of the hills and the river Ganges. Their specific relationship with the Savariya will be elaborated later on. Meanwhile, it can be suggested that Savariya society has remained locked into an exploitative relationship with them since the colonial era when the money-lender first evolved as a middleman between the colonial government and the Savariya. The colonial interest in acquiring *sabai* grass (*Ischaemum angustifolium*), which, though originally wild, is now cultivated heavily in the northern Savariya territory and is used as pulp in paper manufacture, was the context in which the money-lender's role materialised. Until 1909, the Mahajans had controlled the production of this grass, by acquiring long leases for the hillsides where the *sabai* grass grows, and employing the Savariya themselves as labourers. The District Gazetteer (1965, p. 274) records that "the Paharias [Savariyas] became so indebted to them [the Mahajans], that they were practically their bond slaves and received a bare subsistence". It also records that the colonial government, seeing this state of affairs, in 1909 dispensed with the Mahajans as middlemen. But, after four years of government management the production of *sabai* grass dropped and the Mahajans had to be handed back their contracts, if with restrictions.

Today, eighty-odd years later, this relation of exploitation persists. For the Savariya of the study villages, the money-lenders in question are mainly the people of the nearby plains village of Mahadeoganj, although in the course of this study an occasional Santhal, or even a Savariya, was to be found lending at usurious rates of interest. The fact that a Savariya may himself perform the money-lender's role indicates that there are different levels of affluence and associated power within Savariya society.

Savariya economy as a pathological credit economy

It is now apposite to assess the extent to which the ethnographic portrayal of the Savariya is adequate and consonant with the present day situation. A fuller criticism of the study cannot be accommodated here, but we can dwell on the crux of Vidyarthi's studies and main arguments. His general concern with the demonstration of sociocultural integration and stable equilibrium leads to the one basic assertion that the Savariya are functioning in a state of cultural and economic equilibrium. The fact that the Savariya are in the midst of a severe economic and cultural disruption resulting from a prolonged state of dominance, control, and interference from the neighbouring societies, casts doubts on such assertions.

The only socioeconomic survey conducted in the region (Ray 1974) contradicts Vidyarthi's portrayal of the Savariya as an 'integrated' people. We will note some of the survey findings and then tie them together to analyse their meaning and implications for the Savariya society.

1. Today, in terms of occupation, the Savariya are largely associated with agriculture, but also significantly employed as wage-labourers in the lowland agricultural sector, and in mining and quarrying operations within and outside Santal Parganas (Ray 1974, p. 40).

2. The annual per capita production of cereals (maize and paddy) comes to 65 kg, and this by itself is sufficient only for a short time. There is no surplus, but some of the produce is sold because money is required for other purchases. Further, although a tenth of the total production needs to be saved as seeds for the next crop, half of this is given to the money lenders in loan repayment (*ibid.*, p. 36).

3. Loans are taken out for input cost on agriculture and for the utilisation of cultivable land, medical aid, marriage and to avoid starvation. "62.84% of the Savariya are in constant debt to the money lenders" (*ibid.*, p. 70).

4. The survey clearly identifies the firm bond between the Savariya economy and the market economy, which comes about through the sale of forest and agricultural produce (and again, this is not surplus). Indeed, this is so evident that Ray employs in the survey the decidedly unprimitive idea of 'income' in rupees, and examines the distribution along this dimension. It estimates four-fifths of the families of the modal group as using agriculture as a primary or secondary mode of subsistence. But wage-labour and forest produce marketing emerge as the primary or secondary source of subsistence for 66 to 43% of the families (*ibid.*, p. 37).

The immediate implication of the above survey is that the term 'primitive' cannot be used accurately to describe the Savariya economy. Survey findings 1 and 4 suggest that using the term 'shifting cultivators' for the entire Savariya population is inappropriate because a large part of the population subsist mainly on the sale of forest produce and through employment as labourers. Survey findings 2 and 3 are directly related to our argument about the non-independent status of Savariya shifting cultivation and the money-lenders' control over it.

In the villages of this study, agricultural loans are normally taken out at the time of sowing. The lender advances three kinds of loans: cash, grain and a half-cash/half-grain loan. The rate of interest is variable but is normally up to 50% p.a. Inability to repay the loan the same year results in the increase of the rate of interest. The cultivator uses the loan to buy seeds for sowing, as well as to provide food for his family during the 'hunger period', stretching through the months when the fields are being prepared and the previous year's produce has either been consumed or lost in repayment of a previous loan. The crop, when ready, is sold for loan repayment to the money-lender at the low prices that prevail during the harvesting season, even before it is used for eating. The portion sold often includes the quota of seeds for the next crop. This transaction thus makes it necessary for the cultivator to take another loan, and the vicious circle continues, usually until a year when the crop fails and the loan cannot under any circumstances be repaid, leading to the money-lender increasing his rate of interest. Bondage and slavery for the money-lender is then the only means open to the Savariya to 'work off' the debt.

The loan market from which a majority of the Savariya

get their loans is an unlicensed and an unorganised money market. This is so because the local loan market is entirely dominated by private loan-givers (such as the Mahajan) rather than by the government loan agencies. Ray (1974, p. 74) estimates that 83% of the loans taken by the Savariya, for consumption and for input costs on cultivation, are from the money-lender. Government lending agencies account for only 11.57% of the total amount of loans taken. The credit-worthiness of the Savariya is fixed on collaterals like standing crops, future crops, fruit orchards and, in the case of none of these being available, a promise of undertaking unpaid labour on the money-lender's land. The general unmarketability of the Savariya assets in an organised money market leaves their evaluation to the reckoning of the money-lender, who, using his superior economic position, always undervalues them. It is common practice for the lender to use violence and his better knowledge of, and access to, the legal machinery to keep his usurious rates of interest intact. The personal relationship between the Savariya and the lender is marked by the dominance of the latter and is always potentially violent. The Savariyas' perception of the nature of this relationship is very clear, the money-lender's strategies being common knowledge. His consistent efforts to transcend his distinct domain by learning the Savariya language, attending all the festivities and marriages, and professing his function as one of a 'helper' in the time of economic hardship, are, although helplessly, regarded with cynicism by the Savariya. In this instance, Bhaduri's description of the rural money market in Bengal (1977, p. 5), which is "inextricably woven with personal power relations in the villages . . . giving such markets their personalised character" is relevant.

Damin-i-Koh in a historical perspective

In c. 1771, the boats of British merchant capital sailed upriver on the Ganges, from Fort William at Calcutta to Rajmahal, which had recently been wrested from the Mughals after the battle at Oudwanullah. On arrival at Rajmahal, the East India Company found itself inextricably drawn into establishing 'order' over a regional sociopolitical universe which it did not fully understand. The 'Jungleterry districts', as they were then described, were an 'unhealthy', forested and hilly countryside; utterly ravaged and desolate on account of the Bengal famine of 1770, which had reduced its previous lowland population of 18,000 to no more than "a few hundred people" (Hodges 1793, p. 95). Damin-i-Koh (a Persian phrase meaning 'a skirt of hills') seems to have existed as a definite political formation since Mughal times, when it was applied loosely to the area of the Rajmahal Hills and its interlying valleys (see fig. 8.2). Until the arrival of the East India Company the Damin-i-Koh was only nominally divided between revenue areas assigned to the Zemindars (landlords) of the Jungleterry. Its main inhabitants, the Paharia, far from paying feudal dues, were actually at war with the Zemindars. Although colonialism had arrived, it did so with no anticipation of the phenomenal, ethnic, geographic and economic variability of the Jungleterry,

which conformed very poorly to the existing colonial knowledge of Mughal splendour and the wretchedness of the peasant at Calcutta, Murshidabad and even Rajmahal. Neither did gunpowder, cannons and musket charges as forms of subjugation and 'government' meet here with any success. The rationale of the pre-colonial geopolitics and social order, as yet poorly understood, had not entirely declined with the Empire of the 'dark' century. Historians of eighteenth-century India have only recently begun to appreciate and highlight the variety of regional, and smaller, structures that existed for a long time under the Mughal 'state', while retaining their cohesiveness and logic as systems wielding considerable power on the periphery of urban centres. We are arguing, in this research, that the Paharia constituted one among the many other regional power groups. Along with similar groups in the plains, such as the Bhuiyan, they continued to exist as culturally invisible, but controlled from their hilly position the strategic passes and, more crucially, trade, till well after the Company's arrival.

Two central causes of change within Paharia agriculture during the years of colonial rule were derived from profound alterations created within the original demography, ecology and tenurial relations that existed before the arrival of the Company. From 1764 to 1780, Captains Brooke and Browne had dealt with Paharia raids militarily and failed. In contrast, when Augustus Cleveland took over as Collector, from 1780 to 1783, the solution adopted was at a complete tangent from its precursor. The 'Hill System' of Cleveland, which was for 'pacification', involved, in the main, cooption of the Paharia elites through monthly payment of stipends, amounting to a total of 15,000 rupees annually. For the entire Damin-i-Koh the total expenditure was as high as 52,000 rupees annually (Sherwill 1851, p. 606). Political stratification, which among the pre-colonial Paharia was notional and negotiable, became rigid, as the Company set about casting the not unwilling hill chiefs in the image of the lowland feudal Zemindars.

The logic of this policy was threefold. First, this was the only means by which Company's position at Rajmahal could be safeguarded against the event of Maratha raids. The Maratha border, which in 1770 lay just south of Rajmahal Hills, and the successful raids across it in 1742 and 1751 by Balaji Rao and Raghuji Bhonsale, made the question of defence of primary importance to the Company. Major Browne, involved actively in studying the strategy for the Company, aptly summarised the policy to be adopted. He, addressing himself to Governor-General Warren Hastings, pleaded eloquently: "The Mahrattah districts are divided from ours, generally speaking, by an ideal line, the Zemindars on both sides are in many places closely connected . . . If they [the Marathas] offered powerful bribes, while our borderers, generally dissatisfied, are also impoverished, and by no ties united to the state, do you think, Sir, they would have the virtue enough to resist the temptation, or indeed would it be any virtue to do so?" (1788, p. 65). Second, while 'pacification' of the Zemindars, by reduction of rents demanded from them, would strengthen the Company's frontier with the Marathas, the pacification of the

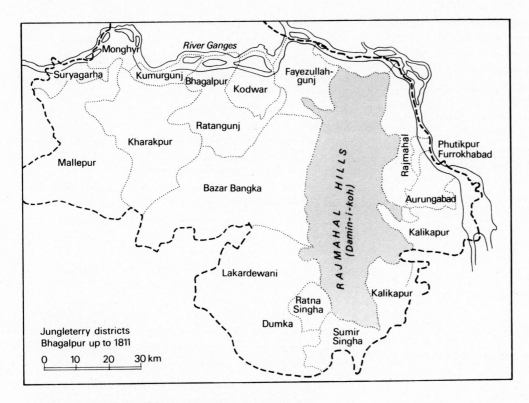

Fig. 8.2 The Jungleterry districts, Bhagalpur, up to 1811

Paharia would allow the rest of the rent settlement operations within the district to proceed unhindered by their raids on the lowland villages. Finally, once the latter was achieved, the Paharia could be themselves persuaded to descend to the plains and take up their new role as a plough cultivating 'peasantry' of the Company which in its own view was now the supreme 'landlord' of Jungleterry.

The latter wish of the Company held no attraction for the Paharia, who had staved off the dire consequences of the 1769–70 famine, by means of their forest based economy. They continued, then, till the opening decades of the nineteenth century, to enjoy the benefits of the 'pacification'. The valleys within Damin-i-Koh remained to be entirely devoid of settlement except for the occasional village of, interestingly enough, the Paharia themselves (Sherwill 1851, p. 576). The Company, for which the payment of stipends now appeared as extortion, while the Jungleterry continued to be far less rent-productive than its potential, looked happily at the windfall solution provided by a most significant population movement. This was the Santhal immigration into the Jungleterry, an event which was in the near future to change the geographical and political face of the district.

The news of the growing tide of Santhal immigration into the southern bounds of the region, from Birbhum and other southern districts, received confirmation around 1810 when Buchanan came across their newly founded villages in Lakardewani (Walsh 1910, p. 30). For the Santhal, who were escaping the "annoyance received from Zemindars" (*ibid.*,

p. 30), immediately south of Damin-i-Koh, a new haven of peace and prosperity was promised within Damin-i-Koh, and the Company hastened to fill the 'peasant' vacuum created by the famine of 1770. This population movement became so important to the Company that its earlier agreement with the Paharia to maintain Damin-i-Koh as a separate rent-free enclave for them was now consciously ignored. The Santhals, who were by 1810 steadily clearing the 'unhealthy' forests, bringing the land under plough, and creating ever increasing villages, were looked upon with extreme benevolence. Santhal villages expanded, filling the inner valleys of the Rajmahal Hills, displacing the occasional Paharia settlement. They also expanded up the foothills, right into what most certainly were the long fallow and buffer zones of shifting cultivation. Boserup has indicated (1966, p. 18) that there is a recurring pattern to the colonial lack of understanding that shifting cultivation requires a constant presence of large uncultivated zones which are of several crucial economic uses, not least to make long fallow possible. The reduction through encroachment in the fallow areas of the Savariya was only too obvious, even though the land use within shifting cultivation was not understood by the Company nor later by the colonial government. This tilted the balance in the favour of the Santhals as far as the grant of and legal recognition of occupancy rights was concerned. Sherwill, surveying the hills in 1851, noted (p. 589):

> The hill-men in my Company on coming within sight of the Sonthal clearings, complained bitterly ... of the

encroachments of their lowland neighbours; they said that the Sonthals were occupying all their vallies [sic] . . . The fact is that the hill-men will not cultivate the valleys and do not like to see any one else cultivate them. Mr. Pontet freely invites the hill-men to take the Sonthals' fields and use the land rent free, but if they do not use the land . . . he immediately allows the Sonthal to take possession.

The necessity of having their own lands demarcated through revenue surveyors, for nominal rents to the government, was the only course now open to the Paharia. This despite the fact that the demarcation package contained within it strict proscriptions on the practice of shifting cultivation, and more crucially on the felling and sale of 'protected' species of trees like *sal* (*Shorea robusta*), teak (*Tectona gradis*), and several other hardwoods. Indeed, this was the basis on which the Santhals were also being settled. The boxing-in of shifting cultivation zones, which the population growth had itself not fully achieved, would now be done by the revenue demarcation, which would also put 'shifting' to a final 'rest'.

The first Paharia villages to be thus settled (ninety-two in all) were in the Pakaur subdivision. Known as the 'Pakaur Paharia settlement' (of 1879) in the documents, this was considered paradigmatic for its 'benefits', as far as occupancy rights of the Paharia were concerned. In 1882, W. B. Oldham, the Deputy Commissioner, seeing the earlier 'success' of the 1879 (J. Wood's) settlement, prepared a draft plan for the settlement of the entire Paharia lands in the Damin-i-Koh. The Paharia headmen who gathered in Dumka in 1882, surprisingly enough, refused to accept the terms of the settlement, which then fell to the ground. By 1895, however, there seems to have been a capitulation to needs of tenurial security, because in that year the headman of eighty-seven unassessed villages applied for and were given settlement. This settlement, while clearly demarcating the territory of each village from the next, further stipulated that shifting plots had to be terraced, and that, while firing the forests, care had to be taken to save "Government Forests from injury" (Walsh 1910, p. 164). Equally significant, this settlement of private property to Savariya holders was an unequal one: the largest chunks of lands and forests were given to the 'Manjhi' (chiefs) who had earlier been drawing stipends and enforcing Cleveland's 'hill-system'.

The question of reserving government forests within Damin-i-Koh, as the second crucial source of change within native agriculture, had arisen with the growing interest in the commercial value of Rajmahal timber, which had till now been exploited in railway constructions only. "There are several advantages", recommended Oldham in his 1882 proposal:

The Conservator of Forests for Bengal has lately visited the Damin and pronounced the forests to be most valuable. One of the advantages of demarcation will be to hand over to the Government considerable tracts of land, which are now unoccupied but if left unresumed may

shortly be encroached upon by the Paharias who now lay no claim to them.   (quoted in Walsh 1910, p. 162)

There was thus no doubt that settlements for land revenue before the mid-nineteenth century and those after were different in this crucial respect. This also explains why despite the fact that they offered security against encroachments that the Paharia continued to be reluctant. That is because, clearly, the reservation of forests would seal off the portion of forests that had till now survived the Santhal migration.

The developments in the demarcation of Government forests in Damin-i-Koh went hand in hand with the overall growth of state forest policy in India. The first Forest Act of 1865, therefore, allowed for the government laying claim to forty square miles of forests, south of the Bansloi river in Dumka subdivision, as 'Reserved' (fig. 8.3). 'Old Reserve', as it came to be known, did not, because of popular opposition, pass under the control of the Forest Department till the first act was revised in the Forest Act of 1878. The Act of 1878 revised the loose control envisaged in its predecessor, by establishing the legal basis, through legislation, of the state's authority to proclaim ownership and control over forests. The attitude to shifting cultivation was itself made very clear (p. 9):

> . . . and no fresh clearings for cultivation or for any other purpose shall be made in such land (except in accordance with rules prescribed by the local Government).
> And further:
> The practice of shifting cultivation shall in all cases be deemed a privilege subject to control, restriction and abolition by the Local Government. (*ibid.*, p. 11)

The 'Old Reserve', at the expense of uprooting forty-eight Paharia villages existing within it, was removed from the domain of all subsistence activities. The use of it, even for cattle grazing, was now considered a punishable offence. As Guha points out (1983, p. 1940), the only provision of the Act of 1865 retained in the Act of 1878 was the one pertaining to the Government's right to arrest offenders without warrants. The full extension of the latter Act to Santal Parganas, Damin-i-Koh especially, was achieved in 1894 when the Paharia lands not already demarcated by revenue surveys were declared 'protected' forests (see fig. 8.3). In 1895 the latter areas, in which the number of protected species of trees was increased, was placed under the control and supervision of the Forest Department. The plight of the local economy was further exacerbated as the 'removal and sale of forest produce by the Paharia raiyats was surrounded by stricter conditions than hitherto obtained' (Walsh 1910, p. 164).

Acting within the limits already described by the Forest Act, the land settlement divided these small village forests into privately owned plots. It followed, then, that all 'shifting' had to be done within the small portions of land held by individuals or families. Quite apart from the core changes caused within the social and economic fabric of the Paharia society by the introduction of private property into the indigenous system of land use based on hereditary use-rights, it is clear that within a

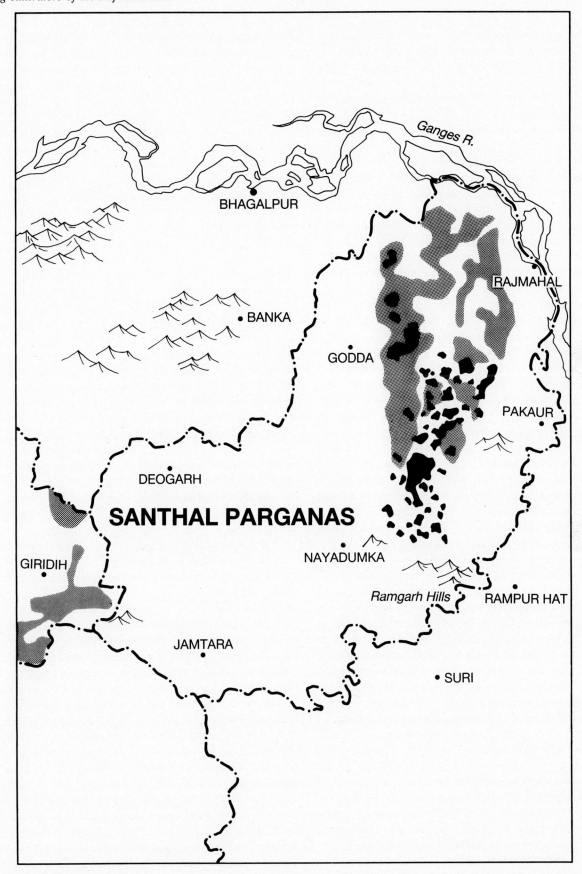

Fig. 8.3 Map of Santhal Parganas, showing government estates, unclassed and private forests (shaded zones) and 'protected' forests (dark zones). Source: A. Decubes (1908)

very small span of time, regular shifting cultivation would result in most Rajmahal forests turning into bush and grasslands, as is the present form. The reduction of the eight to ten year fallows recorded by Buchanan in 1810 (in Oldham 1930, p. 103), to the present three to four years, has therefore a definite historical origin and explanation.

With the land and forest revisions coming into operation, and the government making full use of them, the basic structure of state control and interference within shifting cultivation became legally sanctioned, rigid and permanent. From within, the total fixity of villages and the unequal distribution of property became the catalysts of marked social stratification and of rapid deforestation in the vicinity of settlements. From the outside, the regional immobility created by the reserved and protected zones, and the density of Santhal settlements, left the Paharia stranded in the lateritic zones of their hill-top villages to carry on with an economy now stripped of its life-support mechanism.

A large-scale adoption of the plough and paddy cultivation which is found in association with shifting cultivation today can now be put into perspective. Is this change simply 'evolution'? Or even simply 'commercialisation', which as a rational move for 'risk-minimisation' could be the adaptation thesis in a more sophisticated guise? The conclusion of this field study is that to establish any simplistic evolutionary basis for this change, first of all, one would have to explain away the reality: that shifting cultivation is being practised even when the optimal ecological conditions for its functioning have long since disappeared. The answer to this, perhaps, lies in seeing this not simply as a backward extension of economic principles and facts known to characterise 'Homo Economicus'. There is rather in Uchibori's (1984) sense the need to see economy as related to and determinant of even the identity consciousness of those who engage in it. In Uchibori's view, the loss of the 'economy' is, equally, a loss of identity. In fact, the incorporation of the labour and capital intensive annual cropping within Savariya economy is done with a conscious view to relieving pressure on the 'shifting' grounds, allowing them to regenerate vegetation and fertility. Plough agriculture, at this moment, is a necessary means towards the functioning of the 'ideal' economy: shifting cultivation. Vidyarthi's (1963) observation demonstrates this 'ideal' very explicitly. He recorded that "though they have converted all their lands into *joth bari* (plough lands) . . . still the villagers under force of tradition continue to call them *khallu bari* (shifting plots) in general conversation . . ." (p. 51, emphasis and parentheses mine).

Shifting cultivation among the Savariya

The Rajmahal Hills, described as the 'classic ground for the study of Indian geology' (Ball 1880), stretch for a hundred miles from north to south, and are composed of bedded basaltic traps of cretaceous origin. In the hilly zones of shifting cultivation the primary soil is reddish, and associated with the development of primary and secondary laterites. Although the undulating topography allows for small alluvial nests of a more productive blackish soil (weathered granite-gneisses), these are used for paddy rather than shifting cultivation. There is no indication till 1910, when the Colonial government decided not to bother with "that sterile soil", that agricultural production did not suffice for the domestic consumption needs of the Savariya. Indeed the sale of food crops, in the eighteenth-century Savariya trade with the plains, indicates that production was above the needs and was being channelled into acquisition of goods from the plains. It is also the further evidence, that during the famine of 1769–70 "a very considerable number of lowland population fled to the hills, where the hardy grains of Muckye [maize], Borah [beans] &c. wanting little water, were very plentiful . . ." (Browne 1779, pp. 83–4), that we must accept the present fall in productivity to be of recent origin. Soil-wash (under 54 inches of annual rainfall) and soil exhaustion caused by the increasing permanency and parcelisation of land, are both of late nineteenth-century origin. These factors now permanently inhibiting Savariya economy are, in no uncertain terms, related to the catastrophic ecological decline of the Rajmahal flora and fauna, resulting from the sudden inflation, through immigration, of the low population densities of the eighteenth century. In 1810, Buchanan estimated the population of Lakerdewani, Phutikpur and Kalikapur at 471,300 individuals. Less than a hundred years later, at the time of 1901 census, the population has leapt up to 1,031,421 individuals, a 120% increase. There is, however, a variation in regional densities, where the hilly portions of the district are estimated at 140 per square mile (FAO/UNFPA India 1980, p. 17), and the plains at around 500 per square mile. It is within this new context, then, that the following discussion of Savariya shifting cultivation is situated.

It is not every individual in the Savariya society who can farm his own land, and the significance of this need hardly be underlined. Scarcity of cultivable land has given rise to tenurial relations that are not even considered as being likely in shifting cultivation systems, i.e. tenancy and even landlessness. The wide occurrence of both of these within Savariya agriculture has been recorded by both Vidyarthi and Ray. Separation from land, the primary means of production, surely further disqualifies Savariya agriculture as a primitive one. Further, even though fallow land might be available, the initial capital investment that goes into the buying of seeds, hiring of the community work team to carry out the task of weeding, sowing and harvesting, as well as the capital needed to maintain oneself and family through the period when no substantial food resources are available, prevents a few from having their own fields cultivated.

All descriptions and estimates provided are for a plot of one acre, which is the more commonly selected size. Only a few families in comparative affluence reckon in terms of plots between three and five acres. There are, in this respect, starker contrasts. Almost every village of this study has one or two families that hold over a hundred acres of land and cultivate about forty acres every year. This fact, which has little

Table 8.1. *Agricultural calendar*

Stages	Approximate dates
Cutting the jungle	2 Feb–30 March
Burning the jungle	Feb, March, Apr
Burning the remainder	Feb, March, Apr
Clearing weeds (I)	15–20 May–30 June
Sowing seeds	15 June–15 July
Clearing weeds (II)	30 June–30 July
Clearing weeds (III)	10 July–10 Aug
Watching crops	Sept, Oct, Nov, Dec
Harvesting	Oct, Nov, Dec

analylical significance in Vidyarthi's study, will be discussed in the following section.

The main Savariya crops consist of maize (*gangi*, *tekallo*), beans (*kusre*, or *barbatti*), lentils (*rahar* and *suthri*) and millets (*nanto* or *bajra*). Each plot receives a fixed proportion of all the seeds. The time schedule for the successive stages of the cycle is shown in table 8.1.

The selection of a fresh plot for cultivation is based on several microgeographic and vegetational factors. From the total area available for cultivation, the plot that has already been exhausted, and the area overgrown with *khur* (a long-bladed wild grass used for roof-thatching and basketry) are not considered. *Khur* is an essential raw material, and also clearing it requires additional costs. Of the remaining area, the land adjoining the previous plot, especially if it has a substantial forest growth, is considered ideal. Experience has it that the plot with biggest trees gives rise to minimal weed growth after the monsoons, and is in the long run the most cost-effective. Although the choice of a plot is also regulated by its proximity to the village, a somewhat distant but good plot causes a nuclear family to shift, and build a temporary home next to the site selected for cultivation. Keeping in view the property settlements mentioned before, the question of villages shifting, amoeba-fashion, does not arise. The only instance of a village shifting recorded in the course of this study was on account of frequent infant deaths, and not for gaining new forests for cultivation. Even in this instance, the new village was constructed within five hundred yards of its previous location.

It is believed that felling of the trees, or *darrinirpahara*, helps to protect the crop. Most trees, except the fruit-bearing ones, are cut down, on the principle that if the trees are left they would take all the nutrition from the soil and leave nothing for the crop. After the larger trees have been felled, the bushes are cut next, and then left to dry for at least one month. The timber is taken away and sold, but a small quantity is left lying there to be burnt when the jungle is set on fire. At the end of the month, when the cut wood is dry, the forest is set on fire, with no obvious means of control. The burning is erratic and the fires die out in a few days. The weeds which normally survive the burning, and the incompletely combusted wood, are then managed with the help of hired labour. The wage-labourers, who are in all cases Savariya themselves, uproot the weeds (*palhamari*) and gather the unburnt wood into heaps and burn them a second time. This second burning is known as *gaggappehhe*, after which the cleared plot is left alone till the pre-monsoons arrive in April. The overall shape of the plot is not predetermined, its final contours resulting from the periodic visual estimates which the cultivator makes, when felling is in progress. Therefore there is a considerable variation in plot shapes (see table 8.2).

The pre-monsoonal showers bring along a fresh weed growth. Since sowing is not done till mid-June, the weeds invade the plot considerably and have to be removed. On this occasion, however, the weeds are not burnt but uprooted and left to rot in the rain-drenched soil, to provide manure for the crops. This stage is very important because if the weeds are not uprooted now, then *nikowni* (weeding when the crop has started growing) will have to be done soon after the sowing. Completing the weeding beforehand leaves the workers more time to relax between the sowing and the next two weedings.

To initiate sowing, or *kalchakkai*, the first seeds are planted in by the husband and the wife, as a symbolic gesture, after which the rest of the family share the task. For plots larger than an acre, a larger work-force is solicited from the village. Sowing is done exclusively with the aid of digging sticks or *jugri*. These have iron tips, or are simply wooden sticks with sharpened points. In each hole punctured, two or three seeds of maize, one each of beans, lentils and millet, are sown. Some space is arbitrarily maintained between the holes. It is believed in relation to sowing that if the seeds are sown next to the stumps of trees, they grow into strong plants and will not fall in storms that are frequent during the monsoons (see table 8.3).

The third (mid-monsoonal) weeding, or *nikowni*, is carried out when the crop are a foot or so above the ground, and the weeds sprout up again. Before this weeding is carried out, the cultivator has to slaughter a pig exclusively for the consumption of the work-force. Although this is customary it is not at all mandatory. If the cultivator does not have the means to provide this feast, usually no boycott is made. What is more rigid is that each cultivator has to pay ten rupees to the headman, which goes to an inter-village community fund maintained for festivals. Fifteen days after the third weeding, a further weeding is sometimes necessary. This is less expensive than the previous one even if labour is hired, as the weeds are not very thick or large and can be rapidly uprooted by hand. This final weeding is done in mid-September, by which time the heavy monsoon dissipates, leaving the crops to grow freely.

The next two months, October–November, are spent watching over the growing crops (*khallkappe*). A temporary shelter, overlooking the fields, is built for this purpose. Some cultivators retain residence in the village, watching only in stretches, while nuclear families sometimes shift permanently to the fields till the harvest. Usually it is the adolescent males who, armed with bows, arrows and drums, are assigned the task. Threat of damage to the crops from wild boars,

Table 8.2. *Preparing a plot from the forest (all estimates for a one acre plot)*

	No. of people normally required	Hours per day	No. of days required	Total time spent (hours)	Calendar schedule
1 Cutting the forest (*Darrinirpahara*)	27	Less than 8	Less than 1	108	Early Feb to end Mar
2 Burning	1	1.5	Depends on the weather	—	Feb, Mar, Apr
3 2nd burning	8 to 10	4	3	32 to 40	Soon after above, before the rains start
4 Weeding (*Palhamari*)	27	4	2 to 3	216 to 324	Middle May to middle June, after the first showers

Table 8.3. *Sowing*

No. of people normally required	Hours of work per day	No. of days required	Total time spent (hours)	Calendar schedule
27	4 to 5	1	108 to 135	Middle June to middle July

Table 8.4. *Weeding*

	No. of people normally required	Hours per day	No. of days required	Total time spent (hours)	Calendar schedule
Weeding (II) (*Nikowni*)	10	4	8	320	15 days after sowing, end June to end July
Weeding (III) (*Nikowni*)	5–8	4	5	100 to 160	1.5 weeks after the above, early July to early Aug

Table 8.5. *Watching over crops*

No. of people normally required	Hours of work per day	No. of days required	Calendar schedule
Done by the family	24	3 months	Sept, Oct, Nov, Dec

porcupines, bears and sometimes an enemy, requires a constant vigil. Small, locally made explosives have proved effective deterrents for the occasional snooping boar.

At the end of November, those farmers who have sown earlier in the year, begin their harvesting (*torre*). However, before any of the new crop is harvested or eaten, *eddovay* is performed. This is a sacrifice dedicated to the ancestors and the divine *khallgosain*, who have together preserved the crops. A goat or pigeon is sacrificed at the edge of the field. Though maize matures and is harvested first, sometimes the beans are ready before it, and have to be plucked. However, the plucking of the beans is not associated with any ritual, maize being the only 'sacred' crop of the harvest. Maize is followed by that of the beans, lentils and finally the millets. Millet is reaped with a light sickle to avoid dispersing its seeds. This sequential harvesting lasts for about fifteen days, and the task is managed without hired help. The plant stems remaining in the field serve as fodder for the domestic goats, cows and pigs. They are also used as building material for houses, or sold in the market. Usually, however, the stems are stolen by the constantly fuel-starved plainsmen or the Santhals.

Normally some grain is stored for the next year's sowing. Together with this, an extra stock is stored for consumption in the 'hunger period' which sets in just before the next season of sowing. Occasional loans to families in dire need are also made from this. Within two or three days of the harvest, if not on the same day, the money-lender comes up to collect his due.

Labour, land and 'landlord'

The labour pool for all cultivation-related tasks is the village itself. However, the seasonal migration of kin living elsewhere in the hills, to help their original families on specific agricultural tasks, is also frequent. But there is no evidence of plainsmen being inducted into any of the agricultural tasks in the hills. The labour for most cultivation-related tasks is organised within two forms, the household and kin, and community work groups. The household labour by itself suffices for very few of the plot-related tasks, the most significant of which is watching of the crops. Community-level labour, which consists of *bewa* (reciprocal unpaid labour) and *majuri* (wage-labour), are the main form of labour deployment which can ensure the successful completion of the cycle, from forest felling to harvest. For instance, weeding, as shown in tables 8.2 and 8.4, requires a labour input far above any other activity, and is clearly impossible without a community-level work group.

Historical sources do not mention *bewa*, although oral testimonies locate it as the oldest and the 'traditional' form. *Bewa* can be solicited from the village by a cultivator at any stage during a year's cycle. This entails, very simply, that all households of the village send one worker to donate labour, for a day only, to the cultivator's plot. At the end of the day's 'free labour' the work team does in fact receive payment, in the form of 250–500 grams of rice and 50 grams of lentils each. Especially when *bewa* is performed at mid-monsoonal weeding or sowing, it is customary that the cultivator whose lands are to be worked on slaughters a pig for the consumption of the work team. This, however, is still seen as not constituting payment. Also contained within this is the guarantee of reciprocal labour for each member of the work group, when their cycle is under way. Thus whenever *bewa* is solicited each household is sure to send a representative. This system is dependent on the social ties that are maintained between a cultivator and his kin, and also with the rest of the village.

Bewa, being done on the first day of any particular task, helps only the start of the operation. The completion of these jobs, such as sowing or harvesting, is then dependent on at least some of the previous work group returning as hired hands. *Bewa* is obligatory, but wage-labour is not. Most often, working on a hired basis helps to supplement the meagre household budgets, and therefore labour is mostly available. The existence of *majuri* (although not by this name, which is really a plains terminology for wage-labour) can be traced back to 1810, when Buchanan observed that "Rich men occasionally hire people to sow and reap . . . [who] get two paisas, or the value in maize . . . In harvest they will gather forty to sixty baskets of ears of which . . . they get one for their own labour" (in Oldham 1930, p. 137).

Although *bewa*, in contrast to *majuri*, has a flavour of pristineness, this impression fades away when set in the context of the unequal distribution of land and other means of production. As the main consumers of the labour potential of any given village, the largest landholders stand to benefit the most from any labour form that is based on 'obligation'. The existence of *bewa*, which is obligatory, and even wage-labour, which can be made obligatory, are to the benefit of the Savariya 'landlord' who depends, more than any others, on the yearly deployment of a large work team. It has been noted earlier on in this essay that money-lending is not restricted to the plains lenders. This is, in fact, a very crucial point. The lenders within are none other than the large landholders, who have customarily advanced seed and grain loans to poorer members of the village, claiming interest on them which are no less than the Mahajans'. The qualitative difference, definitely present in this internal loan-network, is that the usury is masked, if not more humanely articulated than that of the Mahajan. It is also elusive, to the casual observer, or to research that sets out to find an egalitarian 'tribal' system.

The constant presence of the Mahajan, as a lending competitor to the Savariya 'landlord', has some interesting consequences. For the landlord himself, while engaged in the same relationship, the need to project himself as different and well-intentioned means that he uses methods of persuasion other than violence for loan recovery. The need to keep the Mahajan away, means that he has to lend even to those who are not credit-worthy, merely to demonstrate the essential difference between him and the Mahajan. By presenting a better option than the Majahan, and by extending regular loans despite the uncertainty of recovery, the landlord can make even wage-labour on his enormous shifting cultivation plots obligatory from his 'clients', the perpetually indebted Savariya smallholders. Further, with the increase of Savariya population, the landlord has 'settled' cultivators on his land as his own tenant farmers, thereby creating 'goodwill' and relations of obligation.

It emerges, even from this brief discussion of Savariya economy, that even though economics based on hunting, gathering and shifting cultivation are practised today, the contemporary basis on which each of these is organised makes it necessary to assess them in their modern context rather than proclaiming them as miraculous survivals of the past. That, denies us the knowledge of why and on what basis they continue to exist within the twentieth century, which, to say the least, is antagonistic to their proper functioning. The case, therefore, for shifting cultivation being "perforce a study of adaptation" (Kirch 1978, p. 105) is rather weak. In the approach suggested in the latter study, shifting cultivation, 'defined' a priori, is clinically removed from the nexus of inter-territorial economic relations in which it is naturally found and logically entrenched. It is then suspended, for a 'diachronic' analysis, in a theoretical but sterile t1–t2 time space which seemingly replicates 'history'. In the final analysis, then, the ultimate dynamics of shifting cultivation becomes a process of its adaptation within progressively altered environmental loci, which causes the system to alter its structure to minimise 'risk'. But what, then, is to be concluded from the fact that 200 million people in the tropics and subtropics continue to practise it even today, when the 'fit' between 'organism' and 'habitat' was lost centuries ago? Why despite the new forces regulating 'adaptation', such as the uniformly found 'state' antagonistic to its proper functioning, have the actual numbers of cultivators increased?

History, ethnographic reality and shifting cultivation

The methodological shift towards history (ethnohistory) as a necessary prerequisite in the process of constructing analogue models either for testing or for the interpretation of the archaeological record is essential, although it obviously extends considerably the archaeologists' involvement in the ethnographic realm. Charlton (1981), in his review of the genealogy of the 'interface' in question here, argues that history, as in 'ethnohistoric data', has long been applied in archaeology for the construction of what are known as direct historical analogies. It is our contention that a greater proportion of the actual 'interface' consists of a hit or miss, or 'piecemeal' use of ethnohistory where the focus of

archaeologists' attention is merely a particular event or archaeological feature about which historical information is available. Binford's seminal 'Smudge pits . . .' (1967), despite its theoretical input, clearly makes very limited use of documentary evidence, or ethnohistory. In considering the use of ethnohistory, therefore, it will be useful to make the distinction between the scales at which historical data and analysis are being envisaged. Going beyond the question of hypothesising about specific features of the archaeological record, to the level of 'economy', for instance, it is impossible to see how the ethnographic record could be more appropriately examined for its structure and coherence, than by looking at it historically. There is in this respect a qualitative difference between the terse, unproblematising entity – the ethnohistoric data base – and an historical study.

Last but not least, relating history to archaeology also involves the additional questions that must then be put to the existing ethnography. The problems arising from an insufficient historical dimension to the works on the Hanunnoo of the Philippines (Conklin 1957), the Iban of Sarawak (Freeman 1955), and the Kachin of Highland Burma (Leach 1954) can here be briefly indicated. Conklin classifies the general occurrence of shifting cultivation into two significant types – partial systems, and integral systems. He emphasises that the difference between them lies in the partial type having "strong sociocultural ties outside the immediate swidden area into which they bring permanent-field agricultural concepts of land use and ownership . . ." (Conklin 1957, p. 3). The integral systems are those that carry on their operations along isolated and therefore independent patterns such as pioneering (reclaiming new forests). First of all the whole notion of integral systems seems doubtful because of the common colonial past of most of the areas in the tropics and subtropics where shifting cultivation occurs. Even if direct colonial contact did not affect these systems the local, neighbouring populations would undermine their integral status. It is of moment to note that even in the integral Hanunnoo system there are definite signs of paid labour (Conklin 1957, p. 54). Although this exists in a smaller ratio to the traditional community form, does its presence indicate incipient commercialisation, contact with settled agriculturalists, or that the largely integral system is changing into the partial? In fact, what Conklin asserts to be two different types of shifting cultivation may well have been successive stages, historically, in the same area. Freeman and Leach note the element of contact and interference in the Iban and Kachin societies. But the all too brief notice of this historial fact seem to be largely insignificant to their main enterprise of discussing the realities of these contemporary systems. Leach (1954, p. 25) notes that the 'past political events' could well have created the local concentration of population which resulted in a 'substantial' shortening of the ideal fallow period of twelve years and a declining fertility. But this rupture is not of any analytical significance in the rest of the study. Freeman (1955, pp. 11–26) records that the land ownership of the Iban underwent considerable change under the impact of the colonial resettlement, but that this would have had some fundamental effect upon the structure of shifting is not incorporated in his analysis.

To conclude, it will be appropriate to look at the recent criticisms of the archaeologist as a mere consumer of ethnographic data. Wobst (1978), Schrire (1980), and Hodder (1982b) have emphasised the need to see the contemporary context in which traditional forms of subsistence exist as analytically important. Schrire's (1980) attempts to reconcile the image of San hunter-gatherers as presented in ethnography with the historical reality lend considerable support to the argument being made here. She argues that the San are not as isolated as they sometimes seem and their economic strategy has only recently remained locked into hunting-gathering. Historically, the San sometimes kept stock, sometimes lost it, their subsistence depending on changing political, social and environmental circumstances. The reason, therefore, for the San still being seen as replicates of primitive hunter-gatherers is to be found in the strong evolutionary bias that characterises Lee and DeVore's (1976) study. Wobst (1978) stresses that the 'silence' that ethnography maintains about the conflict and harmony of the studied group with its neighbours deprives it of a regional perspective, and all phenomena are attributed to the most local and internalised stresses, resulting in what he terms a model of parochial causation. It can now be suggested that parochial causation as well as stereotypic portrayals of traditional economies can be overcome only from a perspective which assumes that their present form is complicated enough to make a historical approach necessary.[1]

Note

1. While the shortcomings of the paper are entirely my own responsibility, its present shape owes a lot to the several criticisms of F. R. Allchin, Mihir Shah, Nandini Rao, Ian Hodder, Gina Barnes, Keith Ray and Sunil Chander.

Acculturation, diffusion and migration as social-symbolic processes

Chapter 9

Problems in the analysis of social change: an example from the Marakwet

Henrietta Moore

This paper is concerned with the process of modernisation in traditional societies, a topic of widespread relevance in archaeology since 'modernisation' is a process that has occurred throughout history as different cultures have interacted with each other, often on the basis of differential power. In this instance, Moore is specifically concerned with 'westernisation' amongst the Marakwet in Kenya. She argues that even if acculturation appears similar (because similar items are adopted), the processes of change may be very different, in different concrete historical traditions. The Kapsowar area in Marakwet has seen colonial and missionary interventions for seventy years, although young and old view the varied changes and influences differently. The economic independence of the young, linked to the privatisation of land, has undermined the communality of labour and land holding which underpinned the authority of the elders. Also, the involvement of men in wage-labour outside the area has led to a greater dependence on wives for the maintenance of the household, land and stock. But in this new situation the patriclan is actually reinforced in relation to the selection of marriage partners in order to maintain control over women as wives. This is an example of 'continuity through change'. 'Change through continuity' is seen in the way that the use of modern, western items within the traditional bridewealth system has created a demand for individualised capital and economic success. Displays of wealth provide a new base for male prestige and status.

Introduction

There is a considerable body of literature concerned with the study of social change in colonial and post-colonial Africa. A substantial proportion of this work has been preoccupied with 'Europeanisation' or 'westernisation', a phenomenon sometimes referred to as 'acculturation'. In spite of the diversity of indigenous African societies and of the colonial impact upon them, an implicit tendency has emerged in the literature to assume that the general features of the process of acculturation are known. In this article, I want to argue that generalised notions like acculturation do not actually help to explain processes of social change, and that this is especially true of post-colonial Africa. In spite of very significant differences between colonial Africa and the successor states, it would appear that essentially the same conceptual frameworks are used for the study of social change in both contexts. This is partly because the indices of social change – for example, electrical and manufactured goods, 'western' clothes and foodstuffs, square houses and household furnishing – are a recognisable feature of changing life-styles in both colonial and contemporary contexts. However, similarities in the indices of social change should not be allowed to mask the potential differences between the processes of change they represent. An additional reason for continuity of approach between the colonial and post-colonial periods is the fact that many of the modern state institutions and administrative structures have necessarily strong links with their colonial predecessors. It would of course be a mistake to assume that this is always so, since the transition from colony (or protectorate) to nation state has often been both abrupt and bloody. A valid argument for continuity of approach can certainly be made, but I would suggest that it is an argument which must be established and not assumed. Furthermore, even when the validity of such continuity has been proven, the value of generalised notions like 'acculturation' and 'westernisation' for the explication of social change should still be strongly questioned.

'Acculturation' and 'westernisation'

I want to discuss the notions of 'acculturation' and 'westernisation' in tandem because in much of the relevant literature on Africa the former is taken to correspond to the latter. The concept of acculturation is not well defined – as befits a broad and trans-historical construction – but a number of processes are normally implied in the use of the term: for example, culture contact between groups, emulation, borrowing and the possible absorption of one group by another. The idea of some hierarchical relation between the groups concerned, often with an implicit notion of 'progress', is also frequently understood: hence the identification of 'acculturation' with 'westernisation' in the case of colonial and independent Africa. Since the notion of progress is strongly implied in the term 'westernisation', an easy dichotomy with 'tradition' and the 'traditional' is established. This dichotomy overlaps with other sets of contrasts: for example, rural/urban, traditional/modern, tribal/detribalised, customary/progressive and past/present. These contrasts are not of course absolutes, but are part of a general 'evolutionary' scheme which places industrialisation and urbanisation at the most developed point in such a progression. Terms like 'westernisation' and 'detribalisation' are therefore used to refer to the workings out of such a scheme in the context of African society.

My main criticism of the concepts 'acculturation' and 'westernisation' is that they do not provide a sufficient theoretical basis for an explanatory model of social change, because they do not specify the concrete historical conditions within which change takes place. Furthermore, the 'smaller-scale' activities – like emulation and borrowing – which comprise the larger process of acculturation carry with them a number of assumptions which effectively hinder an understanding of their historically specific forms. Both Banton (1961, p. 121) and Magubane (1971, pp. 424–6) have criticised the assumption that the adoption of certain 'European' goods and behaviour by Africans was simply 'the emulation of the way of life of the socially dominant Europeans' (Mitchell and Epstein 1959, p. 211). To see the adoption of certain 'European' items as a straightforward desire to emulate Europeans is misleading. Many of the studies which use 'Europeanisation' as an index of social change have been concerned with urbanisation and the growth of 'urban elites'. The value of such a concept when studying urban communities is in doubt (Mariotti and Magubane 1976, pp. 254–8), but its significance for a study of rural African groups is even more questionable. A second, and very important point, is that the process of 'westernisation' or 'Europeanisation' cannot be considered as continuous from colonial times to the present day. However 'westernisation' may or may not be defined, it is

clear that it means something very different in relation to the existing nation states than it did during the colonial period. In the material which follows, I discuss the penetration of industrially manufactured goods into a rural community in Kenya and argue that an understanding of this process must be based on the particular historical context of the group concerned – the ecological and political context, as well as the cultural. In order to understand how specific items and activities are taken up and why, it is necessary to link such 'choices' to the social strategies and possibilities of the group concerned, rather than to the external structure of 'European' prestige. The use of 'western' styles and artifacts as 'symbols of legitimation' is a complex process which cannot be explained in terms of the mere imitation or emulation of foreign models. In order to explain social change it is essential to specify how the changing values and opportunities which material 'westernisation' signifies are linked to the intervention of alternative social, economic and political relations.

My second criticism of generalised notions like 'acculturation' and 'westernisation' is that they lay undue emphasis on exogenous forces of social change. The most obvious manifestation of this in relation to Africa is the opposition of 'westernisation', and all that it implies regarding progress and modernisation, to the notions of 'tradition' and the 'traditional society'. In both Marxist and non-Marxist evolutionary schemes, capitalist and tribal societies are ranked hierarchically. The progression from one to the other is not necessarily thought to be straightforward or unilinear, but it is nevertheless thought to be a progression. The result in African studies is a more or less established link between 'westernisation' and 'detribalisation'. The process of social change – of becoming modern – is somehow analogous to the deconstruction, if not the actual destruction, of the 'tribal' way of life. The concept of 'detribalisation' brings immediate problems because it predicates the study of social change on a number of disputed – and sometimes discredited – assumptions and ideas.

The concept of the 'tribe' has been severely criticised by anthropologists for its over-simplicity and incoherence (Fried 1967; Leach 1954; Southall 1970). But in spite of such criticisms it remains, as Arens has pointed out (1976, p. 65), "a conceptual mainstay" of the discipline. This is not the place to detail the arguments concerning the concept of tribe or the related discussion on ethnicity, except to raise two points which affect the study of social change in colonial and post-colonial contexts. Firstly, it is now accepted by scholars (cf. Arens 1976) that many 'tribes' in Africa, and other parts of the world, are of recent origin, having emerged as a reaction to colonial rule. The existence of self-defining groups, whose members recognise that they share a core of practices and beliefs with an acknowledged degree of historical continuity, is not in doubt. What is in doubt however is whether these groups fit into the European model of a tribe and whether their changing relations with colonial powers and national governments are best understood as a process of 'detribalisation'. Secondly, the emergence of defined entities called 'tribes', with their associated 'traditional' practices, encouraged an idea that 'tribal life' was essentially unchanging. In fact, the notion of the traditional nature of 'tribal life' was advanced by colonial administrators, who often stressed the value of continuity of custom, while at the same time complaining of apathy and stubbornness. The result has been that studies of social change have tended to focus on the impact of 'westernisation' and on exogenous forces of change. The implication is that traditional indigenous societies are essentially passive and respond primarily to change from outside. Many anthropologists have been at great pains to reject this view of a 'static equilibrium' (e.g. Bailey 1969; Gluckman 1958; Leach 1954; Parkin 1978; Moore and Myerhoff 1975), but it is nevertheless pervasive enough to have moulded the study of social change by characterising indigenous, rural communities as "mired in tradition" (Arens 1976, p. 5). The result has been a view of 'acculturation' which stresses the impact of the 'dominant' colonial and national 'cultures', but which pays relatively little attention to the dynamic, strategic responses of rural communities.

The idea of indigenous communities as 'passive' or 'static' has tended to encourage a particularly restricted perception of the process of 'cultural borrowing'. Van den Berghe argues (1964, p. 64) that "much of what is sometimes interpreted as culture borrowing is in fact the result of internal readaptation to change". The idea of 'borrowing' as indicative of 'detribalisation' or 'cultural absorption' is problematic. The adoption of certain items or practices and the abandonment of

others may be part of a strategy to maintain group cohesion and identity, rather than an attempt to emulate or become identified with other groups. The main point here, as Gluckman (1958) first pointed out, is that the effect of change may paradoxically be either to make things different or to ensure that they stay the same: "continuity through change; and change through continuity". Parkin uses an example of changes in burial custom to point out that when we talk of continuity and change it is important to distinguish between (a) the persistence of certain practices in changing circumstances, and (b) changing practices which are actually designed to maintain key attitudes and strategies (Parkin 1978, p. 21). Studies concerned with 'acculturation' and 'westernisation' tend not to consider these sorts of distinctions, except to divide aspects of 'cultural life' into areas which are thought to be more or less susceptible to the forces of change: for example, belief systems are often thought to be more resistant to change than political structures. The idea of resistance or susceptibility to change is always portrayed as structurally or psychologically determined because the impact of individuals or groups in the construction of change is rarely taken into account. It is in emphasising that the construction of change may be part of individual or group strategies that it becomes possible to comprehend how changes in the material world are linked to changing values and opportunities and thereby to alternative social and economic relations. The case material which follows is based on my research among the Marakwet of Kenya and provides an interesting example of some of the points I have raised in this first section.

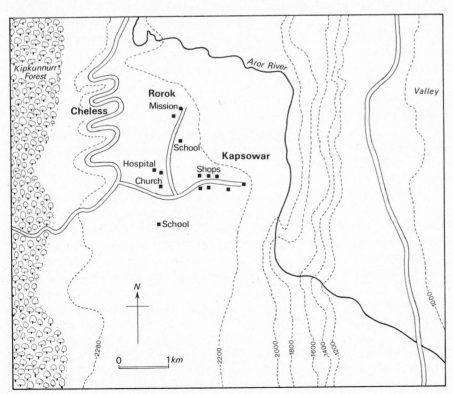

Fig. 9.1 The location of Cheless and Rorok villages

The Marakwet

The Marakwet are a Highland Nilotic-speaking group, who live in the Cherangani hills and along the western edge of the Kerio valley in north-west Kenya. Prior to the colonial period the Marakwet did not exist as a single, coherent unit ('tribe') and the word Marakwet is a corruption of the term Markweta, which originally applied to only one section of the present day group (Kipkorir and Welbourn 1973, p. 1; Sutton 1973, p. 6). The Marakwet number about 81,397 persons (Kenya Population Census 1969: vol. 1) and occupy approximately 1,595 sq km in the adminstrative district of Elgeyo–Marakwet in the Rift Valley Province. Within this area there is a marked difference between the well-watered highlands of the Cherangani range and the semi-arid environment of the Kerio Valley. This article is based on research carried out in two villages adjacent to the settlement of Kapsowar in the Cherangani hills region (see fig. 9.1).

Kapsowar lies close to the Aror river, between the Kipkunurr forest and the edge of the Kerio escarpment, at an altitude of approximately 2,300 m. The topography of this area has had a very decisive effect on settlement patterns. The western direction of the drainage has produced a series of ridge and valley systems which cut the terrain into rounded nazes, divided from each other by steep sided valleys. Most of the settlements are to be found clustered along the tops of the ridges, while the sides and floors of the multitudinous valleys are used for cultivation. Each cluster of family compounds forms a defined social and topographical entity (a *kor*), which may be termed a village. In the past each village would have been occupied by a single patrilineal clan group or by one or more lineages of a particular clan – depending on the size of the lineages. Informants continue to speak of clans and lineages as though they are residentially localised, whereas in fact, due to land registration and enclosure and the clearing of former forest land, clans and lineages are now somewhat mixed. However, it is still possible to say that most villages have a single minimal lineage as their core, even if the rest of the village is made up of people from different lineages and clans.

The Marakwet are a patrilineal society, where marriage is virilocal and the basic unit of consumption and production is the household. Villages are made up of a number of compounds, consisting of one or more houses and a number of related structures enclosed within a defined space. Each compound is occupied by a single household, comprising a man and his wife or wives and their children. Sometimes households also include an elderly relative or a child who has been sent to help the family. The people of the Kapsowar area have a long history of contact with governments and missions, both past and present. As a result, the area has experienced a considerable degree of change in the last seventy years. In the section which follows I describe how ecological, historical and contemporary circumstances have defined the process of social change. In so doing, I take the acknowledged indices of 'westernisation' – industrially produced goods, 'modern' household items and square houses – and I show that the process of 'acculturation' can be understood only with reference to the changing values and concerns of the Marakwet themselves.

The historical background

1912–13 was the first year of colonial adminstration in Marakwet District. At this time Elgeyo and Marakwet were administered as separate districts and the government station for Marakwet was established at a place called Marakwet, later to be renamed Kapsowar (Marakwet Annual Report 1933). Kapsowar (Marakwet) was – and remained for some years – the only government station in the district, and was considered both small and remote. In an effort to reconstruct some of the history of Kapsowar and the surrounding area I have relied for my information on the colonial records and on the testimony of informants. Both these sources have their problems, but the colonial records in particular are very patchy and eclectic in the material they present. In the main these documents cover such items as stock numbers, agricultural problems, climatic fluctuations, land issues and judicial and fiscal matters. In addition they sometimes contain haphazardly acquired information on 'tribal' customs and beliefs, as well as comments on the Marakwet's relations (often ambivalent) with other tribes and the colonial government.

During colonial times the whole Marakwet district was a Native Reserve which was bounded on the north and west by the gazetted 'highlands'. These were the famous 'White Highlands' of Kenya – large areas of land leased by the government to white settlers, first on terms of 99 years and later (amidst great opposition) on 999 year leases. However, none of these farms lay close to Kapsowar, for between them and the government station came a large part of the Cherangani hills and a certain area of Native Reserve Forest.[1] It was not, therefore, the proximity of the white farms which had the greatest impact on the Marakwet, but their consistent demand for native labour. The importance of such labour to the white settlers is clear, and the question of labour emerges from the colonial records as a persistent theme. In the first Annual Report from the Marakwet district the following hope was expressed:

> Their numbers are too small for them ever to affect the labour supply of East Africa, but in the next two or three years it is expected that they will make an addition to the local labour supply on the farms in the Trans Nzoia and the northern end of the plateau nearest their houses.
> (Marakwet Annual Report 1912/13)

However, it was not until just before the Second World War that a significant number of Marakwet were employed in regular out-labour, and in 1950 it was still possible to say that the main attraction of employment for the Marakwet was "good feeding" (PC/RVP/3/1/2. Handing Over Reports, 1944 and 1950). The Marakwet's apparent dislike of out-labour was always considered by the colonial administration to be the produce of a close attachment to a particular way of life, as well, of course, as being the inevitable result of apathy. "Their

chief desire was and still is to be left undisturbed in their hills":
this and similar statements provide a common theme which
links many of the colonial documents (Marakwet Annual
Report 1912/13). In spite of the concern with employment as
an index of 'progression' – not least because it provided the
"natives" with the means to pay their hut and poll taxes – it is
very difficult to establish what the actual number of
out-labourers from any particular part of the district was, at any
one time.[2]

It seems probable that quite a high proportion of men
would have served in the army, given that 97,000 Kenyan
Africans served in one capacity or another during the Second
World War (Clayton and Savage 1974, p. 232). But
unfortunately, information collected during my research forms
an insufficient basis from which to draw firm conclusions on this
matter. In the two villages I sampled, nine men of *kaberur*
age-set (c. 60 years) and older were interviewed: all of them
had either served in the security forces or had worked for
settlers, three had done both. Obviously this sample is not easy
to assess, since it says nothing about what proportion of men of
this age-group worked as labourers, soldiers or policemen.
However, the people of Kapsowar say that they have a long
history of working for the 'Whites' and/or the government.
When enquiring about the history of governmental and
European influence in the area I was frequently told that many
local men had worked for white settlers, and that there had
been – and still is – a consistent flow of young men out of the
District to join the police and the army. Research from another
Marakwet group has also confirmed that the people of the
Kapsowar area are well-known for their involvement in
'out-labour' of various kinds (Moore 1983b).

The African Inland Mission (A.I.M.) and Marakwet attitudes to change

In 1931 Elgeyo and Marakwet were amalgamated into
one District and in 1933 the government station at Kapsowar
(Marakwet) was closed and the buildings sold to the A.I.M., on
condition that they provide some sort of medical service for the
area (PC/RVP/2/4. Marakwet Annual Report 1931; and
Elgeyo–Marakwet District Annual Report 1933). Apart from a
Roman Catholic outpost attached to the school at Tambach,
this was the first mission in the District. A minister, Mr
Reynolds, and a nursing sister immediately took up residence in
Kapsowar (Marakwet) and work began straight away. In 1934
Marakwet was officially renamed Kapsowar and the mission
took over from the government as the main European presence
in the area. This was also the year when the first trading centres
were gazetted: one at Tambach, one at Kapsowar and one at
Chesegon (Elgeyo–Marakwet District Annual Report 1934).
From a small beginning, both the trading centre and the
mission hospital flourished. In 1938 the Annual Report notes
that it was unfortunate that 'the A.I.M. hospital at Kapsowar
had no resident Doctor after April, as Dr Ashton reports that
the Marakwet were just beginning to use the hospital for
maternity cases' (Elgeyo–Marakwet District Annual Report

1938). However, relations between the Marakwet and the
mission were not always easy, particularly over the question of
circumcision. Successive assistant District Commissioners note
the mission's intolerant attitude to circumcision and point out
that this prevented many Marakwet from making use of
educational and medical facilities provided by the mission.[3] In
1939 the Annual Report notes that the A.I.M. bush schools
were failing to attract more than a handful of pupils, "this
failure must be attributed in some measure to their [the
mission's] antipathy to circumcision, a ceremony which plays a
large part in the lives of these people" (Marakwet Annual
Report 1939).

In spite of problems the A.I.M. continued to expand its
activities and by 1950 it was possible for the District
Commissioner to write:

> the A.I.M. at Kapsowar has a strong contingent. One
> surgical specialist, one G.P. (a rugger International), two
> nursing sisters and teacher cum social worker (Miss
> Halliday). Attendances have gone up enormously here
> and the locals have shown their appreciation by providing
> money for a water supply to the very inadequate hospital.
> (Handing Over Report: Carson, Simpson, 1950)

It would be quite impossible to say exactly which
institutions and which policies have had the greatest impact on
the people of Kapsowar over the last seventy years; but I would
suggest that the colonial government, the army, the police, land
enclosure, compulsory primary schooling and waged labour
have been some of the most important agencies and/or results
of change. Until the last decade, the greatest external pressure
for change was surely that stimulated by the advent and
intervention of the Europeans . In the seventy years since
Europeans first came to Kapsowar, their most enduring
presence has been in the form of the A.I.M. mission, its
hospital, schools and churches. This is a fact borne out by the
attitude of the older generations, who feel that many of the
major changes which have affected their lives have been due,
either directly or indirectly, to the 'white man'. This
identification of the Europeans with change itself is
unsurprising, but is reinforced by an oral tradition which
divides the recent past into 'before' and 'after' the 'white men'.
There are, however, two further reasons for the conceived
homology between Europeans and social change. The first is
the very specific impact the missionaries had – or tried to have –
on certain Marakwet practices and beliefs. The Marakwet, like
the other Kalenjin peoples, were very resistant to any attempt
to interfere with circumcision and equally unhappy about the
attitude the church took towards polygamy. It should be said
that the colonial government itself was very much against
mission attitudes to circumcision, but in areas like Kapsowar
where (at least after 1933) the European presence was
maintained almost entirely by missionaries, there was little it
could do. To this day the situation is difficult and the present
African Inland Church continues to take a very strong stand
against female circumcision. While it is true that in recent
years, with the increasing influence of western education and

culture, some Marakwet girls have begun to refuse circumcision, all the informants I spoke to in the Marakwet region claimed that circumcision was still the main area of disagreement between themselves and the 'whites'. By condemning circumcision the church was not merely attacking the 'traditional' belief system of the Marakwet, but was actually striking out at an institution which supports two very important structural features of Marakwet society: namely, the power of the elders over the young and the control of women's productive and reproductive potential by men (Moore 1983a).

The second reason why the Europeans are identified with change is that with the advent of colonialism there came a very significant change in the material basis of Marakwet life. This change was expressed in many ways, but as far as informants are concerned, the three most significant changes were opportunities for wage-labour, land enclosure and the influx of western goods. Even at the present time, the people of Kapsowar maintain that, along with education, it is the continuing developments in these areas which bring about some of the most significant changes in their lives. Questioning informants in Kapsowar I found – not surprisingly – that change could be expressed only in either structural or material terms. By this I mean that either change was discussed in terms of its impact on behaviour and beliefs, or it was expressed in terms of changing life-styles and standards of living.

Attitudes to change are complex and tend to vary slightly from group to group. In Kapsowar this is most noticeable with regard to the difference between old and young. If the older generations identify change with the colonial government and the church, the younger generations see change in the context of a developing Kenya which is becoming increasingly industrialised and commercialised. It is not easy to summarise the different positions, but the older generations do seem to view change in terms of its relations with the past, while the young use change to preserve their vision of the future. These different attitudes to change are crucial in any attempt to understand the conflicts and tensions which shape modern Marakwet society, and they will form a common theme in the sections which follow.

Labour and land: economic change in the Kapsowar area

In the past all land was owned by the clans, even though the usufruct rights to individual plots were inherited through the male line. Grazing land was held in common and all members of the clan had the right to graze their animals anywhere within the clan land. In the Kapsowar area problems with land enclosure were not particularly marked until the 1950s. The colonial government recognised that the elders were 'an indigenous authority with a particular function as a land authority' and were, therefore, aware that tension between elders and young men would be expressed in terms of conflict over land issues (African Affairs Department, Annual Report 1951: ch. 3). In fact, in 1953 the District Commissioner wrote, "the main challenge to the elders' authority comes from the young men who want to enclose the high grazing land on the escarpment to form small holdings while the elders wish to preserve it as communal grazing" (Elgeyo–Marakwet District Annual Report 1953). The colonial government's own attitude to land enclosure and registration was somewhat confused and was often further complicated by an inadequate knowledge of traditional systems of land holding. In the Kenya Land Commission Report for 1933, it was stated that the regulations governing tenure of land in the native reserves should be built up on the basis of indigenous customs (Kenya Land Commission Report 1933, p. 420). In line with this attitude, the report went on to suggest that the actual registration of right-holdings in the native areas (apart from Kiambu District) would be premature and that a policy of simple demarcation should be adopted where necessary. Nevertheless, this did not prevent the Commission from stating its support for what it saw as an emergent trend towards the private holding of land (Kenya Land Commission Report 1933, pp. 423–5, esp. 423, section 1663). This half-and-half policy was followed throughout the colonial period in Marakwet District, where land registration did not actually get under way until after Independence.[4] However, nearly all the land in the Kapsowar area has now been registered.

The break-up of the traditional land holding system in the Kapsowar area has affected the organisation of settlements and the strength of the patrilineal clan group. The increasing fragmentation of residential clan groups and the privatisation of land holdings has encouraged the individualisation of production and reproduction. The emphasis is now on the household rather than on the community of the lineage or patriclan . In many ways, of course, the present day mode of production reflects the past. The family is still the basis for agricultural work and the individual household surrounded by its land (*shamba*) is still the locus of economic activity. In this sense the pre-colonial roots of social organisation and traditional land tenure systems are still discernible. However, the household is more isolated as an economic and social unit than it was in the past and, as a result, within the household the social relations of labour have undergone a profound change. The communality of labour has declined, partly because of the disappearance of communal grazing land and partly because wage-labour and education have had a considerable impact on the allocation of work and responsibility within the community. Traditionally such allocations were made according to age and sex as principles of differentiation, and these divisions were also crucial for the allocation of tasks and responsibilities within the individual household. Some of these features still exist, but age as a determinant of work responsibilities has declined in importance because of the increasing importance of non-agricultural labour and an increasing emphasis on education/qualifications rather than on age as such. Thus, young men with salaries are less dependent on their fathers and are able to set up their households as independent units of production much earlier than in the past. The economic independence of the young and the privatisation of land have undermined the communality of labour and land holding which underpinned the structure of the clan and the authority of the elders.

Within the household the sexual division of labour has also undergone a certain amount of change, particularly in response to the introduction of cash crops and the increasing compulsion to produce agricultural surplus for sale in the marketplace. Hitherto, the family land had been serving subsistence needs and sometimes producing a little surplus for the market. The present situation is that there is an increasing separation between subsistence agriculture and market produce as spheres of production. While this process is still only in its embryonic stages in the Kapsowar area, it has meant that women's work load has increased. Women still have to supply the food for the family, as well as providing labour for cash and market crops. This has had an impact on gender relations, since for the first time unpaid family labour relations are involved, not just in subsistence activities, but in work processes with a marketable value. Once labour has a market value then the nature of communal work is affected because in this new situation labour can be used for the accumulation of private capital. This shift in the nature of labour relations within the family ties the woman more firmly to her husband, since he now has a commercial interest in the control of her labour, as well as an interest *vis à vis* production and reproduction within the family unit. But, the present day structure of the sexual division of labour does retain some of its previous features; for example, men are still concerned more with livestock than crop production. However, men do have new roles and these are primarily defined by the increasing compulsion to earn cash and by new systems of prestige which are associated with 'western', industrially manufactured, goods.

Western goods as indices of change

> Before the white man came there was no sugar, tea or bread . . . 'modern' items came with the *wasungu* (white men); *mongwo* (gourd container) has now been totally replaced by *kikombe* (mug). Traditional items are fewer and will soon disappear.
> (Kapsowar informant)

The first introduction of 'western' goods in the area was associated with the arrival of the Europeans. The identification of 'western' goods with the 'white man' is still so strong that many older informants will say "things of the white man" when they merely wish to refer to an item as industrially produced. This homology between the European and the modern is hardly remarkable and is merely another way of expressing the intimate relationship, which the Marakwet perceive, between the Europeans and certain aspects of social change. The following extract illustrates the point:

> The ways of the grandfathers have gone. In the house modern items have replaced old ones. In the past there were two types of cups – one for men and one for women. Men were not allowed to drink from the woman's cup. Nowadays everything is mixed up and you don't get the same cup twice. In the past there were also

two *kosum* [water pots] – one for the circumcised and one for the uncircumcised.

The informant is bemoaning the passing of certain status distinctions based on age and sex. In traditional Marakwet society these distinctions were particularly salient with regard to eating and drinking because only people of the same status could eat or drink together. The sharing of food was considered to be a statement of equality and communality. By linking the introduction of modern items with changes in traditional custom, the informant illustrates the point that material changes in Marakwet life have been accompanied by changing values and behaviour. As far as the Marakwet are concerned 'western' goods may be understood as being indicative of change in two senses: firstly as the physical replacement of traditional goods and foodstuffs, and secondly as the material expression of changing values and social structures. This dual sense is not difficult to grasp and is exactly what is implied in the phrase 'a changing life-style'.

If 'western' goods somehow symbolise change in general, they are also explicitly linked to two other forces of change, education and wage-labour. It is unsurprising that the Marakwet – like the anthropologists – should link 'western' items with other agencies of acculturation, of which education and wage-labour must surely be the most formidable. The task of analysing the transformation and commercialisation of the rural community with regard to its increasing integration into the emerging capitalist system is beyond the scope of this article. I shall therefore restrict myself to a discussion of the way known 'forces of acculturation' (education and the necessity to earn cash) have encouraged the 'adoption' of certain 'western' traits and goods as part of a strategy for coping with changing circumstances. I shall illustrate this discussion with reference to the organisation of domestic space and the concomitant changes in the range and type of household items.

The changing organisation of domestic space
Sample choice

The villages of the Kapsowar area are defined geographical and social entities (see above). I chose two villages for this study, Cheless and Rorok. Each village is occupied (at least, ostensibly) by a minimal lineage of the *Kapiosei* clan, although Rorok also contains members of the *Siaban* and *Kabitok* clans. The links between the two villages are strong and the lineage affiliation is not completely clear cut. For example, there is one man who lives in Rorok, while his eldest son has one compound (for his first wife) in Cheless and a second (for his second wife) in Rorok. These villages lie on each side of the main road and therefore face each other across a small valley. Rorok is contiguous with the modern centre of Kapsowar and occupies an area of land immediately behind the mission (see fig. 9.1).

The villages of this area usually occupy hill ridges and the settlements are clustered along the spine of the ridge, so that the sides and floors of the valleys are left free for cultivation.

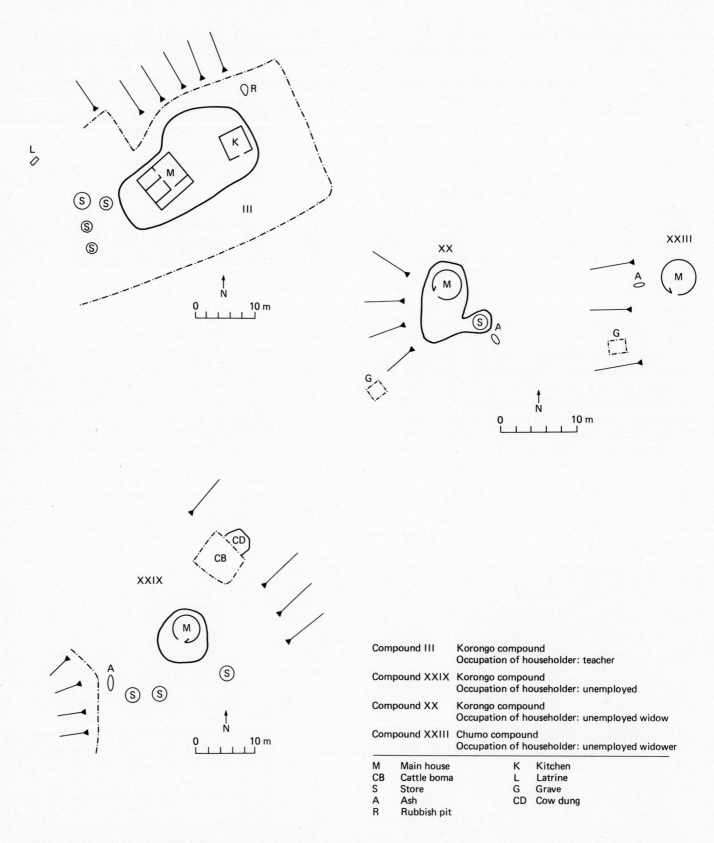

Fig. 9.2 Compounds of individuals aged 55–70 years, showing the position of structures and refuse areas, and the variation in compound size and house type according to age and occupation of householder

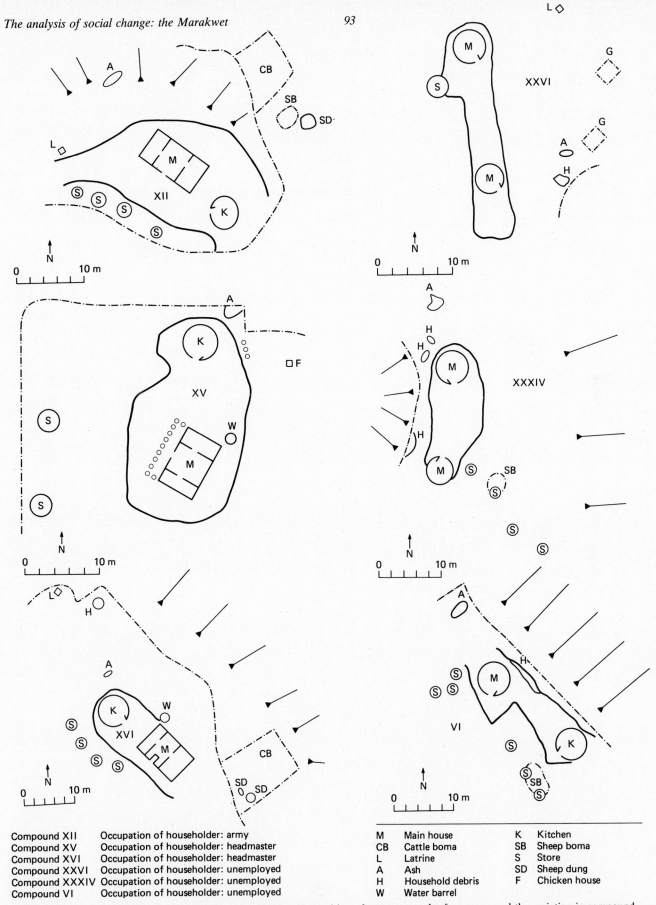

Compound XII	Occupation of householder: army		
Compound XV	Occupation of householder: headmaster		
Compound XVI	Occupation of householder: headmaster		
Compound XXVI	Occupation of householder: unemployed		
Compound XXXIV	Occupation of householder: unemployed		
Compound VI	Occupation of householder: unemployed		

M	Main house	K	Kitchen
CB	Cattle boma	SB	Sheep boma
L	Latrine	S	Store
A	Ash	SD	Sheep dung
H	Household debris	F	Chicken house
W	Water barrel		

Fig. 9.3 Compounds of individuals aged 40–55 years, showing the position of structures and refuse areas, and the variation in compound size and house type according to age and occupation of householder

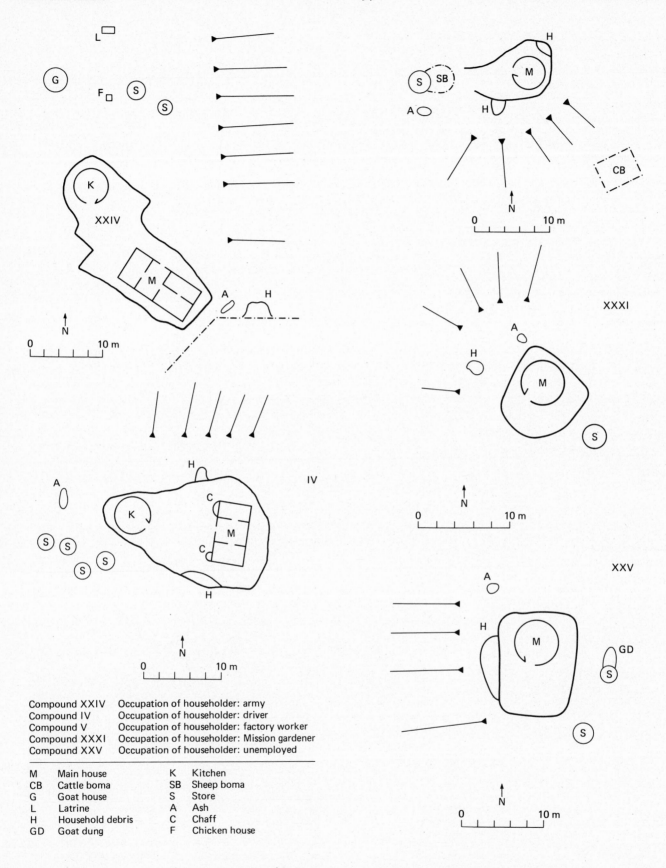

Fig. 9.4 Compounds of individuals aged 25–40 years, showing the position of structures and refuse areas, and the variation in compound size and house type according to age and occupation of householder

Both Cheless and Rorok are sizeable villages and occupy more than one such ridge. I therefore decided to take a vertical half kilometre transect through each village, in order to cover the houses clustered along the spines of two ridges. In the case of Cheless, the longitudinal dimensions of the transect were defined by the road on the one hand and the edge of the forest on the other. In the case of Rorok, the length of the transect was determined by the position of the road and the boundary with the mission (see fig. 9.1). Taken together, there are a total of thirty-five compounds within these two transects and these compounds constitute my sample.

The decision to base my sample on the villages of Cheless and Rorok provided me with an opportunity to study compounds so close to the mission that they are contiguous and yet be able to compare them with compounds a little distance (approximately 1 km) away. I found that the immediate proximity of the mission had a negligible effect on house form, house contents, land use and type of employment. In all other respects – principally, proximity to the road, historical development, size, settlement composition and size of land holding – the villages are extremely similar and there are no major variables which affect their comparability.

The shape and form of compounds

Each compound is occupied by a single household, comprising a man and his wife or wives and their children. Unlike the compounds of other Marakwet groups (see Moore 1983b), the shape and orientation of the compounds in Cheless and Rorok are not primarily determined by topographical features. However, compounds do tend to have a linear form based on the arrangement of houses and are always placed so that the land slopes away from one of the long sides of the compound (see figs. 9.2, 9.3 and 9.4). Comparing the shape and form of compounds is complicated by the fact that since land registration more and more compounds have been fenced. This produces a situation where the houses occupy a cleared area, usually oval in shape, while all other structures (stores, latrines, etc.) may be placed anywhere within the fenced area. This means that individual structures may be dispersed over quite a large area and that their position in the compound is consequently much more variable than is the case with similar structures from other Marakwet groups (Moore 1983b). House types and the presence of certain structures, like latrines, can be correlated with the age and occupation of the household head. The compounds in figs. 9.2, 9.3 and 9.4 show this correlation well, and it is immediately clear that the old and the unemployed have smaller compounds, with traditional round houses and fewer structures. There are employed men who still live in round houses, but they have bigger compounds and bigger houses than their unemployed peers.

Informants say that in the past compounds contained one house for the man and one house for each wife. Nowadays houses are no longer divided according to gender principles, but instead they are distinguished on the basis of function. There are two reasons for this change. The first is that the government has been very concerned about the ill-effects of sleeping and cooking in the same house and has encouraged families to build separate kitchen houses, in order to improve health and hygiene. The second reason is that many families in the area have built square houses. Square houses differ from traditional houses not only in shape and size, but also in function. These 'new' houses are status objects. Their size, shape and position in the landscape signal things about their owners. This display function has further ramifications because, although these houses are used (naturally enough) for ordinary, quotidian family activities, they are also used for entertaining. The utilisation of square houses in this way separates them irrevocably from their circular predecessors and means that they very rarely contain a kitchen or cooking area. Cooking is an activity which, in line with government attitudes, is carried out in an adjacent circular house. The people of the Kapsowar area view the separation of cooking from other activities, such as sleeping and entertaining, as an indication of 'modernity'.

House types and building materials

In the past, all the houses of this area were of the traditional sub-circular form, with thatched roofs. In recent years there has been a growing inclination to build square houses, and this has produced a change in the materials and techniques used for building. In traditional Marakwet society every adult man would have known how to build a house, and special knowledge was required only for building the roof. However, traditional knowledge does not provide for constructing square houses, and those families who want to build such houses have to pay quite large sums (anywhere from 500 to 2,000 Ks (£1=18 Ks)) for a *fundi* (expert) to come and set the wall angles and build the ridge roof. Square houses are therefore a considerable investment and figs. 9.2, 9.3 and 9.4 show that only men who were employed in wage labour own square houses. But the fact that some employed men still live in round houses is an indication of the size of the investment required to build a square house.

The round houses of the Kapsowar area are similar to those of other Marakwet groups; they are usually sub-circular, with a single wooden door and a wooden window. The walls are between 1.5 and 1.8 m high and the roofs are thatched. There are two types of house: (a) post and daub (*kimagen*), and (b) wattle and daub (*kokom*). Houses of post and daub are rare in other areas but extremely common in the Kapsowar region. Of forty-seven round houses surveyed in Cheless and Rorok, forty-four were of post and daub.

Square houses are built in three types of materials: (a) post and daub, (b) vertical wooden slats, and (c) cement blocks. All three types of house have *mbati* (tin) roofs, which are supported with wooden frames. In Cheless and Rorok, there are ten square houses: four are built of post and daub, three of wooden slats and a further three of cement blocks. The most prestigious material to use is cement and the least prestigious type is the house of post and daub, because the construction recalls its traditional origins. Owners of square post and daub and wooden slat houses speak of a desire to rebuild in cement. I recorded only one case (fig. 9.3, compound XV), where a wooden house (built c. 1962) had been replaced by a cement house (built 1980). The other two cement houses were built from scratch in the late 1970s. The cost of building a square house is augmented by the fact that many of the materials are not available locally and have to be brought from distances of 25 to 65 kilometres away.

Stores, animal pens and other structures

The compound of a married man will contain three or four stores (*kapchogo*: they will usually be of wattle and daub construction, with a single entrance half-way up the side). These stores are always elevated on wooden stilts (approximately 40 cm high), to protect the contents from animals and damp. In the past, there would have been separate stores for the man and for his wife (or wives). Nowadays the situation is more complex; some families claim that their stores are differentiated only by use. In such cases, old stores are used for keeping calabashes, broken pots, plastic jerry cans and the like, while those in good repair are used for storing maize and sometimes millet. However, many families divide their stores into those for the father, those for the mother and those for the children. The man's store contains the grain which he takes as his share and which he can dispose of as he pleases; this grain will not be used to support the family. The woman's store contains that food which she has put aside to use for such things as buying clothes or items for the house, contributing to school fees or purchasing essentials, like flour, fat and salt, which she cannot produce herself. The food in the so-called children's store is the food which the family will eat. In some families, where the husband has a substantial wage income, there is no store for the man because he does not earn his cash by selling agricultural produce. Among the thirty-five households I sampled in Cheless and Rorok, there were no families who were engaged in producing what would properly be termed 'cash crops' (e.g. cotton, sisal, tea). Most households, however, were engaged in producing maize, beans or vegetables for sale in Kapsowar centre and other nearby markets.

Whatever governs the allocation of stores, the positioning of these structures within the compound remains constant. Stores must always be placed on the upper side of the compound, away from the rubbish areas which will be on the lower side (see figs. 9.2, 9.3 and 9.4). Some stores have a small pen attached to them for keeping sheep, goats or calves: stores and animal pens occupy similar positions within the compound. The people of the Kapsowar area own many cattle; there is much more rain for grass in this highland region, and the cooler climate means that cattle are less prone to disease. In Cheless and Rorok each household owned an average of five cows. Cattle are much more highly prized than sheep or goats. In fact, the people of Kapsowar see no particular reason to keep goats. Only 50% of households owned sheep, with an average of four animals per household, and only 11% of households owned any goats, with an average of 0.8 per household.

Although sheep and goats may be kept in the compound, cattle *bomas* (enclosures) are usually a little distance from the main part of the compound and, if there is a fence, they are always outside the fenced area (see figs. 9.2, 9.3 and 9.4).

Other structures include such things as chicken runs, drying racks and latrines. Chicken runs and drying racks are normally found on the lower side of the compound (see fig. 9.3, compound XVI), but their positioning is somewhat variable. Latrines do not have a specific position in the compound, but they are usually at the furthest point from the houses, close against the fence. In Cheless and Rorok there were seven latrines all of which were in compounds with square houses. Latrines are of the pit type and are considered to be a particularly modern innovation.

The spatial ordering of household refuse

In the past, the Marakwet recognised three kinds of rubbish which were spatially and semantically distinct: ash, animal dung and chaff from finger millet and sorghum. The semantic distinctions persist, but the contemporary situation with regard to spatial segregation is more complex. Rubbish of all types is usually disposed of on the downward slope of the compound, away from the houses and the stores which are in the upper part of the compound. Informants say that, in the past, the three types of rubbish would have had specific disposal positions relative to each other and to compound activities. This claim is borne out by comparative work with another Marakwet group, the Endo, where the disposal of 'rubbish' is strongly linked to the organisation of the family compound and to the 'symbolic gender' ascribed to particular structures (Moore 1983b). It is also supported by an excerpt from the colonial records:

> Each Marakwet with his family has a separate *boma* [I take the author to mean compound]. Each man has a hut for himself besides one for each of his wives. . . . Garbage and waste is thrown in heaps in the bush at least 50–100 yds from the boma. A separate heap is kept for the different kinds of garbage, such as goat manure, *wimbi* husks [millet] etc.
> (Elgeyo–Marakwet Political Record Book 1918: vol. II)

Although the three types of rubbish no longer have specific disposal positions within the compounds, they are still kept absolutely separate from each other. The reason for this continuing separation is the link which the Marakwet perceive between refuse and burial.

> Must keep rubbish separate, but the most important is to keep ash away from dung because old men must be buried under cow dung and women under the *morir* (chaff).

> Ashes are bad because women are also buried near ashes as well as being buried near the *morir* (chaff).

There are other regulations governing the disposal of the dead which are related to ideas about gender. For example, when a man dies he will be buried just outside the compound, a little way down on the right from his house. A woman, on the other hand, will ideally be buried just down and to the left of her house. However, the positioning of burials *vis-à-vis* the positioning of houses is not as crucial as it (apparently) was in the past because houses no longer have the same sort of gender affilation. The 'lack' of gender principles in the spatial ordering of the compounds is another reason why the specific disposal locations for certain types of rubbish are no longer as important as they were. This is a point I shall return to later.

House interiors

The internal arrangements of all sub-circular houses are similar and follow a regular pattern. Figure 9.5, house XX, is an example of the interior of a traditional circular house, belonging to an old lady (see also fig. 9.2). Figure 9.5, house XXVI, is the interior of the same type of house, belonging to a married man and serving as the main family house (see also fig. 9.3). These two houses contain rather different types of objects and there is some variation with regard to the position of the fireplace, but the underlying principles of organisation are the same. This is because all houses are divided into three areas: (a) *kaptinyo* (area of bed), (b) *kapkoschio* (area for cooking), and (c) *kuti ya tobot* (area beneath the entrance to the roof store). The location of these three areas is the same in all houses because the division of space within the house is

organised according to a scheme which dictates the positions these areas must take *vis-à-vis* one another. The bed must always be behind the door, the fireplace should be towards the back centre of the house and, since the entrance to the roof store must never be over the bed or the cooking area, it is usually on the opposite side of the house from the bed. As a result all houses are organised according to a system of principles.

In the past, the relative positions of the cooking area, the sleeping area and the entrance to the roof store were invariant, but nowadays the principles which govern the organisation of space are changing in response to changing spatial and conceptual requirements. Since many families no longer carry out their activities in a single living space, some houses will be without certain features. For example, a house which is used only for sleeping or entertaining does not need a roof store or a centre post and may not have a fireplace. A house which functions solely as a kitchen will not need to have beds and once there is no need to organise the rest of the space around the position of the bed, the positions of other structures (particularly fireplaces and store entrances) are no longer fixed. This is not just a matter of changing functional and spatial requirements. The area around the bed is the area of 'private' space within the house; when there is no bed, there is no private and hence no public space. When a house no longer has a hearth, then the gender associations (female/hearth, male/centre post) which link the woman as provider with the hearth and the man as father and supporter of the family with the centre post (see Moore 1983b, ch. 6) are no longer appropriate ways of ordering space. The situation is similar

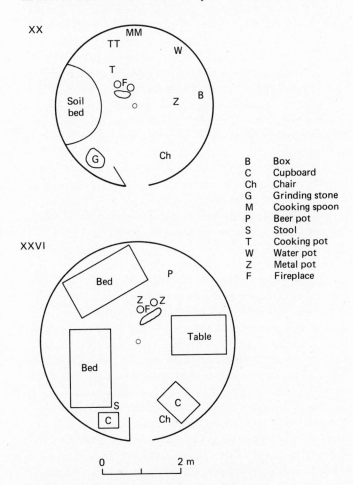

B	Box
C	Cupboard
Ch	Chair
G	Grinding stone
M	Cooking spoon
P	Beer pot
S	Stool
T	Cooking pot
W	Water pot
Z	Metal pot
F	Fireplace

Fig. 9.5 The interiors of two traditional round houses

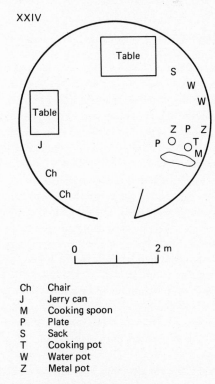

Ch	Chair
J	Jerry can
M	Cooking spoon
P	Plate
S	Sack
T	Cooking pot
W	Water pot
Z	Metal pot

Fig. 9.6 The interior of a kitchen house

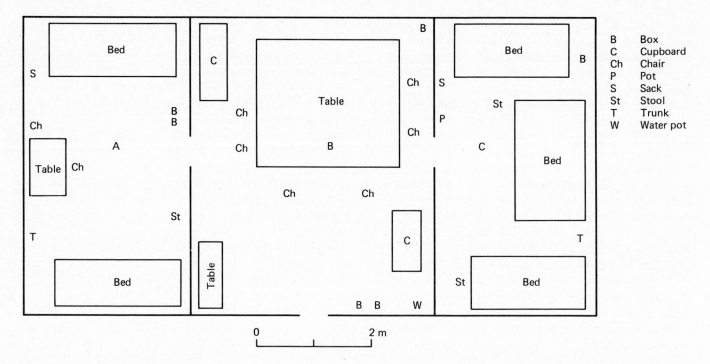

Fig. 9.7 The interior of a square house

with regard to kitchen houses, because although such houses have fireplaces, the fireplace does not need to be in the back centre of the house, since the space it occupies is no longer conceptually differentiated from the space occupied by the bed or the centre post. For example, see fig. 9.6 which is a plan of the interior of the kitchen house from compound XXIV, fig. 9.4

Square houses

The interior organisation of square houses is very different from that of circular houses. Figure 9.7 shows the interior arrangement of a square house which has three rooms. Of the ten square houses in the sample, six had three rooms, two had four rooms and the remaining two were single-room strucures used as kitchens. The three-roomed house is usually oblong-shaped, with two internal partitions, a single window in each room, a wooden outside door and an earthen or concrete floor. The roof, which is ridged, will be covered in tin.

Room B is the room used for entertaining, and contains tables, chairs, cupboards and stools. Displayed in this area will be pictures of the family, calendars, mirrors and the radio. Other objects such as plates, knives and cups may be kept in a glass-fronted cupboard, through which they are visible. This is the room into which visitors are invited to take tea or to eat. It may also contain a water pot and tinned or bottled foodstuffs, like orange juice, which guests may be offered or just allowed to look at. All flat surfaces will be covered with decorated cloths and surfaces not in use may have vases, books or magazines on them.

Rooms A and C are for sleeping. The number of beds is variable and there are usually as many beds as wall space will

allow. Tin trunks, sacks and plastic jerry cans are also familiar items. The walls are usually decorated with calendars, pictures from advertisements and magazines, and mirrors. Clothes are hung on strings which stretch across the room, and smaller items of clothing and shoes are usually kept in boxes under the bed. Flat surfaces are covered with decorated cloths. School books, combs and other such items are to be found on convenient surfaces all round the room. There may also be one or two chairs, and the occasional spear or beer pot may even be in evidence.

The positioning of items in all three rooms is extremely variable and, aside from a tendency to place water pots in the corners of rooms, I could ascertain no underlying themes of organisation. The Marakwet themselves merely remark that the sleeping rooms are organised according to the number of people who have to make use of them, and that the main room is 'made to look nice for visitors'. Any recurrent order in spatial arrangements seemed to be related to wall space, the position of doors and problems of crowding. So far as I am aware, the conceptual ordering of space in square houses is nothing like as overt as in the case of round houses. The space inside a square house has a quality which emanates from its 'squareness' and from the objects it contains. This is not the case with round houses, where different spaces have different associations and qualities (e.g. male or female, public or private). There is, of course, a distinction in square houses between the sleeping rooms and the main room, but it is important not to view this public/private division from a European perspective. For example, the sleeping arrangements inside houses are often complex, particularly since a woman cannot sleep in the same house as her sons once they reach the age of eight and a man cannot sleep in the same house as his daughters once they reach a similar age. This means that the older boys often sleep with relatives or in the animal enclosure. It may also mean that if the father is working away, the family's sleeping arrangements have to be revised on his return. In one particular case, when the father came home all the daughters had to move out and sleep in the kitchen. Items like beds and blankets are not thought of as belonging exclusively to particular individuals. Thus, sleeping rooms are not private space in the European sense. Sleeping places are usually assigned on the basis of gender and, in many of the families I studied, one room was for the mother and daughters and the other for the father and sons.

Household contents

I first decided to investigate household goods as indices of social change when I realised that the Marakwet view them as such. When an informant speaks of 'the time before there were modern cups', attention is drawn to a way of classifying and quantifying the movements of history and change. The Marakwet also have very specific views about which items are 'modern' and which are 'traditional'. This division is a common one and roughly corresponds to a distinction between those items which are made locally, with local materials, and those which are not. The exceptions to this guiding principle are tables, chairs and stools, which are made locally, with local materials, but are definitively 'modern' items. I decided therefore to study household inventories from the Kapsowar sample. Some items are not reliable as indicators of changing preferences and requirements. The most important items which fall into this category are pots. Cooking pots, water pots, medicine pots and beer pots come in a range of types and sizes; in the past a Marakwet house would have had some, but not all, of the types and sizes available. One reason for this is that the number and size of pots is related to the size of the family. Another reason is that an old man would probably possess several of the large ceremonial pots and would lend them out to other members of his clan when necessary. On the other hand, he and his wife would not have anything like a representative range of other types of pot, because they would not need them. In the context of the Kapsowar villages, it is precisely large beer and cooking pots which continue in use, because they are traditional items which are required (although less and less frequently) for ceremonial occasions. Medicine pots are also owned by a large percentage of families, as a sort of 'amulet' against the consequences of forsaking traditional medicine for its European counterpart. The variables with regard to pottery were just too numerous and ambiguous to control and pottery is, therefore, excluded from the following tables. Table 9.1 illustrates the average number of items per household and the percentage of households which possessed the item. The first two sections of table 9.1 are concerned with items which the Marakwet would designate as modern. The third section is an analysis of calabashes by type, and these are items which the Marakwet would consider traditional. The

Table 9.1. *Household items from Cheless and Rorok*

	No. per household	% of total households with the item
(1) Beds (modern)	1.8	92
Mattresses	1.7	93
Frying pan	0.5	47
Lamp	1.1	96
Radio	0.6	65
Mirror	1.0	93
Tables	1.5	89
Chairs	3.3	89
Stools	2.7	89
(2) Sufurias (metal cooking pots)	5.4	100
Mugs	12.0	100
Bowls	8.3	100
Spoons	9.7	100
Metal bowls (karias)	1.7	84
Forks	6.1	100
Plates	8.5	100
Glasses	5.6	82
Knives	2.4	100
(3) *Calabashes*		
Brewing beer	0.4	31
Water	0.2	17
Milk	1.5	51
Beer	0.2	14
Honey	0.3	25
Carrying water	0	0

average household size was five in all three samples. The number of items has to be taken in conjunction with the percentage of households in which they are found. For example, section 2 shows that some items are now so commonplace as to be found in all homes (e.g. *sufurias* and tin mugs), while others are much less common (e.g. knives).

Section 3 shows the declining number of traditional calabashes in the Kapsowar sample. The only calabash still used regularly in the Kapsowar area is the one for milk, and this is because of the continuing importance of milk in the local economy.

These lists of items obviously do not contain all the items which are found inside houses, but they do contain those items which are in constant use in the house and compound, with the exception of pottery and plastic jerry cans. I specifically excluded items like grinding stones, cooking sticks, spears, bows and arrows which have a strong gender affiliation and which are preserved in a changing context because of their association with enduring values and concepts. I also excluded all textiles, photographs and decorative items.

Table 9.2. *Household inventories for individuals of 55–70 years*

Compound	III	XXIX	XX	XXIII
Occupation	Teachers	Unemployed	Widow unemployed	Widower unemployed
No. of children	6	6	0	0
Sufurias	8	4	2	1
Karias	3	2	0	0
Kettles	3	2	1	0
Spoons	20	12	2	2
Forks	12	12	0	0
Knives	8	4	0	0
Cups	25	14	4	2
Plates	12	12	0	0
Bowls	10	10	3	2
Glasses	8	6	1	0
Frying pan	1	0	0	0
Lamps	2	1	0	1
Radio	1	0	0	0
Mirror	2	0	0	0
Beds (modern)	3	2	0	0
Mattresses	3	2	0	0
Tables	6	2	0	0
Chairs	6	3	0	0
Stools	4	2	0	1
Car	0	0	0	0

Tables 9.2, 9.3 and 9.4 give the same items as table 9.1 (with the addition of kettles and cars) for the compounds illustrated in figs. 9.2, 9.3 and 9.4; the number of items can be seen to vary according to age and occupation of the head of the household. There are differences in the numbers of certain items between those families where the man is employed and those where he is not. This corresponds to the employed/unemployed distinction illustrated in figs. 9.1, 9.2 and 9.3, where only employed men have square houses. Tables 9.2, 9.3 and 9.4 show that there is no discernible variation in the number of household items with regard to age, with the exception of the widow and the widower, who both have very few items. This is partly related to the size of their households and partly to the fact that elderly people often give away unwanted household items to younger members of their family. However, I would argue that the small number of items they possess overall is related to the lack of cash income, and that the absence of certain items, like modern beds and frying pans, is an age-related preference. Old people in the Kapsowar area frequently say that it is much warmer and more comfortable to sleep on a traditional bed of packed mud than it is to sleep on a modern iron bed.

So far I have outlined some of the material indices of social change in the Kapsowar area. What remains is to put the building of square houses and the acquisition of certain industrially produced or 'modern' items into the wider context of changing social and economic conditions.

The analysis of change

It is usual to link 'westernisation' to the emergence of alternative prestige systems, which arise when the sub-dominant culture emulates the dominant one. However, as Banton says (1961, p. 121), "It may be doubted . . . whether the association between prestige and Europeanisation is not more apparent than real". In the case of the Marakwet of the Kapsowar region it is possible to recognise the emergence of a 'new' prestige system based on the acquisition and display of certain 'modern' items.

The emergence of this system is linked on the one hand to the decreasing influence of the clan *vis-à-vis* the increasing individualisation of the household, and on the other to a growing commitment to a notion of 'modernity' which finds a partial expression in changing house types and functions. The decreasing influence of the patrilineal clan and lineage groups is primarily due to a change in the established relationship between labour and land. The communality of land holding used to be reflected in the communality of labour and in the joint social responsibility which rested with the elders. Land registration has fundamentally altered the communality of labour and land holding, while wage-labour and education have

Table 9.3. *Household inventories for individuals of 40–55 years*

Compound	XII	XV	XVI	XXVI	XXXIV	VI
Occupation	Army	Teacher	Teacher	Unemployed	Unemployed	Unemployed
No. of children	6	6	6	6	7	6
Sufurias	6	6	8	5	6	4
Karias	2	3	3	2	1	2
Kettles	3	3	3	2	1	1
Spoons	15	15	20	12	4	10
Forks	7	9	20	4	2	6
Knives	3	3	3	2	2	2
Cups	15	15	20	12	8	7
Plates	12	20	15	8	6	4
Bowls	16	20	10	6	4	3
Glasses	8	15	11	4	0	4
Frying pan	1	1	1	1	0	0
Lamps	4	2	2	1	1	1
Radio	1	1	1	1	0	1
Mirror	3	2	3	1	1	1
Beds (modern)	3	3	3	2	1	2
Mattresses	3	3	3	2	1	2
Tables	3	2	3	2	2	2
Chairs	4	4	8	3	2	4
Stools	6	6	4	2	2	6
Car	1	1	1	0	0	0

undermined a system where work and responsibility were allocated on the basis of age. Young men value their modern education over the traditional knowledge of their fathers, and their increasing ability to earn cash guarantees their economic independence. In turn, this independence is reflected in the increasing individualisation of the household. Production and reproduction are now confined to the household, and the role of the clan and the lineage in economic production and reproduction has declined.

The decline of communal land holding units and an increasing emphasis on the individual and the individual family are often described as an effect of 'westernisation'. Insofar as this relationship is spelled out, it is thought to be the result of the structure and values of capitalist/industrial society eroding 'traditional' values and structures. In the case of the Marakwet it is not enough to say that the 'old value system' associated with the clan and the communality of male agnates has broken down. The lineage, and to a lesser extent the broader patriclan, remain crucial to the selection of marriage partners. Lineages are exogamous and the interrelation of bridewealth payments with the inheritance of ownership rights to registered land perpetuates a high rate of ethnic endogamy. In other words, Marakwet men marry Marakwet women and their reasons for so doing maintain the importance of the lineage and the wider agnatic group even in a situation where the clan is apparently decreasing in significance. In fact, it is possible to say that the

importance of the lineage and clan in the selection of marriage partners is retained precisely because the importance of both groups as communal land-holding units and reserves of labour is declining. In a situation where a number of men are employed in wage-labour and where land is owned by individual men, wives become important as 'land guardians'. In the past, the responsibility for land or stock during a long absence would have been invested with close male agnates. But where an increasing number of close agnates work outside the area and where each man is concerned with the maintenance of his own resources, this is not such a desirable practice. The result is an increasing dependence on wives as 'temporary' heads of households with responsibility for decisions concerning land and stock.

This last point is related to the significance of women as rural labourers and producers. Men who are wage earners do not use their wages for the day-to-day maintenance of the household and family members. None of the employed men in Cheless and Rorok sent money regularly to their wives or families. Wages are used to fulfil ritual and kin obligations, to maintain expensive structures like houses and to purchase manufactured goods. Few women have access to substantial sums of money, and of thirty-five women interviewed only one admitted purchasing manufactured goods other than metal cooking pots (*sufuria*). The purchase of manufactured items and of general household fittings – particularly if it is a square house

Table 9.4. *Household inventories for individuals of 25–40 years*

Compound	XXIV	IV	V	XXXI	XXV
Occupation	Army	Driver	Factory worker	Mission gardener	Unemployed
No. of children	5	4	3	2	2
Sufurias	7	8	4	4	5
Karias	3	2	1	2	2
Kettles	2	2	1	2	1
Spoons	12	15	8	12	8
Forks	8	15	3	5	7
Knives	3	3	3	2	3
Cups	14	20	9	10	10
Plates	15	20	3	8	5
Bowls	13	20	4	7	4
Glasses	10	11	3	2	4
Frying pan	1	1	1	0	1
Lamps	2	2	1	1	1
Radio	1	1	1	1	0
Mirror	2	2	1	1	1
Beds (modern)	3	3	2	2	1
Mattresses	3	3	2	2	1
Tables	3	3	1	2	0
Chairs	5	6	2	3	2
Stools	6	6	2	2	1
Car	0	0	0	0	0

– is considered the responsibility of men. Women may earn a little money from craft activities or selling produce in Kapsowar market; this money is generally used for purchasing clothes or imported foodstuffs like vegetable oil, and for school fees. In this situation the wife's labour is essential for the maintenance of the household, for it is she who must produce food for the children to eat, and sell her surplus produce on the market to buy basic foodstuffs and clothes for the children. The responsibility for the maintenance of the household has always rested with women to a large extent, but increasing involvement in wage-labour has meant that husbands are more dependent on their wives in this respect than they were before.

The additional dependence on wives and the immediate 'nuclear' family has paradoxically not meant that agnatic ties have been weakened. The importance of securing control over women as wives has maintained the necessity of agnatic ties between young men. Bridewealth and lineage exogamy are the two crucial determinants in the selection of marriage partners. The payment of bridewealth among the Marakwet, as among other groups, establishes a man's rights in his wife and in all children born to her. It is only by 'safeguarding' unmarried daughters and sisters as wives and child-bearers for other men that fathers and brothers can convert this authority into their control as husbands over women and children. In a situation where land and labour are becoming increasingly capitalised the issue of paternity remains crucial.

This brief discussion goes some way to showing how the famous maxim 'continuity through change; and change through continuity' may actually be observed to work in practice. The significance of the clan and the lineage is maintained in changing circumstances by using the strengths of these institutionalised structures to help the Marakwet – as individuals and as a group – to adapt to a changing situation. As an example of 'continuity through change', the maintenance of clan and lineage structures should be viewed alongside changes in bridewealth associated with employment and the acquisition of 'modern' items, which may be seen as an example of 'change through continuity'.

The value of bridewealth has increased since Independence, in spite of complaints from young men that it is too high and in spite of active discouragement by both the national government and the church. The amount of bridewealth paid varies considerably, but wealthier families are expected to pay more and poor families may still make all or part of the bridewealth payment in stock. The distinction between poor and rich is not easy to make, but in the contemporary situation it roughly corresponds to those families where the head of the household is employed and those families where he is not. (There were no examples of women employed in wage-labour in Cheless or Rorok.) Bridewealth transactions are extremely difficult to document accurately, because even where the payment is said to be entirely monetary there are a number of transactions which take place between husband and wife-to-be which affect the actual amount of money exchanged. Bridewealth payments vary from 2,000–4,000 Ks (£1=18 Ks), but there is a marked increase in the number of women who demand the 'modern' furnishing of the house as part of the payment. All the women from the sample who have married in the last ten years spoke of the household furnishings – and sometimes even the house itself – as part of what they received at marriage. Although transactions between spouses may not be properly understood as comprising part of the bridewealth (in the case of the Marakwet they are akin to Goody's (1976, p. 11) "indirect dowry", they are nevertheless a significant part of the agreement because both families take such provisions into account when assessing the actual amount of money to be paid. The tendency to provide household furnishings is a practice encouraged by the church, which makes much of the link between cash bridewealth and 'purchasing women'. In this way bridewealth is characterised as an undesirable 'traditional' practice, while material provision for the wife shows proper commitment and also has the advantage of being thought 'modern'.

Formerly, a woman would have been expected to provide most of the movable household objects herself, with the help of her mother-in-law. The increasing emphasis on the provision of these items by men as part of the bridewealth is linked to employment and the wider significance of the acquisition of large numbers of expensive 'modern' items is possibly only for men who are employed, but this itself is an important point. Employment appears to bring an overt concern with the display of the wealth of the individual household. An employed man is at great pains to build a square house, plant flowers in his compound and provide iron beds and modern mattresses for his family. He is equally concerned to equip the house in a way which is thought to be modern, that is, to provide plates, bowls, knives, forks and glasses. The cooking area is separated from the main house; the room for entertaining is furnished with tables and chairs and decorated with cloths and other items. All in all a considerable amount of money is spent on doing and being seen to do three things: (a) building a square house, (b) equipping the house, and (c) providing for the family.

The concern with modernity, which is avowed by the display of certain items, is a concern with privatisation and the control of capital. In this context, land and stock are obviously a capital resource, but so are women. Not only do women produce children, but their labour has a market value, because it is their labour which maintains the household and produces agricultural surplus for the market. Conventionally, the Marakwet say that a man brings land and stock to a marriage, while a woman brings her ability to bear children and her domestic and agricultural labour. This convention expresses the complementarity of male and female roles within marriages. The provision of 'modern' household furnishings as part of the 'bridewealth' has become part of the complementarity of the marriage agreement and thus, in part, gives the husband rights over his wife's productive and reproductive labour. However,

the buildings of square houses and the provision of 'modern' and expensive items is bound up with an expressed 'isolation' of the individual household and the increasing 'privatisation' of land and capital. Displays of wealth were not a feature of Marakwet society prior to the intervention of the purchasing power of wages. The success of an individual household (i.e. productive unit) was expressed in children and stock. Both animals and children are still highly valued in Marakwet society, but the determinants of status and prestige have shifted slightly. A man's prestige is increasingly bound up with the display of status, which is recognised predominantly in the building of square houses and the provision of 'modern' and expensive items: radio and cars are highest on the list. Status is ultimately created through a combination of progressiveness and prosperity. Progressiveness is a strategy which both produces and is the product of the prosperity of the household unit. In the conspicuous display of 'modern' items the opposition between what is 'traditional' and what is 'modern' is set up. This opposition is not inherent, nor is it notional. It is a strategy which forms part of the Marakwet's active response to changing circumstances. There is not sufficient room here to discuss all, or even most, of the manifestations and ramifications of this strategy. The most notable omission is a discussion of the relation between 'elders' and young men. However, it should be said that the conflict between what is 'traditional' and what is 'modern' is one of the most powerful metaphors for the conflicts which exist between old and young. Young men seek to emancipate themselves from the control of their elders. The increasing individualism of the household and the provision of furnishings as part of the bridewealth are part of this emancipation, and link it indisputably to the strategy of 'modernisation'.

Conclusion

It would not be possible to generalise from the Kapsowar material to the experience of other Marakwet groups. The specific historical development of the region is crucial to any understanding of social change. Kapsowar was the site of the first government station, the first mission hospital and the first secondary school in the north of Elgeyo–Marakwet District. These factors mean that the people of the area were much in contact with potential forces of change and, even more importantly, that they had to do much to adapt to changing circumstances. From the statements of informants, it is clear that during the colonial period Marakwet attitudes to change were predominantly shaped by contact with the 'whites'. Changes in agricultural practices were accepted speedily; attempts to interfere with circumcision and marriage were ignored. In other parts of Marakwet, colonial attempts to introduce new crops were unsuccessful. This does not mean that the people of Kapsowar were necessarily more 'progressive', but it does mean that they were more accessible to colonial officials and that their well-watered and well-drained environment was better suited to the introduction of maize, potatoes and green vegetables. The changes which took place further differentiated the people of the Kapsowar region from other Marakwet groups and have had a determining influence on subsequent reactions to changing circumstances.

The question we have to ask is whether conceiving of changes in terms of 'emulation', 'borrowing', 'Europeanisation', 'detribalisation' or 'westernisation' actually helps us to understand what is going on in the villages of Cheless and Rorok. Does it actually help to explain either the scale or the nature of the observable social changes? The Marakwet of the Kapsowar region are clearly not trying to emulate Europeans. The material changes which took place during colonial times were not so much an attempt to imitate the 'whites', as a process of making use of what seemed appropriate or useful even if the categories 'appropriate' and 'useful' were defined in part by the impinging 'white' culture as well as by the existing Marakwet culture. The impact of government and mission policies should never be underestimated, not least because authority and coercion provide an environment which can determine what is appropriate or useful.

In the contemporary situation, material changes have to be seen both in the context of factors which lie beyond the control of the Marakwet, like government policy, and in terms of internal changes which are the produce of individuals' construction of change. Change is not necessarily something which people have to be forced into. External pressures may sometimes be better understood as enabling internal changes, rather than as forcing them. Concepts like 'westernisation' and 'detribalisation' do not help us to understand changes in the way of life of the Marakwet because they do not specify the particular social and historical circumstances of change; because they emphasise the enforcement of change from the outside; and because they leave no room for the Marakwet construction of change which alone accounts for the way material changes are linked to changing values and opportunities and thereby to alternative social, economic and political relations.[5]

Notes

1. In the report of the Kenya Land Commission 1933, the total area of the Native Reserve was given as 732 sq m in native use and 20 sq m as Native Reserve Forest (Report of the Kenya Land Commission 1933, p. 262).
2. Out-labour of the kind referred to here falls into the category of voluntary contractual labour, which was the general legal status of most native workers in colonial Kenya. The official line was that natives were to be induced or 'encouraged' to work for private employers. In fact, taxation, population increase and pressure from chiefs and colonial administrators all combined to act as a coercive force. The increasing demand for labour in the face of the Africans' dislike for permanent work became reflected in penal provisions in employment legislation and in the *kipande* identity system (see Clayton and Savage 1974, pp. 131–9).
3. For a discussion of the identification of the church with colonialism see Welbourn 1971.
4. During the 1950s the Dow Commission urged that steps towards the freehold tenure of African lands should be taken. However, the only area to undergo extensive land consolidation and conversion to freehold tenure was the area of the Kikuyu reserves (Clayton and Savage 1974, p. 352).
5. The fieldwork on which this work is based was carried out in Kenya during 1980 and 1981. My research in the field and in Cambridge was supported by the Department of Education and Science. I would also like to thank the British Institute in Eastern Africa, Nairobi; the Smuts Fund, Cambridge; the Anthony Wilkin Fund, Cambridge; and the Tweedie Exploration Fund, Edinburgh. My special thanks to Ian Hodder, who read earlier drafts of the work and patiently supervised the thesis on which this article is based.

The following colonial records in the Kenya National Archives were consulted: Records of the Provincial Commissioner, Rift Valley Province (PC/RVP); District Commissioner, Baringo District (DC/BAR), Elgeyo–Marakwet (DC/ELM); miscellaneous reports and correspondence; Annual Reports of the Native Affairs Department, District Political Record Books (PRBs), Handing Over Reports (HORs) concerning Baringo and Elgeyo–Marakwet Districts were consulted in the Seeley Historical Library, Cambridge.

Chapter 10

A contribution to the study of migrations in the archaeological record: the Ngoni and Kololo migrations as a case study

David Collett

While some papers in this volume emphasise the importance of diffusion in the interpretation of cultural meanings (for an example, see Chapter 11), another component of culture history that has been recently neglected, since it is supposedly non-explanatory, is migration. Collett examines the material culture effects of the migrations of Ngoni and Sotho (Kololo) groups into south-central Africa. While some aspects of material culture style (such as settlement layout and associated cosmology) do 'reflect' the migrations, others (such as pottery style) do not. The reasons for this variation can be shown to lie in the expectations and perceptions of the incoming dominant group. There had been an historical tradition within the migrant groups that linked power and authority to the symbolic ordering of settlement space. Pottery decoration, on the other hand, did not have such significance in the homeland, and so the decoration used by subordinate peoples could be reinterpreted as decoration rather than as a socially active statement. As in Greene's chapter (Chapter 11), the same 'things' had different meanings viewed from different social positions (see also Chapters 3, 4 and 9).

When I was an undergraduate one of the major problems in the study of the later prehistory of eastern and southern Africa was the recognition of migrations (Clark 1962, 1964; Clark and Fagan 1965; Cole 1954; Cooke 1965; Fagan 1965; Huffman 1970; Oliver 1966; Phillipson 1968; Posnansky 1961, 1968; Soper 1971a, 1971b) and it is still a major concern for some archaeologists working in Africa (Ambrose 1983; Huffman 1974, 1978, 1979, 1980, 1983; Phillipson 1974, 1975, 1976, 1977; Soper 1983). This emphasis on migration struck a responsive chord in me because it corresponded with my own peripatetic existence as the child of colonial civil servants. However, there has been some scepticism about the population movements that have been inferred by African archaeologists (Gramly 1978; Lwanga-Lunyiigo 1976; Onyango-Abuje and Wandibba 1976; Robertson 1981; Vansina 1980) and this corresponds to a wider questioning of migration hypotheses in archaeology (Binford 1962, 1965, 1968; Clark 1966; Hodder 1978; Renfrew 1973, 1979a). In some cases these criticisms have served as a prelude to suggestions that there should be a change in the focus of archaeological research: a switch from the elucidation of the history of cultures to the study of culture processes. However, my early and more recent experiences in Africa lead me to believe that history and process are intimately connected and that the recognition of a migration (in my case the British colonial occupation of Africa) may be important in the understanding of the subsequent changes in the material culture of an area. The impact of colonial societies on indigenous African communities provides an example for what Rouse (1972, chapter 1) has said about the importance of culture history in the study of culture process.

The suggestion that distinguishing between autochthonous and allochthonous development is important does not imply that archaeologists should invoke migrations as a full or adequate explanation of culture change, but ignoring the problem of migration may mean that an archaeologist is in the unfortunate position of explaining how one culture develops into another when the reality is that one culture system has been replaced by another which developed elsewhere. This shows that the problem of recognising migrations – cultural replacement – is fundamental to archaeological research and that it should be critically examined.

Rouse (1972) has suggested two criteria for recognising migrations: (1) a demonstration that the material culture in an area occupied by a migrant group is similar to that found in the area from which the group originated, and (2) the ability to show that the migrants are younger in the newly occupied area than in the area of origin. The second has been technically feasible since the inception of radiocarbon dating and the main problem lies in the recognition of cultural similarity.

Traditionally archaeologists have compared lists of traits to assess and quantify the similarity between assemblages. This approach equates cultural similarity with a developmental relationship and ignores the problem of parallel evolution (Binford 1968; Renfrew 1979a, p. 14). This problem has been addressed by Binford (1968) in his discussion of African rock art. He suggests that style and style boundaries can be used to make inferences about the genetic relationships between cultures. This is a common strategy (Dunnell 1978; Sackett 1973) which rests on the assumption that style reflects group identity. The importance of style in identifying archaeological traditions in Africa has been stressed by Huffman (1980, 1983) who has suggested that ceramics should be used to identify the relationships between archaeological entities because they show the greatest stylistic variation. He has attempted to illustrate this point by comparing samples of pottery from known ethnographic groups in South Africa and Zimbabwe (Huffman 1980). While two of the stylistic analyses produce groupings which reflect the ethnographic 'reality', the third, based on the techniques used to produce geometric motifs (incision, comb-stamping, painting), produces a confused grouping of samples. However, the choice of a particular technique is clearly stylistic because all the techniques have the same function and therefore style *per se* cannot be seen as a reflection of group identity.

If neither stylistic variables nor simple comparisons of trait lists can be used to establish cultural relatedness then the possibility of establishing archaeological traditions, and consequently the separation of autochthonous and allochthonous development, seems very remote. One possible way out of this impasse is to examine the changes in material culture after known migrations, a procedure which has been advocated by Alexander (1981). In the present paper I will examine the changes in material culture associated with the migration of two Ngoni groups (Mombera's and Mpezeni's) and a Sotho group (the Kololo) into south-central Africa.

A history of the Ngoni and Kololo migrations

The simultaneous rise of a number of 'states'[1] during the late 1700s and early 1800s in the areas occupied by the northern Nguni (Natal) was associated with a number of major conflicts

between the rival power blocks. Initially, the two major confederations were ruled by the Mthethwa and Ndwandwe clans who used physical coercion or peaceful alliance to extend their power over subordinate groups. Some groups, for example, the Swazi, avoided incorporation by moving away from the group that threatened them (fig. 10.1). These early movements did not necessarily involve any long-distance migrations and the Swazi moved less than 100 km (H. Kuper 1947, p. 13; Omer-Cooper 1966, p. 49).

The defeat of the Mthethwa by the Ndwandwe did not end the internecine warfare because the Zulu, under Shaka, filled the vacuum left by the demise of the Mthethwa confederation. The triumph of Shaka over the Ndwandwe was followed by a major exodus of groups led by the defeated Ndwandwe 'generals'. Three of these migrant groups – the Gaza led by Soshangane, the Maseko/Msene led by Nxaba and the Jere led by Zwangendaba – moved north into Mocambique where they settled, but the peace was short lived. Soshangane was attacked by the Zulu and he moved northwards, where he

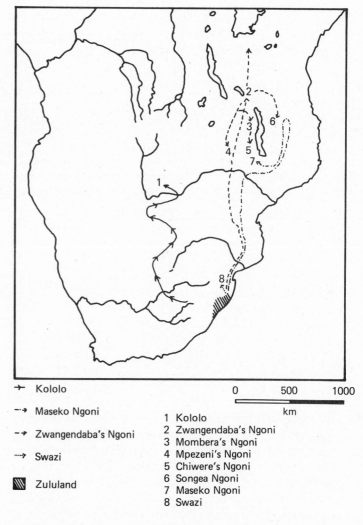

→	Kololo
--→	Maseko Ngoni
-→	Zwangendaba's Ngoni
·····→	Swazi
▨	Zululand

0   500   1000
km

1 Kololo
2 Zwangendaba's Ngoni
3 Mombera's Ngoni
4 Mpezeni's Ngoni
5 Chiwere's Ngoni
6 Songea Ngoni
7 Maseko Ngoni
8 Swazi

Fig. 10.1 The movement of the Kololo, Ngoni and Swazi during the *mfecane*

came into conflict with Zwangendaba. The latter was defeated by the combined powers of the Gaza and Maseko/Msene and he led his group northwards (Omer-Cooper 1966, p. 58). The alliance between the Gaza and the Maseko/Msene was brief and when fighting resumed Nxaba was defeated and the Maseko/Msene followed the Jere northwards. Soshangane was left in control of central Mocambique where he established the Gaza empire, which was powerful enough to force some of the Portuguese settlements to pay annual tribute (Omer-Cooper 1966, p. 58).

The northward movement of Zwangendaba's Jere continued with periodic stops of a few years until the group reached the Fipa plateau and it was here that Zwangendaba died in the late 1840s (Omer-Cooper 1966, p. 68). His death was followed by a series of succession disputes, with one group (the Tuta) moving away to the north, a second (the Gwangara) moving to the east, and the main body moving away to the south-west. There was a second dispute in the main body which then split into two groups. The group led by Mombera settled in northern Malawi, while Mpezeni's group settled in south-eastern Zambia (Barnes 1967, pp. 26–7; Omer-Cooper 1966, pp. 72–3; Read 1956, pp. 10–11). A further secession from Mombera's group occurred with the leader, Chiwere Ndhluvo, settling in central Malawi (Omer-Cooper 1966, p. 86; Read 1956, pp. 8–9).

The descendants of Zwangendaba were not the only northern Nguni group to settle in south-central Africa. It has already been pointed out that after his defeat by Soshangane, Nxaba led the combined Maseko/Msene group northwards. During this movement the Maseko and Msene separated, with the former settling in the Songea district of Tanzania. They were defeated by the Gwangara and moved into southern Malawi where they settled. This group is also interesting because the death of the original leader, Ngwane, does not seem to have been followed by any major fissioning of the group (Omer-Cooper 1966, p. 75).

All the northern Nguni groups who settled in south-central Africa (Chiwere Ndhluvo's group, the Gwangara, the Maseko, Mombera's Jere and Mpezeni's Jere) are referred to as the Ngoni. However, the Ngoni were not the only group to migrate to south-central Africa. Some of the groups that left the northern Nguni area in Natal displaced other groups who were living in the interior of South Africa. One such group were the Fokeng of Sebetwane, a Sotho group living near the Sand river in the Orange Free State. They crossed the Vaal river and joined a second Fokeng group. The continuation of the disturbances on the Highveld resulted in the combined Fokeng group, under the leadership of Sebetwane, moving in search of a new home where they could live in peace (Omer-Cooper 1966, p. 115). The pattern of movements made by the Kololo was similar to that described for Zwangendaba's Jere. Initially the group moved to the west and then turned north. They crossed the Zambezi and conquered the Lozi of south-western Zambia, and it was here that the Kololo settled (fig. 10.1).

Virtually all of the groups that migrated from Natal or the adjacent areas relied on their military power to obtain land which they could occupy. One of the consequences of this militaristic approach was the subjugation of some or all of the indigenous population in the areas where the migrant groups settled. It is clear that a substantial proportion, and probably a majority, of people in the Ngoni groups were incorporated during the intermittent stops on the northward migration (Omer-Cooper 1966, p. 70; Read 1956, p. 10). In contrast, the Kololo did not appear to incorporate any substantial number of subject people (Omer-Cooper 1966, p. 123). However, once the Kololo settled in south-western Zambia they became a minority, and Sebetwane had to force a coherent group out of the diversity of peoples that he ruled.

There was a tremendous variety in the policies that the rulers of the migrant communities adopted towards subject groups. These ranged from attempts at complete incorporation as practised by Mpezeni (Barnes 1967, p. 27) to systems in which there was a segregation of people with different ethnic origins as in the Gaza empire (Omer-Cooper 1966, p. 59). In some cases the leaders of groups that submitted to the Ngoni and Kololo were allowed to 'rule' their own people while in other cases the conquered groups were incorporated into the migrant communities. Where the indigenous 'rulers' remained in charge of their own people they sometimes sent their children to live with the 'king' or an important Ngoni family where the children were taught the Ngoni 'way of doing things' (Read 1956, p. 10). It is also clear that the subordinate groups normally accepted their inclusion in the conquering group and accepted or positively valued their description as Ngoni or Kololo (Barnes 1967, p. 27; Omer-Cooper 1966, p. 123).

Thus, the history of the Ngoni and Kololo shows that they migrated long distances and that during the course of these migrations or when they finally settled a large number of people with different ethnic origins were incorporated into the groups. In virtually all cases the subject communities came to accept or value their inclusion in the Kololo or Ngoni 'states' and in one case, that of Chiwere Ndhluvo, an individual who was incorporated into the Ngoni founded an Ngoni 'state'.

Migrants and changes in material culture

Ngoni and Kololo sites in south-central Africa have not been the subject of intensive archaeological research. However, Phillipson (1974) has reported a distinctive ceramic tradition, the Linyanti Tradition, from sites occupied by the Kololo. This pottery is decorated in a different way to the autochthonous Lungwebungu Tradition pottery, and the style seems to be similar to that recorded for Sotho pottery in South Africa. This observation seems to confirm the importance of style for the recognition of cultural similarity. However, this pattern is not found in the Chipata area of Zambia where Mpezeni's Ngoni settled and the ceramics from Ngoni sites belong within the autochthonous Lwangwa Tradition (Phillipson 1974). Phillipson has suggested that this difference may be related to the composition of Kololo and Ngoni groups. He suggests that pottery is made by both Ngoni and Kololo women but that there were more 'Sotho' women in the Kololo group than 'Ngoni' women in the Ngoni group. Thus, the Ngoni had to use the local style of pottery because they did not have enough women who knew how to make Ngoni style pottery. Unfortunately, this hypothesis ignores the fact that both the Ngoni and Kololo 'rulers' married women who had migrated from the homeland of the group and women from groups that had been incorporatd during the migration (Omer-Cooper 1966, p. 123; Read 1956, p. 142). It seems likely that there were similar proportions of Kololo/Ngoni women to women from incorporated groups living in the settlements occupied by the 'rulers' of the Ngoni and Kololo. Thus, the 'group composition' argument seems intuitively implausible. More importantly, pottery is not the only medium available for the expression of culture, and I will now examine a second set of information, settlement organisations before the search for cultural similarity between the Ngoni and other northern Nguni groups is dismissed as unproductive.

Anthropologists who have worked on the Ngoni in eastern Zambia and Malawi cite early descriptions of Ngoni settlements which indicate that the huts were built around a central cattle byre (Barnes 1951, p. 1; Read 1956, pp. 19–21). There were other features of significance in this traditional pattern: the back of the hut was a 'sacred' area where ritual objects were stored and offerings were placed for the ancestors (Read 1956, p. 200); the heads of sacrificed animals were displayed above the doorway of the *indlunkulu* hut at the back of the settlement, behind the cattle byre (Read 1956, p. 166); and finally, important males were buried on the edge of the cattle byre (Read 1956,p. 23). The consistent articulation of these features as an organised whole is common to both the northern Nguni of Natal and the Ngoni of south-central Africa (Read 1956, p. 23), and stands in marked contrast to the pattern among those groups displaced by the Ngoni, and the matrilineal groups to whom the displaced groups were related. The settlements of the latter groups consist of a dispersed pattern of huts without a central cattle byre, and the dead are buried outside the settlements (Mitchell 1960, Appendix B; Read 1956, p. 23; Richards 1939, end map; Stefaniszyn 1964, p. 29). Thus, the historical relationship between the northern Nguni and the Ngoni is demonstrable through the similarities in the spatial arrangement of their homesteads.

It is of course possible to argue that the organisation of settlements is a stylistic variable and that it should therefore show the cultural affinities of the Ngoni. It is also possible to suggest, on the basis of the Ngoni evidence, that settlement 'style' is a better predictor of cultural affinities than ceramic style. However, this approach ignores the problem hinted at in the analysis of modern African pottery (Huffman 1980), namely, why are some stylistic variables more appropriate for identifying cultural affinities than others, and why are these stylistic variables not always reliable predictors of cultural affinities? If these problems are to be addressed it is first necessary to define what is meant by the term culture and then

to re-examine the northern Nguni and Ngoni material (settlements and ceramics) with this definition in mind.

Geertz (1973, p. 5) has described culture in semiotic terms:

> Believing, with Max Weber, that man is an animal suspended in webs of significance he himself has spun, I take culture to be those webs, and the analysis of it to be ... an interpretive one in search of meaning.

Material culture forms part of the 'webs of significance' in which man is embedded and any interpretation of the material aspects of culture must focus on the meaning encoded in the *gestalten* of artifacts. The analysis of domestic space is particularly appropriate in this context because 'the house and the settlement ... may be like a model of the cosmos as conceived by a people' (Cunningham 1973, p. 234).

Attempts to analyse the symbolic significance of domestic space among the Nguni are not new. A. Kuper (1980, 1982, ch. 10) has produced an analysis which ends by presenting a set of linked triads which represent the symbolic dimensions of

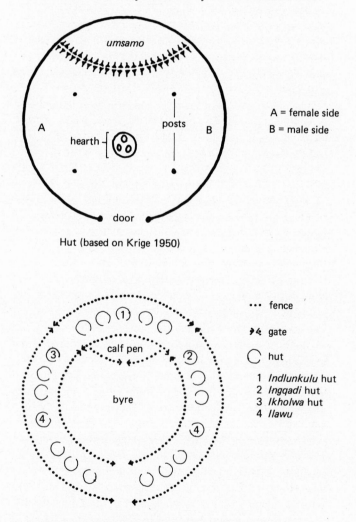

Hut (based on Krige 1950)

A = female side
B = male side

Homestead (after Holleman 1940 and Krige 1950)

··· fence
⁊⁌ gate
◠ hut

1 *Indlunkulu* hut
2 *Ingqadi* hut
3 *Ikholwa* hut
4 *Ilawu*

Fig. 10.2 The ordering of domestic space in the Zulu hut and homestead

social space. Unfortunately, he employs a set of structural divisions which have 'universal significance' – the same divisions can be found in Amerindian and Javanese villages (cf. Lévi-Strauss 1962, as cited in Kuper 1980, 1982) – and one loses any sense of the cosmological basis for the unique ordering of Nguni domestic space. In order to avoid gross generalisations about the order in Nguni settlements I will begin by exploring how the cosmology of a particular northern Nguni group, the Zulu, is encoded in the spatial ordering of the homestead, and how this is used to maintain the cultural dynamic. I will briefly outline the Swazi data to show that the system of meanings encoded in the Zulu settlement is found in other northern Nguni groups. Finally, I will discuss the Ngoni homestead to show that this conforms to the cosmological pattern found among the related groups (Zulu and Swazi) who live in the areas from which the Ngoni migrated.

The Zulu

The Zulu are a partrilineal[2] group and post-marital residence is virilocal (Gluckman 1950, pp. 169–71). They organise social space according to a symbolically significant set of principles. These principles are realised at a number of levels and the two levels which will be considered here are the hut and the homestead. In both cases the outer boundary (the walls of the hut and the outer fence of the homestead) creates a circular space which is divided into two halves by a central axis.

In the hut the central axis is delineated by three features: the *umsamo* at the back of the hut; the fireplace in the centre; and the doorway which is the entrance to the hut (fig. 10.2). This axis divides the hut into two halves, one used by males and the other by females (Berglund 1976, pp. 102–10; Krige 1950, pp. 44–7). The division of the hut into two halves can be seen as a division into members of the lineage who are 'constantly' associated with the homestead, and those members who will ultimately live in homesteads of other lineages (daughters/sisters) or members of other lineages who have come to live in the homestead (wives). The sociological and cosmological significance of this 'male'/'female' division has been discussed in the context of the pollution of birth and death (Ngubane 1977, ch. 5; Sibisi 1976).

The divisions of the homestead mirror the divisions of the hut. The central axis is formed by the *indlunkulu* hut at the back of the homestead, the cattle byre in the middle and the main entrance to the homestead in the front (fig. 10.2). This axis divides the homestead into two halves, which are the equivalent of the 'male'/'female' divisions of the hut. The *ikholwa* section is the equivalent of the 'female' side and this section has the right to move out of the homestead and establish a new settlement before the death of the homestead head (Krige 1950, p. 41). The *ingqadi* section is like the 'male' side of the hut, and it remains in the homestead until the head of the homestead dies. The *ikholwa* and *ingqadi* sections of the homestead are not described as female and male respectively, but their 'behaviour' is analogous to the behaviour of women and men in Zulu society.

Zulu concepts about, and their use of, domestic space are intimately associated with their cosmology, in which the ancestors have a central role in both biological and social 'reproduction'. The central axes are the focus of ritual activities which enable the ancestors to 'reproduce' Zulu society, and the cosmological significance of space is exemplified in the use of this axis in ritual. I will use two rituals, the 'strengthening of the child' after birth which is carried out in the hut, and the *thomba* (male puberty) ritual which is carried out in the homestead, to show the system of meanings which underlie the ordering of Zulu domestic space.

'Strengthening the child' and the symbolism of the Zulu hut

When a child is born two holes are made in the *umsamo* of the hut. The placenta is buried in one and the second is plastered with dung and made into a shallow basin. This basin is filled with 'medicated' (*intelezi*) water and the child is then washed in the bowl. This ritual washing is the first step in a process which transforms the neonate into a 'social being'. At this point the mother and child are in a liminal state and the only people allowed into the hut are the 'midwives' and the 'doctor' (Krige 1950, p. 69; Sibisi 1976). The restrictions on who may enter the hut continue until the child is strengthened by being repeatedly 'smoked' in the fire. The strengthening smoke is produced by burning animal charms mixed with some of the dirt scraped from the father's arm. The father's dirt is particularly important because it confers a portion of the *Thongo*, the ancestral spirits, on the child (Krige 1950, p. 67). Married women are now allowed to visit the mother and child but males, including the father, and unmarried women are not allowed to enter the hut. This period of isolation is terminated by a cleansing ritual. The mother and child are sprinkled with *intelezi* water, the hut is swept clean and the floor is replastered. Then the father is called and the child is presented to him, after which the mother and child are free to leave the hut without being covered.

The *umsamo*, the place where the child is washed, is the area where offerings are presented to the ancestors, who are thought to like this area because it is cool and dark (Berglund 1976, p. 102). The arch of the hut above the *umsamo* is called the *ufindo*, which is also the name for the arch in the spine where the gall bladder and kidneys are located (Berglund 1976, p. 115). The gall bladder is particularly liked by the ancestors because the black, bitter gall is said to be sweet, 'like sugar' to the ancestors (Berglund 1976, p. 110). The darkness of the *umsamo* and the explicit link with the area of the gall bladder indicates that this is an area liked by the ancestors. However, to see this as a residence for the ancestors is inadequate. Gall is sprinkled on people after a ritual sacrifice has been conducted for them and this black gall makes them sweet to the ancestors who descend and brood (Berglund 1976, p. 130). The washing of the child in the *umsamo* places the child in an area especially liked by the ancestors who descend on the child and brood.

But the hearth is also associated with the ancestors. It is

here that the ancestors warm themselves and lick the remains of the evening meal (Berglund 1976, pp. 103–4). The fire is also linked to the activity of the ancestors in procreation – Zulu talk of the ancestors 'moulding the child in the heat of sexual intercourse' and the fire being 'like the heat of moulding' (Berglund 1976, pp. 117, 123). The heat of intercourse is also associated with the strengthening of the unborn child and it is said that: 'When the man puts water [ejaculate] into the womb the shades make the child strong. It eats the water' (Berglund 1976, p. 117). Thus, it seems that the fireplace is associated with an 'active' aspect of the shades. It is here that they mould and transform things and this moulding and transforming may require heating. The repeated 'smoking' of the child is thus analogous to the moulding and strengthening of the embryo during repeated intercourse.

The final point on the axis is the doorway, and once more it is associated with the ancestors, although the nature of the ancestors' presence is not clear from the ethnographies. The Zulu draw an explicit connection between the entrance of the hut and the entrance to the woman's vagina (Berglund 1976, p. 117). Thus, the movement of the child from the hut at the end of the 'strengthening' ritual is analogous to the passage of the child from the womb to the outside world during biological birth.

The conceptual linkage between the hut and the womb is clearly recognised by the Zulu, and the hut is sometimes described as a womb (Berglund 1976, pp. 117, 168; Sibisi 1976). The creation of new huts in a homestead also exemplifies this connection between the hut and the womb. A new bride has no fire in her hut and no utensils or cattle for her own use. She is under the control of her mother-in-law until she has given birth to her first child, an event which takes place in the hut of her mother-in-law. It is only after the birth that the new wife acquires a fire, utensils and cattle for her own use. Thus the acquisition of a complete 'home', with its complex symbolic representation of reproduction, is dependent on successful biological reproduction.[3]

The Thomba ritual and the symbolism of the Zulu homestead

When a Zulu boy has his first nocturnal emission, he gets up before dawn and drives the cattle to some far spot by a stream where he bathes before sunrise. He then herds the cattle secretly until he is found by a search party. The cattle, with the boy in their midst, are then driven back to the homestead. At this stage the boy is considered 'about to be born' and, on getting his first genital discharge, he is described as 'nothing but a beast' – the boy has moved into a liminal state and he is like a beast, not a man. Once the child is in the byre a fire is made at the entrance to the byre and 'strengthening medicines' are put on a potsherd and boiled on the fire. The boy drinks the boiling medicine from his finger tips. He is then taken to the seclusion hut (either the *indlunkulu* hut or the associated *ilawu* or bachelors' hut) where he sits in the *umsamo*. Once beer has been brewed the boy is returned to the byre and an ox or bull is

slaughtered. Special parts of the animal are cut off and placed in the *umsamo* of the *indlunkulu* hut. While this is being done the father may fetch the boy to sit at, not in, the *umsamo* while he reports on the boy's stage of development to the ancestors. The slaughtered animal is then cooked and general feasting follows, although the boy and his age mates return to the seclusion hut. At the end of the feasting the boy is taken to a river and he dives into the water. When he emerges he is considered to be newly born and is given a new name by his age mates. While the boys are at the river the seclusion hut is cleaned and the floor is replastered. This marks the end of the seclusion period and the boy is brought out as a young man in the *umgonqo* dance.

Thus the boy washes away the 'pollution' of a sexual emission and his status as a boy. This is followed by his transformation into an extreme state of liminality via a heating and strengthening process which takes place in the cattle byre. Once the 'initiate' has entered this extreme state of liminality he is secluded in the *umsamo* of the *indlunkulu* or associated *ilawu*[4] and it is here that the ancestors descend on him and brood. The second half of the ritual reverses this process. The 'initiate' is brought from the seclusion hut into the byre where an animal is sacrificed. The Zulu describe meat as 'hot' and this shows that the ritual slaughter of the animal is the equivalent of a heating process which transforms the initiate. The liminal period is ended when the boy emerges from the water and this can be seen as a washing away of the ancestors and a rebirth into a new social status, that of young man.

The interpretation presented above indicates that the three points along the central axis of the homestead are directly equivalent to the three points along the central axis of the hut: the *indlunkulu* hut = the *umsamo*; the byre = the hearth; and the main entrance = the doorway. The link between the *indlunkulu* and the *umsamo* is based on the ritual 'purity' of this hut when it is used as a seclusion hut. The fire does not burn and the hut is cool and dark; the sort of place that the ancestors like (Krige 1950, p. 291). The skulls of sacrificed animals are also displayed above the doorway of this hut, which can be seen as the equivalent of presenting a portion of the sacrificed animals in the *umsamo* of a hut.

The linkage between the byre and the hearth also appears to be straightforward. However, the Zulu draw an explicit analogy between the byre and a hut (Berglund 1976, p. 112). They suggest that the areas at the back of the byre, and in particular the calf pen, are like the *umsamo*. While I would accept that the byre can be seen as the house of the cattle, I feel that if there was a strict analogy then the 'initiate' would be secluded in the calf pen, which is the equivalent of the *umsamo*.

Berglund (1976, p. 112) admits to some surprise at the absence of a special name for the back of the byre, but the lack of a name suggests an even stronger link between the byre and the fireplace. The hearthstone at the back of the fireplace is not given a special name but it is intimately tied to the ancestors:

[The stone is] religiously left in its place, none ever daring to remove it . . . because it is from it that the

shades watch the hearth. That is the place that they
occupy.   (Berglund 1976, p. 104)
It should also be noted that the left-over, cooked food is placed
by this stone for the ancestors to lick at night (Berglund 1976,
p. 103). There is an equivalent to this pattern in ritual sacrifice.
The fire on which the men cook their portion of the meat from
a ritual sacrifice is close to where the animal was killed, and the
men eat the meat in the upper part of the byre (Berglund 1976,
p. 218; Krige 1950, p. 295). Thus, the byre appears to be the
equivalent of a hearth, but one used by the homestead as a
whole, and the back of the byre is probably similar to the
hearthstone at the back of the fireplace.

Discussion

The analyses presented above illustrate the common
symbolism underlying the central axis in the hut and the
homestead. The huts are symbolic wombs embedded in a larger
symbolic womb, the homestead. The former are used in the
social reproduction of individuals while the latter is used in the
social reproduction of the lineage. This can be seen most clearly
in the progressive movement of individuals along the course of
these central axes during the course of their life cycles.

Young children, before they have their ears pierced, sit at
the back of the hut on the female side while their parents (the
'owners' of the hut) sit on either side of the fireplace (Krige
1950, pp. 48-9). Visitors, including the older children, sit
between the fireplace and the doorway. The movement of
children from the front to the back of the hut after the
qumbuza (ear piercing) ritual is associated with the beginning
of their 'official' involvement in communal activities. Although
they remain under the control of their parents, they are now
also subject to the communal control of their age mates.

The same direction of movement is seen at the level of
the homestead during the course of the male life cycle. Young
children live in their parents' house until their ears are pierced.
The boys then move to the *ilawu*, which is below the huts
occupied by the wives of the homestead head (Holleman 1940).
Once the young men marry they build huts for their wives near
the main gate to the homestead. They are now nascent
homesteads and they move away to become independent
homesteads on the death of the homestead head.[5] The men
move to the back of the new homesteads because, like the
ancestors, they are reproducing new lineages.

The Swazi

The settlements of the Swazi are almost identical to those
of the Zulu (Marwick 1940, pp. 13–15). The huts are divided
into male and female halves by a central axis consisting of the
same three features that are found in the Zulu homestead: the
umsamo at back, the hearth in the centre and the doorway in
the front. There is also a ritual 'smoking and strengthening' of
the child which is virtually identical to the Zulu ritual (Kuper
1947, pp. 74–6). However, in this group it is only the 'royal'
children who are 'smoked and strengthened' in the fire.

Similarly, the homestead is divided into two halves, the
kunene and *likholwa* sections,[6] by a central axis which consists
of the *indlunkulu* hut at the back, the byre in the centre and the
main entrance to the homestead in the front (Marwick 1940,
pp. 11–33). The Swazi do not have an elaborate male
puberty/nubility ritual but the central axis is used in ritual
transformations in a number of other contexts, for example in
marriage (Marwick 1940, pp. 101–12) and the first fruits
ceremony (Kuper 1947). In both these cases the ritual takes
virtually the same form as the equivalent ritual among the Zulu
(cf. Krige 1950, pp. 120–58, 249–60).

Unfortunately, the ethnographers who have worked on
the Swazi have not reported the way in which the Swazi
conceptualise the different features which form the central axis
of the hut and the homestead. The only exception is the
symbolism of the *umsamo*, which is clearly conceptualised in
the same way as the *umsamo* in the Zulu hut (Kuper 1947,
pp. 11–13). However, the central axes have the same 'function'
in both the Swazi and Zulu rituals, and the Swazi settlement

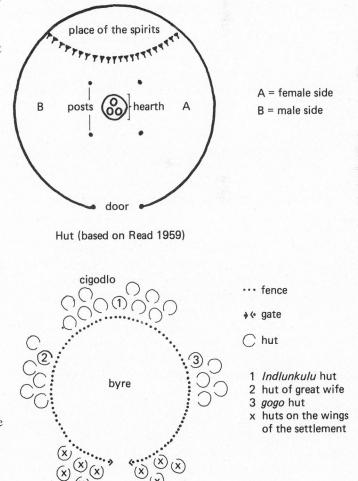

Fig. 10.3 The ordering of domestic space in the Ngoni hut and
homestead

can also be conceptualised as a number of wombs, the huts embedded in a larger womb, the homestead. Thus, the organisation of domestic space among the Zulu and Swazi appears to be based on very similar, but not identical, cosmologies.

The Ngoni

The Ngoni hut (fig. 10.3), like that of the Zulu, is divided into male and female halves by a central axis which consists of the 'place of the spirits' – a raised area at the back of the hut, the hearth in the centre, and the doorway in the front (Read 1956, pp. 82, 200; 1959, pp. 19–20, 73–5). Unfortunately, there is almost no description of the symbolism associated with these points on the central axis and any comparison must be based on how these points are used. The 'place of the spirits' is used to store ritual objects (the spear, gourd cups for blood, baskets and platters) and is also the place where sacrificial meat is presented to the ancestors (Read 1956, pp. 199–200). This corresponds to the uses of the *umsamo* among the Swazi and Zulu. It is also clear that the Ngoni concepts about the fire are similar to those found among the Zulu and Swazi, and this can be seen in the treatment of people who are ill. The person who is ill is placed in the *indlunkulu* hut and special cuts of meat from a sacrificed animal are burnt on the fire (Read 1956, p. 200). The same practice is found among the Zulu (Berglund 1976, pp. 231–4) and this indicates that the Ngoni and the Zulu probably conceptualise the central axis of the hut in a similar way. Thus the Ngoni hut can be thought of as a symbolic womb.

A similar central axis is also found in the Ngoni homestead. The *indlunkulu* hut, at the back of the homestead (fig. 10.3), appears to be an important ritual centre and it is here that the sacrificial meat is normally offered to the ancestors (Read 1956, p. 200). This can be seen as the 'place of the spirits' for the whole homestead. Similarly, the byre is associated with sacrifice and rituals which transform an individual from one social status to another. This area can be seen as the equivalent of a hearth, an equivalence which is represented in the male puberty ritual (Read 1956, p. 164; 1959, pp. 110–11). When a boy's voice has broken (not on the first nocturnal emission as among the Zulu) his father slaughters an animal. Some of the chyme is mixed with the bitter *uludengele* root and this is put on the fire near the gate of the byre. When the mixture starts to boil the boy dips the tips of his fingers in the liquid and licks the liquid off. He does this repeatedly until the liquid is finished. In between drinking the liquid he jumps over the fire.

Although the Ngoni male puberty/nubility ritual is different from the one described among the Zulu it clearly represents the idea of the creation of a new social being – an adult as opposed to a child – through a heating process that takes place in the cattle byre.

Finally, the central axis of the Ngoni homestead – *indlunkulu*/byre/entrance – divides the settlement into two halves. The *gogo* section (see p. 113 below) is on the 'female'

side of the homestead while the section headed by the great wife is on the 'male' side of the homestead (fig. 10.3). Thus the divisions of the hut are reproduced in the homestead and the Ngoni homestead, like that of the Zulu, can be conceptualised as a number of wombs, the huts, embedded in a larger womb, the homestead. It is within these symbolic wombs that the ancestors transform the social status of individuals.

The basic system of beliefs which is encoded in the social organisation of domestic space among the Zulu, Swazi and Ngoni is very different from the cosmology encoded in Central Bantu settlements, and it was representatives of the latter group who were displaced by the migrant Ngoni. The first point to be noted about the Central Bantu settlements is that there is no apparent organisation of the homestead: it consists of a dispersed pattern of huts (Mitchell 1966, Appendix B; Richards 1939, end map; Stefaniszyn 1964, p. 29). Thus the symbolism of the larger symbolic womb associated with the social reproduction of the homestead is absent in these groups. An examination of the symbolism of Central Bantu huts also shows a number of differences between them and northern Nguni/Ngoni huts. It is clear that the 'ancestors' are associated with Central Bantu huts but their presence is more pervasive and there is no particular spot where offerings are presented to them (Richards 1939, p. 357; Stefaniszyn 1964, p. 144). Thus the idea of a central transforming axis is also absent. However, it is clear that the Central Bantu believe that fire is an important agent in ritual transformation, and this is shown in a number of rituals including the Chisungu rite among the Bemba (Richards 1982). What is different is the elaborate cosmology linking the settlement with the activity of the ancestors in social reproduction at a number of different levels.[7]

Discussion of the homestead data

It is clear from the discussion presented above that the northern Nguni groups who migrated into south-central Africa maintained their ancestral organisation of domestic space. It is also clear that the ordering of domestic space among the migrant communities encodes a cosmology which is central to their existence as a northern Nguni/Ngoni society. The maintenance of this ideology is at least partly linked to the fact that the Ngoni were conquering groups and this ideology set them apart from the neighbouring Central Bantu groups whom they despised. However, this observation illustrates the importance of a second event that has already been noted, namely the adoption of Lwangwa Tradition pottery by the migrant Ngoni groups. It is to this problem that I will now turn.

Ceramic continuity and the arrival of the Ngoni

The acceptance of an autochthonous pottery tradition, the Lwangwa Tradition, by the migrant Ngoni needs some explanation because other migrant communities, for example, the Kololo, introduce a new ceramic style into the areas where they settled.

It has been noted on a number of occasions that geometric motifs and other forms of surface treatment may be used as symbols by 'Bantu' communities in southern and south-central Africa (Brelsford 1937; Drourega 1927; Earthy 1933, p. 105; Goodall 1946; Huffman 1984; Stead 1947) and these symbols are presumably important in particular cultures. If this is true then a migrant group, which brings a new system of meanings with it, should be associated with a change in ceramic decoration, and this model would account for the correlation between the Kololo and Linyati Tradition.

But why do the Ngoni adopt the local pottery tradition on their arrival in south-central Africa? Swazi and Zulu pots are normally plain (Maggs 1980; Marwick 1940, p. 83), and pottery decoration does not seem to be central in their culture. Therefore, the decoration on Lwangwa Tradition pottery does not conflict with any of the beliefs which are central to being Ngoni, and ceramic decoration can be reinterpreted as decoration rather than as a culturally meaningful statement. This form of reinterpretation is fairly common and can be seen in our own reinterpretation of artifacts from the Third World as 'primitive art'.

It could be argued that Lwangwa Tradition pottery is used by the subject population to maintain their own system of beliefs and to separate them from the conquering Ngoni. However, this model fails to take into account the power of the Ngoni women who were responsible for the maintenance of domestic etiquette and who clearly despised many of the cultural beliefs about 'correct domestic practice' held by the Central Bantu (Read 1959). Furthermore, the northern Nguni/Ngoni women produced the pottery in their homeland and the acceptance of Lwangwa Tradition pottery can hardly be blamed on ignorance. Thus the acceptance of Lwangwa Tradition pottery by the migrant Ngoni groups is probably based on a reinterpretation of a symbolic 'statement' which is culturally meaningful in a Central Bantu context but which does not conflict with the Ngoni cosmology.

Culture, sociology and homesteads: the problem of reinterpretation

The discussion of the ordering of domestic space among the Zulu, Swazi and Ngoni indicates that historical relationships can be detected by an analysis of the cosmology underlying the articulation of remains on a site. This analysis cannot be confined to one aspect of material culture but should be incorporated to cover all aspects of the material remains. Treating sites as *gestalts* may help to overcome some of the problems of reinterpretation hinted at in the discussion of the Ngoni acceptance of Lwangwa Tradition pottery. If motifs are symbolically significant then one might expect to find some pottery types in specific contexts. However, if another group, which did not understand the meaning of the symbols, used the same pots one might expect to find them in unusual contexts. Unfortunately, it is not possible to give an example of this for the Ngoni, as the ethnographies do not examine the use of decorated pottery in any detail.

However, there is a second and more subtle problem of reinterpretation which has not been dealt with, namely the

reinterpretation of the cosmology by migrant groups. This is linked to the sociological significance of the cosmology, the aspect that is central to an anthropological analysis (Cunningham 1973; Tambiah 1969). It has been pointed out by those working on Frontier Theory that sociological changes are common in migrant communities (Billington 1967), and reinterpretations of the symbolism and cosmology should be expected. The Ngoni and Swazi provide an example of this type of reinterpretation.

The Zulu (Krige 1950, pp. 42–4), Swazi (Marwick 1940, pp. 13–15, 28–9) and the Ngoni (Read 1956, p. 20) divide the huts in the homestead into three sections but there are differences in who lives in which section and consequently in the way in which the divisions are conceptualised. For example, the mother of the headman occupies the *indlunkulu* hut among the Swazi and Ngoni, while the Zulu install the great wife in this hut. Kuper (1980, 1982, ch. 10) has suggested that the Swazi practice emphasises the continuity of the homestead and that this is also found in the marriage rules, where there is a preferential alliance with the descendants of one's grandparents' generation (i.e. FMBSD or MMBSD).[8] This model might work in Mombera's kingdom where there is preferential marriage into the mother's clan (basic continuity of homestead structure) but would not work in the Ngwane kingdom where one 'marries-up' but where there is no explicit preferential marriage rule (Read 1956, p. 142). An alternative would be to see 'marrying-up' as the important criterion. 'Marrying-up' is the attempt to marry wives from 'aristocratic' or important families and this has important consequences for the succession to a particular title or position because the status of a male is dependent on the status of his mother's family. This is symbolised by the installation of the mother in the *indlunkulu*. If a Zulu man marries the daughter of a chief then she becomes his great wife even if she is not his first wife (Krige 1950, p. 156), and the status of a son is thus dependent, at least partly, on the status of his mother's family. However, it has been suggested that the Swazi put the mother in the *indlunkulu* because her son's status is dependent on the status of her family, but the status of a Zulu man is also dependent on the status of his mother and he installs his great wife in the *indlunkulu* hut.

The Zulu and Ngwane examples seem to contradict any neat kinship interpretation, but this is only because preferential marriage rules and 'marrying-up' are seen in terms of a system of marriage rules and not in terms of the sociology of the women who are married. This can be illustrated by comparing the 'behaviour' of the analogous *ikholwa* and *gogo* sections in the Zulu and Ngoni homestead. Both of these sections are on the 'female' side of the homestead and yet they behave very differently. Among the Zulu the *ikholwa* has the right to move away and build a new homestead before the head of the homestead has died, while the *gogo* section in the Ngoni homestead remains in the same settlement even when the homestead head has died.

It has already been pointed out that the behaviour of the

ikholwa section is like that of a daughter who leaves the homestead of her father when she marries. The conceptual link between the 'female' half of the homestead and daughters underlines the importance of the marriage of daughters in establishing alliances with other homesteads. These alliances are summarised in the Zulu terms *umphini wekhuba* (the handle of a hoe) which is used to describe a son-in-law because 'the *umkhwenyana* is, like the hoe, a friend and helper to his people-in-law' (Krige 1950, p. 121). A man had to give his father-in-law one beast every time a brother of his wife got married, and he could be called on to provide cattle as and when they were needed. Unfortunately, there is no description of the relationship between a new *ikholwa* homestead and the father's homestead, although Ngubane (1977, p. 40) does say that siblings (from different sections) may be expected to assist one another.

However, a different link is apparent in the behaviour of the 'female' half of the Ngoni homestead. The term *gogo* means grandmother, an elderly female attendant or a house where ancestral spirits are guarded (Read 1956, p. 205). In this case the 'female' half of the homestead is likened to a woman who has married into the lineage and who tends to the needs of the lineage. This is further emphasised in the idea that the *gogo* section is left behind to take care of the ritual and ceremonial duties (Read 1956, p. 15).

The importance of the *gogo* section in the ceremonial and ritual life of the Ngoni appears to be odd because ritual is normally controlled by males rather than females, and the *gogo* section is symbolically 'female'. However, Read (1956, p. 142) points out that women were responsible for the training of young children of both sexes and girls until their marriage. Once a girl was married it was the responsibility of her mother-in-law to teach her correct behaviour and this was considered essential by the Ngoni of Mombera's kingdom and was used to emphasise why they married-up (Read 1956, p. 143). The emphasis on correct behaviour among wives is not hard to explain because eating and drinking amongst the Ngoni were characterised by a formal etiquette:

> [the etiquette] was maintained by the organisation and forethought of the . . . big wives and mothers . . . who planned the work of their own households and supervised that of the lesser wives who were attached to the two main houses.   (Read 1956, p. 86)

Thus women who married into a lineage (wives and mothers) were central to the maintenance of culturally correct behaviour. A similar point is made by Marwick (1940, pp. 64–5) when he cites the Swazi petition to the Union of South Africa Parliament in March 1932:

> [A man's] mother's hut is the chief hut in every Kraal. It is the home of all the children of the Kraal. They all love to sleep and eat there with 'grandmother' who teaches them all about their clan and customs.[9]

Thus the emphasis on marrying-up in both the Ngoni and Swazi appears to be associated with an emphasis on wives and mothers as teachers and guardians of traditional practice. They are as responsible as men, if not more so, for the maintenance of 'Ngoniness' or 'Swazihood'.

Both the Ngoni and the Swazi were migrant groups who settled in areas occupied by alien cultures. Both groups also draw a clear distinction between 'true' Ngoni or Swazi and those groups who were indigenous to the area. In both cases marrying-up means marrying a woman who is a 'true' Ngoni or Swazi and this ensures that the wife knows 'correct behaviour'. Similarly, installing one's mother in the *indlunkulu* hut means that one who knows 'correct behaviour' is in charge of one's wives and the day to day running of the homestead. Evidence which supports my contention that these reinterpretations are a consequence of migration is provided by Swazi oral tradition which indicates that Somtjalose Simelane (the mother of Sobhuza I, the 'king' who migrated to Swaziland) won a special place in ritual and government for the mother of the Dlamini ruler (Kuper 1947). Thus, marrying-up and the installation of the mother of the homestead head in the *indlunkulu* can both be explained by the importance of women in the maintenance of the etiquette which served to distinguish the migrant communities from the alien groups around them.[10]

In this case the reinterpretation is probably not detectable in the material culture residues left on a site, although it is apparent in the behaviour of extant communities. However, this subtle form of reinterpretation may be important in the differential historical development of communities. Unfortunately it is not possible to illustrate this in the Swazi or Ngoni case because the European colonial powers arrived and disrupted the cultural systems.

Discussion

This chapter has been concerned with the archaeological recognition of migrations and it has used a particular series of historically documented movements, the Ngoni and Kololo migrations, to explore this problem. The first point that should be emphasised is that migrations need not produce a complete change in the material culture of an area. Only some aspects may change. This is shown particularly clearly by the Ngoni in the Chipata area of Zambia where there is a drastic change in settlement organisation but a continuation of the pre-Ngoni ceramic style. Furthermore, the types of change cannot be arranged into a neat typology which links them to types of migration or the composition of the migrant group (cf. Alexander 1981; Phillipson 1974). Both the Ngoni and the Kololo had a similar history of movement after they left their original homeland (Omer-Cooper 1966, chs. 5 and 8) and yet there are different patterns of change in the two groups. In the former case there is ceramic continuity despite the arrival of a new group, while the Kololo are associated with a new pottery style (Phillipson 1974). It has been suggested that the different patterns of change are associated with the significance of different aspects of material culture in different communities, and it has been argued that the absence of any significance attached to pottery decoration among the Ngoni enabled them to 'accept' Lwangwa Tradition pottery. Given the above, then there can be no *sine qua non* for the recognition of migrations, and suggestions that only ceramic style can be used to establish the historical relationships between 'Iron Age' cultures in southern Africa (Huffman 1983, p. 134) cannot be accepted.

It is clear from the Ngoni data that the changes in material culture associated with the arrival of a new community are linked to the way in which the new group represents its system of beliefs in material culture. If archaeologists want to infer a migration then they must undertake a detailed contextual analysis to establish the cultural significance of different aspects of material culture and then try to show that the new system of beliefs represented in the material culture is more easily derived from elsewhere. Within this framework it is the articulation of artifacts that encode cultural 'messages' and it is these 'messages', not the artifacts *per se*, which are important in the recognition of migrations. This has an important corollary: conceptualising the changes in material culture associated with a migration in simple mechanical terms – how many migrants moved and who made what (e.g. Phillipson 1974) – is clearly an untenable form of explanation. The important determinant of change is the dominance of a particular ideology and the ability and desire of the migrants to enforce this 'official' system of beliefs. This is particularly clear in the case of the Ngoni migrants where the 'true' Ngoni were probably always in a minority (Read 1956, p. 10). In the case of the Ngoni it is also clear that 'non-Ngoni' accepted the Ngoni system of beliefs and in one case, that of Chiwere Ndhluvo a 'Nsenga' war leader, a 'non-Ngoni' who had been assimilated established a new Ngoni 'kingdom' (Omer-Cooper 1966, p. 83).

However, to see assimilation and cultural uniformity in the area occupied by a migrant community as an inevitable outcome of migration would be wrong. The migrant community might use their culture, including their material culture, to mark themselves off as a separate ruling 'elite'. In the African context this can be seen most clearly in the case of South Africa, where 'being white' (which is partly determined by social acceptance, as the boards for racial classification illustrate), a member of a migrant community, entails both a physical and a cultural separation from the 'non-white' masses. The cultural differences are represented in material culture as well. For example, 'Black' housing in the vicinity of 'white' towns is government controlled and built to different specifications from the 'white' housing in the towns. Similar examples could be drawn from many of the British colonies and Protectorates during the colonial period. Thus, the pattern of change may also represent the relationship between the migrant and indigenous communities and this may be linked to the policies (overt or covert) of the ruling group. This serves to further reinforce the idea that each possible migration must be examined as an historical phenomenon and understood in its own terms and not in terms of a general model of migration or an overarching typology of migration. The cultural and historical realities which produce archaeological data are too complex to be reduced to anything except the most trivial of generalisations.

The recognition that cultural systems may be reinterpreted as a consequence of the experiences of the migrant group raises two issues. Firstly, some of these reinterpretations may not be detectable in the archaeological record: for example, the status of the person occupying the *indlunkulu* hut. This indicates that archaeologists can never hope to write a complete history of cultures or provide a complete understanding of a past culture.

The second issue relates to the recognition of a similar cosmology in the area occupied by a migrant group and in the area from which they moved. If the system can be reinterpreted, then how is it possible to demonstrate that a new system of beliefs has entered an area and that this system of beliefs had its origin elsewhere? On the basis of the Ngoni data it is possible to argue that one can decipher an overarching system of beliefs, a general ethos, into which all the discrepant interpretations fit. Once more this can be illustrated by comparing the *gogo* section of the Ngoni with the *ikholwa* section among the Zulu. These analogous sections are given mutually exclusive interpretations because the metonym of mothers/wives standing for female automatically excludes the metonym sisters/daughters standing for female. However, they are mutually compatible at the level of one side of the homestead's being like a 'female'. Here one can see that the specific interpretation, which is sociologically significant, is a synecdoche for the concept 'female', and the particular part that stands for the whole can be reinterpreted as long as the whole does not change. If subtle reinterpretations are not always recognisable but are consistent with an overarching system of beliefs then one may be able to recognise that a migrant community is derived from a particular major cultural grouping. Thus one could infer that the Ngoni were a northern Nguni group, but one would not be able to say where they came from within this cultural grouping.

It is now possible to return to the original problem with which the present paper was concerned, namely the recognition of migrations in the archaeological record. It is fairly clear from the Kololo and Ngoni data that migrations can be recognised from changes in material culture but only when material culture is seen to be part of systems of belief. This in turn means that archaeologists have to move away from a trait list or stylistic approach to inferring migrations and must, to rephrase Geertz (1973, p. 5), attempt to interpret the webs of significance which are represented in material culture residues which the archaeologist uncovers; and this implies a particularist and historical approach to archaeology.[11]

Notes

1. The terms 'general', 'state' and 'kingdom' have been placed in inverted commas to indicate that they are not necessarily synonymous with the English concepts to which the terms normally refer.
2. There is some controversy about the existence of lineages in Southern Bantu communities (cf. Hammond-Tooke 1984 and

Kuper 1983). However, I would agree with Ngubane (1977, pp. 13–17) that lineages do exist but that they have a very shallow depth. In this case I think that the reasons for the shallow depth of the lineages might form the basis for a more interesting discussion than whether or not the Zulu 'lineage' corresponds to the exact anthropological definition of a 'lineage'.

3. Women without children may have a child put into their 'house', which makes them sociologically but not biologically reproductive.

4. Seclusion huts have to be ritually pure, i.e. without a fire. Thus a hut with a woman and child, which always has the fire burning, cannot be ritually pure. It is possible to argue that huts that are ritually pure are missing the central axis and that there can be no connection with the ancestors. However, this would ignore the fact that ritually pure huts are equivalent to the *umsamo* where the ancestors are quiescent, and the absence of the fire serves to further emphasise the quiescent nature of the brooding shades.

5. The social reproduction of the lineage is very reminiscent of the reproduction of viruses.

6. The *likholwa/kunene* divisions of the Swazi homestead do not appear to be sociologically significant (see Kuper 1947; Marwick 1940). Any attempt to do justice to this problem would have turned this paper into a monograph and I hope to deal with this aspect of the Swazi settlement at some future time.

7. The idea that huts and homesteads are symbolic wombs may be a feature in Bantu groups that are patrilineal, and the symbolism could be interpreted as an attempt by the patrilineages to control fertility. If this is the case, then the symbolism would be largely redundant in the matrilineal Bantu, where individual and lineage reproduction are centred in individual houses. However, any attempt to examine this hypothesis would require a detailed analysis of the symbolism of huts and homesteads in a number of matrilineal and patrilineal Bantu groups. This is clearly beyond the scope of the present paper.

8. These symbols follow the conventional anthropological procedure for representing kinship ties (see Kuper 1982, p. 9, for further details).

9. In this case 'Kraal' means homestead.

10. The emphasis on women and etiquette among the Zulu is reminiscent of our ideas about the British *memsahib* but without the negative connotations. This indicates the importance of women in the maintenance of culture (hardly surprising given their 'normal' role as child bearers and educators of young children), an importance which is clearly recognised and valued in migrant communities where the 'naturalness' of cultural beliefs and values are constantly challenged by the existence of 'alien others'.

11. I would like to thank John Alexander and Ian Hodder for their comments on an early draft of this paper. My special thanks go to Joan Knowles who provided the intellectual stimulation that made this paper possible. While I am sure that she does not agree with all aspects of my interpretation I hope that this paper reflects the concern for 'real people' which she has emphasised in our discussions (even though my work is concerned with dead 'real people').

Chapter 11

Gothic material culture

Kevin Greene

Around AD 500, Ostrogoths and Visigoths held power in Italy, Spain and much of southern France. Through a long and complex history, the structure of Gothic society, waxing and waning in influence, underwent significant alterations. The Goths were everywhere in a minority in relation to those they ruled, and material symbols played a role in the maintenance of power. Yet the meaning and social significance of items such as the Gothic 'eagle-brooches' can be understood only by tracing the history of their use. The form of the eagle-brooches refers back to important influences upon the Goths – the Roman Empire (where the model is the imperial Roman eagle) and the Huns (where the eagle presents an image of strength and predation). Other influences concern the change from horse-gear to female brooch depictions, and the use of lavish polychrome. These symbolic associations played a part in the legitimation of the highest level of the Gothic elite. This elite, however, maintained a contradictory position in relation to Romans. As a minority, the Goths expressed their rule as an imitation of the Romans. Yet Goths had sacked Rome and they maintained an 'heretical' religion. The style of the eagle-brooches played on this duality, meaning different things to Goth and Roman. There is similar potential for linking culture history to social process through the interpretation of symbolic meanings for the whole range of Dark Age metalwork.

Introduction

This paper attempts to explain the adoption, transmission, and eventual abandonment of certain forms of artifacts and artistic idioms in early medieval Europe. It will examine ways in which tribal identity could be defined, reinforced or abandoned, and will argue that abstract concepts about society were displayed by decorated metalwork. Prehistorians have of course long been interested in the problems of correlating peoples with things, whether on a general 'cultural' level, or simply when similar artifacts or motifs are found over a wide geographical area. However, increasing numbers of archaeologists are realising that historical periods may be very important for testing hypotheses developed in other contexts where no independent evidence for a historical and cultural framework exists.

The elucidation of problems encountered in past studies of correlations between artifacts and society has been a consistent feature of ethnoarchaeological analyses of the contexts of material objects in anthropological settings, whether by Binford in Alaska or Hodder in Africa. An early result of such research was the observation that the same artifact could possess different 'meanings' in different social settings, which could by implication change through time or even coexist within a single society which was itself changing: "reference to the history of a particular cultural trait is fundamentally important in the interpretation of its position and use within a new phase" (Hodder 1982a, p. 217). For the purposes of early medieval archaeology, Gothic metalwork may demonstrate that similar interpretations can be derived from its known historical and cultural context, without the necessity of recourse to other, albeit interesting, ethnoarchaeological analogies.

The concept of 'cultures' has been at the forefront of

theoretical and practical research in archaeology for several decades (e.g. Hodder 1978, 1982a, pp. 1–12). In the Migration period (*Völkerwanderungszeit*), the phase of late Roman and early medieval history which was characterised by the movements of large numbers of principally Germanic peoples (Musset 1975), a simplistic 'Childean' view of cultures, with more or less explicit ethnic overtones, has implicitly underlain much archaeological research (Greene 1983, p. 161, fig. 89). However, Shennan's case study of Beaker 'culture' (1978) has demonstrated the dangers involved in making superficial comparisons between different geographical areas in terms of artifacts. The results of his quantified presentation of the features of four separate European areas of 'Beaker culture', where Beakers are the only consistent element amongst a range of traits with different spatial distributions, seem to parallel the kind of variations likely to have resulted from the manner in which migration, division and absorption took place amongst ethnic groups in early historic Europe (Wenskus 1977, pp. 431–7, 471). Barbarian tribes were by no means static; they branched out in complicated ways involving different numbers of people. A successful settlement by a few individuals in a new area could lead to the arrival of further groups, and the accretion of unrelated groups and native populations, who might all eventually adopt the name and traditions of the founders.

In addition to the problem of cultures, another recent preoccupation of prehistorians has been explanation, used as an antonym of description. European Bronze Age Beakers illustrate the changing tide of interpretation, from a diffusionist extreme where Beakers marked the progress of intrusive metallurgists, to a 'package deal' where the idea of using Beakers spread without 'Beaker People' (Burgess 1980, p. 63). Many early medieval artifacts have a widely dispersed distribution which can be related to historically documented events and processes which have remained unpopular amongst prehistorians for nearly two decades: invasion, migration and diffusion (J. G. D. Clark 1966). Other less direct cultural interactions may also be attested, and the symbolic nature of artifacts may be more important than their precise geographical locations and ethnic affiliations. Thus, the lesson of historical archaeology is the same as that of ethnoarchaeology: identical cultural traits may be explicable in very different ways depending upon their geographical, chronological and social contexts. The application of ethnoarchaeology should perhaps be optimised not in prehistoric archaeology but in the historical period; occasional enlightenment may be extended into real understanding and explanation.

The Goths

There are serious difficulties in the use of the term 'Goths' before the fifth century AD. Not only is there the problem of the date and significance of the division into Ostrogoths and Visigoths, but also the relationship between Goths and other eastern Germanic relatives and offshoots such as Taifali or Gepids. A full discussion of the problems involved

has been provided by Wolfram (1979, pp. 32–136; see also Wenskus 1977, especially pp. 462–85). In this paper, 'Gothic' is used in its widest sense, justified by the evidence which Wenskus assembles for the broad concept of overall unity held by the Goths themselves before their entry into the Roman Empire in the fourth century, and still embodied in the writings of Jordanes in Italy in the sixth (*ibid.*, pp. 474–5).

The Goths in south-east Europe

Although the story is shrouded by mythology and retrospective simplification by the sixth-century historian Jordanes (*Gothic History* IV. 25), it seems reasonable to assume that having crossed the Baltic from their original Scandinavian homeland, the Goths gradually spread south from Poland to the Black Sea by the third century AD (Wenskus 1977, pp. 462–9). Around AD 270, Rome abandoned the province of Dacia, and Goths filtered into the area which is now Romania; for the following century, they shared a common frontier with the Empire along the lower Danube. By 376 the Asiatic nomadic Huns had overrun not only the Ostrogoths in south Russia but also the Visigoths in Romania. Many Goths, along with other peoples, continued to live in these areas under Hunnic rule, but others, notably the Visigoths, sought refuge inside the Empire in exchange for military service (Ammianus xxxi. 3–4). This relationship broke down, and led to a rebellion by the Visigoths which resulted in the defeat of the Roman army at the catastrophic battle of Adrianople in AD 378.

The Goths in western Europe

Two invasions of Italy involving Goths took place in the early fifth century AD. An assortment of Germans including Ostrogoths under Radagaisus were defeated, but a major invasion by Visigoths led by Alaric actually resulted in the sacking of Rome in AD 410. These Visigoths then moved north on Rome's behalf in 411 to attack the British usurper Constantine III, who had recovered Gaul after the great invasion by Vandals, Alans, and Suebi in 406–7. Having successfully defeated Constantine, the Visigoths were once more a threat to the Romans. After being blockaded and starved out of southern Gaul and forced into Spain, they settled in parts of Aquitaine in 418 with official Roman approval, and founded a Gothic kingdom centred upon Toulouse. Italy itself fell to the Ostrogoths in 488, when Theodoric invaded from Hungary to displace Odovacer, a German who had ruled Italy since the last western emperor was deposed in 476. The Ostrogothic kingdom flourished under Theodoric, but a Byzantine army intent on reconquest invaded in 536. A protracted series of bitter and destructive campaigns ensued which so weakened the country that it fell to yet another barbarian group, the Lombards, in AD 568.

The Visigothic kingdom based on Toulouse in Aquitaine expanded steadily after its creation in 418, and soon reached the Loire and the Rhone. At its greatest extent, it shared a common border in southern Gaul with the Italian Ostrogothic

Fig. 11.1 Metalwork from the Ostrogothic kingdom of Italy (Ashmolean Museum, Oxford, 1909, 775–6). Brooches and buckles of this form with cast decoration were the commonest items buried with deceased Gothic women in the later fifth and sixth centuries AD, from Hungary to Spain. After the initial extravagance of the very large cast brooch (fig. 11.4, 4), Gothic brooches show a remarkable uniformity of size, form and decoration from Spain to south Russia (*ibid.*, nos. 5–6). Scale 1:1

kingdom of Theodoric (James 1977, pp. 7–8). The Frankish king Clovis conquered most of the kingdom in 507, leaving only a narrow strip of territory along the Mediterranean coast north of the Pyrenees in Visigothic hands (James 1982, pp. 15–21). Because the Gothic kingdom had also been expanding southwards across the Pyrenees since 475, its capital was moved south, eventually to Toledo. The Spanish Gothic kingdom survived much longer than the Italian, and weathered a partial Byzantine reconquest in the sixth century, before finally succumbing to the Arabs in the early eighth.

Thus, at their greatest extent around AD 500, Ostrogothic and Visigothic kingdoms incorporated Italy, Spain, and much of southern Gaul. In his study of the Ostrogoths, Burns divided their history into three phases: (1) the gradual spread from Scandinavia to south Russia; (2) the experiences on the frontiers of the Roman Empire (c. AD 250–450); (3) the Gothic kingdom of Italy (AD 488–568). He saw the different circumstances of each phase as crucial to the transformation of the structure of Ostrogothic society (1974, pp. 8–10). Thus, the Ostrogoths developed from agrarian peasants into richer, more hierarchically organised enemies/allies of Rome, and finally became the minority rulers of the former heart of the Roman Empire. How are these developments expressed in the archaeology of the Goths?

Gothic material culture

The historical outline given above makes it clear that the Goths were one of the most important barbarian peoples involved in the disappearance of the western Roman Empire. Their authority grew and contracted dramatically in Gaul, Italy, and Spain between AD 400 and 700. Archaeologically, the Goths are significant because they formed a link between the Asiatic Huns, the surviving eastern Roman Empire, and the western Germanic Franks and Lombards. They also continued to be influenced by the western Romans, and in fact did much to preserve the structure of Roman law, administration, and land-holding in their kingdoms (Goffart 1980). Goths were everywhere in a minority in relation to the Romans they ruled, and this fact may explain their tenacious adherence to some specific types of metalwork.

The range of artifacts which can be associated with the Goths through their date and distribution includes several types of brooches and buckles, most frequently found in the graves of aristocratic women (Bierbrauer 1975, pp. 63–8, 72–83). Unlike the western and North Sea Germanic peoples, in the Roman Iron Age the Goths had adopted the practice of inhuming their aristocratic dead in small, rich cemeteries, in which only the graves of women contained objects. Their cemetery archaeology is therefore much poorer than that of the Franks, Lombards, or Anglo-Saxons, who appear to have buried all of their dead with grave goods in large cemeteries. Bierbrauer assembled the evidence from the whole of Ostrogothic Italy, and found that only 126 graves could be assigned to this period with confidence. Few Gothic burial places have been examined archaeologically, but the small cemetery investigated at Acquasanta (Ascoli Piceno) is probably typical of the many known only from accidental finds (Annibaldi and Werner 1963). Gothic burial practice thus creates a bias in the recovered evidence – there is not a great deal of it, but the material quality is high.

The commonest set of artifacts found buried with the female dead consists of a pair of brooches with semicircular

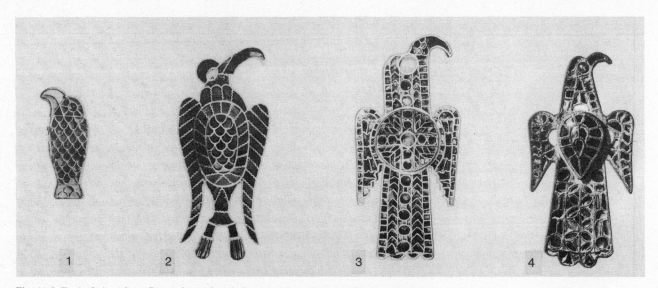

Fig. 11.2 Eagle fittings from Romania, and eagle-brooches from Italy and Spain. Scale 1:2.
1. Conçesti, Moldavia, Romania (Kühn 1939–40: Taf. 57b. 6, p. 140). Size: 6.00 cm. Gold, inlaid with red stones and mother of pearl.
2. Apahida, Cluj, Romania (Horedt and Protase 1972: Taf. 49–50 and pp. 187–8). Size: 11.5 cm. Gold, inlaid with red almandines; green stone in eye.
3. Domagnano, San Marino, Italy (Bierbrauer 1973: Taf. 35–6. 1a–b, 1 and p. 68). Size: 12 cm. Gold, inlaid with red almandines and white paste details including wing tips. Provenance frequently quoted as Cesena (Prov. Forli).
4. Alovera, Guadalajara, Spain (Roth 1979: Abb. 57b and p. 147). Size 11.5 cm. Bronze, gilt, inlaid with red almandines.

heads and rhombic feet (see below, p. 126), and a buckle with a rectangular plate (fig. 11.1). Other items, including ear-rings, bracelets, and toilet instruments, occur more sporadically (Bierbrauer 1975, pp. 64, Abb. 7, 65, Abb. 8, 73, Abb. 9). It is important to note that the brooches and buckles are not of a traditional ethnic form stretching back into the Roman Iron Age, but can be seen to have been adopted in the fourth and fifth centuries AD in south Russia and Romania (Diaconu 1973, pp. 266–8, Taf. IV–VI).

Eagle-brooches

A particularly distinctive brooch in the form of a highly stylised eagle is found in Italy and Spain (fig. 11.2: 3–4; distribution, fig. 11.3). It allows us to investigate the effects of Hunnic and eastern Roman influences upon the Goths. Eagle-brooches are of considerable importance in illustrating the active role of cultural choice in the adoption of artifacts, and have clear implications for the use of distinctive items for social purposes. They were worn in symmetrically opposed matching pairs, of which the remains of seventeen have been found, three in Italy, eleven in Spain, two in France, and one in East Germany. Those from France are almost certainly imports from Spain, while the German example may well have come from Italy. In isolation, they tell us little; their significance is revealed only by an investigation into their earlier development in Romania.

Origins of eagle-brooches Substantial numbers of Goths, in particular Ostrogoths, lived in south-eastern Europe under Hunnic domination from the later fourth century AD until the rebellion of these subject peoples which culminated in the battle of Nedao in Romania in 454 (Pohl 1980, pp. 252–61). Only three years earlier, under the leadership of Attila, the Huns had threatened the whole of Gaul and Italy; after their defeat at the battle of Châlons in eastern France, Attila moved south into Italy, before eventually withdrawing to Hungary, where he died in AD 453. During this brief domination of much of Europe and Russia, the Huns had presented an image of a horse-borne nobility decorated with flashy polychrome jewellery, even possessing objects from China such as jade sword chapes and silver mirrors (Werner 1956a, Taf. 3.13, Taf. 13). Their distinctive reflex bows and wooden saddles, essential to their mounted archery, were frequently sheathed in decorated metal, sometimes gold (*ibid.*, Taf. 16).

Many Goths and other Germans undoubtedly shared in the spoils of Hunnic raids on Persia, Syria, and the Roman Empire, as well as the rich pickings to be gained from Roman bullion diplomacy and ransoms. The taste for polychrome

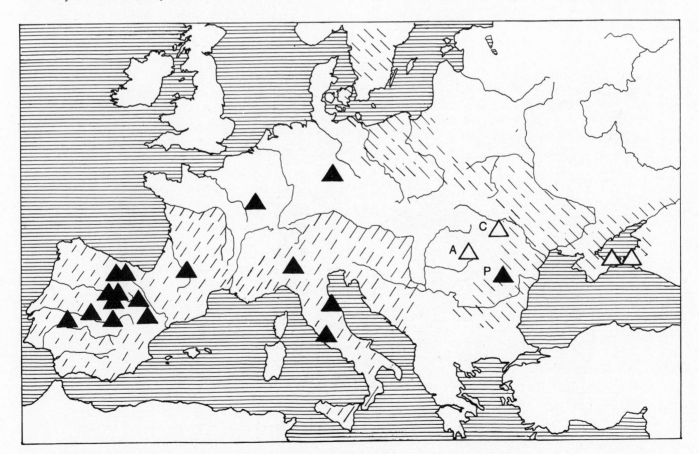

Fig. 11.3 Areas of migration/settlement, and the extent of kingdoms of the Ostrogoths and Visigoths (shaded areas): after Wolfram 1979: Karte 7). Solid triangles indicate eagle-brooches.
C = Conçesti, P = Pietroasa, A = Apahida, Romania. Drawn by Sarah Mawson

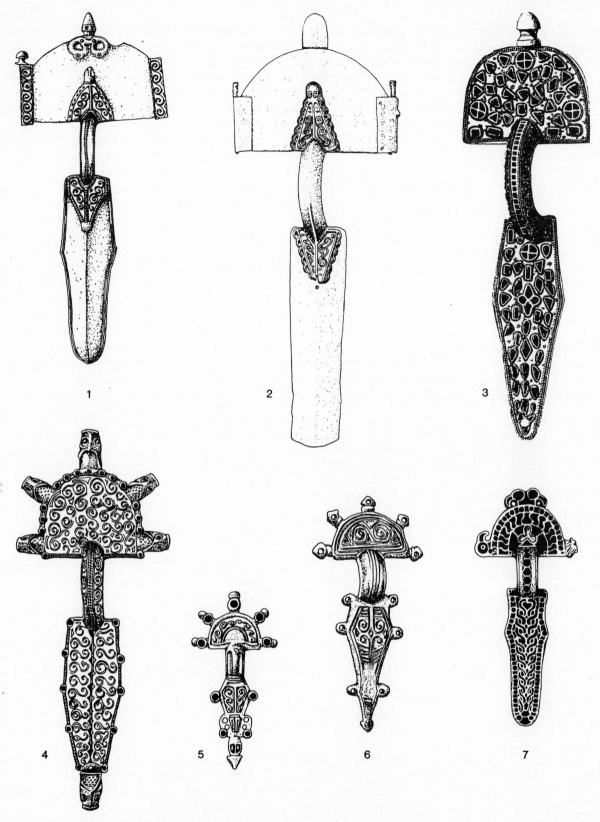

Fig. 11.4 Gothic plate-brooches of developed forms: 1: Gyula, Kom. Békés. Hungary. Sheet-silver, with repoussé and cast decorative fittings. 2: ?Castiltierra, Segovia, Spain. Sheet silver, with repoussé and cast decorative fittings. The form of the foot is characteristically Spanish, although the overall concept of this brooch closely resembles that of no. 1. 3: Simleul Silvaniei (Szilágysomlyó), Salaj, Romania. Sheet silver covered with gold foil, decorated with filigree wire and cabochon stone settings for red almandines and green glass. 4: Gáva, Kom. Szabolcs-Szatmár, Hungary. cast silver, gilded; some niello inlay, and small garnets set around edges of plates. 5: South Russia. Cast silver, lightly gilded, with cast spiral decoration; some small almandines set into projecting knobs. 6: ?Castiltierra, Segovia, Spain. Cast bronze, with cast spiral decoration, and plain holes without stone settings. 7: ?Desana, Vercelli, Italy. Cast silver or bronze plates with gold cloisonné settings for red almandines and green glass; the round cells contain domed pieces of green glass.
Drawn by William Hubbard, after Roth 1979: Taf. 34, 55, 39b, 56c, and 72a (nos. 1–2, 4, 6–7); Kühn 1974: Taf. XX.26; Werner 1961: taf. 26.109 (no. 5). Scale approximately 1:2

metalwork which continued to characterise the highest levels of Germanic society down to the Carolingian period was no doubt enhanced by this formative experience. The polychrome style itself was not intrinsically Hunnic, of course, but derived from eastern Roman and Persian sources. The former Greek and Roman cities on the south-Russian coast of the Black Sea presumably acted as the foci for the production of richly decorated artifacts under Ostrogothic or Hunnic patronage. Polychrome decoration is found on Gothic plate-brooches in the fifth century AD in the second treasure from Simleul Silvaniei (fig. 11.4: 3; Harhoiu 1977, fig. 2.1). Current opinion now links the burial of this and other Romanian treasures with the break up of Attila's empire in the mid-450s AD, rather than with the arrival of the Huns in the previous century (*ibid.*, pp. 3–6). The emergence of the eagle-brooch as a distinctive Gothic artifact can be traced in this varied cultural context, and its origins reflect the two most important influences upon the Goths – the Roman Empire and the Huns.

The imperial Roman eagle provided many examples of both three-dimensional eagles with folded wings and two-dimensional spread-eagles, including some used as brooches (e.g. Werner 1961, Taf. 49. 323; Thiry 1939, Taf. 1L). Such emblems must have been familiar to young Goths, such as the future ruler of Italy, Theodoric, serving as hostages in the court of Constantinople. They may also have been visible on Roman military buildings and other monuments left behind in Dacia. From the Huns came a different notion of the eagle, never represented whole, but either by its head and beak or simply by a stylised representation of its overlapping feathers (e.g. head – Werner 1956a, Taf. 14.9; feathers – *ibid.*, Taf. 7.3). These occur throughout south Russia and Europe, and correlate well with other Hunnic artifacts assignable to the time of Attila (fig. 11.5).

To Romans, the eagle embodied the notion of royalty. To the aggressive nomadic Huns and earlier nomads such as the Sarmatians, it would have provided a more extensive symbol of power combined with strength and predation, presumably enhanced by the practice of falconry. Indeed, the modern Khazakhs of western China even managed to maintain the tradition of hunting with eagles from horseback through the Cultural Revolution of the 1960s. Some Sarmatian eagles are represented whole, and bear stylised imbricated feather patterns (Phillips 1965, p. 89, figs 100–1), but for some reason complete representations of the bird were not used by the Huns. Whether this was a result of conscious avoidance is difficult to decide, but of course partial representation need in no way have diminished the symbolic power of the eagle.

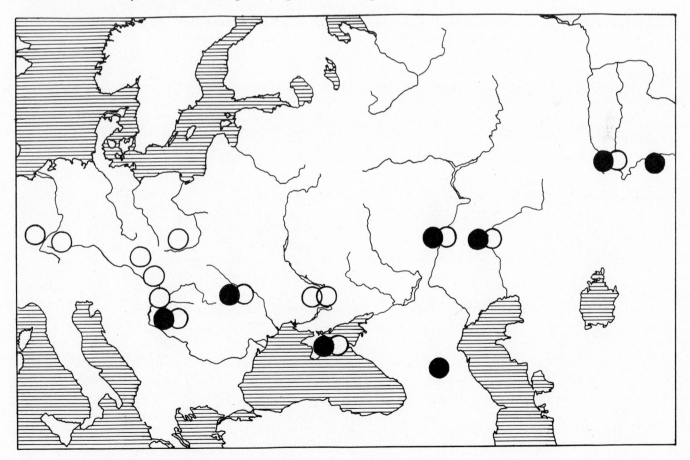

Fig. 11.5 Distribution of gold eagle motifs (filled circles) and feather-pattern decoration (hollow circles) on artefacts associated with the Huns (drawn by Sarah Mawson after Werner 1956a: Taf. 72, Karte 7).

Eagle fittings (fig. 11.2: 1–2) Simple fittings or appliqués in the shape of eagles, presumably made during the fifth-century Hunnic domination of the Ostrogoths, have been found in south Russia and Romania (Kertsch – Thiry 1939, Taf. 6.27; Conçesti – fig. 11.2:1). These eagles have a head and body of rudimentary form, and do not possess wings. In an abstract typological sense, they provide a bridge between Hunnic and later Gothic forms. They are small and simple, and have *cloisonné* decoration made up of cells which copy the feather pattern frequently used by the Huns to adorn the sheet-metal fittings of their wooden saddles. The first 'Gothic' eagles with wings also occur on fittings, likewise found in south Russia and Romania (?Taman – Thiry 1939, Taf. 1 F; Apahida – fig. 11.2:2).

Apahida The most significant eagle fittings were a pair found in burial no. 2 at Apahida, near Cluj in Romania (fig. 11.2:2; for full details of burial, see Horedt and Protase 1972). This grave contained a male body accompanied by a sword, purse, other personal items, and a magnificent set of horse-gear contained in a chest. These eagles have been interpreted by Horedt as originally adorning the front panel of a wooden saddle of Hunnic type (*ibid.*, p. 203, Abb. 10). They display the full Roman form complete with outspread wings and legs, but, like the Conçesti eagle, possess very stylised heads. Furthermore, their *cloisonné* work includes panels arranged in an imbricated feather pattern. These fittings are 115 mm in length, and are therefore closer in size to eagle-brooches than to the other fittings discussed above. Many decorated items amongst the Apahida horse-harness also include eagles' heads, of the same stylised form (*ibid.*, p. 201, Abb. 8).

There is a sharp contrast between these grave goods and those found in another grave discovered at Apahida in 1889 (grave 1), which included Byzantine utensils and personal ornaments of a Christian character, including a gold crossbow brooch (Harhoiu 1977, fig. 10). Horedt has postulated that these male burials diverge from the pure Gothic tradition of placing goods only in female graves because of the identification of the deceased individuals with Hunnic and Byzantine power; he dates grave 2 to the Attila period, and grave 1 to a later period of renewed contact with Constantinople. It is conceivable that Apahida 2 is the grave of the Gepid king Ardaric, one of the closest allies of Attila, who led the revolt in which the Huns were defeated at Nedao in AD 453 (Horedt and Protase 1972, p. 216). Some of the finds from graves 1 and 2 at Apahida, including one of the eagles, are illustrated in colour by Condurachi and Daicioviciu (1971, pls. 186–91).

It must be stressed that the eagles from Apahida are not brooches, but fittings from part of a saddle or other horse-gear. The transition from fitting to brooch seems to have taken place in Romania in the fifth century AD, however, and is demonstrated by a curious set of brooches found in the treasure found at Pietroasa (Petrossa) in 1837 (Harhoiu 1977; Odobescu 1976). Like the Simleul Silvaniei hoards, the typology of the objects does not allow it to be dated as early as the arrival of the Huns in the area in the late fourth century AD, and current thinking suggests that it should belong instead to the mid-fifth century, when Hunnic power collapsed. The precise date is not crucial, for its importance lies in the variety of metal objects included in the treasure, which illustrate the range of influences present in Gothic/Hunnic Romania. Odobescu's publications

Fig. 11.6 The manner in which the brooches found in the Pietroasa treasure may have been worn (drawn by Helen Tustain, after Brown 1972: 114–15, figs. 2–3)

contain full illustrations in colour, and some items are included in coloured photographs by Condurachi and Daicioviciu (1971, pls. 180–5), whilst Harhoiu (1977) makes all of the objects readily accessible in monochrome.

The treasure includes Roman gold bowls and flagons decorated in a classical manner, and Persian bowls with leopard handles and *cloisonné à jour* stone settings; for the purposes of this paper, the most significant objects are the remains of four extraordinary eagle-brooches. The largest has a three-dimensional neck and head whilst its body curves smoothly down to a splayed tail finished off with jewelled pendants. Surface enrichment is provided by *cabochon* stones, *cloisonné* work, and (on the hollow neck) inset stones *à jour* in the Persian manner. Brown (1972) has elucidated the manner in which this brooch was worn, perched very naturalistically on a man's shoulder (fig. 11.6). Brown emphasised its late Roman imperial connections, which doubtless inspired imitation by Gothic royalty, and Harhoiu has conveniently illustrated several Roman representations of brooches worn in this way (1977, fig. 17). The remaining eagle-brooches (one pair joined by a chain, and a single smaller brooch which probably also once had a counterpart) were more suitable for wearing in pairs by women in the Germanic manner (fig. 11.6). These pairs are complex in design and workmanship, and have no parallels or successors. The fully developed eagle-brooches of Italy and Spain (fig. 11.2:3–4) demonstrate the adaptation of much simpler Hunnic-influenced mounts such as those from Conçesti and Apahida to the role of brooches.

The role of eagle-brooches in Gothic society It would seem that the eagle was adopted by the Goths because of its significance to both Romans and Huns. Werner lays considerable emphasis upon the shamanistic significance of eagles to nomads, and the role of birds of prey in Germanic religion (1956a, pp. 69–81). Whatever the religious background of the eagle may be, it seems unnecessary to look beyond the obvious references to Roman imperial power and the speed and predatory nature of a hunting eagle for its primary symbolic purpose. Furthermore, the ability of a high-ranking individual to provide essential gifts to his followers in order to maintain status must have depended largely upon access to the Roman sources of wealth, such as diplomatic payments or plunder; symbolic eagles could have provided a convenient visual reinforcement of their owners' ability to claim a relationship with both Romans and Huns. Thus, the simplified and stylised Hunnic form was maintained, but grafted onto the Roman spread-eagle; it was then adorned with *cloisonné* stones in the prevailing lavish polychrome manner. The rich associations of several of the earliest examples indicate that this symbol was adopted by the very highest level of Gothic society. Unlike the contemporary and similarly impressive jewelled plate-brooches (fig. 11.4:3), they have no simpler counterpart in plain sheet silver or cast bronze (fig. 11.4:1–2, 4–6). It is tempting to associate eagle-brooches with members of the ruling or even royal elite, whose emergence has been independently charted by Burns (1974;

above, p. 120). Only much later, in the different circumstances of Visigothic Spain, are comparatively plain eagle-brooches without all-over stone settings found (Thiry 1939, Taf. 5. 24–24a).

'Gothic' metalwork owes little or nothing to Germanic tradition, but everything to the adoption of desirable characteristics of the metalwork of three major contemporary powers, the Huns, Persians, and Romans. The results were carried westwards to Italy and Spain, where some spectacularly rich examples have been found. In Italy, the position of the Ostrogoths in relation to the Roman population was dominant in a military sense, but remained inferior in relation to the prevailing perception of the superiority of Roman culture. Theodoric wrote to the Byzantine emperor Anastasius in 508/9: "Our royalty is an imitation of yours, a copy of the only Empire on earth; and in so far as we follow you do we excel all other nations" (Bullough 1965, p. 168). Yet Theodoric, as a Goth, can obviously be closely identified with the Visigoths, who had slain a Roman emperor in the fourth century and sacked the eternal city of Rome in the fifth. We shall see (below, p. 127) that plate-brooches as well as the rarer eagle-brooches reflect this contradictory situation extremely well.

In the religious sphere, continuing adherence to Arianism – a brand of Christianity considered heretical by Romans – provided a spiritual demarcation between Goths and Romans. It was emphasised by the construction of separate churches and baptisteries, although they were necessarily constructed in a Roman style by Roman builders. The wearing of Gothic buckles and brooches by aristocratic women in a style different from that of Roman women represents a parallel physical expression of separation on a more personal level. Indeed, if the resources required to obtain the materials and craftsmanship involved in the making of eagle-brooches were under the control of male Goths, they may have had the further purpose of visually underlining the legal restrictions upon intermarriage, by effectively 'labelling' well-born Gothic women. This need may well have been felt most strongly amongst the most 'Romanised' male Goths, who were tending to receive Roman-style burials marked by Latin inscriptions in royal and administrative centres. Indeed, the finding of eagle-brooches in Rome itself, at Milan, and near Ravenna (fig. 11.3; Bierbrauer 1973) emphasises the exclusive proximity of their wearers to the traditional seats of Roman authority.

The etymology of the name 'Visigoth' implies that it may in fact mean 'good/real/original-goth' (Wenskus 1977, pp. 322–3), a self-designation adopted by a branch of the Pontic Goths who had moved into the former Roman province of Dacia in the late third century AD. Within the Roman Empire, a combination of material artifacts (mainly connected with female dress) and a 'heretical' religion would certainly maintain Gothic identity both in a visual and spiritual sense. This involved inevitable contradictions, such as the adoption of a brooch form largely derived from Roman models because of the high status of Roman culture in order to reinforce the fact that Goths were not Roman. In Spain, eagle-brooches disappeared from the archaeological record along with other items of tribal dress precisely at the time when history shows that religious and legal barriers between the Roman and Germanic populations were disappearing, and that intermarriage was taking place.

We have seen that the jewelled eagle emerged in Romania, where some Goths evidently prospered as sub-rulers within the 'empire' of the Huns. The eagle as a brooch began life as a symbol of qualities emulated or admired by Goths (Hunnic hunting, Roman imperial authority) and was then transformed into a symbol of Gothic self-awareness, of the kind documented by Wenskus (1977, p. 474), in situations where Roman culture dominated. Indeed, from the evidence of Italy and Spain, I would argue that the eagle-brooch may *only* have acted as a special symbol of 'being Gothic' in a *Roman* context, for in Romania or south Russia there is no evidence of any development beyond the simple fittings and the strange brooches found at Pietroasa, which all belong to the fifth century AD. That this was not simply a result of geographical separation is shown by the broadly parallel typological development of plate-brooches and buckles which continued in south-eastern Europe as well as Italy and Spain (fig. 11.4).

Gothic plate-brooches (figs. 11.4, 11.7)

Eagle-brooches are rare and exceptional, although their interest is by no means diminished by their scarcity. In common with other Germanic peoples in the migration period, the commonest brooch forms found amongst the Goths were bow-brooches (*Bügelfibeln*), worn in pairs by women. These brooches underwent a succession of stylistic and technical changes from the fourth to the sixth centuries AD. Essentially, all bow-brooches consist of three necessary parts if they are to function on the safety-pin principle: a headplate or fitting to hold a spring and pin; the bow into which a fold of cloth is gathered; and a catchplate to secure the pin (fig. 11.7). The dominant principle in the design of early medieval bow-brooches, in contrast to many of their Iron Age and Roman counterparts, is the use of plates of metal over the spring and catch as a decorative feature which went far beyond purely functional requirements.

The commonest brooch types associated with the Goths are distinguished by a semicircular or subrectangular head, plain bow, and a rhombic foot (Kühn 1974, Taf. 218–33). They may be made from bronze or silver, the former normally cast and the latter either cast or hand-worked from a single sheet of

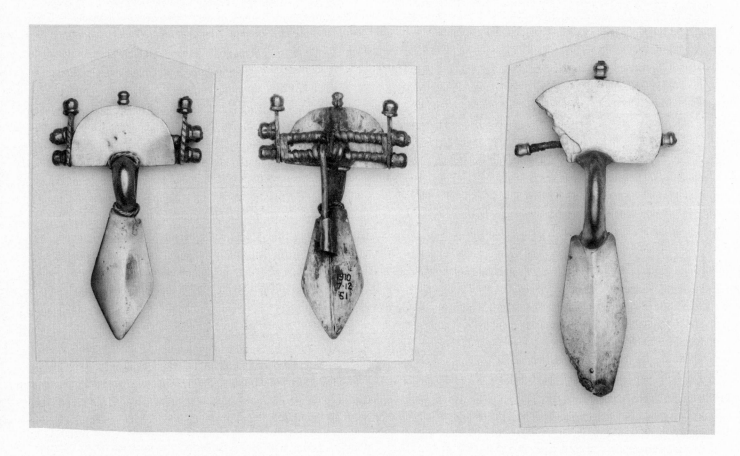

Fig. 11.7 Early silver plate-brooches from south Russia, late fourth – early fifth century AD (British Museum, London, 1910, 7–12, 51 and 13). The relatively low maximum width of the foot is an early characteristic found in the Sîntana-de-Mures/Cherniachov culture, while the longer (incomplete) brooch would belong to Bierbrauer's Villafontana horizon. The brooches are made from single sheets of silver, to which the catch plate and spring fittings have been soldered. At this stage of development, the cast knobs were fitted individually to the springs and head plate; later, they were integrally cast (fig. 11.4 nos. 5–6). Scale 1:1

metal (fig. 11.7). Their size and shape vary considerably, and fittings such as filigree wire, knobs, and additional pieces of applied decorated metal are all encountered (fig. 11.4:1–2). Occasionally, the entire brooch might be encased in sheet gold and set with *cloisonné* or *cabochon* garnets and other stones (fig. 11.4:3, 7). In the later fifth century AD, cast brooches are found in Italy and Hungary with elaborate 'chip-carved' decoration all over the plates, and integral knobs on the head-plate (fig. 11.4:4). The Franks, Lombards, Anglo-Saxons and other peoples also wore cast bow-brooches during this period, bearing more or less elaborate decoration, but only the Goths maintained the plain plate-brooch alongside cast varieties, further adorned if necessary with the kinds of additional fittings described above.

A considerable amount of work has been devoted to plate-brooches by German scholars, initially in gathering together the dispersed material evidence (e.g. Kühn 1974), and more recently towards interpretation in social and cultural terms (Bierbrauer 1975, 1980). The present writer is engaged in an attempt to obtain a firmer base for future study of plate-brooches by providing accurate numerical descriptions, and through the exploration of methods of classification and analysis similar to those which have been applied to Iron Age brooches by Hodson (Doran and Hodson 1975, pp. 218–37). In this paper, I hope simply to integrate the useful work of Bierbrauer with the style of interpretation which was applied to eagle-brooches above.

Bierbrauer has recently outlined the development of Gothic material culture in south-eastern Europe in relation to cemetery evidence, and has emphasised the gradual rather than abrupt divisions of the 'horizons' which he has defined (1980, p. 132). Of particular interest is the gradual change to be found in the cemeteries of the Sîntana de Mureş/Cherniachov culture in the fourth century AD in south Russia and Romania. In essence, there is a move from cremation to inhumation, accompanied by a decrease in the practice of placing grave goods with the dead. However, this decrease coincides with an increase in the richness of goods, so that in the early fifth-century Villafontana horizon, larger silver plate-brooches are found (fig. 11.7) with buckles and fine drinking vessels in the graves of the few, invariably female, deceased who were buried with goods (*ibid.*, pp. 132–4). These changes do of course coincide very well with Burns' independent observation that Gothic society became more stratified, with greater divisions based upon wealth, as a result of proximity to and contact with the Roman Empire (above, p. 120).

In symbolic terms, the contrast between the larger precious metal brooches combined with specialised drinking vessels, and the smaller brooches (fig. 11.7) but wider range of vessels found in the fourth century AD, could be seen as a reinforcement of a social elite by specialised practices in both life and the treatment of the dead. In the fifth century, the experience of domination by the Huns led to greater wealth and an intensification of elite burials, in separate burial places rather than cemeteries. Towards the middle of the fifth century

(in Bierbrauer's Untersiebenbrunn/Laa an der Thaya horizon) a small number of graves of spectacular wealth, including some of men, far outstripped the accompanied graves of the later Sîntana de Mureş/Cherniachov culture and Villafontana horizon. These are characterised by the use of gold and semi-precious stones for the adornment of plate-brooches (fig. 11.4:3) and other grave goods. The grave of a woman at Untersiebenbrunn and a man at Aphida (grave 2) typify this group; Hubert *et al.* 1969, p. 214, pl. 223 illustrates the superb pair of gold and polychrome brooches from Untersiebenbrunn. The less spectacular elite graves of the Untersiebenbrunn/Laa an der Thaya horizon contain some very large and elaborate plate-brooches with elaborate extra fittings (fig. 11.4:1), which in Italy and Hungary are followed by cast brooches in Bierbrauer's Domolospuszta/Bacsordas horizon (fig. 11.4:4). Casting was a novelty for large brooches, and for a while the new technique presumably allowed a re-emphasis of status through exclusivity.

In Italy, I would suggest that the level of society which had previously been distinguished by the rich burials of the Untersiebenbrunn/Laa an der Thaya horizon and the Domolospuszta/Bacsordas horizon expressed their status in different ways because of their completely new position of power in what had been the heart of the Roman Empire. Bierbrauer has shown that many aristocratic Ostrogoths near the centres of power adopted Roman burial customs, indicated by Latin inscriptions rather than grave goods. Those who still buried jewellery with the dead used either the eagle-brooch or an Italian form of plate-brooch which, like the eagle-brooches, was entirely covered with stone settings in a rather Roman manner (fig. 11.4:7; Hubert *et al.* 1969, p. 230, pl. 243). These were of course capable of conveying an ambiguous symbolism, embodying Gothic qualities in the eyes of a Roman, but Roman qualities in the eyes of a Goth, and thus reflected the position of the Gothic aristocracy very well. The remainder of Goths who were buried with goods (still, exclusively, relatively wealthy women) received the standard set of a pair of bow-brooches and a rectangular buckle without any notable variation in quality (figs. 11.4:4–6 and 11.1).

In Spain, the plate-brooch had an extended life (Palol n.d., p. 146, pl. 97). Large examples derived from those found in south-eastern Europe in the Untersiebenbrunn/Laa an der Thaya horizon are plentiful, and appear to have been made well into the sixth century (compare fig. 11.4:1–2). Cast brooches also abound, some of modest size similar to those of Italy (compare fig. 11.4:6 with fig. 11.1), others versions of the large plate-brooches (Kühn 1974, Taf. 232–3, 201–16). Such Gothic items were progressively abandoned as barriers between the Roman and Visigothic populations disappeared. Indeed, given the *Reihengräberfeld* burial mode in Spain, which resembles that of Frankish rather than Gothic territories, one may wonder whether many of the dead were even of Germanic origin at all. In comparison with Italy and south-eastern Europe, Spanish finds do not give an impression of great wealth or differentiation; this is a very relative view, however, for the availability of precious metal and stones may have been more restricted in Spain.

Conclusions

Most of the brooch forms associated with the Goths have origins in the area of the Sîntana de Mureş/Cherniachov culture in south Russia and Romania in the fourth century (fig. 11.7). This paper has examined their development and significance in the western areas occupied by Ostrogoths and Visigoths. Not all Goths left south Russia, however, and cemeteries continued in use in the Crimea at least down to the late sixth century AD (Brenner 1912, pp. 280–2). What is remarkable is that the development of large sheet-metal plate-brooches and smaller cast bow-brooches was broadly parallel in all of these areas, with understandable regional differences (figs.11.4:4–6, 11.1). This observation reinforces the view that plate-brooches were significant to the Goths, both socially and tribally. The use of modern statistical studies of form and distribution promises to elucidate the similarities and contrasts between different areas. At the moment, this paper must be seen as a preliminary exercise in which the interpretation of Gothic metalwork has been subjected to analysis in symbolic terms. The results, which are undoubtedly simplistic in many details, are I hope of sufficient credibility to establish that this approach may enhance the interest of the whole range of Dark Age metalwork. This field of study has tended to stagnate into hyper-typology or chronological hair-splitting since the essential groundwork was carried out by scholars such as Salin and Aberg. Further attempts to improve the quality of archaeological information and its importance to the historical understanding of the Goths in the manner of scholars such as Bierbrauer are to be welcomed, but they must be based on an even more rigorous attention to the details of the material artifacts.[1]

Notes

1. I wish to thank Newcastle students Bill Hubbard, Sarah Mawson and Helen Tustain for their drawings, and Dafydd Kidd and David Brown for helping me to obtain photographs of objects in the British Museum, London, and the Ashmolean Museum, Oxford. Ian Hodder has provided a general stimulus to my thinking through his ethnoarchaeological research, and a specific stimulus by inviting and commenting upon drafts of this paper. Detailed comments were also received from David Boyson, University of Newcastle, and Dr Edward James, University of York, from whose knowledge of Visigoths, Burgundians and Franks I have greatly benefited. A grant from the Research Fund of the University of Newcastle enabled me to pursue obscure publications of brooches in the library of the Römisch-Germanisches Zentralmuseum, Mainz, where Dr Kurt Weidemann provided valuable assistance.

   My research into Gothic metalwork is conducted with the help of database software (DBase III) donated by Ashton-Tate (UK) Ltd, and a grant from the Research Committee of the University of Newcastle.

Catalogue of Eagle fittings and brooches

This list is numbered in the same order as figs. 11.8 and 11.9, and arranged geographically rather than typologically. All provenances and descriptions are based entirely upon published accounts, which frequently disagree, particularly in the case of dimensions. Although what appears to be the most reliable source has been used in each case, the catalogue is not intended to be complete or definitive. All of the eagles are reproduced at approximately 1:2 scale, from a number of sources of unequal quality (an asterisk precedes the reference to the publication from which the illustration has been taken). This is considered worthwhile because of the difficulty of access to the illustrated catalogues published by Thiry and Kühn in 1939 and 1940/1. The writer intends to carry out further research on the typology and dating of these artifacts, which it is hoped will allow a more accurate catalogue to be compiled. Only one eagle from each pair is illustrated; not all pairs survive complete.

Fig. 11.8: Eagle fittings and brooches from Russia, Romania, East Germany and France

Eagle fittings

1 Kertsch (Kerch), Crimea, Russia: Hermitage Museum, Leningrad.
   *Thiry 1939, Taf. 6.27 & p. 69; Kühn 1939–40, Taf. 57a & p. 140. Size unknown. Gold with red stones; white elements on beak and tail. A very close parallel to 2, unless it is a bad drawing of the same fitting which has acquired a false provenance.

2 Conçesti, Moldavia, Romania: Hermitate Museum, Leningrad. Thiry 1939, Taf. 6.28 & p. 70; *Kühn 1939–40, Taf 57b & p. 140; Werner 1956a, Taf. 29.6. Size: 6 cm. Gold, with red stones and mother of pearl (beak, tail, 2 feathers).

3 Taman, Kuban, Russia: Römisch-Germanisches Museum, Köln. Thiry 1939, Taf. IF & p. 66; *Kühn 1939–40, Taf. 57c & p. 140. Size: 4.2 cm. Gold, with almandines.

4 Apahida, Cluj, Romania: Cluj Museum.
   *Horedt and Protase 1972, Taf. 49–50 & pp. 187–8; Condurachi and Daicioviciu 1971, pl. 191; Roth 1979, Abb. 51 a–b. Size: 11.5 cm. Gold, red, almandines and green stone in eye.

Eagle brooches

5 Ossmanstedt, Kreis Weimar, E. Germany: Weimar Museum. Behm-Blanke 1973, Taf. 65 & pp. 54, 60, 342; Roth 1979, Abb. 303. Size: 6.3 cm. Gold, with red almandines backed by gilded silver foil.

6 Domagnano, San Marino, Italy: Nürnberg Museum, and private collection, Paris.
   *Bierbrauer 1973, Taf. 35–6.1 a–b, a & p. 68; Thiry 1939, Taf. 4.17–18 & p. 68; Kühn 1939–40, Taf. 57 2 a–b & p. 140; Bierbrauer 1978, Tav. CI, fig. 15.1 & p. 215; Roth 1979, Abb. 75a. Size: 12 cm. Gold, with red almandines; white paste wing tips, etc. Provenance frequently given as Cesena (Prov. Forli).

7 Rome, via Flaminia, Italy: Museo Capitolino.
   *Bierbrauer 1973, Taf. 39 3a–4c & p. 509; Thiry 1939, Taf. 5. 25 & p. 69; Kühn 1939–40, Taf. 57a & p. 140; Bierbrauer 1978, Taf. CI. fig. 15.2–3 & p. 215; Roth 1979, Abb. 78b. Size: 4.6 cm. Gold with red almandines and crystal eye.

8 Milan, Sant'Ambroggio, Italy: Sant'Ambroggio Museum, Milan.
   *Bierbrauer 1973, Taf. 39.1 & pp. 510–11; Bierbrauer 1978, Tav. XCI, fig. 5.8 & pp. 220–1. size: 8 cm? (no dimensions are given in Bierbrauer 1973, while those in Bierbrauer 1978 conflict). Bronze, with one surviving red almandine, and trace of green and white stones.

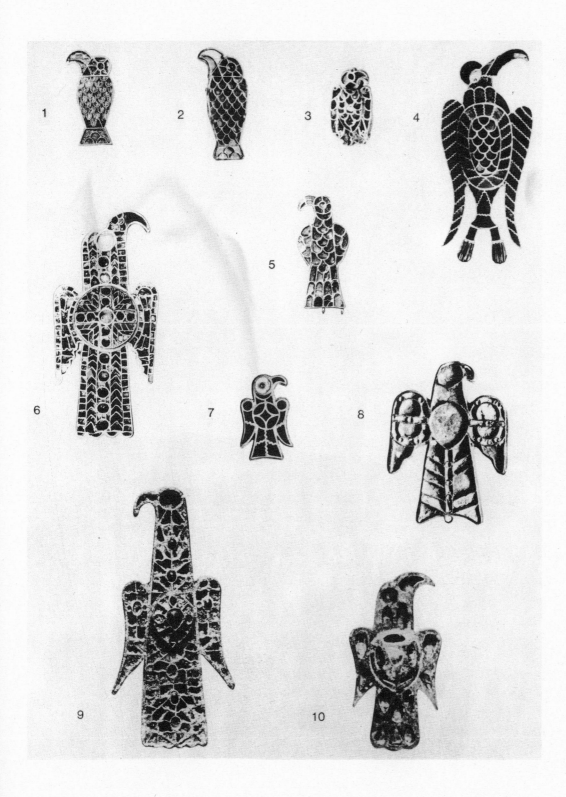

Fig. 11.8 Eagle fittings (1–4) and brooches from eastern Europe (1–5), Italy (6–8) and France (9–10). Scale c. 1:2

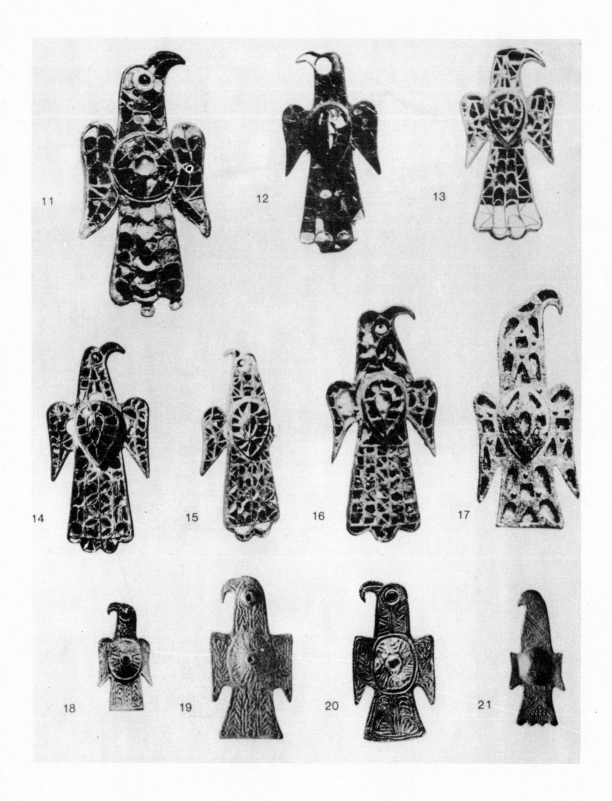

Fig. 11.9 Eagle brooches from Spain. Scale c. 1:2

9 Valence d'Agen, Dép. Lot et Garonne, France: Musée de Cluny, Paris.
>Thiry 1939, Taf. 3.15 & p. 67; Kühn 1939–40, Taf. 60.8 a–b & p. 142; *Santa-Olalla 1940–1, Lam. 4.10–11 & p. 52. Size: 14 cm. Bronze, various coloured stones or glass inlays.

10 Ville-sur-Cousance, Dép. Meuse, France: Römisch-Germanisches Museum, Köln, and Römisch-Germanisches Zentralmuseum, Mainz.
>Thiry 1939, Taf. 3.13 & p. 67; Kühn 1939–40, Taf. 65.16 a–b & p. 143; Santa-Olalla 1940–1, Lam. 7.20 & p. 53; *Werner 1961, Taf. 39.203, Taf. 50D & p. 42. Size: 9.7 cm. Bronze, gilt, with green glass inlays.

Fig. 11.9: Eagle brooches from Spain

11 Tierra de Barros, Badajoz, Estremadura, Spain: Walters Art Gallery, Baltimore.
>Thiry 1939, Taf. 3.16 & p. 68; Kühn 1939–40, Taf. 58 & p. 141; Santa-Olalla 1940–1, Lam. 1.1–2; Santa-Olalla 1936, Taf. 12.3–4, 48, Abb.1; *Ross 1961, fig. 48 & p. 100; Roth 1979, Abb. 57a. Size: 14.5 cm. Bronze, gilt, with garnet, crystal blue, and green inlays. Eye made from amethyst and meerschaum, central boss crystal.

12 Calatayud, Zaragoza, Spain: Madrid, National Museum.
>Thiry 1939, Taf. 4.21 & p. 68; Kühn 1939–40, Taf. 59.6 & p. 141; *Santa-Olalla 1940–1, Lam. 2.4 & p. 51; Zeiss 1934, Taf. 6.2. & pp. 19, 104–5; Pidal 1940, facing p. 640. Size: 11.1 cm. Bronze, gilt, with red glass and white mother of pearl inlays. Colour plate in Pidal 1940.

13 Herrera de Pisuerga, Palencia, Spain: Römisch-germanisches Museum, Köln.
>Thiry 1939, Taf. 4.20 & p. 68; Kühn 1939–40, Taf. 59.5 & p. 141; Santa-Olalla 1940–1, Lam. 3.8–9 & p. 52; *Werner 1961, Taf. 40.205 & p. 42. Size: 10.6 cm. Bronze, gilt, red glass inlays.

14 Alovera, Guadalajara, Spain: Madrid, National Museum.
>Roth 1979, Abb. 57b & p. 147. Size: 11.5 cm. Bronze, gilt, with red almandines. Another photograph of the same brooch is *ibid*. 57d, in error for one from Deza (no. 18 below).

15 Herrera de Pisuerga, Palencia, Spain: Walters Art Gallery, Baltimore.
>Thiry 1939, Taf. 4.22 & p. 68; Kühn 1939–40, Taf. 59.7 & p. 142; *Santa-Olalla 1940–1, Lam. 3.7 & p. 52; Zeiss 1934, Taf. 6.3 & pp. 19, 104–5; Ross 1961, p. 103 fig. 49 & p. 102. Size: 10.8 cm. Bronze, gilt, with red, blue, and white (mother of pearl) inlays.

16 (Probably Spain): Römisch-Germanisches Museum, Köln.
>Thiry 1939, Taf. 4.19 & p. 68; Kühn 1939–40, Taf. 59.4 & p. 141; Santa-Olalla 1940–1, Lam. 2.5–6 & pp. 51–2; *Werner 1961, Taf. 40.204 & p. 42. Size: 13 cm. Bronze, gilt, with red, blue, and green glass inlays and ?pearl eye.

17 Talavera de la Reina, Toledo, Spain: Madrid, National Museum.
>*Thiry 1939, Taf. 3.14 & p. 67; Kühn 1939–40, Taf. 65.15 & p. 143; Santa-Olalla 1940–1, Lam. 5.12 & p. 52; Zeiss 1934, Taf. 6.1 & pp. 19, 104–5; Roth 1979, Abb. 57c. Size: 13.3 cm. Bronze; all inlays lost.

18 Deza, Soria, Spain: Madrid, National Museum.
>Santa-Olalla 1940–1, Lam. 8.21–4 & p. 53; *Thiry 1939, Taf. 5.24 & p. 69; Kühn 1939–40, Taf. 60.9 & p. 142; Zeiss 1934, Taf. 6.4 a–b, 5 & pp. 19–20, 104–5. Size: 6 cm. Bronze, with sapphire eye and almandine boss.

19 Castiltierra, Segovia, Spain.
>Santa-Olalla 1940–1, p. 40, fig. 27 & p. 54; *Pidal 1940, p. 131, fig. 50. Size: 9 cm. Bronze.

20 Castiltierra, Segovia, Spain: Barcelona Museum.
>*Santa-Olalla 1940–1, Lam. 7.18–19 & p. 54; Thiry 1939, Taf. 5.24a; Kühn 1939–40, Taf. 60.10 & p. 142; Santa-Olalla 1936, Taf. 12.1–2. Size: 9 cm. Bronze with almandines.

21 Castiltierra, Segovia, Spain: Madrid, National Museum.
>Santa-Olalla 1940–1, Lam. 8.25–6 & p. 53; *ibid*., p. 47, fig. 28; Pidal 1940, p. 133, fig. 51; Roth 1979, Abb. 57e. Size: 7.5 cm. Bronze.

REFERENCES

Aberg,N. (1922) *Die Frankenund Westgoten in der Völkerwanderungszeit*, Uppsala

Alexander, J. A. (1981) 'The archaeological recognition of migrations', paper read in Mexico City

Allanson, H. (1912) *Final Report of the Survey and Settlement Operations in the District of Sonthal Parganas [Third Programme] 1898–1910*, The Bengal Secretariat Book Depot, Calcutta

Allchin, B., and Allchin, F. R. (1982) *The Rise of Civilisation in India and Pakistan*, Cambridge University Press

Ambrose, S. H. (1983) 'Archaeology and linguistic reconstructions of history in East Africa', in C. Ehret and M. Posnansky (eds.), *The Archaeological and Linguistic Reconstruction of African History*, University of California Press, Berkeley, pp. 104–7

Annibaldi, G. and Werner, J. (1963) 'Ostgotischer Grabfunde aus Acquasanta, Prov. Ascoli Piceno', *Germania* 41: 356–73

Anonymous (1836) 'The Cornish farmer and the labouring classes', *The Penny Magazine* (1836), 196–9

Arens, W. (1976) 'Changing patterns of ethnic identity and prestige in East Africa', in W. Arens (ed.), *A Century of Change in Eastern Africa*, Mouton, The Hague, pp. 65–75

Asad, T. (1973) *Anthropology and the Colonial encounter*, Ithaca Press, London

Ascher, R. (1961) 'Analogy in archaeological interpretation', *Southwestern Journal of Anthropology* 17:317–25

Axford, E. C. (1975) *Bodmin Moor*, David and Charles, Newton Abbot

Baby, R. S. (1969) 'An Adena effigy pipe', *Ohio Archaeologist* 19(1): 16–17

Bäckman, L. (1978) 'Types of shamans: comparative perspective', in Bäckman and Hultkrantz (eds.) 1978

Bäckman, L., and Hultkrantz, Å. (eds.), (1978) *Studies in Lapp Shamanism*, Stockholm Studies in Comparative Religion 16, Almqvist and Wiksell, Stockholm

Bailey, F. G. (1969) *Stratagems and Spoils: A Social Anthropology of Politics*, Blackwell, Oxford

Bainbridge, R. B. (1911) 'The Saorias of the Rajmahal Hills', in *Memoirs of the Asiatic Society of Bengal*, Vol. 2, Baptist Mission Press, Calcutta

Bakka, E. (1975) 'Bergkunst i barskogsbeltet i Sovjetsamveldet', *Viking* 1975: Oslo, 95–124

Ball, V. (1880) *Jungle Life in India or The Journeys and Journals of an Indian Geologist*, Thos. De La Rue and Co., London

Banaji, J. (1970) 'The crisis of British anthorpology', *New Left Review* 64 (Nov.–Dec.)

Banton, M. (1961) 'The restructuring of social relationships', in A. Southall (ed.), *Social Change in Modern Africa*, International African Institute, Oxford, pp. 111–25

Barnes, J. A. (1951) 'Marriage in a changing society', *Occasional Papers of the Rhodes-Livingstone Institute*, 20, Livingstone

(1967) *Politics in a Changing Society: The Political History of the Fort Jameson Ngoni*, Manchester University Press

Baudou, E. (1978a) 'Kronologi och kulturutvekling i mellersta Norrland under Stenålderen och Bronsålderen', *Studier i norrlandsk forntid*, pp. 8–18

(1978b) 'Archaeological investigations at L. Holmsjon Medelpad', *Early Norrland*, 11, pp. 1–4, Kungl. Vitterhets Historie och Antikvitets Akademien, Oslo

Behm-Blancke, G. (1973) *Gesellschaft und Kunst der Germanen*, Dresden

Benveniste, E. (1969) *Le Vocabulaire des Institutions Indo-Européens*, Editions de Minuit, Paris

Berger, J. (1979) *Pig Earth*, Writers and Readers, London

Berglund, A.-I. (1976) *Zulu Thought Patterns and Symbolism*, Hurst, London

Beverley, R. (1705) *The History of and Present State of Virginia*, London

Bhaduri, A. (1977) 'On the formation of usurious interest rates in backward agriculture', *Cambridge Journal of Economics* 1, no. 4

Bierbrauer, V. (1973) 'Die ostgotischen Funde von Domagnano, Republik San Marino', *Germania* 51: 499

(1975) *Die Ostgotischen Grab- und Schatzfunde in Italien*, Spoleto

(1978) 'Reperti ostrogoti provenienti de tombe o tesori della Lombardia', *I Longobardi e la Lombardia*, Milan, pp. 213–40

(1980) 'Zur chronologischen, soziologischen und regionalen Gliederung des ostgermanischen Fundstoffs des 5. Jahrhunderts in Südosteuropa', in Wolfram and Daim (1980), pp. 131–42

Billinge, M. (1977) 'In search of negativism: phenomenology and historical geography', *Journal of Historical Geography*, 5: 55–67

Billington, R. A. (1967) 'The American frontier', in P. Bohannan and F. Plog (eds.), *Beyond the Frontier*, The Natural History Press, New York

Binford, L. R. (1962) 'Archaeology as anthropology', *American Antiquity* 28: 217–25

(1965) 'Archaeological systematics and the study of culture process', *American Antiquity* 31: 203–10

(1967) 'Smudge pits and hide smoking: the use of analogy in archaeological reasoning', *American Antiquity* 32(1): 1–12; reprinted in *An Archaeological Perspective*, Seminar Press, New York (1972)

(1968) 'Archaeological perspectives', in L. R. Binford and S. R. Binford (eds.), *New Perspectives in Archaeology*, Aldine, New York, pp. 5–32

Blakeslee, D. J. (1981) 'The origin and spread of the calumet ceremony', *American Antiquity* 46(4): 759–68

Böhme, H. W. (1974) *Germanische Grabfunde des 4. bis 5. Jahrhunderts zwischen unterer Elbe und Loire*, 2 vols., München

Bonte, P. (1977) 'Non-stratified social formations among pastoral nomads', in J. Friedman and M. J. Rowlands (eds.), *The Evolution of Social Systems*, Duckworth, London

de Boor, H. (ed.) (1972) *Das Nibelungenlied. Nach der Ausgabe von Karl Bartch*, Wiesbaden

Boserup, E. (1966) *The Conditions of Agricultural Growth*, George Allen and Unwin Ltd, London

Bowers, A. W. (1965) 'Hidatsa social and ceremonial organization', *Smithsonian Institution Bureau of American Ethnology Bulletin* 194: 1–493

Brackert, H. (ed.) (1970) *Das Nibelungenlied* I and II, Frankfurt am Main

Bradley-Birt, F. B. (1905) *Story of an Indian Upland*, Smith, Elder and Co., London

Brasser, T. J. (1980) 'Self-directed pipe effigies', *Main the Northeast* 19: 95–104

Braudel, F. (1958) 'Histoire de sciences sociales, la longue durée', *Annales, Economies*: 725–53

(1973) *The Mediterranean and the Mediterranean World in the Age of Philip II*, Collins, London

Brelsford, V. W. (1937) 'Some reflections on Bemba geometric art', *Bantu Studies* 11: 37–45

Brenner, E. (1912) 'Die älteste germanischen Gräberfelder in Sudrüssland und Siebengurgen', *Bericht. Röm.-Germ. Kommission* 7, pp. 262–82 (part III of 'Der Stand der Forschung über die Kultur der Merowingerzeit', *ibid*, pp. 253–352

Brewster, C. (1975) *Bodmin Moor – A Synoptic Study and Report of a Moorland Area*, Institute of Cornish Studies, Camborne

Bricker, V. (1981) *The Indian Christ, the Indian King: the Historical Substrate of Maya Myth and Ritual*, University of Texas Press, Austin

Broner, S. J. (1979) 'Concepts in the study of material aspects of American folk culture', *Folklore Forum* 12

Bronson, B. (1978) 'Angkor, Anuradhapura, Prambanan, Tikal: Maya subsistence in Asian perspective', in P. D. Harrison and B. L. Turner II (eds.), *Pre-Hispanic Maya Agriculture*, University of New Mexico Press, Albuquerque

Brown, D. (1972) 'The brooches in the Pietroasa treasure', *Antiquity* 46: 111–16

Browne, Maj. J. (1788) *India Tracts: containing a description of the Jungleterry districts . . .* Logographic Press, Blackfriars, London

Bullough, D. (1965) 'Germanic Italy: the Ostrogothic and Lombard kingdoms', in Talbot-Rice (ed.) 1965, pp. 157–74

Burenhult, G. (1980) *Götlands Hällristningar I*, Theses and Papers in North European Archaeology 10, Institute of Archaeology, University of Stockholm

Burgess, C. (1980) *The Age of Stonehenge*, Dent, London

Butt, A. (1966) 'To dance among bird-women', in S. Wavel, A. Butt and N. Epton (eds.), *Trances*, George Allen and Unwin, London

Calame-Griaule, G. (1955) 'Notes sur l'habitation du Plateau Central Nigérien', *Bulletin de l'Institut Française d'Afrique Noire, B* 17: 477–99

(1965) *Ethnologie et langage: la parole chez les Dogon*, Gallimard, Paris

(1968) *Dictionnaire Dogon*, Librairie C. Klincksleck, Paris

Carse, M. R. (1949) 'The Mohawk Iroquois', *Bulletin of the Archaeological Society of Connecticut* 23: 3–53

Castellis, M. (1983) *The City and the Grassroots*, Edward Arnold, London

Catlin, G. (1841) *The Manners, Customs, and Condition of the North American Indians*, 2 vols., London

Census of India (1981), New Delhi

Chafe, W. L. (1964) 'Linguistic evidence for the relative age of Iroquois religious practices', *Southwestern Journal of Anthropology* 20: 278–85

Chang, K. C. (1967) 'Major aspects of the interrelationship of archaeology and ethnology', *Current Anthropology* 8(3): 227–43

Charlevoix, P. F. X. de (1761) *Journal of a Voyage to North America*, 2 vols., London

Charlton, T. H. (1981) 'Archaeology, ethnohistory, and ethnology: interpretive interfaces', in M. B. Schiffer (ed.), *Advances in Archaeological Method and Theory*, Vol. 4, Academic Press, New York

Childe, V. G. (1925) *The Dawn of European Civilization*, Kegan Paul, London; 6th edn 1957

(1951) *Man makes himself*, New American Library, New York

(1956) *Piecing Together the Past*, Praeger, New York

Clare, M. (1955) 'The significance of the pipe to the Gros Ventres of Montana', unpublished M.Ed. thesis, Montana State University

Clark, J. D. (1962) 'The spread of food production in sub-Saharan Africa', *Journal of African History*, 3: 211–28

(1964) 'The prehistoric origins of African culture', *Journal of African History* 5: 161–83

Clark, J. D. and Fagan, B. M. (1965). 'Charcoal, sands and channel decorated pottery from Northern Rhodesia', *American Anthropologist* 67: 345–71

Clark, J. G. D. (1952) *Prehistoric Europe: The Economic Basis*, Cambridge University Press

(1966) 'The invasion hypothesis in British archaeology', *Antiquity* 40: 172–89

Clarke, D. L. (1973) 'Archaeology: the loss of innocence', *Antiquity* 47: 6–18

Clayton, A., and Savage, D. C. (1974) *Government and Labour in Kenya*, Methuen, London

Coe, M. D. (1978) *Lords of the Underworld*, Princeton University Press

Cole, S. (1954) *The Prehistory of East Africa*, Penguin, London

Collingwood, R. G. (1946) *The Idea of History*, Clarendon Press, Oxford

Condurachi, E. and Daicioviciu, C. (1971) *The Ancient Civilization of Romania*, Barrie and Jenkins, London

Conkey, M. W., and Spector, J. (1984) 'Archaeology and the study of gender' in M. Schiffer (ed.), *Archaeological Method and Theory* 7, Academic Press, New York

Conklin, H. C. (1957) *Hanunnoo Agriculture: A Report on the Integral system of Shifting Cultivation in the Philippines* (vol. 2 of the F.A.O. series on shifting cultivation), F.A.O., Rome

    (1961) 'The study of shifting cultivation', in *Current Anthropology*, 2 (1): 00–0

Cooke, C. K. (1965) 'Evidence of human migration from the rock art of Southern Rhodesia', *Africa* 35: 263–85

Crawford, T. C. (1928) *Hand-Book of Castes and Tribes Employed on the Tea-Estates in North-East India*, Catholic Orphan Press, Calcutta

Crouch, D. E. (1965) 'Types of Hopewell effigy pipes', unpublished M.A. thesis, Department of Art, State University of Iowa

Cunningham, C. E. (1973) 'Order in the Atoni house', in R. Needham (ed.), *Right and Left: Essays on Dual Symbolic Classifications*, University of Chicago Press, pp. 204–38

Curtin, J. (1923) *Seneca Indian Myths*, E. P. Dutton, New York

Dalton, E. T. (1872) *Descriptive Ethnology of Bengal*, Government Printing Press, Calcutta

Davis, D. D. (1981) 'Some problems in applying Hodder's hypothesis', *American Antiquity* 46: 665–7

Deetz, J. (1977) *In Small Things Forgotten*, Anchor Press, New York

Demoule, J.-P. (1980) 'Les Indo-Européens ont-ils existé?', *L'Histoire* 28: 108–20

    (1982) 'Le Néolithique, une révolution', *L'Homme. Debat* 20: 54–75

Diaconu, G. (1973) 'Über die Fibel mit halbkreisförmiger Kopfplatte und rautenförmigern Fuss aus Dazien', *Dacia* 17: 257–75

Dieterlen, G. (1956) 'Parenté et mariage chez les Dogon', *Africa* 26: 107–48

Dobkin de Rios M. (1972) 'The anthropology of drug-induced altered states of consciousness: some theoretical considerations', *Sociologus* (Berlin) 22(1): 147–51

    (1973) 'The non-western use of hallucinogenic agents', in *Drug Use in America. Problem in Perspective*, Appendix, Volume 1, Second Report of the National Commission on Marihuana and Drug Abuse, Washington, D.C.

    (1975) 'Man, culture and hallucinogens: an overview', in V. Rubin (ed.), *Cannabis and Culture*, Mouton, The Hague

    (1976) *The Wilderness of Mind: Sacred Plant in Cross-Cultural Perspective*, Sage Publications, Beverly Hills

    (1977) 'Plant hallucinogens, out-of-body experiences and New World monumental earthworks', in B. M. Du Toit (ed.), *Drugs, Rituals and Altered States of Consciousness*, A. A. Balkema, Rotterdam

Domini, G. and Ford, G. B. (1970) *Isidore of Seville's History of the Goths, Vandals and Suevi*, Brill, Leiden

Donley, L. (1982) 'House power: Swahili space and symbolic markers', in I. Hodder (ed.) *Symbolic and structural archaeology*, Cambridge University Press

Doran, J. E., and Hodson, F. R. (1975) *Mathematics and Computers in Archaeology*, Edinburgh University Press

Dorsey, J. O. (1884) 'Omaha sociology', *3rd Annual Report of the Bureau of Ethnology to the Secretary of the Smithsonian Institution* (1881–2)

Dray, W. H. (1958) 'Historical understanding as re-thinking', *University of Toronto Quarterly* 28: 200–15

    (1980) *Perspectives on History*, Routledge and Kegan Paul, London

Dronke, U. (ed.) (1969) *The Poetic Edda*, vol. 1, *Heroic Poems*, Oxford University Press

Drourega, M. (1927) 'Initiation of a girl in the Acenga tribe, Katondwe mission, Luengwa district, Northern Rhodesia', *Anthropos*, 22: 620–1

Dumézil, G. (1977) *Les Dieux-Souverains des Indo-Européens*, Gallimard, Paris

Dunnell, R. (1978) 'Style and function: a fundamental dichotomy', *American Antiquity* 43: 192–202

Earthy, E. (1933) *Valenge Women*. Oxford University Press

Eliade, M. (1964) *Shamanism: Archaic Techniques of Ecstasy*, Princeton University Press

Engelstad, E. M. T. (1984) 'Diversity in Arctic maritime adaptation. An example from the Late Stone Age of Arctic Norway', *Acta Borealia* 1(2): 3–24, University of Tromsø

    (1985) 'The Late Stone Age of Arctic Norway', *Arctic Anthropology* 22(1): 79–96

Ewers, J. C. (1979) *Indian Art in Pipestone: George Catlin's Portfolio in the British Museum*, British Museum Publications and Smithsonian Institution Press, Washington, D.C.

Fagan, B. M. (1965) *Southern Africa During the Iron Age*. Thames and Hudson, London

FAO/UNFPA (1980) *Population Data regarding Forestry Communities Practising Shifting Cultivation, (India)*, RAS/77/P09, S. Bose and V. Saha (eds.), Anthropological Survey of India, Calcutta

    (1980) *Population in the Forest Communities Practising Shifting Cultivation (Thailand)*, RAS/77/P09, Faculty of Forestry, Kasetsart University (ed.), Bangkok

Fenton, W. N. (1953) 'The Iroquois eagle dance an offshoot of the calumet dance', *Smithsonian Institution Bureau of American Ethnology Bulletin* 156: 1–222

Finch, R. G. (ed.) (1965) *The Sage of the Volsungs*, Nelson's Icelandic Texts, London

Fitzhugh, B. and Kaplan, S. (1982) *Inua, Spirit World of the Bering Sea Eskimo*, Smithsonian Institution Press, Washington D.C.

Flannery, K. V. and Marcus, J. (1983) *The Cloud People*, Academic Press, New York

Fletcher, A. C. (1884) 'The "Wawan," or pipe dance of the Omahas', *Annual Report of the Trustees of the Peabody Museum of American Archaeology and Ethnology* 3: 308–33

    (1904) 'The Hako: a Pawnee ceremony', *22nd Annual Report of the Bureau of American Ethnology* (1900–1) Part 2

Fox, C. (1932) *The Personality of Britain*, National Museum of Wales, Cardiff

Fox, W. A. (1982) 'The Calvert Village: Glen Meyer community patterns', *KEWA, Newsletter of the Ontario Archaeological Society, London Chapter* 82 (7); pp. 5–9

Francklin, W. (1821) 'A journey from Bhaugulpoor through the Raj Muhal Hills in the months of December and January 1820–1', *Calcutta Annual Register*, Calcutta

Freeman, J. D. (1955) *Iban Agriculture: A report on the Shifting Cultivation of Hill Rice by the Iban of Sarawak*, Colonial Research Studies 18, London

Fried, M. (1967) 'On the concepts of "tribe" and "tribal society"', in J. Helm (ed.), *Essays on the Problems of the Tribe*, Proceedings of the American Ethnological Society

Furst, P. T. (1965) 'West Mexican tomb sculpture as evidence for shamanism in prehispanic Mesoamerica', *Antropologica (Caracas)* 15: 29–80

    (1973–4) 'The roots and continuities of shamanism', *Stones, Bones and Skin: Ritual and Shamanic Art*, *Artscanada* Special 30th Anniversary Issue 184–7: 33–60

    (1974) 'Archaeological evidence for snuffing in prehispanic Mexico', *Botanical Museum Leaflets* 24(1): 1–28, Harvard University

    (1976) *Hallucinogens and Culture*, Chandler and Sharp, Novato, California

    (ed.) (1972) *Flesh of the Gods: The Ritual Use of Hallucinogens*, Praeger, New York

Fussell, G. E. (1958–9) 'Cornish farming A.D. 1500–1910', *The Amateur Historian* 4: 338–45

Geertz, C. (1973) *The Interpretation of Cultures*, Hutchinson, London

Ghurye, G. (1943) *The Aboriginal 'so called' and their Future*, Gokhale Institute of Politics and Economics, Poona

Giddens, A. (1979) *Central Problems in Social Theory*, Macmillan, London

Gilmore, M. R. (1933) 'The Dakota ceremony of presenting a pipe To Marshal Foch and conferring a name upon him', *Papers of the Michigan Academy of Science, Arts and Letters* 18: 15–21

Gjessing, G. (1932) *Arktiske helleristninger i Nord-Norge*, Instituttet for Sammenlignende Kulturforskning, ser. B XXI, Oslo

(1945) *Norges Steinalder*, A. W. Brøggers boktrykkeri A/S, Oslo

Gluckman, M. (1950) 'Kinship and marriage among the Lozi of Northern Rhodesia and the Zulu of Natal', in A. R. Radcliffe-Brown and D. Forde (eds.), *African Systems of Kinship and Marriage*, Oxford University Press, pp. 166–206

Gluckman, M. G. (1958) *Analysis of a Social Situation in Modern Zululand*, Rhodes-Livingstone Papers 28, Livingstone

Goddard, D. (1979) 'Anthropology: the Limits of functionalism', in R. Blackburn (ed.) *Ideology in Social Science*, Fontana, London

Goffart, W. (1980) *Barbarians and Romans, A.D. 418–584: The Techniques of Accommodation*, Princeton University Press

Gombrich, E. (1966) *Norm and Form: The Stylistic Categories of Art History and their Origins in Renaissance Ideas*, Phaidon, London

(1979) *Ideals and Idols*, Phaidon, London

Goodall, E. (1946) 'Rhodesian pots with moulded decorations', *NADA* 23: 37–8

Goody, J. (1976) *Bridewealth and Dowry*, Cambridge University Press

Gould, R. A. (1974) 'Some current problems in ethnoarchaeology', in C. B. Donnan and C. W. Clewlow Jr (eds.), *Ethnoarchaeology*, Institute of Archaeology, Monograph 4, University of California, Los Angeles

(1978) 'Beyond analogy in ethnoarchaeology', in R. A. Gould (ed), *Explorations in Ethnoarchaeology*, University of New Mexico Press, Albuquerque, pp. 249–93

(1981) 'The archaeologist as ethnographer: a case study', *World Archaeology* 3: 143–77

Gould, R. A. and Schiffer, M. B. (1981) *Modern Material Culture: The Archaeology of Us*, Academic Press, New York

Government of India (1903) The Indian Forest Act, 1878 (VII of 1878), Government of India Legislative Department, Superintendent Government Printing, Calcutta

Graceva, G. N. (1982) 'A Nganasan shaman costume' in V. Dioziego and M. Hoppal (eds.), *Shamanism in Siberia*, Akademiai Kiado, Budapest

Gramly, R. M. (1978) 'Expansion of Bantu-speakers versus development of Bantu languages in situ: an archaeologist's perspective', *South African Archaeological Bulletin* 33: 107–12.

Green, S. W. (1980) 'Towards a general model of agricultural systems', in M. B. Schiffer (ed.), *Archaeological Method and Theory* 3, Academic Press, New York

Greene, K. (1983) *Archaeology: An Introduction*, Batsford, London

Greenhalgh, M., and Megaw, V. (eds.) (1978) *Art in Society*, Duckworth, London

Griaule, G. (1954) 'Remarques sur l'oncle utérin au Soudan', *Cahiers Internationaux de Sociologie* 16: 35–49

Grierson, G. (1927) *Linguistic Survey of India*, I, part I, Calcutta

Groube, L. M. (1977) 'The hazards of anthropology', in M. Spriggs (ed.) *Archaeology and Anthropology*, B. A. R. Supplementary series, 19, Oxford

Guha, R. (1983) 'Forestry in British and post-British India', *Economic and Political Weekly*, No. 44: 1882–96; No. 45 & 46: 1946–7

Gurevich, A. (1968) 'Wealth and gift-bestowal among the ancient Scandinavians', *Scandinavica, an International Journal of Scandinavian Studies* 7 (2): 126–38

(1974) 'Representations of property during the high Middle Ages', *Economy and Society* 6 (1): 1–30

Gurina, N. N. (1980) 'Imitative art of ancient tribes on the Kola Peninsula', *Fenno-Ugri et Slavi 1978*, Stencil 22, Dept of Archaeology, University of Helsinki

Hætta, O. M. (1979) *Samelands eldste bosetning. Same tema I*, Emnehefte 10, Skoledirektøren/Høgskolen i Finnmark

(1980a) *Fra Steinalder til Samisk Jernalder. Same tema II*, Emnehefte 11, Skoledirektøren/Høgskolen i Finnmark

(1980b) *Eldste skriftkiler om Samer. Same tema III*, Emnehefte 12, Akoledirektøren/Høgskolen i Finnmark

Hagen, A. (1976) *Bergkunst. Jegerfolkets helleristninger og malninger i norsk steinalder*, J. W. Cappelens forlag A/S, Oslo

Hahn, P. (1963) 'Where is that vanished bird', *Royal Ontario Museum Publications*, University of Toronto Press

Halifax, J. (1979) *Shamanic Voices: A Survey of Visionary Narratives*, E. P. Dutton, New York

Hall, R. L. (1977) 'An anthropocentric perspective for eastern United States prehistory', *American Antiquity* 42(4): 499–518

(1984) 'The evolution of the calumet-pipe', unpublished manuscript in author's possession

Hallowell, A. I. (1966) 'The role of dreams in Ojibwa culture', in G. E. von Grunebaum and R. Caillois (eds.), *The Dream and Human Societies*, University of California Press, Berkeley, pp. 267–92

Hallström, G. (1960) *Monumental Art of Northern Sweden from the Stone Age*, Almqvist and Wiksell, Stockholm

Hamilton-Jenkin, A. K. (1945) *Cornwall and its People*, Dent, London

Hammond-Tooke, W. D. (1984) 'In search of the lineage: the Cape Nguni case', *Man* 19: 77–93

Handsman, R. (1980) 'Studying myth and history in modern America: perspectives for the past from the continent', *Reviews in Anthropology* 7: 255–68

(1983) 'Historical archaeology and capitalism, subscriptions and separations: the production of individualism', *North American Archaeologist* 4: 63–79

Hanson, F. A. (1975) *Meaning in Culture*, Routledge and Kegan Paul, London

Hanson, J. R. (1980) 'Structure and complexity of medicine bundle systems of selected Plains Indian tribes', *Plains Anthropologist* 25: 199–216

Harhoiu, R. (1977) *The Fifth-Century A.D. Treasure from Pietroasa, Romania, in the Light of Recent Research*, B.A.R. S24, Oxford

Hart, G. (1978) *Hart's Prehistoric Pipe Rack*, Hart Publishers, Bluffton, Indiana

Harvey, K. (1970) *The Industrial Archaeology of Farming in England and Wales*, Batsford, London

Hatto, A. T. (1965) *The Nibelungenlied. A New Translation*, Penguin, Harmondsworth

Haudricourt, A. (1962) 'Domestication des animaux, culture des plantes et traitement d'autrui', *L'Homme* 2: 40–50

Haudry, J. (1981) *Les Indo-Européens*, Presses Universitaires de France, Paris

Hawkes, C. (1954) 'Archaeological theory and method: some suggestions from the Old World', *American Anthropologist* 56: 155–68.

Heber, R., Bp of Calcutta. (1828) *Narrative of a Journey through the Upper Provinces of India, from Calcutta to Bombay . . .*, London

Helskog, E .M .T. (1983) *The Iversfjord Locality. A study of behavioral Patterning during the Late Stone Age of Finnmark. North Norway*, Tromsø Museum Skr. 19. University of Tromsø

Helskog, K. (1974) 'Two tests of the Prehistoric Cultural Chronology of Varanger, North Norway', *Norwegian Archaeological Review* 2, pp. 97–103

(1977) 'Et reingjerde fra Steinalderen', *Ottar* 101: 25–9, Tromsø Museum, University of Tromsø

(1978) 'Late Holocene tide levels seen from prehistoric settlements', *Norsk Geografisk Tidskrift* 32: 111–19

(1980) 'The chronology of the Younger Stone Age in Varanger, North Norway, revisited', *Norwegian Archaeological Review* 1: 47–60

(1983) 'Helleristningene i Alta i et tidsperspektiv – en geologisk og multivariabel analyse', in J. Sandnes, A. Kielland and I. Sterlie (eds.) *Folk og Ressurser i Nord*, Tapir forlag, Trondheim

(1984a) 'Helleristningene i Alta. En presentasjon og en analyse av menneskefigurene', *Viking* 1983: 5–41

(1984b) 'Younger Stone Age settlements in Varanger, North Norway. Settlement and population size', *Acta Borealia* 1:39 – 71, University of Tromsø

(n.d. a) 'Boats and meaning. A study of change and continuity in the Alta fjord, Arctic Norway, from 4200 to 500 years B.C.', *Acta Boralia*, University of Tromsø

(n.d b) 'Altaristningenes kronologi', paper presented at seminar on multivariate statistical analysis in Nordic archaeology, University of Århus, 24–26 November 1984

Hennepin, L. (1698) *A New Discovery of a Large Country in America, Extending above Four Thousand Miles, Between New France and New Mexico . . .*, London

Herring, P. C. (forthcoming) 'Post-Prehistoric Landscape of Bodmin Moor', M.Phil. thesis, Dept of Prehistory and Archeology, University of Sheffield

Hewitt, J. N. B. (1895) 'The Iroquoian concept of the soul', *The Journal of American Folklore* 8: 107–16

(ed.) (1918) 'Seneca fiction, legends, and myths', *32nd Annual Report of the Bureau of American Ethnology* (1910–11)

Hine, R. C. (1972) 'The changing structure of agriculture and the position of the small farmer', in W. E. Minchinton (ed.), *Farming and Transport in the South-West*, Exeter Papers in Economic History 5, pp. 47–60

Hodder, I. (1978) 'Simple correlations between material culture and society: a review', in I. Hodder (ed.) 1978, pp. 3–24

(1979) 'Economic and social stress and material culture patterning', *American Antiquity* 44: 446–54

(1981) Reply to Davis, *American Antiquity* 46: 668–70

(1982a) *Symbols in Action: Ethnoarchaeological Studies of Material Culture*, Cambridge University Press

(1982b) *The Present Past, An Introduction to Anthropology for Archaeologists*, Batsford, London

(1982c) 'Theoretical archaeology: a reactionary view', in I. Hodder (ed.) 1982, p. 1–16

(1986) *Reading the Past*, Cambridge University Press

(ed.) (1978) *The Spatial Organisation of Culture*, Duckworth, London

(ed.) (1982) *Symbolic and Structural Archaeology*, Cambridge University Press

Hodges, R. (1982) *Dark Age Economics*, Duckworth, London

Hodges, W. (1793) *Travels in India 1780–1783*, J. Edwards, Pall Mall, London

Holleman, J. F. (1940) 'Die twee-eenheidsbeginsel in die sosiale en ploitieke samelewing van die Zulu', *Bantu Studies* 14: 31–75

Holm, B. (1965) *Northwest Coast Indian Art: An Analysis of Form*, University of Washington Press, Seattle

Holtsmark, A. (1970) 'Sigurdsdiktningen', *Kulturhistorisk leksikon for Nordisk Middelalder* 15: 224–31

Horedt, K. and Protase, D. (1972) 'Das zweite Fürstengrab von Apahida (Siebenburgen)', *Germania* 50: 174–220

Hoskins, W. G. (ed.) (1970) *History from the Farm*, Faber and Faber, London

Hubert, J., *et al.* (1969) *Europe in the Dark Ages*, Thames and Hudson, London

Hübener, W. (1970) 'Zur Chronologie der westgotenzeitlichen Grabfunde in Spanien', *Madrider Mitteil ungen* 11: 187–211

Huffman, T. N. (1970) 'The Early Iron Age and the spread of the Bantu', *South African Archaeological Bulletin* 25: 3–21

(1974) 'The linguistic affinities of the Iron Age in Rhodesia', *Arnoldia (Rhodesia)* 7 (7): 1–14

(1978) 'The origins of Leopard's Kopje: an 11th century difaquane, *Arnoldia (Rhodesia)* 8 (23): 1–23

(1979) 'African origins', *South African Journal of Science* 75: 223–37.

(1980) 'Ceramics, classification and Iron Age entities', *African Studies* 39: 123–74

(1983) 'Archaeology and ethnohistory of the African Iron Age', *Annual Review of Anthropology* 11: 133–51

(1984) 'Expressive space in the Zimbabwe culture', *Man* 19: 593–612

Hultgreen, T. (1983) 'Stiurhelleren i Sør-Sjona', *Årbok for Rana* 16: 113–19

Hultkrantz, Å. (1953) 'Conceptions of the soul among North American Indians', *Statens Etnografiska Museum Monograph Series* No. 1, Stockholm

(1978a) 'Means and ends in Lapp Shamanism', in L. Bäckman and Å. Hultkrantz (eds.) 1978

(1978b) 'The relations between the shaman's experience and specific shamanistic goals', in L. Bäckman and Å. Hultkrantz (eds.) 1978

(1979) *The Religions of the American Indians*, University of California Press, Berkeley

Hunter, W. W. (1868) *Annals of Rural Bengal*, London

Iversen, J. (1941) 'Land occupation in Denmark's stone age', *Danmarks Geologiske Undersoglese* 2, 66: 1–68

(1973) 'The development of Denmark's nature since the last glacial', *Danmarks Geologiske Undersoglese* 5, 7–C; 7–126

James, E. (1977) *The Merovingian Archaeology of South-West Gaul*, B.A.R., S25, Oxford

(1982) *The Origins of France from Clovis to the Capetians 500–1000*, Macmillan, London

Janiger, O., and M. Dobkin de Rios (1976) 'Nicotiana an hallucinogen?', *Economic Botany* 30: 149–51

Johansen, O. S. (1979) 'Early farming north of the Arctic Circle', *Norwegian Archaeological Review* 1: 22–32

(1982) 'Det eldste jordbruket i Nord-Norge', in T. Sjøvold (ed.), *Introduksjonen av jordbruket i Norden*, Det Norske Videnskaps Akademi, Universitetsforlaget, Oslo

Johnson, F. R. (1967) *The Tuscaroras*, 2 vols., Johnson Publishing Co., Murfreesboro, North Carolina

Jones, W. (1852) 'Preface', *Journal of the Asiatic Society of Bengal*, vol. 20

Kahn, J., and Lobera, J. R. (eds.) (1981) *The Anthropology of Pre-Capitalist Societies*, Macmillan, London

Karsten, R. (1935) 'The head-hunters of Western Amazonas', *Societas Scientiarum Fennica*, Helsingfors

(1955) *The Religion of the Samek, Ancient Beliefs and Cults of the Scandinavian and the Finnish Lapps*, Brill, Leiden

Kennedy, C. C. (1984) 'Did Champlain stalk a Carolina Parakeet in Southern Ontario in October 1615?', *Arch Notes, Newsletter of the Ontario Archaeological Society* 84 (6): 55–62

Kent, S. (1983) 'The differential acceptance of culture change: an archaeological test case', *Historical Archaeology* 17: 56–63

Kenya Land Commission. 1933. HMSO, London

Kenyon, W. A. (1982) *The Grimsby Site: A Historic Neutral Cemetery*, Royal Ontario Museum, Toronto

Kipkorir, B. E., and Welbourn, F. B. (1973) *The Market of Kenya: A Preliminary Study*, East African Literature Bureau, Nairobi

Kirch, P. V. (1978) 'Agricultural adaptation in the humid tropics', in R. A. Gould (ed.), *Explorations in Ethnoarchaeology*, University of New Mexico Press, Albuquerque, p. 00–0

Kirchner, H. (1952) 'Ein archäologischer Beitrag zur Urgeschichte des Schamanismus', *Anthropos* (Freiburg) 47: 244–86

Kleppe, E. J. (1974) 'Samiske Jernalderstudier ved Varangerfjorden', unpublished Magister thesis, University of Bergen

(1977) 'Archaeological material and ethnic identification. A study of Lappish material from Varanger, Norway', *Norwegian Archaeological Review* 1–2: 32–59

Kramer, C. (1979) *Explorations in Ethnoarchaeology: Implications of Ethnography for Archaeology*, Columbia University Press, New York

Krige, E. J. (1950) *The Social System of the Zulu*. Shuter and Shooter

Kühn, H. (1939–40) Die grossen Adlerfibeln der Völkerwanderungszeit, *Jb für prähistorische und ethnographische Kunst* (= *IPEK*) 9: 126–44

(1974) *Die Germanischen Bügelfibeln der Völkerwanderungszeit in Süddeutschland*, 2 vols., Graz

Kuper, A. (1980) 'Symbolic dimensions of the Southern Bantu homestead', *Africa* 50: 8–23

(1982) *Wives for Cattle*. Routledge and Kegan Paul, London

(1983) 'Lineage theory: a critical retrospect', *Annual Review of Anthropology*, 11: 00–0

Kuper, H. (1947) *An African Aristocracy*, Oxford University Press

La Barre, W. (1970) 'Old and New World narcotics: a statistical question and an ethnological reply', *Economic Botany*, 24: 73–80

(1972) 'Hallucinogens and the shamanic origins of religion', in P. T. Furst (ed.), *Flesh of the Gods: the Ritual Use of Hallucinogens*, Praeger, New York, pp. 261–78

(1975) *The Peyote Cult*, 4th edn, Schocken Books, New York

Lafitau, J.-F. (1724) *Moeurs des sauvages amériquains, comparées aux moeurs des premiers temps*, Paris

LaFlesche, F. (1884) 'The sacred pipes of friendship', *Proceedings of the American Association for the Advancement of Science* 33: 613–15

Lane, P. J. (in press) 'Dogon house form and material culture patterning', in K. Ray & J. A. Alexander (eds.), *Studies in African Archaeology and Material Culture*, B.A.R. International Series, Oxford

Langdon, E. J. (1979) 'Yagé among the Siona: cultural patterns in visions', in D. L. Browman & R. A. Schwarz (eds.), *Spirits, Shamans, and Stars: Perspectives From South America*, Mouton, The Hague, pp. 63–80

Larsen, G. Mandt. (1972) *Bergbilder i Hordaland*, Årbok for Universitetet i Bergen, Humanistik serie, 1970(2), Bergen University Press

Lasko, P. (1971) *The Kingdom of the Franks*, Thames and Hudson, London

Latham, B. (1971) *Trebartha: The House by the Stream*, Hutchinson, London

Latta, M. A. (1976) 'The Iroquoian cultures of Huronia: a study of acculturation through archaeology', unpublished Ph.D. dissertation, Department of Anthropology, University of Toronto

Leach, E. R. (1954) *Political systems of Highland Burma: A study of Kachin social structure*, Bell, London

Lechtmann, H. (1984) 'Andean value systems and the development of prehistoric metallurgy', *Technology and Culture* 25: 1–36

Lee, R. B. and DeVore, I. (1976) *Kalahari Hunter-Gatherers: Studies of the !Kung San and their Neighbours*, Harvard University Press

Leone, M. (1982) 'Some opinions about recovering mind', *American Antiquity* 47: 742–60

Le Page du Pratz, A. S. (1758) *Histoire de la Louisiane . . .*, 3 vols., Paris

Lévi-Strauss, C. (1962) *The Savage Mind*, Weidenfeld and Nicolson, London

Lifszyc, D. and Paulme, D. (1936) 'Les fêtes des semailles en 1935 chez les Dogon de Sanga', *Journal de la Société des Africanistes* 6: 95–110

Linton, R. (1923) 'Purification of the sacred bundles, a ceremony of the Pawnee', *Field Museum of Natural History Anthropology Leaflet* 7: 1–11

Lowie, R. H. (1919) 'The tobacco society of the Crow Indians', *Anthropological Papers of the American Museum of Natural History* 21(2): 101–200

Lowther, G. R. (1961) 'Relations between historical theory and archaeological practice in the work of R. G. Collingwood', *Anthropologica*, New Series 3: 173–81

Lwanga-Lunyiigo, S. (1976) The Bantu problem reconsidered. *Current Anthropology* 17: 282–6

McClintock, W. (1948) 'Blackfoot medicine-pipe ceremony', *Southwest Museum Leaflets* 21: 1–11

Macfarlane, A. (1978) *The Origins of English Individualism*, Blackwell, Oxford

McKern, W. C. (1928) 'A Winnebago war-bundle ceremony', *Yearbook of the Public Museum of the City of Milwaukee* 8(1): 146–55

Maenchen-Helfen, J. O. (1973) *The World of the Huns*, University of California Press, Berkeley

Maggs, T. M. (1980) 'The Iron Age sequence south of the Vaal and Pongola rivers: some historical implications', *Journal of African History* 21: 1–15

Magubane, B. (1971) 'A critical look at indices used in the study of social change in colonial Africa', *Current Anthropology* 12(4–5): 419–45

Malmer, M. (1981) *A Chorological Study of North European Rock Art*, Kunliga Vitterhets och Antikvitets Akademien Antikvariska Serien 32, Stockholm

Manker, E. (1938) *Die Lappische Zaubertrommel I*, Acta Lapponica I, Almqvist and Wiksell, Stockholm

(1950) *Die Lappische Zaubertrommel II*, Acta Lapponica II, Almqvist and Wiksell, Stockholm

(1971) *Samefolkets Konst*, Askild and Karnkull, Halmstad

Mariotti, A. and Magubane, B. (1976) 'Urban ethnology in Africa: some theoretical issues', in W. Arens (ed.), *A Century of Change in Eastern Africa*, Mouton, The Hague, pp. 249–73

Marstrander, S. (1963) *Østfoldske Jordbruksristninger*, Instituttet for Sammenlignende kulturforskning, ser. B, Skrifter, Oslo

(1970) 'A newly discovered rock-carving of Bronze Age type in Central Norway', in E. Anati (ed.), *Valcamonia Symposium*, Capo di Ponte

Marwick, B. A. (1940) *The Swazi*, Cass, London

Mason, J. A. (1924) 'Use of tobacco in Mexico and South America', *Field Museum of Natural History Anthropology Leaflet* 16: 1–15

Mathews, Z. P. (1976) 'Huron pipes and Iroquoian shamanism', *Man in the Northeast*, 12: 15–31

(1978) *The Relation of Seneca False Face Masks to Seneca and Ontario Archaeology*, Garland Publishing, New York

(1980) 'Of man and beast: the chronology of effigy pipes among Ontario Iroquoians', *Ethnohistory* 27(4): 295–307

(1981a) 'The identification of animals on Ontario Iroquoian pipes', *Canadian Journal of Archaeology* 5: 31–48

(1981b) 'Art historical photodocumentation of Iroquoian effigy pipes', *Annals of the New York Academy of Sciences* 376: 161–76

Mead, M. (ed.) (1955) *Cultural Patterns and Technical Change*, UNESCO Mentor Books, Paris

Meillassoux, C. (1972) 'From reproduction to production: a Marxist approach to Economic Anthropology', in *Economy and Society* 1: 93–105

(1978) 'The economy in agricultural self-sustaining societies: a preliminary analysis', in D. Seddon (ed.), *Relations of Production*, Cass, London

Merriman, N. (1987) 'An investigation into the archaeological evidence for Celtic spirit', in I. Hodder (ed.), *The Archaeology of Contextual Meanings*, Cambridge University Press

Mitchell, J. C. (1960) *The Yao Village*, Manchester University Press

Mitchell, J. Clyde, and Epstein, A. L. (1959) 'Occupation as prestige and social status among the urban Africans in northern Rhodesia', *Africa* 29: 23–39

Mohan, H. (1959) 'Economic organisation of the Saoria Paharia', in *Bulletin of the Bihar Tribal Research Institute* I, no. 1

Molinero Perez, A. (1948) 'La necropolis visigoda de Duraton (Segovia)', *Acta Arqueologica Hispanica* 4, Madrid

Moore, H. L. (1983a) 'Anthropology and development: some illustrations from the Marakwet of Kenya', in B. E. Kipkorir, R. C. Soper and J. W. Ssennyonga (eds.), *The Kerio Valley: Past, Present and Future*, Institute of African Studies, Nairobi, pp. 132–8

(1983b) 'Men, women and the organisation of domestic space among the Marakwet of Kenya', unpublished Ph.D. thesis, Cambridge University

Moore, S. F., and Myerhoff, B. G. (eds.) (1975) *Symbol and Politics in Communal Ideology*, Cornell University Press, Ithaca

Moosbrugger-Leu, R. (1967) *Die frühmittelalterliche Gürtelbeschläge der Schweiz*, Basel

Morris, J. (1973) *The Age of Arthur: A History of the British Isles from 350 to 650*, Weidenfeld and Nicolson, London

Mulk, I. M. (1985) *Kulturhistoriska undersøkingar efter Langas och Stora Lulejavre*, Rapport 3 (1982), Institusjonen för arkeologi, University of Umeå

Murray, R. A. (1962) 'A brief survey of the pipes and smoking customs of the Indians of the Northern Plains', *Minnesota Archaeologist* 24: 4–41

Musset, L. (1975) *The Germanic Invasions. The Making of Europe, A.D. 400–600*, Batsford, London

Neckel, G., and Kühn, H. (eds.) (1962) *Edda. Die Lieder des Codex Regius nebst verwandten Denkmälern* 1 and 2, Heidelberg (References in ch. 7 are made to this edition)

Neihardt, J. G. (1972) *Black Elk Speaks*, Pocket Books, New York

Ngubane, H. (1977) *Body and Mind in Zulu Medicine*, Academic Press, London

Nicolaisen, W. F. H. (1979) '"Distorted Function" in material aspects of culture', *Folklore Forum* 12: pp. 223–35

Noble, W. C. (1975) 'Van Besien (AfHd-2): a study in Glen Meyer Development', *Ontario Archaeology* 24: 3–95

(1979) 'Ontario Iroquois effigy pipes', *Canadian Journal of Archaeology* 3: 69–90

Nowakowski, J. A. (1982) 'Abandoned farmsteads in an upland area: a behavioural approach', unpublished B.A. dissertation, University of Sheffield

Nummedal, A. (1929) *Stone Age Finds in Finnmark*, Instituttet for Sammenlignende Kulturforskning, ser. B, Skrifter, Oslo

Odner, K. (1983a) *Finner og Terfinner, Etniske prosesser i det nordlige Fenno-Scandia*, Occasional papers 9, Dept of Social Anthropology, University of Oslo

(1983b) 'Reflection on autonomy – thoughts on European cultural development', *Norwegian Archaeological Review* 16: 1–13

Odobescu, A. (1976) *Opere IV: Tezaurul de la Pietroasa*, Bucharest

Oldham, C. E. A. W. (1930) *Journal of Francis Buchanan, kept during the survey of the district of Bhagalpur in 1810–1811*, Superintendent Government Printing, Bihar and Orissa, Patna

Oliver, R. (1966) 'The problem of the Bantu expansion', *Journal of African History* 6: 361–76

Olsen, B. (1984) 'Stabilitet og endring. Produksjon og samfunn i Varanger 800 f.Kr.f – 1700, e.Kr.f', Unpublished Magister thesis, University of Tromsø

Olsen, H. (1967) *Osteologisk materiale, innledning: fish–fugl*, Varangerfunnene VI, Tromsø Museum Skrifter VII, Tromsø

Olsen, M. (ed.) (1906) *Volsunga Saga ok Ragnars Saga Loðbrókar*, Samfund til udgivelse af gammel nordisk litteratur, København

Omer-Cooper, J. (1966) *The Zulu Aftermath*, Longman, London

Onyango-Abuje, J. C. and Wandibba, S. (1976) 'The palaeoenvironment and its influence on man's activities in East Africa during the latter part of the Upper Pleistocene and Holocene', *Hadith* 7: 24–40

Orlandis, J. (1956) 'El cristianismo en el reino visigodo', in *I Goti in Occidente*, Settimane di Studio . . . sull'Alto Medioevo, Spoleto, pp. 153–71

Orme, B. (1981) *Anthropology for Archaeologists*, Duckworth, London

Palol, P de (n.d.) *Hispanic Art of the Visigothic Period*, Barcelona

Panofsky, E. (1957) *Meaning in the Visual Arts*, Doubleday, New York

(1968) *Idea – A Concept in Art Theory*, University of South Carolina

Parker, A. C. (1924) 'Fundamental factors in Seneca folklore', *The University of the State of New York, New York State Museum Bulletin* 253: 49–66

Parker Pearson, M. (1984) 'Economic and ideological change: cyclical growth in the pre-state societies of Jutland', in D. Miller and C. Tilley (eds.), *Ideology, Power and Prehistory*, Cambridge University Press

Parkin, D. (1978) *The Cultural Definition of Political Response: Lineal Destiny among the Luo*, Academic Press, London

Pathy, J., Paul, B., Bhaskar, M., and Panda, J. (1976) 'Tribal studies in India: an appraisal', *Eastern Anthropologist* 29(4): 399–417

Paulme, D. (1940) *Organisation Sociale des Dogon (Soudan Française)*, Domat-Montchrestien, Paris

Peacock, D. P. S. (1982) *Pottery in the Roman World*, Academic Press, London

Pease, T. C., and Werner, R. C. (1934) 'The French Foundations 1680–1693', *Collections of the Illinois State Historical Library*, vol. 23, French Series, Volume 1

Phillips, E. D. (1965) *The Royal Hordes: Nomad Peoples of the Steppes*, Thames and Hudson, London

Phillipson, D. W. (1968) 'The Early Iron Age in Zambia – regional variants and some tentative conclusions', *Journal of African History* 9: 191–211

(1974) 'Iron Age history and archaeology in Zambia', *Journal of African History* 15: 1–25

(1975) 'The chronology of the Iron Age in Bantu Africa', *Journal of African History* 16: 321–42

(1976) 'Archaeology and Bantu linguistics', *World Archaeology* 8: 65–82

(1977) *The Later Prehistory of Eastern and Southern Africa*, Heinemann, London

Pidal, R. M. (ed.) (1940) *Historia de Espana, III, Espana Visigoda (414–711 de J.C.)*, Madrid

Podro, M. (1982), *The Critical Historians of Art*, Yale University Press, New Haven

Pohl, W. (1980) 'Die Gepiden und die Gentes an der mittleren Donau nach dem Zerfall des Attilareiches', in Wolfram and Daim 1980, pp. 239–301

Posnansky, M. (1961) 'Iron Age of East and Central Africa: points of comparison', *South African Archaeological Bulletin* 16: 136–8

(1968) 'Bantu genesis: archaeological reflections', *Journal of African History* 9: 1–11

Pounds, N. J. G. (1945) 'The historical geography of Cornwall', unpublished Ph.D. thesis, University of London

Pratap, A. (1986) 'Savariya Paharia ethnohistory and the Archaeology of the Rajmahal Hills', Ph.D. dissertation, Cambridge University

(1987) *The Origin and Transformation of Paharia Identity*, forthcoming

Prevec, R. (1984) 'The Carolina Parakeet – its first appearance in Southern Ontario', *KEWA, Newsletter of the Ontario Archaeological Society, London Chapter* 84(7), pp. 4–8, reprinted in *Arch. Notes, Newsletter of the Ontario Archaeological Society* 84(6): 51–4

Preziosi, D. (1979). *The Semiotics of the Built Environment*, Indiana University Press, Bloomington

Ravdonikas, V. I. (1936) *Les Gravures rupestres des bordes du lac Onega et de la mer Blanche*, Moscow

Ray Choudhary, P. C. (1965) *Bihard District Gazetteers: Santal Parganas*, Secretariat Press, Patna, Bihar

Ray, S. N. (1974) 'Sauria of Santal Parganas', *Bulletin of the Bihar Tribal Research Institute*, S. P. Gupta (ed.), Special Issue, 'Paharias of Santal Parganas', vol. 16, 1–2, Ranchi

Read, M. (1956) *The Ngoni of Nyasaland*, Oxford University Press

(1959) *Children of Their Fathers*, Oxford University Press

Redfield, R. (1953) *The Primitive World and its Transformations*, Cornell University Press, Ithaca

(1956) *Peasant Society and Culture*, University of Chicago Press

Reid, C. S. (1975) 'The Boys Site', *National Museum of Man Mercury Series, Archaeological Survey of Canada Paper* 42

Relph, E. C. (1976) *Place and Placelessness*, Pion, London

Renfrew, C. (1973) *Before Civilisation: The Radiocarbon Revolution and Prehistoric Europe*, Penguin, Harmondsworth

(1979a) *Problems in European Prehistory*, Edinburgh University Press

(1979b) 'Transformations' in C. Renfrew & K. L. Cooke (eds.), *Transformations: Mathematical Approaches to Culture Change*, Academic Press, London

Renouf, M. A. P. (1981) 'Prehistoric coastal economy in Vanangerfjord, north Norway', unpublished Ph.D. dissertation, University of Cambridge

Reymert, P. K. (1980) *Arkeologi og etnisitet. En studie i etnisitet og gravskikk i Nord-Troms og Finnmark i tiden 800–1200*, unpublished Magister thesis, University of Tromsø

Richards, A. I. (1939) *Land, Labour and Diet in Northern Rhodesia*, Oxford University Press

(1982) *Chisungu: A Girl's Initiation Ceremony Among the Bemba of Northern Rhodesia*, Tavistock, London

Ricoeur, P. (1981) *Hermeneutics and the Human Sciences*, Cambridge University Press

Riegl, A. (1923) *Stilfragen: Grundlegungen zu einer Geschichte der Ornamentik*, 2nd edn, Berlin (1st edn 1893)

Risley, H. H. (1891) *Tribes and Castes of Bengal*, Calcutta

(1892) *Ethnographic Glossary*, vol. 2

(1908) *The People of India*, Thacker Spink & Co., Calcutta

Ritchie, W. A. (1980) *The Archaeology of New York State*, rev. edn, Harbor Hill Books, Harrison, New York

Ritchie, W. A. and D. W. Dragoo (1960) 'The eastern dispersal of Adena', *New York State Museum and Science Service Bulletin* 379, pp. 1–68

Robertson, J. (1981) 'Archaeology in south-central Africa', in D. Ray, P. Shinnie and D. Williams (eds.), *Into the 80's: Proceedings of the 11th Annual Conference of the Canadian Association of African Studies*, Vol. 1, Tantalus, pp. 00–0

Rogers, R. (1765) *A Concise Account of North America*, London

Ross, M. C. (1961) *Arts of the Migration Period in the Walters Art Gallery*, Baltimore

Roth, H. (1979) *Kunst der Völkerwanderungszeit*, Frankfurt

Rouse, I. (1972) *Introduction to Prehistory: A Systematic Approach*, McGraw-Hill, New York

Rowe, J. (1959) 'Cornish agriculture in the age of the Great Depression', *Journal of the Royal Institution of Cornwall* 3: 147–62

Rowley-Conwy, P. (1981) 'Slash and burn in the temperate European Neolithic', in R. Mercer (ed.), *Farming Practice in British Prehistory*, Edinburgh University Press

Runciman, S. (1975) *Byzantine Style and Civilization*, Penguin, Harmondsworth

Rutsch, E. S. (1973) *Smoking Technology of the Aborigines of the Iroquois Area of New York State*, Fairleigh Dickinson University Press, Rutherford

Rygh, K. (1908) *Helleristninger af den sydskandinaviske type i det nordenfjeldske Norge*, Det Kgl. Videnskabers selskabers Selskab, Skrifter 10, Trondheim

Sackett, J. (1973) 'Style, function and artefact variability in palaeolithic assemblages', in C. Renfrew (ed.), *The Explanation of Culture Change: Models in Prehistory*, Duckworth, London, pp. 317–25

Sagard, G. [1632] (1939) *The Long Journey to the Country of the Hurons*, The Champlain Society, Toronto

Sahlins, M. (1972) *Stone Age Economics*, Tavistock, London

Said, E. W. (1978) *Orientalism*, Routledge and Kegan Paul, London

Salmon, M. H. (1982) *Philosophy and Archaeology*, Academic Press, New York

Sandars, N. K. (1968) *Prehistoric Art in Europe*, Penguin, Harmondsworth

Santa-Olalla, J. M. (1936) 'Westgotische Adlerfibeln aus Spanien', *Germania* 20, pp. 47–52

(1940–1) 'Nuevas fibulas aquiliformes hispanovisigodas', *Archivo Espanol de Arqueologia* 14: 33–54

Sarkar, S. S. (1933) 'The origin of the Malpaharia', *Indian Historical Quarterly* 9: 886–97

Savvateyev, Yu. (1970) *Zalavruga*, Leningrad

(1977) 'Rock pictures (petroglyphs) of the White Sea', *Bolletino del Centro Camuno di Studi Preistorici* 16: 67–86

Sayce, R. V. (1933) *Primitive Arts and Crafts*, Cambridge University Press

Schiffer, M. B. (1976) *Behavioural Archaeology*, Academic Press, New York

(1977) 'Towards a unified science of the cultural past', in S. South (ed.), *Research Strategies in Historical Archaeology*, Academic Press, New York

Schiffer, M. B. (1978) 'Methodological issues in ethnoarchaeology', in R. A. Gould (ed.), *Explorations in Ethnoarchaeology*, University of New Mexico Press, Albuquerque, pp. 229–47

Schrire, C. (1980) 'An inquiry into the evolutionary status of the San Hunter-Gatherers', *Human Ecology* 8: 9–32

Schultes, R. E. (1972) 'The utilization of hallucinogens in primitive societies – use, misuse or abuse?', in W. Keup (ed.), *Drug Abuse: Current Concepts and Research*, Charles C. Thomas, Springfield, Illinois, pp. 17–26

Schultes, R. E., and Hoffman, A. (1979) *Plants of the Gods: Origins of Hallucinogenic Use*, McGraw-Hill, New York

Schweitzer, B. (1971) *Greek Geometric Art*, Phaidon, London

Seamon, D. (1979) *A Geography of the Lifeworld*, Croom Helm, London

Setzler, F. M. (1960) 'Welcome Mound and the effigy pipes of the Adena People', *Proceedings of the United States National Museum* 112 (3441): 451–8

Sharp, L. (1952) 'Steel axes for Stone Age Australians' in E. H. Spicer (ed.), *Human Problems in Technological Change*, Russell Sage Foundation, New York

Shaw, T. (1807) 'On the inhabitants of the hills near Rajmahal', *London Asiatic Researches*, 4

Shefferus, J. (1673) *Lapponia*, Frankfurt; reprinted in Swedish in *Acta Lapponica* VIII, 1956, Uppsala

Shennan, S. (1978) 'Archaeological cultures: an empirical investigation', in Hodder (ed.) 1978, pp. 113–39

Sherwill, Col. T. (1851) 'A tour through the Rajmahal Hills', *Journal of the Asiatic Society of Bengal*, 20: 544–606

Shimony, A. (1970) 'Iroquois witchcraft at Six Nations', in D. E. Walker, Jr (ed.), *Systems of North American Witchcraft and Sorcery, Anthropological Monographs of the University of Idaho* 1: 239–65

Sibisi, H. (1976) 'Some notions of "purity" and "impurity" among the Zulu', *Journal of the Anthropological Society of Oxford* 6: 18–29

Sidoff, P. G. (1977) 'An ethnohistorical investigation of the medicine bundle complex among selected tribes of the Great Plains', *The Wisconsin Archaeologist* 58 (3): 173–204

Siikala, A. L. (1984) 'Finnish rock art, animal ceremonialism and shamanic worldview', in M. Hoppal (ed.), *Shamanism in Eurasia*, Edition Herodot, Gøttingen

Simmons, E. A. (1968) 'The smoking complex in the prehistoric Southwest', unpublished M.A. thesis, Department of Anthropology, University of Arizona

Simonsen, P. (1955) 'Helleristningene ved Tromsø', *Ottar* 5, Tromsø Museum, University of Tromsø

(1958) *Arktiske Helleristninger i Nord-Norge, II.* Instituttet for Sammenlignende Kulturforskning, ser. B., XLIX

(1961) *Varanger-funnene II. Fund og udgravninger paa fjordens sydkyst*, Tromsø Museum Skr. VII: 2, Universitetsforlaget, Tromsø

(1965) 'Settlement and occupation in the Younger Stone Age', in H. Hvarfner (ed.), *Hunting and Fishing*, Luleå

(1967) 'Relations between the Lapps and the Scandinavians in early times – an archaeological survey', in *Lapps and Norsmen in Olden Times*, Instituttet for Sammenlignende Kulturforskning, ser. A, Oslo

(1975) *Veidemenn på Nordkalotten, Yngre Steinalder, Stencil series B – History 14, University of Tromsø*

(1979) *Veidemen på Nordkalotten. Yngre Steinalder og overgangen til metalltid*, Stencil series B – History 17, University of Tromsø

(1982) *Veidemenn på Nordkalotten, Jernalder og Middelalder*, Stencil series B – History 21, University of Tromsø

Skinner, A. (1913) 'Social life and ceremonial bundles of the Menomini Indians', *Anthropological Papers of the American Museum of Natural History* 13 (1)

(1920) 'Medicine ceremony of the Menomini, Iowa, and Wahpeton Dakota, with notes on the ceremony among the Ponca, Bungi Ojibwa, and Potawatomi', *Museum of the American Indian, Heye Foundation, Indian Notes and Monographs* 4

(1926) 'Ethnology of the Ioway Indians', *Bulletin of the Public Museum of the City of Milwaukee* 5 (4): 181–354

Smith, J. L. (1967) 'A short history of the sacred calf pipe of the Teton Dakota', *University of South Dakota Museum News* 28 (7–8): 1–37

Sognnes, K. (1981) *Helleristningsundersøkelser i Trønderlag 1979–1980*, Rapport Arkeologisk Serie, A 1981: 2, D. K. N. V. S. Museet, Trondheim

Soper, R. C. (1971a) 'A general review of the Early Iron Age in the southern half of Africa', *Azania* 6: 5–37

(1971b) 'Early Iron Age pottery types from East Africa: comparative analysis', *Azania* 6: 39–52

(1983) 'Bantu expansion into East Africa: archaeological evidence', in C. Ehret and M. Posnansky (eds.), *The Archaeological and Linguistic Reconstruction of African History*, University of California Press, pp. 223–44

Southall, A. (1970) 'The illusion of tribe', *Journal of Asian and African Studies* 5 (1–2): 28–50

Spencer, J. E. (1966) *Shifting Cultivation in Southeastern Asia* University of California Press, Berkeley

Spriggs, M. (1984) *Marxist Perspectives in Archaeology*, Cambridge University Press

Springer, J. W. (1981) 'An ethnohistoric study of the smoking complex in eastern North America', *Ethnohistory* 28 (3): 217–35

Stahl, G. (1926) 'Der Tabak im Leben südamerikanischer Völker', *Zeitschrift für Ethnologie (Berlin)* 57th year, pp. 81–152

Stead, W. H. (1947) 'Types of clay pot', *NADA* 24: 100–2

Steensberg, A. (1980) *New Guinea Gardens. A Study in Husbandry with Parallels in Prehistoric Europe*, Academic Press, New York

Stefaniszyn, B. (1964) *Social and Ritual Life of the Ambo of Northern Rhodesia*, Oxford University Press

Steward, J. H. (1942) 'The direct historical approach to archaeology', *American Antiquity* 7: 337–43

Stothers, D. M. (1977) 'The Princess Point complex', *National Museum of Man Mercury Series, Archaeological Survey of Canada Paper 58*

Street, B. V. (1975) *The 'savage' in Literature: Representation of 'primitive' Society in English Fiction 1858–1920*, Routledge and Kegan Paul, London

Sutton, J. (1973) *The Archaeology of the Western Highlands of Kenya*, British Institute in Eastern Africa, Nairobi

Swinton, G. (1978) 'Touch and the real: contemporary Inuit aesthetics – theory, usage and relevance', in Greenhalgh and Megaw 1978, pp. 71–88

Talbot-Rice, D. (ed.) (1965) *The Dawn of European Civilization: The Dark Ages*, Thames and Hudson, London

Tambiah, S. J. (1969) 'Animals are good to think and good to prohibit', *Ethnology* 8: 424–59

Taylor, T. (1987) 'Flying stags: icons and power in Thracian art' in I. Hodder (ed.) *The Archaeology of Contextual Meanings*, Cambridge University Press

Testart, A. (1982) 'Essai sur les fondements de la division sexuelle, du travail chez les chasseurs-cuilleurs', circulated mimeo., Paris

Thiry, G. (1939) *Die Vogelfibeln der germanischen Völkerwanderungzeit*, Bonn

Thomas, S. J. (1941) 'A Sioux medicine bundle', *American Anthropologist* 43: 605–9

Thompson, E. A. (1948) *A History of Attila and the Huns*, Oxford, University Press

(1963) 'The Visigoths from Fritigern to Euric', *Historia* 12: 105–26

(1966) *The Visigoths in the Time of Ulfila*, Oxford University Press

(1969) *The Goths in Spain*, Oxford University Press

Thruston, G. P. (1890) *The Antiquities of Tennessee and the Adjacent States and the State of Aboriginal Society in the Scale of Civilization Represented by Them*, reprinted by AMS Press, New York (1973)

Thwaites, R. G. (ed.) (1896–1901) *The Jesuit Relations and Allied Documents: Travel and Explorations of the Jesuit Missionaries in New France, 1610–1791*, 73 vols. Burrows Brothers, Cleveland

Timmins, P. A. (1984) 'An analysis and interpretation of radiocarbon dates in Iroquoian archaeology', unpublished M.A. thesis, Department of Anthropology, McGill University, Montreal

Todd, M. (1975) *The Northern Barbarians, 100 B.C. – A.D. 300*, Hutchinson, London

Tooker, E. (1970) *The Iroquois Ceremonial of Midwinter*, Syracuse University Press

Trigger, B. G. (1978) 'Cultural unity and diversity', in B. G. Trigger (ed.), *Handbook of North American Indians Volume 15 Northeast*, Smithsonian Institution, Washington, D.C., pp. 798–804

(1980). *Gordon Childe: Revolution in Archaeology*, Thames and Hudson, London

Tringham, R. (1978) 'Experimentation, ethnoarchaeology, and the leapfrogs in archaeological methodology', in R. A. Gould (ed.), *Explorations in Ethnoarchaeology*, University of New Mexico Press, Albuquerque, pp. 169–99

Turnbaugh, W. A. (1979) 'Calumet ceremonialism as a nativistic response', *American Antiquity* 44 (4): 685–91

(1984) 'Cloudblowers and calumets', in G. P. Horse Capture and G. Ball (eds.), *Plains Indian Seminar in Honor of Dr. John C. Ewers*, Buffalo Bill Historical Center, Cody, Wyoming, pp. 54–72

Ubelaker, D. H., and Wedel, W. R. (1975) 'Bird bones, burials, and bundles in Plains Archaeology', *American Antiquity* 40 (4): 444–52

Uchibori, M. (1984) 'Transformation of the Iban consciousness', *Senri Ethnological Studies* 13: 211–35, National Museum of Osaka

Van den Berghe, P. L. (1964) *Caneville; the Social Structure of a South African Town*, Wesleyan University Press, Middletown

Vansina, J. (1980) 'Bantu in the crystal ball, II', *History in Africa* 7: 293–325

Vastokas, J. M. (1978) 'Cognitive aspects of Northwest Coast art', in Greenhalgh and Megaw 1978, pp. 243–59

Verma, B. B. (1959) 'Social organisation and religion among the Sauria Paharia of the Rajmahal Hills', *Bulletin of the Bihar Tribal Research Institute* 1: 67–101

Vestergaard, E. (1984) 'Gudrun/Kriemhild – søster eller hustru?' *Arkiv för Nordisk Filologi* 29: 63–78

    (1985) 'Transformations of social relations and power in the Volsunga–Nibelungen tradition' (forthcoming)

Vidyarthi, L. P. (1963) *The Maler: Nature-Man-Spirit Complex in a Hill Tribe*, Bookland Private Limited, Calcutta

Vogt, E. Z. (1964) 'The genetic model and Maya cultural development', in E. Z. Vogt and A. Ruz (eds.), *Desarrollo Cultural de los Mayas*, UNAM, Mexico

    (1965) 'Structural and conceptual replication in Zinacatantan culture', *American Anthropologist* 67: 342–53

von Gernet, A. D. (1985a) 'The Iroquoian pipe tobacco smoking complex: analogy in constructing the past', Ph.D. dissertation (in progress), Department of Anthropology, McGill University, Montreal

    (1985b) 'Petun et Songes: seventeenth-century Iroquoian visionary experiences and the ethnopharmacology of the spirit world', Paper presented at the R. M. Bucke Society of the Study of Religious Experience (Montreal), Seminar series on Visual Imagery in Religious Experience, April 1985

    (1985c) 'Analysis of Intrasite Artifact Spatial Distributions: The Draper Site Smoking Pipes', *University of Western Ontario Museum of Indian Archaeology Research Report* no. 16

von Gernet, A. D. and P. A. Timmins (1985) 'The symbolic significance of an unusual Early Iroquoian assemblage', unpublished manuscript

Vorren, K.-D. (1979) 'Anthropogenic influence on the natural vegetation in coastal north Norway during the Holocene. Development of farming and pastures', *Norwegian Archaeological Review*, 12: 1–21

    (1983) 'Den eldste korndyrking i det nordlige Norge', in J. Sandnes, A. Kjelland and I. Østerlie (eds.), *Folk og Ressurser i Nord*, Tapir forlag, Trondheim

Vorren, K.-D. and Nilssen, E. (1982) 'Det eldste jordbruket i Nord-Norge en paleoøkologisk oversikt', in T. Sjøvold (ed.), *Introduksjon av jordbruket i Norden*, Det Norske Vitenskaps-Akademi, University Press, Oslo

Wallace, A. F. C. (1959) 'Cultural determinants of response to hallucinatory experience', *American Medical Association Archives of General Psychiatry* 1: 58–69

Walsh, E. H. (1910) Commissioner of the Bhagalpur division and the Sonthal Parganas, *Report to the Chief Secretary of the Government of Bengal, Revenue Department*, B. S. Press, Calcutta

Ware, T. (1964) *The Orthodox Church*, Penguin, Harmondsworth

Wassén, S. H. (1965) 'The use of some specific kinds of South American Indian snuff and related paraphernalia', *Etnologiska Studier* (Göteborg) 28: 1–116

    (1967) 'Anthropological survey of the use of South American snuffs', in D. H. Efron (ed.), *Ethnopharmacologic Search for Psychoactive Drugs* 1645, Public Health Service Publication, Washington, D.C., pp. 233–89

Weber, M. (1976) *The Protestant Ethic and the Spirit of Capitalism*, George Allen & Unwin, London

Welbourne, F. B. (1971) 'Missionary stimulus and African responses', in V. Turner (ed.), *Colonialism in Africa 1870–1960*, Cambridge University Press, pp. 310–45

Wenskus, R. (1977) *Stammesbildung und Verfassung: das Werden der frühmittelalterlichen Gentes*, Köln/Wien

Werner, J. (1956a) *Beiträge zur Archäologie des Attila-Reiches*, Bayer, Akad, Wiss, Phil.-Hist, Kl., Abhandl, N.F. 38, Munich

    (1956b) 'Die archäologischen Zeugnisse der Goten in Sudrüssland, Ungarn, Italien und Spanien', in *I Goti in Occidenti*, Settimani di Studio . . . sull-Alto Medioevo, Spoleto, pp. 127–30

    (1961) *Katalog der Sammlung Diergardt, völkerwanderungs-zeitlicher Schmuck I: Die Fibeln*, Berlin

West, G. A. (1934) 'Tobacco, pipes and smoking customs of the American Indians', *Bulletin of the Public Museum of the City of Milwaukee* 17: 1–994

Whitthoft, J. (1949) 'Green corn ceremonialism in the Eastern Woodlands', *Occasional Contributions from the Museum of Anthropology of the University of Michigan, Ann Arbor* 13: 31–77

Whitthoft, J., and W. S. Hadlock (1946) 'Cherokee-Iroquois little people', *Journal of American Folklore* 59: 413–22

Whitthoft, J., H. Schoff and C. F. Wray (1953) 'Micmac pipes, vase-shaped pipes, and calumets', *Pennsylvania Archaeologist* 23(3–4): 89–107

Wilbert, J. (1972) 'Tobacco and shamanistic ecstasy among the Warao Indians of Venezuela', in P. T. Furst (ed.), *Flesh of the Gods: The Ritual Use of Hallucinogens*, Praeger Publishing, New York, pp. 55–83

    (1975) 'Magico-religious use of tobacco among South American Indians', in V. Rubin (ed.), *Cannabis and Culture*, Mouton, The Hague, pp. 439–61

Wildschut, W. (1926) 'Crow war bundle of two-leggings', *Museum of the American Indian, Heye Foundation, Indian Notes* 3: 284–8

    (1960) (J. C. Ewers (ed.)) 'Crow Indian medicine bundles', *Contributions from the Museum of the American Indian, Heye Foundation* 17: 1–177

Williams, W. M. (1963) 'The social study of family farming', *Geographical Journal* 129: 65–75

Willis, D. (1977) *Learning to Labour: How Working Class Kids get Working Class Jobs*, Gower Press, London

Wissler, C. (1912) 'Ceremonial bundles of the Blackfoot Indians', *Anthropological Papers of the American Museum of Natural History* 7(2): 65–289

Withaker, I. (1978) 'Tacitus' fenni og Ptolemeus' phinnoi', in *Kultur på karrig jord*, Festschrift to Asbjørn Nesheim, printed in *By og Bygd. Norsk folkemuseums årbok*, Oslo

    (1983) 'Late classical and early medieval accounts of the Lapps (Sami)', *Classica et Mediaevalia* 34: 283–303, Copenhagen

Wobst, H. M. (1978) 'The archaeo-ethnology of the hunter gatherers or the tyranny of the ethnographic record in archaeology', *American Antiquity*, 43: 303–9

Wolfflin, H. (1950) *Principles of Art History. The Problem of the Development of Style in Later Art*, Dover Publications, New York

Wolfram, H. (1979) *Geschichte der Goten*, Munich

Wolfram, H. and Daim, F. (1980) *Die Völker an der mittleren und unteren Donau im 5. und 6. Jh.*, Ber. Symp. Kommission für Frühmittel-alterforschung, 24, Vienna

Worgan, G. B. (1811) *General View of the Agriculture of the County of Cornwall*, Board of Agriculture, London

Wright, J. V. (1972) *Ontario Prehistory: An Eleven-Thousand-Year Archaeological Outline*, National Museum of Man Canadian Prehistory Series, Van Nostrand Reinhold Ltd., Toronto

Wylie, M. A. (1982) 'Epistemological issues raised by a structuralist archaeology', in I. Hodder (ed.), *Symbolic and Structural Archaeology*, Cambridge University Press, pp. 39–46

Zachrisson, I. (1983) *De Samiska metalldepåerna år 1000–1350 (The Saami Metal Deposits A.D. 1000–1350)*, Archaeology and Environment 3, Department of Archaeology, University of Umeå

Zachrisson, I. and Iregren, E. (1974) *Lappish Bear Graves in Northern Sweden. An Archaeological and Osteological Study*, Early Norrland 5, Kungl. Vitterhets Historie och Antikvitets Akademien, Stockholm

Zeiss, H. (1934) *Die Grabfunde aus dem spanischen Weitgotenreich*, Berlin/Leipzig

Zerries, O. (1962) 'Die Vorstellung vom Zweiten Ich und die Rolle der Harpye in der Kultur der Naturvölker Südamerikas', *Anthropos* (Freiburg) 57: 889–914

INDEX

The Archaeology of Contextual Meanings
Edited by Ian Hodder

This companion volume to *Archaeology as Long-term History* focuses on the symbolism of artefacts. It seeks at once to refine current theory and method relating to interpretation and show, with examples, how to conduct this sort of archaeological work. Some contributors work with the material culture of modern times or the historic period, areas in which the symbolism of mute artefacts has traditionally been thought most accessible. However, the book also contains a good number of applications in prehistory to demonstrate the feasibility of symbolic interpretation where good contextual data survive from the distant past.

In relation to wider debates within the social sciences, the volume is characterised by a concern to place abstract symbolic codes within their historical context and within the contexts of social actions. In this respect, it develops further some of the ideas presented in Dr Hodder's *Symbolic and Structural Archaeology*, an earlier volume in the *New Directions* series.

Contributors: SHEENA CRAWFORD; LIV GIBBS; IAN HODDER; ROBERT JAMESON; NICK MERRIMAN; KEITH RAY; TONY SINCLAIR; MARIE LOUISE SØRENSON; TIMOTHY TAYLOR; LINDA THERKORN; SARAH WILLIAMS.

New Directions in Archaeology

0 521 32924 8

Reading the Past
Current Approaches to Interpretation in Archaeology

Ian Hodder

Ian Hodder's controversial new book focuses on meaning in archaeology, arguing that the interpretation of meaning needs to be closely integrated with adaptive, economic and social factors when we are seeking to explain the behaviour of past societies. Symbolism and ideology are discussed in relation to history and social practice and general accounts are provided of systems theory in archaeology, of structuralist and Marxist archaeology, and of the relationships between archaeology and history. The author then defines what he has termed contextual and post-processual archaeology and examines their implications for practice of the discipline. In particular, he argues that while material culture is not a literary text, an analogy with text offers powerful insights into the nature of archaeological data and into the procedures involved in 'reading the past'.

0 521 32743 1
0 521 33960 X (paper)

Peer Polity Interaction and Socio-political Change
Edited by Colin Renfrew and John F. Cherry

Thirteen leading archaeologists have contributed to this innovative study of the socio-political processes – notably imitation, competition, warfare, and the exchange of material goods and information – that can be observed within early complex societies, particularly those just emerging into statehood. The common aim is to explain the remarkable formal similarities that exist between institutions, ideologies and material remains in a variety of cultures characterised by independent political centres yet to be brought under the control of a single, unified jurisdiction.

A major statement of the conceptual approach is followed by ten case studies from a wide variety of times and places, including Minoan Crete, early historic Greece and Japan, the classic Maya, the American Mid-West in the Hopewellian period, Europe in the Early Bronze Age and Early Iron Age, and the British Isles in the late Neolithic.

Contributors: GINA L. BARNES; RICHARD BRADLEY; DAVID P. BRAUN; SARA CHAMPION; TIMOTHY CHAMPION; ROBERT CHAPMAN; JOHN CHERRY; DAVID A. FREIDEL; RICHARD HODGES; COLIN RENFREW; JEREMY A. SABLOFF; STEPHEN SHENNAN; ANTHONY SNODGRASS.

New Directions in Archaeology

0 521 22914 6

Hunters in Transition
Mesolithic Societies of Temperate Eurasia and their Transition to Farming

Edited by Marek Zvelebil

This book analyses one of the crucial events in human cultural evolution: the emergence of postglacial hunter-gatherer communities and the development of farming. Traditionally, the advantages of settled agriculture have been assumed and the transition to farming has been viewed in terms of the simple dispersal of early farming communities northwards across Europe. The contributors to this volume adopt a fresh, more subtle approach. Farming is viewed from a hunter-gatherer perspective as offering both advantages and disadvantages, organisational disruption during the period of transition and far-reaching social consequences for the existing way of life. The hunter-gatherer economy and farming in fact shared a common objective: a guaranteed food supply in a changing natural and social environment. Drawing extensively on research in eastern Europe and temperate Asia, the book argues persuasively for the essential unity of all postglacial adaptations whether leading to the dispersal of farming or the retention and elaboration of existing hunter-gatherer strategies.

Contributors: TAKERU AKAZAWA; PAUL DOLUKHANOV; CLIVE GAMBLE; STEFAN KAROL KOZLOWSKI; JANUSZ KOZLOWSKI; JAMES LEWTHWAITE; GERALD MATYUSHIN; PETER ROWLEY-CONWY; SLAVOMIL VENCL; MAREK ZVELEBIL.

New Directions in Archaeology

0 521 26868 0

Stone-Age Prehistory
Studies in Memory of Charles McBurney

Edited by Geoff Bailey and Paul Callow

The studies in this wide-ranging volume focus on the analysis of stone artefacts and industries and on the ways these can be used to throw light on human behaviour from the earliest times. They have a broad chronological and geographical spread – from Europe and Africa to Australia and New Guinea – and pay particular attention to the information that may be sought at different levels of investigation, from the detailed examination of individual objects to a regional or even continental perspective. Papers on two parallel lines of enquiry – prehistoric art and the physical development of the early hominids in Africa – demonstrate the wider relevance of many of the theoretical issues raised in the course of the enquiries into lithic technology.

The collection has been produced in memory of Charles McBurney, formerly Professor of Quaternary Prehistory in the University of Cambridge, and its authorship is drawn largely from his former pupils.

Contributors: P. ALLSWORTH-JONES; G. N. BAILEY; A. BILSBOROUGH; B. A. BRADLEY; P. CALLOW; J. G. D. CLARK; J. D. CLARK; J. CLEGG; A. E. CLOSE; I. DAVIDSON; H. DIBBLE; J. A. J. GOWLETT; M. HAYNES; G. Ll. ISAAC; P. A. MELLARS; L. McBRYDE; J. E. PARKINGTON; N. ROLLAND; C. G. SAMPSON; J. P. WHITE; L. P. WILKINSON.

0 521 32132 8

The Palaeolithic Settlement of Europe
Clive Gamble

A major new survey of the prehistoric hunter-gatherer societies of Europe, this book reviews the newest information and interpretations for scientific research. The palaeolithic is at an exciting point of transition. The explosion in ethno-archaeological studies has fundamentally challenged our models and interpretations amongst all classes of data and at all spatial scales of analysis. Furthermore the traditional concerns of dating and quaternary studies have also passed through their own revolutions and palaeolithic archaeology is the direct beneficiary. Dr Gamble presents in an imaginative but comprehensive framework the changing perspectives of Europe's oldest societies.

'This book . . . is a serious discussion of how to use the archaeological record as a bridge to understanding the past. It is a demonstration that patterning at the regional level, while being important and fascinating, is also a necessary empirical framework in terms of which we must approach the task of learning about the past. It both opens up archaeology to new dreams of things to be accomplished and broadly outlines some very new challenges.'
Lewis Binford

Cambridge World Archaeology

0 521 24514 1
0 521 28764 2 (paper)

Specialisation, Exchange and Complex Societies
Edited by Elizabeth M. Brumfiel and Timothy Earle

This book, the first comparative study of specialised production in prehistoric societies, examines both adaptionist and political approaches to specialisation and exchange using a worldwide perspective. What forms of specialisation and exchange promote social stratification, political integration and institutional specialisation? Can increases in specialisation always be linked to improved subsistence strategies or are they more closely related to the efforts of political elites to strengthen coalitions and establish new institutions of control? Are valuables as important as subsistence goods in the development process?

These and other questions are examined in the contexts of ten prehistoric societies, ranging from the incipient complexity of Mississippian chiefdoms through to the more complex systems of West Africa, Hawaii and Bronze Age Europe, to the agrarian states of Mesopotamia, Mesoamerica, Peru and Yamato Japan.

Contributors: GINA L. BARNES; ELIZABETH M. BRUMFIE; TIMOTHY K. EARLE; KATHLEEN F. GALVIN; ANTONIO SILMAN; KRISTIAN KRISTIANSEN; JON MULLER; PRUDENCE M. RICE; MICHAEL ROWLANDS

New Directions in Archaeology

0 521 32118 2

Symbols of Excellence
Precious Materials as Expressions of Status

Grahame Clark

Pithily written, rich in anecdote and superbly illustrated with examples of ancient craftsmanship, this book by an archaeologist of world renown ranges freely over the civilisations of the last five thousand years. The theme is a fascinating one. Why is it, Professor Clark asks, that human beings value precious metals, gems and a few organic materials like ivory and pearls so highly? All are difficult to obtain and largely useless for practical purposes. Yet the prestige associated with possession down the ages is undoubted. Position, sanctity and – by extension – the social and political hierarchies of entire societies have become embodied in these materials. Though first exploited to the full in the service of early cults and rulers, their appreciation has survived social change, and personal jewellery and insignia of rank are today more common that ever before. The reasons why are authoritatively explored in this remarkable book.

'The great clarity of the author's style, the appositeness of his example and the originality of his basic approach, [are] entirely felicitious. This is a handsome book which any archaeologist could read with profit, yet its interest is certainly not restricted to the archaeological reader alone.'
Colin Renfrew, *Antiquity*

0 521 30264 1

Island Societies

Archaeological Approaches to Evolution and Transformation

Edited by Patrick Kirch

Concentrating their attention on the Pacific Islands, the contributors to this book show how the tightly focused social and economic systems of islands offer archaeologists a series of unique opportunities for tracking and explaining prehistoric change. Over the last thirty years excavations in Fiji, the Marianas, and Hawai'i have revolutionised Oceanic archaeology and, as the major problems of cultural origins and island sequences have been resolved, archaeologists have come increasingly to study social change and to integrate newly acquired data on material culture with older ethnographic and ethnohistorical materials. The fascinating results of this work, centring on the evolution of complex Oceanic chiefdoms into something very much like classic 'archaic states', are authoritatively surveyed here for the first time.

Contributors: R. C. GREEN; GEORGE J. GUMERMAN; ROBERT J. HOMMON; TERRY L. HUNT; PATRICK V. KIRCH; BARRY ROLETT; MATTHEW SPRIGGS; CHRISTOPHER M. STEVENSON.

New Directions in Archaeology

0 521 30189 0

Prehistory in the Pacific Islands

A Study of Variation in Language, Customs and Human Biology

John Terrell

How, asks John Terrell in this richly-illustrated and original book, can we best account for the remarkable diversity of the Pacific Islanders in biology, language and custom? Traditionally scholars have recognised a simple racial division between Polynesians, Micronesians, Melanesians, Australians and South-east Asians: peoples allegedly differing in physical appearance, temperament, achievements, and perhaps even intelligence. However, Professor Terrell shows that such simple divisions do not fit the known facts and are indeed little better than a crude, static snapshot of human diversity.

In a fresh and stimulating study that brings to bear a wide range of data drawn from anthropology, archaeology, geography, biogeography, human ecology and linguistics, he poses a whole series of unfolding and interlinked questions about prehistoric life in the Pacific that effectively unite the human imagination with logical and empirical methods of evaluation.

0 521 30604 3

Production and Exchange of Stone Tools

Prehistoric Obsidian in the Aegean

Robin Torrence

The aim of Robin Torrence's important new study is to develop new methods for reconstructing the processes of prehistoric exchange. Recent archaeological work has concentrated on mapping obsidian finds relative to source areas using trace-element analysis and on investigating the effects of trade on particular cultural groups. Dr Torrence, in contrast, draws extensively on ethnographic analogy to develop a new approach which uses differences in the level of efficiency for the acquisition of raw materials and the production of goods to infer the type of exchange. Regional patterns of tool manufacture, specialist craft production at central places and quarrying are analysed in detail in the context of the prehistoric Aegean and previous ideas about the importance of trade in the growth of civilisations are re-assessed.

The methodology developed by Dr Torrence will be applicable to a wide range of artefact types and her book will therefore be of value to archaeologists working in many different places and periods.

New Studies in Archaeology

0 521 25266 0

Prehistoric Adaptation in the American South-West

Rosalind L. Hunter-Anderson

This book is about post-Pleistocene adaptive change among the aboriginal cultures of the mountains and deserts of Arizona and New Mexico. Conceived essentially as a natural science alternative to the prevailing culture history paradigm, it offers both a general theoretical framework for interpreting the archaeological record of the American South-West and a persuasive evolutionary model for the shift from a hunter-gatherer economy to horticulture at the Mogollon/Anasazi interface.

Technical, architectural and settlement adaptations are examined and the rise of matrilineality, ethnic groupings and clans are modelled using ecological and ethnographic data. In the last part of the book, Dr Hunter-Anderson evaluates the 'fit' between her model and the archaeological record and argues vigorously for future research into the evolution of ethnicity in the adaptive context of regional competition.

New Studies in Archaeology

0 521 30751 1